EARTH SWEET EARTH

Also by Darwin Lambert:

Beautiful Shenandoah
Herbert Hoover's Hideaway
Illustrated Guide to Shenandoah National Park
Gold Strike in Hell
Timberline Ancients
Great Basin Drama
The Undying Past of Shenandoah National Park
The Earth-Man Story
Talking Waters
Herbert Hoover's Hideaway, with Reed L. Engle 2011

Darwin Lambert

EARTH SWEET EARTH:
My Life Inside Nature

Artfulpersuasion Press, Spokane WA

Earth Sweet Earth: My Life Inside Nature

By: Darwin Lambert
Production editors:
   Harvey Lambert
   Sylvia Lambert Schneider
   Laura Lambert Rowe
Publisher:
   Brent Schneider, Artfulpersuasion Press
Cover image:
   Darwin Lambert by Eileen Lambert
Back cover image:
   Darwin & Eileen Lambert by Christian I. Schneider

Web: www.darwinlambert.org

Copyright 2014 by Artfulpersuasion Press, Spokane, WA

Printing History: First Edition: January 28, 2014
   ISBN: 978-0-9847795-2-9 (paper)
eISBN: 978-0-9847795-3-6 (e-book)

All rights reserved, including the right of reproduction in whole or in part, in any form except for short quotations in critical essays and reviews unless explicit permission is obtained from the Publisher.

This work is not to be used for commercial purposes.

   Artfulpersuasion Press
   Permissions Department
   418 W 17th Ave.
   Spokane, WA 99203

Email: SupportTeam@artfulpersuasion.net

Birth from earth must humans trace,
not from nation, sect, or race:
heart's wrong symbols these
from half-blindness sprung,
intermediaries
by half-knowledge sung.
    Darwin Lambert, 1947

Foreword

Darwin Lambert was one of the most fortunate men I have ever met. He was able to live the life he chose to live—and lived it for ninety-one years. The first time that I heard of Darwin was when I became the superintendent of Lehman Caves National Monument in 1963. Darwin had been the editor of Ely, Nevada's daily newspaper, and while there had written a number of editorials, articles and personal letters to various government officials proposing the establishment of a Great Basin National Park, which would include Lehman Caves National Monument. We worked together on this park proposal and, today, in the visitor center of the park, hangs a beautiful stained glass window in his honor, and in recognition of the work he did in its creation.

I didn't meet Darwin personally until 1964 when he and his wife Eileen stopped at Lehman Caves to introduce themselves to me. They were moving from Alaska to the Blue Ridge Mountains in Virginia. As a young man he had had the foresight and opportunity to purchase sixty plus acres of land adjacent to Shenandoah National Park—a secluded and remotely located spot in the shadow of the mountains—where he and Eileen had chosen to live out their lives on the edge of civilization and in harmony with the natural world.

In 1972, when I became superintendent of Shenandoah National Park, my wife Phel and I forged a close personal relationship with Darwin and Eileen. We didn't know Darwin singly, as for us it has always been Darwin and Eileen. Darwin, again, had had the good fortune of meeting and loving a woman who, like him, wanted to live a life that was minimally dependent on what most of us consider to be necessities, and instead chose to dedicate their lives to the natural world—living close to the soil and its seeds, and in the society of Mother Nature's creatures.

The many animated conversations we enjoyed over our respective dinner tables allowed us the privilege of learning about other facets of Darwin's life—including a foray into Nevada politics, his tenure as a Lend Lease official in China, and his and Eileen's life in Juneau, Alaska where he served as the editor of the Juneau newspaper.

Darwin's knowledge of the workings of nature, his historical perspective, and his various writings earned him a large following among near-by and national conservationists. He was a careful and thorough researcher and his broad range of local information was most helpful to me throughout my tenure at Shenandoah National Park.

If Darwin were alive today, in our world of instant communication and everyday convenience, I am confident that he and Eileen would still choose to live in Shaver Hollow in their 1845 log house located at the end of a narrow, ungraded mile of bumpy road from a chained gate and their rural mailbox.

Robert R. Jacobsen, November 4, 2013
National Park Service, retired, former superintendent of Lehman Caves National Monument and Shenandoah National Park

The Lambert's 1845 log house, Shaver Hollow, Virginia

Contents

Chapter 1 - Feelings from 86 Years 13
Chapter 2 – Cold Desert Ranch 35
Chapter 3 – Grandma's Place 1925-27+ 53
Chapter 4 – Hot Desert Oasis 1926-27 65
Chapter 5 – Wicked Mining Town 1927-33 80
Chapter 6 – Mormon Capital 1931-34 96
Chapter 7 – United States Capital 1934-36 115
Chapter 8 – New National Park 1936-37 133
Chapter 9 – Wife and Children and War 1938-43 151
Chapter 10 - Round Earth 1943 171
Chapter 11 – China's Wartime Capital 1943 189
Chapter 12 – Loneliness and East West Love 1944-45 210
Chapter 13 – Barbaria in the Blue Ridge 1945 - 49 231
Chapter 14 – The Great Basin Again 1949-61 253
Chapter 15 – "Darwin, You Can't Love Two" 1956-61 273
Chapter 16 – New State of Alaska 1961-64 295
Chapter 17 – Tenting North America 1964 316
Chapter 18 – The Blue Ridge Again 1964-68 334
Chapter 19 – More Letters to Mentors 1968+ 353
Chapter 20 – Earthmanship 1968-72 371
Chapter 21 – Feeling vs. Thinking 1972-84 394
Chapter 22 – Circling and Linking 1985-94 414
Epilog 452
Family Tree 454
People of the Book 457

to Eileen, My Partner in Nature

Chapter 1 - Feelings from 86 Years

My good news when I was reaching age 75 was First Lady Barbara Bush naming me a member of her "Green Team" of leading conservationists. In a magazine of national circulation she credited me with persevering 35 years in my efforts to "create" Great Basin National Park (Nevada). My conservation/environmental efforts on other fronts, including Shenandoah National Park (Virginia), were also mentioned, but she stressed the Great Basin perseverance – more than a third of a century without giving up the effort – and the multi-million circulation of my numerous writings about the proposed park. The magazine (*Countryside* Sept '91) reached me weeks after publication – without my having heard in advance even a whisper of the First Lady's interest in my doings.

At that time I was snagged already in the bad news that was taking weeks to accumulate. Two doctors and a variety of investigative tests and imaging sessions at a hospital forty miles from our home finally proved I had prostate cancer already metastasized in my bones from skull to spine, ribs and pelvis – far too many places to be attacked by surgery, chemicals, radiation, or any other treatment then known. Our family doctor and the urologist feared I might be dead in six months – or just possibly could survive a year or two.

I didn't feel significant pain and couldn't easily believe the findings, but my reaction was immediate and close to frantic. Encouraged by the First Lady's praise and scared by the apparent nearness of death, I felt energized (after years of intention without action) to tell my life story while I still could. I dropped everything else and began searching my old diaries, cobweb-dusty but never forgotten, and was soon rediscovering notes and outlines and rough drafts I'd hoped to use somewhere. I tried to guess what actions or published thoughts had most impressed Barbara Bush.

My aim was to explore my whole life and relate my conservation efforts with the main drives or motivations – love, food, desire for money and property, parental and educational influences, economic struggle and success or failure – whatever makes a person "tick" – thus revealing the central essence of my environmental persistence.

The more I probed in my old papers and in my published works, the more clusters of related details and emotions swirled in my memory. They're swirling vigorously now, so I'll move ahead with this introductory chapter by confessing I can't yet clearly explain – though I have strong clues to pursue. My perseverance doesn't seem to have grown directly from conscious calculation or planning. The best indication now is that it grew from unworded emotions inside me, from the love of nature that was strong in me from childhood as far back as my memory reaches. It didn't grow from my parents, though they helped as well as hindered, and it didn't grow directly from reading or from thoughts easy to express in words.

My mind is fuzziest in relation to influences of my boyhood and youth – apparently the most crucial time, because by age eight I was writing "poems" about nature and at 16 I recorded in one of my intermittent diaries a strong wish to become a naturalist, writing and maybe lecturing about wild creatures and plants, so I needed to study biology in college, and by age 18 I was dreaming of guiding nature walks in national parks. (So far Dad had veered much too briefly off direct routes visiting relatives – but had let us glimpse a fringe of Grand Canyon and watch one eruption of Old Faithful geyser in Yellowstone.).

Seriously now, just how and why had I started falling in love with nature? I was strongly curious about natural surroundings when I first became aware of them – and aware of myself as a living individual. But I had a strange quirk: I loved the familiar but tended strongly to dislike the natural (and human) surroundings when my father moved us to new homes in different kinds of environments.

And *why*, then, gradually, did my feelings reverse and turn to love – step by step, region by region? Something unconscious? Akin to instinct? I invite readers to come along as I re-experience my life, beginning in Chapter 2, feeling as I felt during the long-ago happenings, trying to catch and hold and sort out the meanings.

Ever since I became conscious (aware of memories of myself) I've puzzled over what or who I am and what I'm wanting to do and why. And now, at age 86, I'm getting close to the center of the puzzle. All the experiences seem to say I've spent my life pursuing happiness, and where I've finally caught up with it in the strongest and most lasting forms is along the paths and in the fields, forests and deserts of Earth (the planet including humans and all creatures). Or, shifting the angle, I feel I've found happiness primarily through a continuing effort to win harmony with nature.

Ignoring chronological order, I'll now try a quick flight over my lifetime, hoping to spot events or situations or connections identifying and beginning to explain the key structures and tendencies. Then, from Chapter 2 on through this narrative, I'll re-experience in more intimate language the days and months and years in calendar order, beginning about 1920 when my memory started recording.

I confess the major decisions and perseverances of my life are more from the "heart" than from the "mind" – which makes them harder to understand or explain. In other words, I feel more than I think. I don't mean just active emotions. I feel brightness or dullness of the morning when I wake up, or the songs of birds, or the fragrance of the forest, or some stink of pollution, or the friendliness or its opposite in another person's glance, or the hospitality in sunshine and the abundance of Earth – or, really, it's a blend of many feelings. Nature has sometimes scared me – as when a forest fire raged within 200 yards of our house just this past November – but, in searching memory, I'm surprised such occasions of fear have been few. Much more often I've felt in tune, in harmony, and without conscious thinking I've felt happy.

Long before I ever thought I might learn to think a little, I've felt somehow connected with nature and friendly with other forms of life. Partly for this reason, though partly also because of the family and community I grew up in, my life story interweaves with animals and plants, mountains and streams, biology and geology, with the different tones and rhythms of male and female, and in the mature years with conservation and environmentalism – efforts to save wilderness in both the western and eastern regions of America and efforts to influence personal and family living in ways that might increase humanity's harmony with nature and decrease our strain on the resources of Earth.

The story wanders, of course, yet it keeps returning to the dodging or embracing of responsibility. There's backsliding too often; there's running away from strain. And there's returning to the battle and repeatedly finding the strongest happiness there. It's the story of a striving yet fallible and often-confused human reaching and reaching – or so I've convinced myself – to link my own pursuit of happiness with that of my expanding community – the Great Basin first of all, then the whole West, America, the Allies of World War II and on, and ultimately with the planet and all its inhabitants – Earth, sweet Earth – though I don't mean to claim I love everybody; it's just that, well, I sometimes try – and sometimes seem to succeed.

Mostly, since age 22, when confessing my occupation I've said writer or editor or both. Much of my striving has been as a small-newspaper or small-magazine editor in Virginia, in Nevada, and in Alaska (that has many problems and opportunities resembling Nevada's) or as freelance author of articles or nonfiction books about nature and history (or fiction, one novel published so far, others in draft form).

I've sometimes wanted to identify myself as naturalist/historian, because I've worked in those fields – several years for the National

Park Service as a clerk and then ranger researching and answering visitors' questions, orally and through publications, then decades as a researcher-writer under contract with NPS or its cooperating associations. Also I served a quarter-century on the governing board of National Parks Conservation Association (NPCA). Through writing and speaking and membership in half a dozen nonprofit organizations – Sierra Club, The Wilderness Society, etc. – I've helped further in saving wild and scenic areas in the West, the East, and Alaska.

Almost always I've been a multiple-incentive person. This tendency came close to removing me as a "Green Team" candidate – before Barbara Bush's magazine article was published. I first came to her researchers' attention in connection with Shenandoah National Park (Virginia). Before World War II, Shenandoah had no funds for research or visitor information, and I (officially a senior clerk-stenographer, age 20) volunteered to fill the gap, researching and writing. But then we needed the information printed for distribution. NPS had no money for this purpose, so I got businessmen to contribute, agreeing to print their names in the "nature journal" (no display-type ads). The park Superintendent objected but then came around. Need for the "literature" was most urgent!

The Barbara Bush researchers, more than half a century later, came around too. A picture of me on Old Rag, in Shenandoah, was chosen to be published with the "Green Team" article. At the last minute, the researchers realized my effort for Great Basin was more significant than what I'd done for Shenandoah. So – the text of the Bush article in the magazine turned out to be entirely Great Basin – but with the Shenandoah photograph!

Then the researchers learned – horrors! – a not-quite-so-ancient tidbit, that I'd been manager of the White Pine Chamber of Commerce and Mines at Ely, Nevada, when in the early 1950s I first publicly advocated Great Basin National Park. And my aim wasn't conservation alone but also business. I wanted to help save the region's economy as "Big Copper" was dwindling toward dying.

Thus, for years, I was a "money grubbing" suspect in the minds of many conservationists – because I mixed economics with conservation.

I'd further aggravated the problem when as a state assemblyman I introduced a bill to create a Nevada Department of Economic Development, thinking of Nevada towns so small they couldn't afford a doctor or a public library or equipment for volunteer firefighting – and my bill passed and the Governor named me chairman of the statewide economic development board. But the new state agency helped tremendously in gaining wide recognition for the proposed national park and for Great Basin scenery in general, so the Barbara Bush researchers, much later, saw my economics-conservation mix as having been beneficial – pro-conservation – and had given me merits for it rather than demerits.

The conservation/economics pull and tug and related puzzles get so confusing sometimes in my life that I need to define a few of my much-used words:

> **NATURE** first meant to me the wild animals and plants but soon grew to include domestic animals, then land, air, water, fire, and sky. "Nature" began *absorbing me* too as I kept noticing how much I resembled other life. In most of my decades of writing, I've made myself conform to a meaning that's prevalent – nature is everything except civilized humans and their culture. Finally, though, I give way in words to my persistent feeling that nature *includes* humans and their doings.
>
> **LIFE** is a continuous process made possible by the forces of nature. Using a diversity of these forces, life has great possibilities of variation and growth – as shown voluminously, for instance, by Charles Darwin whose family name my parents borrowed for my given name.
>
> **THE EARTH** is this planet and all that's on or in it.

THE WORLD is this planet's humans and their institutions.

HARMONY is not all sweetness and light but a functioning complexity that goes on sustaining life and creativity while producing more concord than discord. There's a feeling of unity, of considering and balancing all the interests and concerns of a person, and of integrating and adapting them, so the person "sings" with other persons and other creatures and with Earth.

RESPONSIBILITY is a feeling my Dad tried to teach me – applying in his view to our family and our property and to the Mormon Church and its members and property. It's the feeling much of my story builds around. In me, it kept stretching or extending – though too often lost in my weakness or error – until I half-consciously felt a tug, at least, of responsibility for all life and the whole planet. Just now, though, age 86, I no longer try hard to reform the world; I just want to tell, with a slight shrug of indifference because I'm beyond my "active" years, some of the events and feelings of my learning (slowly and confusingly) to feel responsibility in the first place and about my efforts – in some ways but definitely not in others, resembling my Dad's – to infect other people with a similar germ.

MORALITY is a cousin, at least, of responsibility. It is behavior that enhances health and happiness, keeps Earth a hospitable home for human and other life, strengthens survival, and in most people, I believe, generates a feeling akin to happiness.

HAPPINESS is well-being as it reaches consciousness. Differing from pleasure and possibly from joy, happiness implies *long-lasting*.

PURSUIT OF HAPPINESS is the search for the situation in which feeling at home sustains its highest level.

FEELING AT HOME is my sensing of my most desired place or situation that harmonizes natural phenomena including humans and other life forms in communication with and influencing each other. Elements of home include love, meaningful work, beauty, healthful land, air and water, and adequate shelter and food, some drawn directly from Earth by the user.

CONSERVATION is, according to my usage (and my dictionary), "protection from loss, waste, etc." and/or "the official care and protection of natural resources, as forests."

ENVIRONMENTALISM is "working to solve environmental problems, such as air and water pollution ... uncontrolled population growth, etc..."

Learning even a glimmer of responsibility for something I or my Papa or Mother didn't own took me years of trial and error, though I always "loved" wild places and wild creatures. This love of nature was nourished a bit (or awakened?) by Mother when, before I learned reading, she read aloud to me from Robert Louis Stevenson and read stories by Thornton W. Burgess – one echoing in me even now – "'Chug-a-rum,' said Grandfather Frog as he sat sunning himself on his lily pad in the center of the Smiling Pool..." And from the *Bible*, Mother's reading of these words sounds again in me: "The Lord is my Shepherd... I shall not want... He maketh me to lie down in green pastures. He leadeth me beside the still waters. He restoreth my soul..." I feel the Psalmist now showing me nature, beginning to explain how love of nature might grow toward responsibility for protecting nature.

As soon as I could walk independently, I explored the green pastures on our ranch near Metropolis (Elko County, Nevada, near present-day Wells), then tried to explore the tall sagebrush across the irrigation canal. I was caught and "grounded" but kept discovering nature all over the ranch itself (mostly an alfalfa-wheat-potato-dairy farm). I learned to snare squirrels with twine, but I never killed them; I kept them in a steel drum to feed and watch and learn from. I watched cows and calves and our ill-tempered Jersey bull and our immense, sweet-tempered red-brown Durham bull. I learned how calves are created. Papa confirmed my guess. Before I was eight years old I'd learned by chance what I shouldn't have, that human babies are created similarly.

That's when I first began to feel I too am nature, a feeling that wouldn't go away – and got stronger during my World War II years as a U.S. Government civilian in Chungking. My Chinese language teacher taught partly from the *Tao Te Ching* – humans and nature united and male-female togetherness considered so basic that no life can be fully enlivened or interpreted without understanding in some detail both the *yin* (feminine) and the *yang* (masculine). The combination is near the center of life's meaning – in America too – a view that repeatedly revs up my environmentalism and lets me identify my occupation (in my own mind) as *"earthmanship,"* the art and science of living on Earth for maximum health and happiness while enhancing the planet's resources and functions as the home of life.

Even now, after surviving ten years of metastasized prostate cancer and moving into the new millennium, I consider China significant in the way Eileen, my second wife, and I live. We've terraced our vegetable garden, imitating the graceful soil-saving terraces so prominent in hilly parts of the Far East, maintaining soil and its fertility for centuries and millenniums. We've started a smallish variety of bamboo (stalks harvested to support beans, peas, climbing roses and other vines) and so far have kept this aggressive oriental plant from spreading beyond its allotted territory. And we find our "standard of living" (rate of consumption and pollution of Earth's resources) continuing to shrink while our pursuit of happiness prospers.

Though I loved nature in the Elko County years, I'd never heard of conservation. I was having surges of responsibility, however, for the creatures and the land our family owned. I asked Papa: "Who takes care of wild nature?" And he said, "God. He takes care of you too, and all the rest of us humans." I accepted that until God let Mother die when I was nine. I felt then He didn't care about individual persons, just about the system He'd set up with laws of nature in control.

Step by step through boyhood I learned earthly details – experimenting, reading, dreaming, observing. I read Ernest Thompson Seton because he wrote about boys living as Indians in wild places. I read John Muir's *Steep Trails* because Muir hiked in Nevada and introduced me to Wheeler Peak before I'd ever seen it. Because my Uncle Roy had named his son Walden after the pond where Henry David Thoreau lived alone in wild nature, I read Thoreau's most famous book. But his writing was hard for me then, and I don't recall advocacy of conservation, though I gathered Thoreau disliked new trends in commerce and industry. What intrigued my cousin and me in that book was a person enjoying life in wild woods – what both of us boys wanted for ourselves, perhaps beside one of those beaver dams up in the wild Uinta Mountains, west slope, that drain toward Great Salt Lake (part of the Great Basin). Or, yes, my dream that would be long-lasting, to live in a cabin beside a stream or spring in an unspoiled canyon, a cabin I'd later try to build – and not succeed – but ultimately discover and acquire in the Blue Ridge Mountains of Virginia.

My first surge resembling conservation was a bounce-back from guilt. While still unable to stop mourning Mother, I was confronted by a substitute, a housekeeper Papa invited for a home he was trying to pull together at Overton (near Colorado River) where he'd become teacher of agriculture at the high school. This housekeeper told me to dress for Sunday School, a stress situation with me even when Mother was alive, and I ran away instead, mistakenly hating the newcomer – partly, unreasonably, it now seems, because she wasn't Mother. With a walking stick I hurried toward a wild mesa. I was swinging hard with the stick, making hisses and roars in the air, when suddenly I was beating flowers from prickly enemies, thorny blooming cactus.

Catching myself in this savage mistake, I dropped the stick and fell on my stomach and face, crying into the sand.

I ran to an old mine prospect where I'd earlier noticed a rusty bucket by a seeping spring. For Mother then I coaxed and carried water every Sunday morning for two months to revive my innocent victims. Guilt gradually washed away as the plants began making new tissue. I felt a lasting surge of happiness – from having acted-out responsibility. Yet I wasn't thus becoming an activist for wild nature. How could an 11-year-old reach for that much responsibility? A tiny seed, though, must have been planted in me, waiting for the life-season to sprout and grow.

Half a lifetime later, when I was most active on the governing board of National Parks Conservation Association, I probed into the influences and patterns of my conservation-environmentalism – and into the origins and aims of the way of life Eileen and I have followed since 1961, striving to "consume" less rather than more, finding happiness in loving and protecting nature – even capturing spiders and wasps alive inside the house and gently putting them outside to go on living.

In the 1960s and 70s I was writing for conservation magazines, nature magazines, and Earth-citizenship magazines (such as *VISTA*, United Nations Association), and for *Reader's Digest*. Also in the late 1960s (and occasionally in later years) I wrote "letters" to naturalists and diverse conservationists, past and present, to help clarify my own understanding of myself. Most of the letters could never be sent, because I lacked the address of Heaven. Yet I gained from visiting in imagination with people I deeply wanted to visit in person, people who'd pulled or pushed me toward conservation, helping make a nature-protector from one who'd been merely a nature-lover.

Among these were my partly anti-nature Dad (changed from Papa as we kids grew up). Though he knew a lot about nature, he criticized me for making a "big thing" of it – which opposition stimulated my stubbornness, even started me pushing back hard in the direction opposite from his push. Still I loved him, and long after his death I spent a year of snatched time reading word-by-word all through the *Bible*. I gleaned conservation/environmentalism and responsibility from both testaments, surprising myself, almost regretting my frequent Sunday mornings of running away instead of dressing for Sunday School.

Also I wrote to Daniel Defoe, the author of *Robinson Crusoe*; and to Olaus Murie, well-known biologist and leading wilderness advocate and personal friend who'd but recently died; and to Thomas Jefferson whose spirit seems to have survived at Monticello, across the Blue Ridge from Eileen's and my Virginia mountain home. I tried a letter to Walt Whitman but decided instead to just quote him more often in my writing. Two letters I did mail – one to my son Harvey at University of Nevada (Reno), about Buckminster Fuller and "Spaceship Earth," and one to psychiatrist Edward Stainbrook who'd opened up new ground in me at a man-and-nature gathering in Washington, D.C. Those letters of the late 1960s and early 1970s show my sprouting conservation leanings and learnings more strongly than I could word them now in my declining years.

I'll include two here. Though written in my environmentally-active middle-age, they cast light into my much-earlier years when conservation wasn't a word I could even spell:

Planet Earth 1971

Dear Ernest Thompson Seton:

For half a century your magnificent grizzly bear Wahb has been part of my life, continually opening my feelings to the realities of wild nature. Though I'm aware the story of Wahb's life and death (old-age suicide?) – from breathing poisonous gases in a remote gulch in the Yellowstone area – was published as fiction, I feel you must actually have known that bear. You avoided "making him human" as many skilled writers have done with animals, but you did something truer, made him a living member of nature – as I feel you consider yourself to be and as I consider myself.

Wahb and the other bears you wrote about in your life (1860-1946) didn't fit that period's belief in bears' ferocity. The majestic giant Wahb, and other bears you described also in your scientific masterwork, *Lives of Game Animals,* wanted peace with humans and other creatures (unless they'd previously been mistreated by this "enemy"). I feel I could share Earth peacefully with a creature resembling Wahb. Even more, your portrayal of wild creatures bolstered my fondness for wilderness and kept moving me toward conservation and environmentalism – sometimes as if in bear-style paths pointed out to me (bears tending to step always in the same spots, wearing track-bowls on the land) but sometimes, like you, Mr. Seton, heading off through the wilderness, making a trail-trace where no human has walked before.

I'm glad you risked your audience by telling of Wahb's death. I fumed and mourned and protested inside myself at first; you didn't *have to* hit your readers with such tragedy. Yet I told myself as a boy who'd lost his Mother – and I tell myself now – that death is part of the pattern of life, with new individuals continually replacing us. And with the aid of my given-name source Charles Darwin I see this pattern as wonderfully creative.

Though my much-worn book about Wahb has disappeared – was it *The Biography of a Grizzly* first published in 1900? – I kept your *Two Little Savages* close to me through the years of adjusting to Mother's death and believe it's still with me, though boxed with other old books in the attic. I wanted as a ten-year-old boy to run away and live like an Indian (savage?) in wild forest and semi-desert. I kept looking for the right companions to live with and tried runaway days or nights with different ones. We made bows and arrows that functioned – but not well enough to feed us. We gathered and roasted and ate pine nuts. I tried catching and eating crickets. By themselves they weren't delicious. I tried catching masses to make pinenut-cricket bread as Shoshone Indians had in the Great Basin, but I couldn't' catch enough of the insects even to make a test batch. I wanted to join your *Woodcraft League* but never lived where it was active. I became a Boy Scout instead, learning some skills for coping in wild situations. But Dad moved the family to Salt Lake City before I'd advanced far enough.

In my early teens, while rereading parts of *Two Little Savages,* I used a .22 rifle I'd saved money to buy for killing rabbits to eat, preferably cottontails but sometimes jackrabbits. I was both proud of killing and apologetic – unable for years to decide who or what I was becoming or wanted to become. I tried thanking the spirits for allowing me food – as Indians are said to have done – but couldn't get my feelings in that channel so gave up hunting when I first went east from the Great Basin at age 18. Had I outgrown *Two Little Savages,* Mr. Seton, or should I have struggled harder to explain myself to wild creatures'spirits?

Thank you especially for the dignity and reality of your great grizzly Wahb – also for your so honest, perceptive, sympathetic and detailed *Lives of Game Animals* (though I've wished you'd have named the four-volume masterwork "Lives of Wild Animals," not "Game" that seems to reach out and invite sport-hunting-killing). I feel sure you didn't feel Wahb as "game."

D.L. ('71)

Planet Earth, May 1971

Dear John Muir:
I don't suppose you've noticed me when looking down at your favorite Earth-places, but I've been trying to imitate you ever since 1930 or so – and knowing I was falling hopelessly short. I didn't know at first that you'd been the key person in establishing Yosemite National Park, but I'd found your book *Steep Trails* and knew you'd climbed my favorite mountain, Wheeler Peak in eastern Nevada (13,063 ft) – apparently by yourself which was how I mostly hiked, though I welcomed friends when they'd come.

After enjoying the Wheeler country through your words (you called it "the Jeff Davis group of mountains"), I looked for more of your writings and thus spread my love of wild nature to the national park system and dreamed of far Alaska and even farther wilds on the planet.

Your tendency to take long, long walks intrigued me, and I read your *A Thousand-Mile Walk to the Gulf*. I kept wanting to walk like that (and to talk with you on the way) but never could organize my time to devote weeks and months to exploring. (And, of course, you and I were never alive on Earth at the same time.) I've seldom exceeded two or three days in succession of walking-exploring, hiking with a backpack, sleeping in wilderness. Mostly I've taken dawn-to-dark hikes, carrying nothing but peanuts or other easy foods.

I've been amazed by reports (exact source forgotten now in 1971) that you memorized substantial sections of *The Bible* when you were young. I never tried to imitate you in that, but just last year – thinking of you and my Dad, also likely in Heaven – I read the whole *Bible* beginning to end and marked passages that had "Earth-Day" meanings. I found many more such passages than I'd expected.

Reports of your inventions amazed me, too – and your carving of wooden parts and putting together a big clock that actually functioned! I played with imitating you, while knowing I actually couldn't. It was a kind of daydreaming. After Mother died I lived at intervals with Grandma, and she let me try to fix an old Grandfather's clock that hadn't functioned for years. I took it apart in a vacant room of the big old house and cleaned all the parts, finding some of wood, some of metal, and after a couple of weeks I somehow put it back together. I was as amazed as Grandma when it functioned. I hadn't fixed anything, just cleaned and re-assembled.

As you may guess, Mr. Muir, I'm letting myself go sort of wild here, one fourth playing-dreaming, yet the other three-fourths serious. I hope you understand I'm trying to find meanings in my life – and in man-earth relationships – that aren't yet fully conscious in me. One further stroke – to balance my opinion of you that's so high it may sound insincere: On your climb of Wheeler in 1878 you missed two features that are primary in the case for establishing Great Basin National Park. The bristlecone pines ("foxtail?") are strongly there – in the glacial cirque and widely separated other places. One bristlecone cut down "by mistake" in 1964 proved to have been the oldest living tree yet known to science, around 5,000 years alive.

The second feature: I wish I could have been hiking with you, supplementing your Wheeler impression that "every marked feature is a glacier monument – peaks, valleys, ridges, meadows, lakes." I could have guided you to an actual active glacier, studied by the U.S. Geological Survey in 1883 and currently continuing to function, to move and carry fallen rocks and gravel. It was "rediscovered" in 1955. Sure, it's small, but I could have shown you a crevasse so deep in blue ice that the bottom, maybe as much as a hundred feet down, remained lost in shadow – because the sun never shines in that part of this main cirque of what's now called the Snake Range.

Thank you, Mr. Muir, for your patience with me – and for the boost your life here gave to human responsibility for the health and beauty of Earth.

D.L. ('71)

In January 1974, *Readers Digest* and *National Wildlife*, simultaneously, published my article about Eileen's and my effort to live in harmony with Earth, "We Chose to Live with Nature." It won a circulation count that I've reached only a few other times – 34 million copies world-wide. The numerous responses included praise from Jimmy Stewart, Eileen's and my favorite actor. Another high – not so big an audience but lasting three whole months in 1980 – was Ed Merritt reading on public radio WAMU (American University, Washington, D.C.) the entire text, 193 pages, of my book *The Earth - Man Story*. Such rare successes bolstered our enjoyment of trying to live our beliefs that include disagreement with the American rate of consumption – mistakenly called "standard of living." Published in magazine articles, this disagreement with what so many people took for granted, also brought much mail, caused lots of argument, reached no conclusion – and continues on the planet to this day.

I'd make more of this episode and discussion if our one car in my lazy 80s weren't a Jeep Laredo with extra-high wheels that gets only 15 miles to the gallon. We look for an affordable vehicle delivering better mileage while high enough underneath to cope with flooding or unplowed snow on our mile-long driveway (a 150-year-old wagon road worn in places as a narrow gully) but haven't yet found one. So we tell questioners we drive few miles, burn little gas in total, and don't pollute much. Though true, the excuse sounds weak.

As I review this Chapter 1 the feelings that moved me into conservation seem clear, but the thoughts still a bit fuzzy. I think I could have become a naturalist "on my own"; I was born so inclined. But I doubt I'd have become a *conservationist* that way. In tracing motivational channels I've named several men I wrote "letters" to because they influenced me toward accepting conservation-type responsibility. Now, further feelings come.

Many, if not most, of the people who helped me on the front lines of entering conservation, of embracing this extra responsibility, are women. I catch myself wondering if the *yang-yin* energy I mentioned pages back (Chinese) hasn't been working in me without quite entering consciousness – the **motivational mystery** going: **man, woman, children, home, protection, healthful and beautiful environment** – all connected in a natural line of feeling-meaning-action.

Let's explore back. First, those cactus plants I beat down in misplaced anger, then laboriously restored over a period of months. I was alone, true, but Mother, for whom I was still mourning, was somehow in my shadowy, secret psyche gently prodding me. Every time I carried water that long distance, or covered the cactus wounds with damp soil, hoping for new roots, Mother was somehow with me, motivating.

Okay, so that's a personal feeling – mine alone. Does it prove anything? Maybe not – so let's consider more experiences. My next conservation-type spark was in my mid-teens organizing "Pals of Olympus Club" with Peggy Farrell as co-leader. The idea came when Peggy and her brother Bob and I were puzzling what to do about an active moonshine still I'd found, its fire flaming but the moonshiner absent – sneaked away as I approached (?). The site was among dense scrub oak where the red-hot destroyer might roar up the slope of the Wasatch Range's Mt. Olympus, above the Salt Lake suburb where Dad settled after remarrying. We began walking up there so often the moonshiner seemed never to return. Peggy and I drafted a club constitution and invited more members for "wholesome companionship ... in harmony with nature," focusing on learning and protecting trees, flowers, and wild creatures. There were parties at different homes and frequent hikes up-canyon beyond any road – several all the way to the rocky double summit.

So the club was a game played for fun? Well – yes – but we learned essences of Mt. Olympus and the whole Wasatch and whole Great Basin – and together hoped the most scenic parts would always be safely wild. Though Peggy and I never kissed, we walked Wasatch trails hand in hand, coming close to falling in love but feeling, after all, too young to promise forever love. The club's minute book, fattened by snapshots of member-Pals mountain-climbing or examining flowers (club flower was *oxhead*) and by stories of parties and hikes written by different members, has been saved to this remote time. I feel what we did influenced all the Pals – certainly influenced me – and we Pals have influenced others.

At age 18 I got a job in the nation's capital and attended university at night. In two different classes at George Washington U., my eyes and fellow-student Barbara Closs's eyes had been meeting frequently, and when on a geology walk I'd come down a steep step in an old quarry, and she was hesitating up there on a rock shelf, I held out my arms and she stepped into them. Both of us were far from home. Her parents and siblings lived in upstate New York. We started walking together, exploring parts of Washington that interested us, seldom entertainments or restaurants, most likely outdoors, soon half-wild Rock Creek Park. It was friendship in early months, not dating exactly, but we often held hands when crossing streets and did a special lilting leap over curbs up to the sidewalks. She was an artist and art teacher, a graduate of prestigious Pratt Institute in Brooklyn.

In the spring, summer and fall of 1935, urged by botany professor Robert F. Griggs, I spent all possible time collecting wildflower samples in Virginia where Shenandoah National Park would soon become official, making flower-picking illegal. I'd bought a second-hand Ford V-8 and was spending weekends and all my annual leave and some weekday nights in the Blue Ridge.

Barbara, spending non-school time at home far to the north, was much interested in my letters about Virginia's mountain flowers. Next year with the park a reality, we had a long Sunday date in magic mountain haze.

In March 1936 I became the first NPS employee at the new park's headquarters in Luray, Virginia (Civilian Conservation Corps "CCC" had done much work there since 1933). My first title was clerk-stenographer, my central job to set up NPS files and bookkeeping. No naturalist position was yet authorized, so I also pushed into nature research and interpretation. New friends and I, including women hardly older than my 20 years, organized Shenandoah Nature Society and began publishing a quarterly nature journal for park visitors and interested people living near the park. Though still a "boy," I was elected president of the organization and was soon editor of the nature journal. I researched and wrote and Barbara encouraged me and drew illustrations. I was part of a great conservation agency and felt happy "my park" would be protected, but I had nothing to do with policy, and what I was doing beyond office routine was my longtime specialty – nature loving and learning, not actual conservation.

Barbara and I soon married, and our worlds (that had been separate, New England and the Great Basin) became the whole United States. We felt proud of our national park system and worked to protect and advance it – *becoming conservationists.* I wrote and published a guidebook to Shenandoah. Before World War II rationing of gas and tires shut down almost all this park's visitation, we had three children, and both of us hoped they'd grow up to be naturelovers and conservationists.

The idea of conservation – that I feel means most basically the protection of home – simply becomes more fitting and more powerful in the man-woman combination, and more powerful yet when children come. The growth of "home" from one house or apartment or one farm or one town or state or region to an entire nation or continent and on to *one planet* becomes a not-quite-separable part of learning and enjoying responsibility – at least it became so in my case, though I stumbled sometimes and told myself I was but one grain of sand on a continent-sized beach.

My war-time service in China as an agent of non-military lend-lease (economic warfare) readied me for the planetary view. In frequent friendly contact with a young Chinese woman, as teacher and interpreter, I began trying to embrace the whole round Earth – and not just national parks or other wildernesses but the producing land and waters too – in fact, the whole human affair with the totality of nature for food, shelter, health, all of life.

Earthwide conservation-environmentalism (my word became *earthmanship*, a take-off from *seamanship*) surged in NPCA (National Parks *and* Conservation Association then) during the 1958-83 quarter-century when I was on the governing board. Two women in addition to my wife Eileen were primary catalysts for me – Mrs. Casenove (Dorothy) Lee, a widow, NPCA board member and a great hostess with a mansion near NPCA headquarters, and Eugenia

Horstman Connally (GG, now Eugenia Horstman of Arizona), then editor of *National Parks Magazine*.

Mrs. Lee entertained and enlivened the board at her home – after meetings, with refreshing drinks and what foreigners in China call "small chow." Usually there were special guests from outside the board, often nationally known conservationists, the Interior secretary, say, or Justice William O. Douglas, or the chairman of a conservation-oriented committee in Congress. Mrs. Lee was a birder, and she and son Richard accepted our invitations to spend weekends with us in the Blue Ridge, preferring late April or the first days of May – before the forest leafed out and hid migrating birds. Our conversations tended to interweave people and Earth.

GG and her daughter Lara spent many weekends at our Blue Ridge log house or hiking with us in or near Shenandoah National Park. GG is my favorite editor thus far in my long writing career. She embraced and expanded my proposal to co-edit a frequently appearing page called "Exploring Earthman's World." I solicited brief essays from thinkers and writers I admired, essays to help mobilize major divisions of civilization – sciences, religions, universities, governments, corporations – to join in maintaining a beautiful, healthful planet. I suspect – though won't try to prove – that some of those essays of the 1970s helped launch trends that are only now ripening, such as relationship between diverse religions and environmentalism, also the growing earth-man involvement of psychiatry.

GG went beyond reacting favorably to my proposals. She directly challenged me in 1970 to write a future-fiction story dramatizing a new civilization living in harmony with Earth. I researched, interviewed, dreamed, and toiled for months. I imagined pollution and nature-abuse getting so bad that much of Earth's youth blamed their elders and took off into space to find better homes on other planets, thus forcing the elders into such drastic reforms that people-nature relations truly did harmonize. So – survivors on other planets began drifting homeward, finding Earth the best, after all.

With a dozen different women, at least, I've felt partnership in generating and sharing responsibility feelings and actions for conservation, for environmental protection. I've taken wrong turns, or run out of energy-initiative – and somehow been corrected and re-energized in contact with wild nature. My two wives, in turn, have stirred and magnified my feeling of responsibility for the health of Earth, our home. The feeling with them has been both conscious and unconscious. We've thought and talked about home as our shared project. Now, in 2002, I still feel nature-responsibility – but no longer for "saving the world" exactly, as I confess I sometimes felt in the 1960s, 70s, and 80s. Now, with both worry and ambition perceptibly fading, I'm feeling keen responsibility mainly for telling my story as fully as I can to as large an audience as I can – to stress not an *environmental duty* on Earth that others *ought* to embrace but to establish what's been a major reality that's lived for decades with Eileen and me – showing that *a persistent effort to harmonize with nature can be a significant personal and family source of lasting happiness.*

A bit more elaboration: With Barbara, as with my Dad and Mother, the crucial center of responsibility was a personal God. We humans shared only small bits of His responsibility. With Eileen and me, and in our view with fellow humans everywhere, welcoming whatever help can be provided by other species of life, we have direct and primary responsibility for the health of Earth – as much responsibility as is in any way possible. What we think of as God long ago established the system of nature with its energies and rules or habits or customs. We try to learn the way through reading the scripture of nature which, though puzzling at times to the best of scientists, is our most solid source of the needed facts and how they fit together and affect all life.

From this natural scripture, having Eileen with me full-time since 1961, grew my perseverance with Great Basin National Park and Shenandoah National Park and **"earthmanship"** – our stubborn tendency to keep trying to reduce the strain on the resources, health and beauty of **Earth**, our home.

Chapter 2 – Cold Desert Ranch

I'm hiding in tall sagebrush, a forest to me, and I hear Papa calling, "Hey, Doc!" and then Mother, "Yoo-hoo, Darwin." I know what they want – me to get dressed up now so I'll be ready for Sunday School when the family crowds into our canvas-topped car.

Papa calls again, louder but not angrily yet. I pretend I can't hear, but I expect to answer Mother's next call. I always answer Mother sooner than Papa – unless his voice scares me, then I answer at once or sneak farther away so I really can't hear. Mother wants me to go to church but doesn't scold me for liking wild places and creatures, or wasting my time with nature, as Papa puts it. I believe Mother feels as I do about church and nature – both sacred. "The Lord is my Shepherd," she whispers sometimes. "I shall not want. He maketh me to lie down in green pastures; He leadeth me beside the still waters." If the Lord is like that, I can go to church – even if it's crammed with people.

But I'll stay here in the sagebrush long enough to see if these two ants can really drag this big worm, still wriggling, to the ant hill. I favor these two ants, they're struggling so. I thump the ant hill with a stick. Many ants race about looking for the enemy. They mingle feelers with each other, then rush blindly again. They don't see me. Maybe I'm too big for their queer eyes. Anyway, I'm not their enemy, nor the worm's. I start hurting for the worm. Would it be my fault if the ants ate the worm – when I could have saved him?

Papa calls a third time. I don't answer, but I think of the judgment book where – Papa must have told me – an angel records your behavior for God to use in the final judgment. You're "responsible" so must expect punishment for your bad behavior – or, though this wasn't emphasized, reward for good behavior, if any. Papa shifted it at times, saying, "I'm your father, and I'm responsible for you, so your behavior makes a bad mark in my judgment book, too."

I see a wandering ant finding the two with the worm. He helps, pulling once, then he zigzags toward the hill, and I wonder a second or two who's responsible for what ants do, and then I forget whose fault or whose credit anything might be. Soon many ants are helping, and at the base of the hill dozens start pulling the worm apart.

Mother calls, "Yoo-hoo," and I answer, "C-o-m-i-n-g," as if I'm farther away than I really am. Soon I run to her, cutting across the cow pasture after checking that our Jersey bull isn't pawing the ground, making dust, a danger sign.

Mother runs her fingers through my uncombed curls and tells me what to wear. I feel she'd understand, though maybe not approve, if I told her I'm happier watching the ants than getting dressed up for church – though Papa would say, "Stop wasting your time with nature, Doc." I don't know why he calls me Doc. Does he expect me to become a doctor? Would it be my fault if I never became a doctor – if I could have? But I don't tell anybody, even Mother, what I do and feel out in the sagebrush.

The ants-and-worm memory seems my first with me in it. I see now that through such pushings and pullings on the border between the wild desert of the Great Basin and the green farming community, I was finding myself as a person with potential of my own, starting to become a far-out conservationist – or, at least, responsible for something – for the ants maybe? Or the worm? Or, of course, just slightly responsible? (This "re-experiencing" that I'm doing here was learned in 1934 from my professor of literature at George Washington University in the nation's capital, and I've practiced it a lot and found it helps in sorting feelings and helping me understand myself.)

Back on the ranch in the 1920s, Papa kept trying, though not awfully hard, to get my attention off wild nature. He knew a child should have some freedom to play, but when we were alone he'd tell me things a grown-up ought to know about church and society, illustrating with our neighbors and problems on our ranch and in our community. I didn't stop hiding in the tall sagebrush, but I did soon understand him a little. He was feeling responsible for getting his family to church and keeping us good. But most sharply now he was feeling responsible for the worsening failure of this semi-desert agriculture that was supposed to justify the town's name.

Metropolis, Nevada was founded in 1910 by a company centered in faraway New York. The undisturbed soil of this part of northeastern Nevada was extraordinarily fertile. Giant sagebrush was said to prove the fertility. An irrigation system, complete with storage and distribution reservoirs and canals, was created, but only for a limited acreage. The big production and profit were to come from "dry farming." A brick hotel was built, Nevada's most modern. Electric power, water, and sewer systems were readied. A variety of businesses started. Southern Pacific brought in railway and telegraph service and built a splendid depot with an outside fountain.

Though the project was advertised across the country, it attracted mostly Mormons, descendants of Utah pioneers. The dry farming (without irrigation) went well at first. Through leaving the soil idle and heavily mulched one year, the farmers could grow one great crop of Turkey Red wheat the next year, not drawing at all on the canal. During World War I wheat was in constant demand at high prices, and annual precipitation stayed close to 14 inches. The company advertised for more farmers. Dr. John A. Widtsoe, educator and Mormon church leader, had known Papa's work at Utah State Agricultural College, so recommended him to improve the farmers' crops. In 1917, Papa had become county agricultural agent, informally "dry farm specialist" – which Papa denied ever claiming to be. We moved into a small house a mile outside the dreamed city. By the time we were settled, the big war was ending. The wheat price shrank, and so did the clouds overhead, reducing annual precipitation.

Everyone struggled. Papa agonized. In 1919, to experiment at his own expense with alternatives to dry farming, so he might make proven recommendations to the farmers he felt responsible for, Papa had bought a house and 300 acres, soon called our ranch.

A family story of our first move – which I don't remember – shows my love of home – that would ultimately get elephantized/metamorphosed? – love of home, love of Earth! There were five of us then: Papa, Mother, Wendell (born 1914), I (born 1916), and Ruth (born 1918). All but the baby helped unload the wagon and the Model T Ford. When dinnertime came, midday then, I was missing. Papa and Wendell walked the canal banks to see if I'd drowned. Papa drove to recruit searchers. Passing our former home, he found me circling the deserted house, sobbing. I must have run the three miles back to what, in my feelings, was still *home*.

The next day and again the day after that I ran back and had to be forcibly rescued. But soon, somehow, home expanded, and I was feeling good at both places and in between, almost any place from which I could see familiar Trout Creek Mountain. I liked the alfalfa fields, the canal and branching ditches, the sagebrush and rabbitbrush. Soon the domestic and wild creatures were my friends, or kin, creatures of home. Even the tumbleweeds forever bounding across the land or sailing the air, rising in dust devils (junior tornadoes that we kids called "whirligigs") helped me feel at home. And I loved the faraway whistling of steam trains. Paradoxically, though, those trains were calling me to follow to some still-more-magical place, an ever-more-fitting home. I told Mother, and she said emphatically I didn't have to follow. I tried to tell Papa, but he was too busy to listen, too worried about Metropolis's troubles and the mortgage on our ranch and helping Bishop Wolf get enough people to church and responsible for themselves and the community. Everybody, it seemed, had to be responsible for something.

My daytime territory kept expanding, reaching upslope from the sagebrush into the juniper-and-pinenut woodland, and I couldn't guess where or how to anchor my responsibility feeling – or if Papa did or didn't expect me to have such a feeling. From other causes, my nighttime territory shrank. A cow got rabid – a coyote had bitten her, Mother guessed. Papa was off somewhere, and Mother kept warning us, with fear in her voice, not even to approach the pasture fence. The cow ran desperately back and forth for hours as if seeking help. Then she died.

After that, if caught away from the house after dark, I'd run, and the faster I ran the closer behind me I felt coyotes pursuing. In bed, I'd bury my head under the covers. Too often I dreamed of falling into a mine shaft with rabid coyotes howling at the bottom. But I always waked before landing. I waked once with Mother's arms holding me. Papa came and told me few coyotes were ever rabid – "So stop worrying, Doc!" Both Mother and Papa insisted God would take care of me.

The Psalms and the words of Jesus did help me cope with my nightmares – for a while anyway. In Sunday School we were among Mormon families united in reassuring faith and in determination to make this "desert blossom as the rose" despite the severe drought. I remember the rhythm and soaring power of many voices – "Come, come ye saints. No toil nor labor fear, But with joy wend your way," a song that had bolstered morale of the people in wagon trains or pushing handcarts across the Great Plains and the Rocky Mountains. "Though hard to you, This journey may appear... Yet with joy wend your way... Above the rest, Our call shall ring. All is well! All is well!"

Papa's devotion to the church didn't take lasting root in me. Neither did his view of nature as outside real life, a waste of time. But his enthusiasm for education spread through me. He let me play with his portable typewriter. He took time one day, after Wendell had caught the school wagon for first grade, to teach me to type my name and his name and Mother's, Wendell's, Ruth's, and Ona's. (Ona was just months old, born in April 1920). On the typewriter, while I was four, I learned many words. Soon I was typing letters to Grandma. Sometime or other, when I was about six Papa taught me the longest word I ever typed at Metropolis – r-e-s-p-o-n-s-i-b-i-l-i-t-y. I'm quite sure neither Papa nor I at that time made the slightest connection between that big word and nature, or with *conservation*. Or maybe the connection was hiding already in my *unconscious*. It must have been creeping in somewhere. At age eight, typing, I made a poem – that a church magazine published – "In the midst of the wood / The little brook is singing / The prettiest song in the world..." This wasn't conscious conservation either – but the idea, in hiding??

The school wagon was pulled by horses. When snow was deep, the whole wagon box was lifted off the wheels and put on sled runners. The long winters dipped far below zero – once 60 F below! The canvas-covered "bus" had a stove that burned wood. The singing in the bus and in classrooms survives inside me just as does the singing in church - "Springtime in the Rockies," "Night-time in Nevada," "The Spanish Cavalier," "Juanita – Nita, Jua-a-a-nita, Ask thy soul if we should part. Nita, Jua-a-a-nita, Lean thou on my heart."

Papa kept buying dairy cows and raising hay and recommending others do the same. Soon – I'm remembering, slipping into re-experiencing again – there's a truck hauling cream to Elko for making butter. Papa has too many cows, so he calls me to come up beside him while he's milking, on his right side, away from the cow's legs that might kick. I like cows. They're warm, and most cows like to be touched. Papa wants me to squeeze milk from the cow's tits. I grasp a tit with my right hand and squeeze. Nothing comes. "Watch me," Papa says. "You tighten on the top first – see – with index finger and thumb, then close in with the other fingers from the top down." He does that, and a strong squirt splashes. I try again - nothing.

He assigns me a different job, that even an adult could flunk, to take 30 cattle along the fenced road to what had been dry-farm land, and let them graze there but not break into the alfalfa field and get bloated from the green plants and die. Old Sweetie, a middle-aged, steady, brown and white cow, is my helper. She's a genius. She comes when I call, and she opens the board-gate of the corral by lifting the bar from its notch with her nose. She leads along the dusty road to a barbwire gate that she can't open. She looks hard at me, seeming to say *we're in this together*.

Different species understanding each other thrills me, confirms and strengthens my love of nature. I open the difficult gate and let them all in. The mixed weeds please the cows. I sit on the ground between the herd and the alfalfa field. I'm in sunshine, gloriously warm, and I feel I can do whatever's needed. I feel responsible – and find it's a good feeling. Responsibility comes easier if you or your family have ownership of what you're feeling responsible for. More advanced responsibility takes – or took me, anyway – years longer to develop and function; it's a different road. But there's a connection I feel now, a contagion, though the route isn't easy to trace.

If the cows come toward me, trying to walk over me, I'll get up and stand tall. Occasionally, I know, I'll have to yell and fling my arms up, or, once in a while, run at the cows and maybe throw pebbles. But I feel the cows' feelings – and feel they sense mine, if only dimly. One cow starts following a fence. Such behavior, with intermittent bawling, could start others moving – or they could work out their restlessness in fake fights or imitation sex play. Or a cow could be truly in heat, and then our red-brown Durham bull would come sniffing and trying to mount – until at last the cow would hold still for the breeding. I can't remember ever not knowing what starts calves and lambs – and, after a neighbor-girl older than I told me what she'd seen through the keyhole of her parents' bedroom and asked me to participate with her in the same way, what starts people babies. It's natural but also sacred and scary. The girl and I tried in the same bedroom when her parents were away, but I failed – and ran and hid in the sagebrush, wondering how bad a mark the judgment-book angel would give me – for daring to try – or, for failing? Life is endlessly puzzling, I feel – but I don't sense impermeable walls – maybe secret linkings.

While the cows are feeding calmly or chewing their cuds, I watch badgers and ground squirrels. Just outside a badger hole a badger mother lies on her side and lets babies nurse – which is how, Mother told me, I got food from her, as calves do from cows before weaning time. The father badger chases a squirrel, and when the squirrel dives into his hole the badger digs after him, throwing the dirt back. First, I feel responsible for the squirrel and want to help him escape; then I want the badger to catch the meat and let the mother have it to make milk for the babies. I don't learn who wins. I shrug – and can't help scolding myself just a little for failing to take sides or to take any action at all. Soon the hole is closed by dirt the badger pushes behind him.

In some ways I'm like the badger. I snare squirrels, and if the badgers weren't here I'd be snaring now. You tie a lasso-loop knot on a 20-ft piece of twine, the kind that holds bundles of wheat stalks. You put the loop around the squirrel's hole, move back 12 feet and wait. When the squirrel pokes his head out to look around, you jerk the twine tight on his neck. I had a dozen picket-pin squirrels in a steel drum with its top cut out. I felt responsible for them, because I'd caught them, and I fed them wheat and watched them often, hoping I'd catch them breeding to make baby squirrels.

When I was taking the twine off a new one, to drop him in, he panicked and sank teeth into my hand and wouldn't let go. I guess I panicked; I squeezed his neck and killed him, but the teeth stayed locked in me. Papa got me loose with pliers and a screwdriver. While Mother bandaged my bleeding wound, Papa set my leaky drum into the canal and drowned the squirrels. "We fight for the crops we need. They fight against us," he said. I ran away into the tall sagebrush, with tears streaming, and got hold of myself – but stayed anyway until almost dark.

My favorite cow, Old Sweetie, is dead one morning, and I think rabid coyote, but Papa says "her lifespan." Using a horse, Papa drags her into a far field he's planning to plow next year. He buries her, not deep, saying she'll make the soil more fertile. Nightmares about death start up in me again. Mother comforts me, but Papa says

I'll never be a man till I've accepted death. I tell him I do accept death – for creatures we need to eat, even for squirrels the badgers need to eat – but not for Old Sweetie. He looks at me, his dense black hair standing as usual two inches deep, not curly like mine. I feel endlessly, totally, confused, not making sense out of people or cows or nature or anything, yet I know Papa often has kind feelings, even love. He's just pushed too hard now by sharp worries, and I'm pushed too hard too!

"Lend me the shotgun," I say. "I'll prove I accept death – for food." He likes to test me. He says God put us on Earth to get tested – for increasing responsibilities we'll have after being resurrected. He gets his 16-gauge down from its high pegs and hands it to me, not loaded, then hands me one shell.

I walk slowly, the gun heavy in my right hand, the barrel slanting down so close to the ground I watch the end to avoid scooping dirt. Among sagebrush I walk silently as an Indian, studying the ground, approaching a shallow wash. Chicken-like tracks cross the sandy ground. Quietly I shove the shell into the gun chamber. My hand is sweating. I stoop as I move, raising my head only when I stop to reconnoiter. The tracks disappear over the rim of the wash. On my stomach now I'm pushing the gun forward, wriggling and dragging after it, pushing it again. Elbows and toes in the sand move me. I lift my head and see three sagehens down in the wash, tails toward me. I aim.

The butt jolts my shoulder as the shell explodes. Sagehens are flying. But one lies crumpled, and I fear the judgment-book angel is writing about me. Papa doesn't know everything; maybe a person, having learned responsibility beyond personal selfishness (which I hadn't yet but must have been half-consciously considering) wouldn't kill scarce sagehens, even for food. As I carry the dead bird by its feet, I'm seeing myself double – from inside and from outside. I'm ashamed and I'm proud – whichever, I'm the guy responsible. An eggbeater swirls in my stomach. Papa and Wendell congratulate me, and I don't want congratulating. When the sagehen is cooked I can't eat.

My dreams worsen. Coyotes yip and howl in the dark, and death is there – maybe, most disastrous of all possibilities, for Mother. I pull the covers over my head, pretending to muffle my crying, yet hoping someone hears me. Mother comes with a coal oil lamp and puts it on my dresser. Her long hair is down from its bun behind her head, and it swings in the light as far down as her waist. She sits on the bed and caresses me. The Bible is open on her lap, and she reads: "He maketh me to lie down in green pastures; He leadeth me beside the still waters... Yea, though I walk through the valley of the shadow of death, I will fear no evil, for thou art with me..."

There's no more memory – until Papa's hand touches my shoulder before dawn. "You're big enough now, Doc, to help milk." Coyote howls seem far away while I'm holding Papa's hand among the cows in the corral. I choose one I've liked best – after Old Sweetie. Papa hands me a bucket and a one-legged stool. I move toward the cow's right flank. "So-o-o-o-o, Bess." I make my voice as deep as I can, but it trembles. "So-o-o." I touch her, and she's warm. I sit near her, almost under her, and push my head into her flank. She moves her leg out of my way. I rub her hairy skin, her swollen udder, soothing her and brushing off dirt that might fall into the milk.

This time I succeed a little. Within weeks I'm skillful, and I'm responsible for something important. Holding the bucket between my thighs, I'm gripping two tits. My hands are strong, and the streams of milk sing tinnily in the bucket and become heavier. I play them against the resounding metal to impress Papa. The streams go zi-i-i-p, soft and low-pitched now, building up foam on the rising surface. I change tits, right-front and left-rear instead of the right-rear and left-front, squeezing alternately. Playfully I squirt a stream toward my open mouth. It hits my cheek and feels hot. I adjust the aim. The milk is tasty, and I'm hungry – I'm inside nature with this cow, but dutifully I keep filling the bucket, emptying it through a strainer of cloth into the five-gallon milk can, then choosing a different cow. I feel the milk coming through the cow from grass and hay and grain that come from soil and water and sunshine. I'm an important functioning part of a human family, working responsibly inside nature, and happiness flows through me.

Papa lets me feed warm milk to a calf just separated from her mother. You dip two fingers in the bucket, then lift them toward the calf's mouth. He smells your milky fingers, licks them. He sucks your fingers into his mouth, and you feel the strength of a hungry life, yet he has no teeth to hurt you. Gently you lower your hand into the milk. The calf's eager mouth comes along, and as he sucks he draws milk from the bucket. Soon he's drinking life from the bucket even faster than before from his mother.

I'm responsible. I feel I'll get favorable credit in the judgment book for feeding calves. But Papa decides we need veal to eat and chooses a lively, husky male I'd been feeding milk, then shifting him to the seasoned alfalfa hay, which he also relishes. I defend the calf, but Papa kills it. I can't eat the veal. I guess I can't accept death, and I don't want to be responsible for any living creature, ever again.

Intense nightmares start flashing in me. Details scatter as I wake, and I'm left curled deep under the covers sobbing, feeling I'm mourning for Mother, yet knowing she's alive. I try to remember any trip that might have been to a doctor, any hint in any talk that Mother's in danger. Nothing. Nobody comes to me. I don't even tell myself how odd it is that death shifted inside me from a calf to my own Mother. Sleep catches me again.

Next morning Papa calls me earlier than usual. I jerk away from his hand, angry, and my antagonism grows as he tells me I must go out to find a young cow that's run away. Papa's hand on my shoulder feels gentle, but he ignores my confused protests. Okay, I decide, I'll find that cow and take her with me far away and start my own ranch. I'll be responsible for myself alone – only – totally.

Stars still shine. Coyotes howl. I hope they'll get me, then Papa will be sorry. I shuffle through the wet, cold grass and come to land that's squishy with humps and holes where cows have stuck their feet in as they grazed. I wade toward the willows, and each foot sinks, then squishes and pops when I pull it out. I guess Papa knows the young cow is about to give birth – and he still considers me the calf tender. But will he kill this calf too? What will the judgment angel record about Papa?

I move toward the densest willows. Water stands almost everywhere, and I fear I'll find the cow drowned. But no – there she is – on my side of the deepest water. There's a slimy package, the cord showing where it came from its mother. The cow is eating the wrapping. A wet, red-brown head emerges and gasps. The mother licks the face clean, then licks the entire calf. The rising sun warms the three of us, together deep in nature, and the grass and willows steam, the steam rising as mist, halo-like in the sunshine, soon dissolving but not forgotten. My feelings have no words. I don't want to feel responsible for the calf – but I do – yet also feel helpless, useless, and angry at Papa – because, after all, I must obey him.

Though I did my assigned tasks, sometimes gladly, often resentfully, I also kept wandering the semi-desert wilderness. Exploring upstream along the canal, I reached the diversion reservoir and the larger dam up Bishop Creek Canyon that caught snowmelt from the mountains and released it gradually during the growing season. This exploring was also exploring the ways we humans adjust to the ways of water and gravity – a Mormon strong point since Brigham Young's time.

Sunday afternoons, occasionally, Papa drove us all to the hot spring not far from the diversion reservoir. All children of Mormons are baptized, immersed, at age eight. It happened to me in that hot pool. One wall is the rising cliff from which the water springs; other walls are concrete. On less formal days we swam and dived – a little – the hot water not encouraging exertion. I liked the spring's current on me, the deep warmth of Earth, like Mother's arms and bosom when I hurt. I feel baptized in total reality, feel part of everything, but can't hold the feeling or explain it, even to myself.

Tasks associated with crops weren't as quarrel-making as tasks with animals. I remember Papa in rubber boots and me barefooted, irrigating. Alfalfa hay had to be watered regularly. The canal had concrete-lined openings in its downhill bank, closed by sliding gates of wood. Farmers had to take turns. When our turn came, the sliding gates were raised, thus filling the ditches along the upper sides of our fields. Papa would sub-divide the flow into many channels for distribution, wielding a shovel to open the way or to reduce or stop a flow – by deftly placing chunks of sod, for instance, allowing only enough water to reach the foot of the field, soaking in – no overflow, no waste. Wendell and I helped watch the flows – to correct if we could, otherwise to shout for Papa.

Each dry summer Papa watched the fast-lowering water level behind the big dam – the life of all the farms now dry-farming had ended. Trout, grown large in the depths, would begin to die as water receded and warmed. Some would escape downstream. Some we caught, using an old screen door that fit the concrete outlet. In that roaring tunnel that penetrated the big dam, we'd hold the screen against the current, one side on the tunnel floor, the two ends against the tunnel walls. One trout we grabbed by the gills as the screen held it was so big we ate cross-sections, flour-dipped and fried brown.

The dam went totally dry one August. Algae fibers blackened the canal. The mud cracked in polygonal patterns, kept drying until the black cover scaled off and left the dirt defenseless to the wind. Looking up into the leathery face of my father as we watched precious soil blowing from the canal and the fields, I knew a strong man might – just might – I couldn't watch him – cry.

Though I got angry at Papa, I kept wanting to help – and I loved him. One effort I often re-experience: I'm taking Papa's shovel, idle now, and sneaking down over the pasture-slope to a place above fields of potatoes and irrigated wheat. Despite the drought, in the yellow-green of rabbitbrush I smell water. I dig. The soil isn't dusty, yet it isn't swampy here. All around me when I stop digging and look

I see dust blowing. I count 14 dust devils active, in sight at one time, all dense with farmer's soil that should somehow have been held in the fields.

The ground I dig, deepening a small well-shaft, is loose except where roots intertwine. I cut the roots with the sharp shovel. I make a hole two feet wide and four feet long, a size I can stand in and still throw the dirt from a depth of two feet, three feet, four feet. I work through the midday mealtime, pretending I'm far off, hidden. The shovel loads get heavier; soon they're mud. The too-long handle jabs the wall of dirt, each load so heavy I rest after lifting it. A clayey shovel bite resists, almost beyond my strength, then makes a sucking plop when it comes loose. Gravy creeps down the slick place left by the back of the shovel.

I climb out and lie on my stomach, looking down into the hole I've dug. The gravy becomes level and clear on top as the silt settles. More water enters in a dirty swirl resembling a geyser. The level rises. The water becomes blue with white blobs floating – blue sky and white clouds reflecting with my own solemn face and blond hair floating in the depths – an experience to remember forever, the thrill of a well of my own, of seeing myself in the land, a responsible person, baptized in deep reality.

I run and bring Papa to see. My well – I read on his face what I also feel – the water of my well isn't enough to save our wheat crop, or even our potato crop beyond what we'll need to eat at home. But, though pathetic in quantity, this water speaks of Earth's hospitality – and speaks to Papa's deep feelings. He reaches out awkwardly because the gesture isn't customary. His big hands go around my shoulders, and he holds me against him, almost too roughly. He holds me long enough to keep his tears invisible while he blinks and turns his head away to look into far distances.

A friend, Harry Thurston, living a mile away, likes exploring as I do. We talk of climbing Trout Creek Mountain, a landmark rising high from Metropolis Valley. The upper half looks steep yet possible.

Too much distance, though, for smallish boys to walk up and back in a day. I daydream, though, and one morning after the milking, feeling Papa is friendly, I say I want to ride our Old Bay up that mountain. Papa smiles as if at a younger child than I think I am, but after breakfast he saddles the horse, winking at Wendell, apparently testing my courage.

"I'm not sure how long it'll take," I say.

"Doesn't matter," Papa says. "Stay out all night."

Feeling trapped, yet eager, I ride Old Bay toward Thurston's. The climbing sun encourages me. Harry sneaks out two Hudson's Bay blankets, some bread and raisins. We fill a canvas water bag. Harry rides behind the saddle. Old Bay walks fast, maybe twice as fast as *we* could for any distance. We let him rest while we eat wild service berries, then hurry on.

On a high ridge at noon we take another breather. One slope is so steep down we'd roll half a mile among bushes and wildflowers until stopped by an aspen grove. Still farther down, tiny, the Bishop Creek irrigation lake shines in the sun. Our eyes follow the irrigation canal among whirling dust devils. From blue distance come repeating whistles of a steam locomotive, calling me into the unknown. I tell myself we should turn back, and I read the same on Harry's face. But the horse comes to us from his grazing, and, not saying anything to the horse or to each other, we mount and climb again. It's a long, still-rising ridge, steeper and steeper. Old Bay puffs and walks slower, and Harry clings to the saddle straps to keep from sliding off the horse's rear. We'd use our own legs but don't see how to carry everything while leading and holding onto the horse – who's acting excited now, sensing our confusion. We three must stay together. Separated, we're lost, failing responsibility to each other.

Almost no trees grow on the great ridge we're climbing, but in the heads of canyons above us we see more aspen groves, this kind of tree hugging moist places. We find a big snow patch and use sharp-edged rocks to scratch a water basin for ourselves, while Old Bay scratches another with his hooves. We refill our water bag. Neither Harry nor I can say: Turn back! The sun moves toward the western horizon. Our energy increases instead of shrinking, and we take turns walking, leading the horse.

One more steep slope, and we're surrounded by sky. I drop the reins and run into the chilling wind. Ahead, northward, massed beyond a cliff and down declining slopes, is a seemingly endless forest of big pines. We're discoverers! Everywhere are highlights and shadows – more mountains and canyons than I've dreamed could exist. Metropolis Valley back there is dwarfed by unending sagebrush flats and hills leading toward a giant pyramid speckled with white – must be snow. From somewhere, with Papa, I'd seen just the point of that pyramid. He'd said, "Star Valley Mountain." Harry and I might climb it next – if we get down from this one.

We look and look and feel the wind. Westward, the sun hides behind a far black range. We build a fire as dark comes. Exhausted, we roll into our separate blankets with the fire glowing between us. I'm hungry, of course, but that's not important. Harry doesn't mention it, but when yips and howls sound below us he whisper-yells, "Coyotes!" as if asking, what do we do now?

I'm surprised by a laugh rising in me – my area of Earth has greatly expanded, my love of nature too – and I say, "I used to be scared of coyotes in the dark."

"I used to be too," Harry says, also laughing.

Old Bay, nearby, nickers.

When Mother went to Ogden, Utah, in 1925 to visit two sisters, there must have been explanations. A housekeeping woman came to take care of us males as the girls were going with Mother. Even when, on September 16, Papa told Wendell and me we'd be going with him to Ogden next day, he didn't tell us anything was wrong. The talk about Mother being overworked, or over-strained from having too many babies in too short a time, came later.

Papa was more silent than usual as we started the 200-mile drive. He cursed the road and the "damn useless car" when one of those too-fragile tires blew out. He talked about a snake – certainly a rattler – he sighted beside the road near Wendover. Later he talked about the hot day and cursed the glare of the endless white salt flats. But he didn't talk about Mother.

Late in the afternoon we reached Salt Lake City. Papa stopped near an intersection and went into a phone booth. He put coins in the phone, and he talked. When he came out, moving slowly as if with impossible effort, he put one hand and arm down around Wendell's shoulders and pulled him against his leg and hip and whispered something I couldn't hear. Then he similarly held me and whispered, "Your Mother is dead."

I don't remember more of that day. We must have driven on north to Ogden. But my next memory is of Mother in an open coffin at Grandma Lambert's big house in Kamas, Utah. I guess Mother's funeral was held at the church in Kamas, and I must have been there, but that memory is blacked out too. There's a scene, though, at the cemetery – the closed coffin being lowered from bright sunshine into the black shadow, and then the picture blanking out and the sound coming, heavy thuds on the coffin lid, before I escaped by running beyond hearing.

I thought then the Lord is not my shepherd. He's not responsible for me – nobody's responsible – and I won't feel responsible for anything – ever again.

Darwin's parents, Laura and J. Carlos Lambert, ca. 1920

Chapter 3 – Grandma's Place 1925-27+

Following Mother's funeral I live at Grandma's place at Kamas, Utah, mostly in the large kitchen that's also a main living room, but I'm mostly blanked out in nightmares, whether awake or asleep. Grandma's the responsible one. I don't know where Papa is, though I guess he's gone back to Metropolis to take care of our ranch there and to keep serving as county agricultural agent. Grandma's with me or near me all the time, and my brother Wendell's somewhere around. He and I are mostly good friends but not necessarily interested in the same things. Grandma keeps me safe and tries to comfort me. I love Grandma always, but often don't hear what she says. Some memories do rise and live as re-experience.

I'm out back of Grandma's house. Wind blows in the orchard where nearly all the leaves are gone – more than a month, maybe, has passed since Mother's burial – and the few surviving leaves are dried and rattle in the wind. I feel I'm seeing the wind by watching those leaves and the tiny snowflakes like white gnats dancing. I'm stretched out on my back along an almost level limb. One apple hasn't been picked. I reach for it, but Mother's death hits me again, and I don't pick it. Grandma's house has 14 rooms and a round tower. Lombardy poplars on the street-corner sides are taller than the tower. Grandma knows when to call me or come to me and take me in her arms, and she doesn't try to kiss me after I've dodged once. I like her understanding. Visiting women whose names I can't remember, relatives or family friends, pet me and kiss me and keep saying things they can't know, like Mother wasn't in that coffin when the shovelfuls of dirt came down on it; she's home in heaven where we'll live with her again. I don't argue. I just don't know.

But often I pretend I've got to pee, and I hurry out to the backhouse, then deeper into the orchard or roundabout to the old barn that's full of cobwebs.

I help Grandma when I can guess, or she tells me, something she wants. I even wish there were more chores. I do cut and carry firewood – that's a long-time habit. I've become pretty good, too, at taking over the mouse-trapping in the pantry – not as a job, really, just for fun, I guess, or to show off. Grandma smells mice; she hates them and doesn't like touching them or anything they might have touched.

I want to look after her chickens. I always liked doing things with birds and mammals. But she loves feeding the chickens herself, saying "Chick-chick-chick" as she swings her hand - and trickles of grain fly between her fingers. She's letting me bring in eggs, though, from nests I find under bushes or in cobwebby hiding places in the barn, wherever the chickens run free in daylight times; they're always safe inside the coop during darkness.

When Papa was leaving after the funeral – memories do pop up in me, maybe more and more often – he told that story again about my being born in the big kitchen here on a night when 18 inches of snow fell. He talked again too about his grandfathers, converted to Mormonism in Europe: John Lambert of a cattle-growing family in Yorkshire and William O. Anderson, Grandma's father, in Copenhagen, after being imprisoned as a conscientious objector. Both came early to Utah. John Lambert was a friend of Mormon leaders Joseph Smith (having known him before the Far West migration) and Brigham Young (who followed Smith as head of the church). Great Grandpa Lambert was a stone mason in constructing Salt Lake Temple. In 1861 he built the first house in Kamas. Papa emphasized, "They were men of fidelity and honor. Any principle they believed in they'd fight for to the last ditch. Like them and me, Doc, you're a *Pioneer!*"

Being a Pioneer, I guess, is great, but now anyway I'd rather be an Indian. In my room upstairs at the back of Grandma's house, I read a lot of Seton's *Two Little Savages*, about boys living like Indians with the wild animals and plants. Boys don't have to be responsible for anything, except a little maybe for themselves. Grandma does expect that much, and I try to take care of myself – part of the time anyway.

There's a window above the roof of the big north porch, and often I crawl out to be a savage. I slide down the roof and the corner column. I pause in the bushes there to be sure no one's watching, then dash across the dirt street into the willows and drop into the ravine of Beaver Creek. The stream tumbles over rocks between banks thick with wild rose bushes, naked now – no green pastures, no still waters, but I'm hidden and the creek's talk gives more comfort than the caresses of women who aren't my Mother. Each time I sneak out I explore farther up the stream, and someday I'll find where it starts – from beds of sand under hard ground maybe or from cracks in a mossy cliff, some sacred place anyhow.

When Papa comes again I tell him I want to go back to our ranch, the cows and horses and wild creatures, and the little well I dug by myself – for Papa. I tell him he knew Mother in different places, but I remember her alive only at our ranch, and we should live there and make it even more beautiful – for Mother. He's listening, I think, which often he isn't, and he says he'll try to arrange so Wendell and I can live with him there after school's out. "But we've got to be practical, Doc. We can't keep the ranch much longer." He explains it's getting him deeper into debt as the water-short farming is doing to most of the Metropolis families.

Now he takes Wendell and me in his Model T to visit our sisters at Uncle John's. It's a healing visit. We kids are happy being together and wish it could happen more often, and wish soon again we'll have our own home. I say I'll walk to visit the girls soon. What I don't say is, I need to get away from other people part of the time. I need to be alone a little with wild nature. Papa and Wendell wink at each other and look from eye corners at me, silently laughing, I feel, but honestly I think I can walk the distance in about two hours, taking shortcuts across cow pastures and through wild pine-cedar groves and maybe aspens. Papa spends the night at Grandma's and says good-by again in the dark before dawn – the time of so many memories of him at the ranch.

The mystery of far away works on me, almost as did those train sounds in Metropolis. Papa's youngest sister Lorraine stubbornly married a red-headed Jew from Europe, not converted to Mormonism. They have a daughter named Betty, and the family lives upstairs here. My curiosity about the inside of the round tower on the house pulls me up there the first time, but something about Uncle Harry keeps pulling me back. He's been almost everywhere and coped with almost everything, and I dream of doing all that, of soaring as on Trout Creek Mountain beyond the piney horizons, of seeking a combination of persons and forces I can cope with, give and take, earning my food, clothing, shelter, and security without waiting for Papa.

Somehow, along about here, I was suddenly wanting responsibility again – but for myself only. Or was this all fantasy? Uncle Harry, whom I'd imitate, wasn't really real, was he? And I guess I wasn't even sure I was real – or just what was really real. I feel Grandma knew the dream-nightmare confusion I was living in. Perhaps she knew about my wanderings far up Beaver Creek. Perhaps she even knew my vague world dream.

Time and again, when alone for a rare moment with Uncle Harry up in that round tower, the Zieve apartment with windows three-fourths of the circle around us, I wanted to tell this extraordinary uncle my world dream. But I never in those years could quite get hold of it, never could quite begin to put my fear-and-pleasure-streaked longing into words or coherent thoughts.

Nevertheless, my Kamas experience was somehow expanding my horizons, my home territory, as well as deepening my interconnections with nature (I see that now!), and as my territory grew both nature and society grew in space and complication. I had this internal puzzle of humans and nature – with nature not just something to enjoy or watch or study, not just pet-like – to play with or observe. It's also things and processes you work with, accomplish with, interweave your self with, like designs on Indian baskets or pots or rugs. I felt estranged from society's typical attitudes – some of them anyhow. But I couldn't have been so very far outside normal; I felt I was climbing out of a dark tunnel back toward kinfolk and friends.

Grandma never mentioned any judgment-book angel, or used the word *responsibility* in talking to me. She and Wendell and I went to Sunday School together, and I caused no friction. And she sent me to public school – where other kids didn't tease me as if I were an oddball – as they had in Metropolis, at first, because I seemed (and was) too young for my grade.

Neighbor boys in Kamas were soon treating me as one of them, pulling me into games I'd never experienced in Metropolis. We raced handmade toy boats in the tiny streams that, Mormon fashion, ran in grassy channels at the edge of streets. The six-to-eight-inch craft were powered only by the water's current. We competing boys followed on the ditch-bank, prohibited from touching the boats while they were racing. Different shapes acted differently in the flow. My own design was long and narrow, the ends tapering to sharp points for easy penetration of grass and algae fibers in the water. My "patent" – each of us carved differently – was wide notches a quarter-inch deep crosswise on the bottom, to catch the current's thrust. I credited the notches mostly, but also the sharp points, for any victories I won.

The water play with nature was simple compared with the air play, yet both were direct experiments with Earth's ways as youngsters' play tended to be. Some of us made kites – framed crosses of pine wood usually, the sticks thinned with a carpenter's plane (my Grandpa's when he was alive) so light in weight. Newspaper was glued on, and we made tails of string knotted around crumpled bits of newspaper. The main secret was the angle you got from strings tied to the four ends of the cross. If the wind was medium-strong and you had smooth ground to run on, you might keep your kite in the air longer.

A new boy recruited me and Grandma's shop to make airplanes using wound-up rubber for power. I didn't believe it was possible as I hadn't believed Seton's savages, imitating Indians, could make whatever they needed – boys making workable bows and arrows, fire-by-friction gadgets, traps to catch fish, birds, mammals, or insects – directly from nature. My new friend might have been part Indian. Our airplane fuselages would be simple sticks planed down to light weight, usually two sticks per fuselage, spread apart some, to hold a wing and a tail and a propeller - with rubber strands between the propeller shaft and a hook under the tail.

I see, of course, we fudged with the rubber and some of the other materials, but they *did* come first from nature – in South America. (Much later I'd visit the Amazon jungle where rubber grew in native trees.) Wings would have pine edges and tiny ribs of the hard "skin" split off a bamboo stick with a razor blade. You bend a shallow arch into the ribs and glue on tissue paper, and there'll be a lift in the wings as the propeller pulls them through the air.

By far the most work was carving light-weight propellers out of small pieces of pine board. Our pocketknives made blisters from the intricate effort, but after half a day of careful persistence a propeller would be ready.

We kept experimenting with our odd airplanes until other boys, and finally even grown-ups, noticed. Most of our models lasted, with minor repairs, through twelve to twenty landings. We two collaborated on the last plane, what we called a twin pusher. It had its tail in front - no rudder, just the stabilizer, with a shallow angle (dihedral) in the middle. The one big wing, also dihedral, was near the back; so were the two propellers. To launch the craft, you wound the propellers in opposite directions, grasped them and the rear of the frame, and at face level pushed gently into approximate flight speed, preferably into a weak but steady wind. The twin pusher flew best of all, beyond Grandma's house and along the street. Our so-careful work was harmonizing, singing, with Earth's air, balancing gravity with other forces of nature.

Uncle Harry, watching, commented, "You boys will go far in the world." These words sang in me for years.

Not all my Kamas adventures were fun, but all were educational, which didn't necessarily ruin them for me. One friend brought tobacco snatched from his father's store. I'd discovered a tall plant with hollow stems growing in a marsh and suggested we make pipes. From the main stem nearly an inch through, I cut a bowl with the bottom closed solid at a joint typical of this plant. The thin pipestem, from higher up on the plant, was thrust into the bowl where I made the right size hole by stabbing with a small nail. Three other boys made similar pipes.

We hid in an unused woodshed. Pretending we were Indians smoking in a tepee, we stuffed our pipes with tobacco and applied flame (Whitemen's matches, I confess). My pipe lit, and I showed off by blowing puffs at the others – who couldn't get going.

I imitated grownup smokers' movements. But soon the woodshed started to sway, almost to tip over. After a bit I realized it was really me swaying - badly sick. A friend on each side held me up, and we ran home to Grandma. The doctor came (his office was a block away). He aimed sharp eyes at us boys. We confessed our tobacco, quite serious with Mormons, but that didn't satisfy him. He sent a boy running for my pipe. When he saw it, he said, "Water hemlock! Deadly poison!" I spent a week sick, deeply learning the nature lesson. I tried to be more wisely responsible – for myself, I mean, and maybe close family and close friends – no responsibility beyond that.

Discovery of horseradish plants growing half-wild in Grandma's apple orchard launched a different episode. Uncle John had brought my sisters and left them with Grandma for a few days. We dug horseradish roots, thick, almost white, and ground them in Grandma's handle-crank grinder without asking first. Tears came worse than from onions, and Grandma moved us quickly out onto the screen porch. We filled glass jars with the ground root and added vinegar – Grandma's recommendation. The resulting relish was tasty, especially on beef, the main meat in the mountain West, and we sold our nature-production quite easily around the neighborhood. The money went for clothes that Papa hadn't found the time – or maybe the money – to buy for us since Mother died.

Even after we had school-year homes elsewhere with Papa, Kamas continued as Wendell's and my summer home. We lived mostly at Uncle Roy's farm, two miles from town, and helped with the haying and other farm work. Uncle Roy loved wild places and had named his first son Walden. I could sense that, like me, he'd like spending his Sundays out in the mountains but attended church anyhow. Both Uncle Roy and I would later write books and become state legislators. He taught me to identify forest trees and many other Great Basin and Uinta Range plants. He also taught me that the best farmers are also naturalists, students of nature and participants in nature, but he didn't mention conservation, or if he did I don't remember. He and cousin Walden, though, got me puzzling about Henry David Thoreau and the famous book called *Walden*.

Uncle Roy's barn was so big you just kept exploring. The upper space was for hay; the ground floor had room for cows, horses, and sheep. Along with Uncle Roy's and Aunt Zina's children Walden and Corine, we climbed wall ladders and pulled ourselves up thick ropes. We dropped with belly thrills into bouncy hay. We youngsters earned our meals and lodging, getting up, except Sundays, before daylight, we boys doing early chores outside, while Corine and younger sister helped cook breakfast. The kitchen had a sink, a pipe to carry waste water outside, and a pump from a well at the sink (no faucet). Move the pump lever strongly up and down and the water gushes – coming from nature, powered by nature. But I didn't tell anybody; they'd call me a "nut."

Haying was the summer's big job, starting with Uncle Roy himself mowing. He sat on a two-wheeled machine pulled by two work-horses. The mowing blade, lowered to horizontal near ground level when in action, moved invisibly fast back and forth through the longer, guiding teeth of the mowing bar. The noise carried far as Uncle Roy circled the field leaving a continuous swath of cut hay and adding hay fragrance to the breeze.

The next step – that intrigued me more and more because I coveted the job instead of small-boy jobs – was raking. Wendell and Walden had both operated the dump rake. It was a wide thing of slender steel parts. The two metal wheels were taller than I was then and about ten feet apart. Between them the rake itself was big curves of steel (tines), one every few inches filling the whole distance between the wheels. You sat on a metal seat the size of a man's buttocks. I knew I'd feel scared above all those sharp tines, but I was growing up and believed I could cope. And I see now the whole experience with Uncle Roy and Walden was training in "earthmanship": You can't harmonize with nature unless you understand production and human needs as well as the nature of nature and how to conserve natural resources.

Ahead of the metal seat, between the long shafts, was the one horse, to be controlled with your voice and two long leather reins. I watched and did various steps over and over in my mind. You had to hold the reins in your left hand only, because when the rake got full you had to move a lever with your right hand to dump the hay in the windrow to be gathered up by a bigger, more complex machine called a bull rake. You started the windrows when your dump rake was full. The rows of hay would be about 20 feet apart with this crop of average density, and you had to continue them faithfully in lines as straight as possible all across the field by dumping at exactly the right time, in line, with what you'd dumped before.

I kept telling Uncle Roy I was ready, I could cope, but he kept putting me off, telling me raking was dangerous and, anyway, he couldn't spare me from the haystack crew, leading the big horse pulling the big rope that lifted the great netful of hay as high as the stack where it could be dumped as the stacker ordered. But finally my chance did come. What happened was unforgettable and still runs vividly inside me as I re-experience:

I'm scared but proud as I hold the reins in my left hand and climb onto the high metal seat above the curving tines. The horse, Pancho Villa, seems calm. I make the snapping sounds in my throat that I've long practiced, and Villa moves toward the field with the rake in position behind me. We reach the swaths of hay, and I lower the rake into working position, watch as it fills, then move the lower lever with my right hand to dump. I thus start a windrow, and I remember a special need to let the rake down easy so the sharp tines don't jab into the ground.

Bits of hay are blowing out of position, but I'm getting the windrows straight. Soon the work seems automatic. Pancho Villa has pulled this rake in many haying seasons and makes the right moves. My eyes wander. Across the fence there's tall grain ripening. The wind sways the grain, and the field resembles a lake with waves. We turn to start back across the field, and there's a stronger gust. More hay flies. I hear a swish and glimpse the grain field violently agitated in waves and troughs. Pancho Villa sees it too and whirls away from it, running out of control.

I pull on the reins and shout, "Whoa! Whoa!" Villa doesn't seem to hear. He's cutting across the field slantwise. I tighten my legs around the thin steel support of the seat, to anchor myself on. I can't see whether the tines are up or down, and I'm afraid they'll catch in the ground and wreck the machine – and Villa and me! I pull the reins with all my strength and shout "Whoa! Whoa! Whoa!" I hear myself shouting, and the sound is high-pitched with fear. If Villa wasn't already scared, my desperate voice would scare him. I stop shouting and get one rein in my right hand, so – with the other in my left – I can jerk Villa's head from side to side and slow him down.

The big wheels hit an irrigation ditch at a slant, and we lurch crazily and seem to be flying. When we come down we're still right side up and not racing quite so fast. But we cross our field three times before Villa actually stops. I'm trembling, but I guide Villa back to where we left off, and we go on raking. No tines seem broken, and the metal wheels don't look bent. I think I hear distant laughter from others of the hay crew, but all of us go on working.

    The haying and the rake runaway added to my understanding of horse-nature and of wind and soil and plant life. There are ways to do for harmony, and ways not to do, and we learn to survive and improve and live-down our mistakes. Work-pressure slackened. Uncle Roy rewarded us by shifting easily from production-with-nature to recreation-with-nature, taking us hunting and fishing, camping and picnicking. We explored the western half of the high Uinta range where a good road was reaching Mirror Lake. We went skinny-dipping in wild rivers quite different from soaking and floating in the Metropolis hot spring.

    We camped at the western end of the east-west above-timberline range, that drains into Salt Lake (Great Basin). A doctor's wife, who'd walked with him from the campground to the fishing spot he favored, got lost on her way back. She knew the trail, but an impressive big butterfly crossed in front of her and landed. She wanted a closer look, but before this was possible the butterfly took off again. The lady followed and finally saw enough – but couldn't then find the trail she'd left.

    When her husband came back from hours of fishing, he learned she hadn't been seen. Every camper, including us, helped search. Mosquitoes were so thick that one hand stroking down the opposite forearm made black rolls of insect bodies. Darkness deepened. The shouting of searchers between campground and fishing area brought no reply. The lady, somewhat elderly, might be miles away – with bears, cougars, snakes, and mosquito hordes.

    At dawn we were searching again, and recruits were arriving from Salt Lake City to help. I can't remember how many days and nights the lady was lost – perhaps three days, three nights. Someone then – close to me in the spaced lines we formed for efficient coverage – found her sitting on a boulder, conscious but dazed. She refused to get up off that boulder until her husband the doctor came for her. I can't forget the suffering that showed in her face.

And I can't forget the happy feeling I had because I'd gladly shared responsibility for another human – not this time a family member or a friend. Papa's judgment-angel watching me seems to confer happiness immediately, at appropriate times, not just influence on St. Peter at Heaven's gate in the possibly remote future. There's some puzzling psychology here that I'll have to question Papa about – and watch for *carefully* in my further experiencing and re-experiencing.

Chapter 4 – Hot Desert Oasis 1926-27

Wendell and I and Dad – not called Papa any more as that's childish – have a new town. It's Overton, Nevada, where Dad's to teach agriculture in Moapa Valley High School. It's 500 miles south of our Metropolis Valley ranch and a mile lower in elevation. The temperature, ten days before school starts with me in sixth grade, is 125 F. You get burned if you touch a car door in sunshine without gloves. I feel Overton's not as good as Kamas, which wasn't as good as our ranch, but if things work out here, Dad says, we might bring the girls to live with us.

There's a stream in this Moapa Valley, Muddy River. First thing I did outside, wearing an old straw hat as Dad insisted, was walk along it, but it's not the place to get away from continual people – which I like to do, though I also want a friend or two, like Harry Thurston on Trout Creek Mountain or my airplane-making partner in Kamas.

Alone now, I've climbed a dry canyon to a mesa's tabletop. My waterbag feels cold where it touches me, though I'm hot everywhere else. As far as I can see on this flatness there's no other person. The land is pebbles mortared in tan soil. Cactus and knee-high scraggly bushes live here. Lizards disappear with flashy speed so I can't describe them. I'm carrying a long stick, partly for protection against rattlesnakes and fat venomous lizards called Gila monsters. But I don't hate snakes and monsters or want to kill them. If they stay away from me, I'll stay away from them.

I'm trying to think why I resent new homes Dad arranges. Will I stay homesick for Mother and the ranch all my life? The wild places here are so different – no tall sagebrush or pinenut trees or junipers, no aspens. Could a "little savage" imitating Indians survive anywhere near Overton?

I'm walking fast and pointing the stick as a jousting knight would at his enemy, then I'm swinging it like a sword, listening to its buzz as it cuts the air. Feelings shift inside me. Control slips. I'm cutting harder, imagining cobras or tigers or human bandits or the Devil's angels, and the harder I swing the louder the buzz. Thorny cactus plants and dwarf bushes somehow become enemies, and I'm whacking them with the sword.

I'm angry, and with every whack I'm angrier, but I'm slow understanding why. I charge into the thickest patch of vegetation, swinging right and left, bashing enemies. I keep on till my right arm can't fight any more. It hangs aching, barely grasping the stick. I don't hate Dad; he's doing the best he can for us. But I hurt inside from *wanting* to hurt him.

Turning, I look at the destruction. A beautiful cactus, once of keg shape and size, is split almost in two, oozing light-green blood that's gelatin-thick. Half the cactus remains erect with red flowers on top. I feel sick – as when at our ranch I shot the sagehen without giving it even one chance to fly. My muscles, recovered, grip the stick in a different flash of anger. I fling that evil stick from me with all my strength. It whirls end to end, with buzzes fading, and disappears over the edge of the mesa. I drop face down and sob into the hard tan soil. The tears seem right. When I get up, I pour my precious water bag supply to help the worst-injured plants.

I walked and ran northward, running away from Overton, wanting to never come back. I must have covered miles while light lasted. After dark I finally turned, and it was midnight before I found our house. Dad's hands gripped my shoulders while he scolded in anger, mixed, I felt, with fear and love. He wouldn't let me eat anything – "Wait for breakfast!"

But long before breakfast he waked me in the dark, as so often at the ranch, and he gave me a cantaloup, a favorite of mine. While I ate the whole thing, he talked about Overton. Like Metropolis and Kamas, he said, it's a Mormon community, and we can feel at home here. The agricultural water supply is limited but more dependable than at Metropolis. Mormon communities are mostly successful, because of the close-knit organization, the tradition of overcoming impossibilities with persistence, and the church's discouragement of mining and all gambling, drinking, and other weakening habits. At intervals, he'd ask, "What do you think, Doc?" I doubted he really wanted me to answer, but I felt good being asked.

Dad got us a housekeeper, his cousin Hilda Mitchie from Provo, Utah. She cooked well and arranged our things to be handy. She recognized our needs for school supplies and clothes, table space and light for studying, but she was young and had her own life to live, and we youngsters weren't a long-lasting part of it. She was a church person, of course, and she tried to break me of running off to "nature" Sunday mornings.

Our water at the house came from a concrete cistern, refilled at unpredictable intervals by rain channeled off the roof. Our refrigeration was in a "desert cooler," a small cupboard with shelves open front and back – except draped in burlap with its upper end folded down into a bucket, this burlap wicking water, letting it evaporate in the desert air, thus keeping the food cold.

Dad gave us an educational tour – in his Star car that replaced the old Model T. Maybe he was practicing for his teaching. Main crops, he said – as in much of Mormon-land – were hay and livestock, both meat and milk products being sold commercially. I wanted to stop at a dairy farm and touch a cow, but Dad wouldn't even slow down. I noticed palm trees, very tall, the first I'd ever seen, but Dad kept driving, while saying they were date palms, maybe the only grove in Nevada – also that this valley had a few orange trees and last year produced Nevada's first oranges, seven of them. Almond and pomegranate trees are more common, "But none of these oddities is significant in the valley's agriculture." He took us past fields of cantaloups, watermelons, diverse vegetables and berries. "The main crops are shipped to cities," Dad said. "Sugar cane and cotton used to be commercial crops – but not now."

We came back into Overton's dirt streets, supposing our tour was over. Two boys were picking something off a street. "Puncture vine," Dad said, "also called goat-head. Its burs, like jacks girls play with, except sharper, cause flat tires. The town pays kids for goat-heads they bring in." Wendell wanted to stop – he often alerted to money prospects – but Dad pushed on the gas as if remembering something good that wasn't on the program.

Some miles south of town as he drove without talking or hesitating I saw a pond, half-hidden. Two young bodies rose up out there and dived. "Swimming pool," I said. "Let's stop and cool off."

But no. What he had in mind was farther, the Colorado River, biggest stream I'd ever seen. The raging torrent, football fields across, I guessed, was even muddier than the little Muddy. We walked to the edge and couldn't see into the water. Dad helped look for a place where we could at least wade, but everywhere the bank was unstable, the drop-off steep, and the current dangerous. Dad said in consolation, "Big fish in there." But we didn't have anything to fish with.

In the distance, upstream, I saw odd structures – tall, looking old, maybe stone walls plastered with adobe mud. When I pointed, Wendell and Dad saw them. "Must be Lost City," Dad said. "Built and lived in by long-ago Indians. I've heard they raised maize, Indian corn – must have somehow captured water to irrigate with. The ruins are closed to the public to save remaining artifacts."

Dad went on talking, but I was thinking in surprise that, contrary to my earlier angry guess, *some Indians* apparently could thrive not so very far from Overton. Could I learn to love this different face of nature?

When I was listening again, Dad was reminding us that he knew the Governor – "Scrugham – I'll ask him to keep us informed. The ruins are being studied by scientists."

Dad and Scrugham had been Democratic candidates in the 1922 election, and Dad, though not winning a legislative seat, had helped Scrugham carry Elko County. Dad also knew U.S. Senator Key Pittman. Another election was coming in November, and Dad said the Governor and Senator wanted boys to place their posters around town. "They'd pay," he said, and Wendell perked up, and I did too, a little.

I went back, though, to thinking about Indians. If they could raise corn from this hot desert, I could make a start, at least, toward adapting as I learned more about how nature worked here. I went to Sunday School and picked puncture vines off dirt streets and went to school and really studied. And I found pomegranates falling and going to waste. The juicy kernels massed inside, seeds liberally coated with juicy "jello," were yellow in color (not red as in the commercial variety of pomegranate but sweeter and tastier inside the leathery skins). My at-home territory was beginning to grow again as it had in Metropolis and Kamas valleys and mountains. Repeatedly, I carried my water bag, fat and heavy, up that Overton mesa – it served better than trying to get bucketsful from the seepage at the old mine – in my efforts to revive the cactus plants and desert bushes my anger had so damaged.

I like Overton grade school. Miss (Mae W.) Rowe gave me all B the first time, except A in geography, but next time it's all A except B in physical education and drawing. Miss Rowe has become my judgment-book angel – my earlier one tending to fade – and she's doing what I hoped and wanted all along, revealing her judgments in time for me to improve my performance. Dad does this too, in different fields, though not as gently as Miss Rowe. My main complaint is, I haven't found a friend yet to hike with me on the wild mesas or to Lost City.

Maybe a girl would hike with me. My eyes often cling on Eloise whose desk is two rows to my left and three desks toward the front. She has brown hair and smooth skin. I've never dared speak to her, but her right cheek and her right ear up ahead there seem to play peek-a-boo as she turns her head, tossing her hair. Once she turned and our eyes met, and her face after that seemed pink and mine burned. I feel she's sacred somehow, unreachable.

Another girl I watch, everybody watches, is Regina. Kids say she's from Hollywood, staying a while with friends here. She wears crystal beads and a crystal bracelet and noticeable cosmetics. She's usually with other girls, and they seem dazzled by her. I guess she feels Overton boys are small-townish, but sometimes she comes walking alone while I'm playing mumble-peg on our front lawn alone. If I glance up without lifting my head, I catch her watching, but when I move my head she looks quickly away, lifting her gaze, pretending she doesn't know I exist. I don't feel she's unreachable, but if I spoke to her, I think, she'd laugh at me.

One girl, Elaine, already speaks to me. Once when larger boys snatched my wooden top that I'd just learned to spin with a string, she snatched it back for me and stared them down. She sits behind me where I can't watch her, and I don't think of her as either sacred or city-smart. I guess I think of her as another person my age, not as girl or boy. She seems more grown up than I, like an older sibling. She might be a better companion on walks than any boy I know. But I lack initiative to ask if she's interested.

Then she comes to me at recess and says she wants to go to the eighth-grade play but can't be out alone after dark. I say, "Let's go together." She hesitates, then agrees. The date is a week ahead, and I worry. I lie awake at night, though I seem to have sand in my eyes. I think I should cancel, but I don't.

Elaine talks about school as we walk the short distance we know well in daylight. I answer at intervals with one or two words; I never was much of a talker. I buy the tickets and feel important (maybe it's sort of "responsible" that I feel), taking a girl with my own money - that comes from distributing the political posters and picking goat-head plants. We sit quite far from the stage, as near out of sight as possible, surrounded mostly by parents. Elaine whisper-talks into my ear, commenting on people she sees moving by.

    Lights go off except on stage, and the curtain rises. Elaine puts her hand down between us, and I take it. Holding and squeezing it in response to tensions in the play seems better than voice-talking. Too soon, though, the hands feel sweaty. The air is hot, and I'm not hearing all of the characters' words. I ask Elaine what was said, but that doesn't help. While I'm asking for words just past we both miss the current words. Besides, she isn't hearing perfectly either. The play must be a comedy; people in front laugh often. We squeeze hands and laugh along with them – and survive the first act.

    Early in the second act, we solve the hand-sweating, learning to catch and release, squeeze and release – not to hold continuously. All seems well except the characters mumble too much, but then without warning my eyes close and my head nods. I jerk my head up and look secretly to see if anyone noticed. Apparently not. If Elaine noticed she's kind enough not to stare. Eloise and Regina are here – Eloise far to the front with her parents, Regina somewhere behind us with a boy-and-girl gang, giggling behind hands – not, I think, at me, or anything on stage.

    There's a steady hum in the audience, and the voices of the actors and actresses are far off, Their meanings eluding me. My head droops heavily to one side, startling me again into a jerky movement. Elaine takes my hand; she's watching the stage as if entranced. The second act ends with no one staring at us, but the third act seems to last forever. The voices from the stage lack recognizable syllables in my ears. The stage lights glare into my gritty eyes. Every time my eyes close my head nods.

    Elaine keeps watching the stage, knowing, I'm quite sure, that I'm bored-sleepy, but still kind, even motherly. She holds my hand and at intervals squeezes. I don't actually sleep, and finally the play is over. Everyone is clapping and standing up, and I am too, pretending, and guessing many others are pretending too. When the clapping fades, Elaine takes my hand again and leads me out through the crowd. When we're alone in the dark, I expect her to scold me, but she walks beside me, talking about the play, and I pretend I'm getting it straight now. But I'm not – and I don't care very much, and I think Elaine's a kind and intelligent person, but not one to become interested in nature or to hike with me on the mesa.

I feel Elaine's fond of me – as if, say, I'm her kid brother. She gives a tighter squeeze to my hand as we go up her front steps. The hands aren't sweating now. I squeeze back. "Good night," she says, and I say, "Good night." After the door closes, I walk slowly to the front gate. I close it carefully. Then I run as fast as I can all the way home.

My date was gossiped about as amusingly traditional. Searching now into that long-ago time, I see it as helping to hide my somewhat extreme affair with nature – and as a lesson I failed to learn firmly – that all wonderful girls aren't ideal for a boy wrapped up in nature and wanting to live as one of Ernest Thompson Seton's "little savages." She wouldn't understand or care how far or long or eagerly I walked in the desert. She'd laugh gently and stay friendly if I told her I was trying to heal cactus plants I'd injured, if I explained I was feeling guilty, wanting to atone, wanting all the plants to flourish – not only because I enjoyed them but because a direct connection into responsibility, into duty, had been awakened in me – though, of course, I didn't yet – couldn't yet – expect that feeling to grow or to apply beyond making amends for damage I myself had actually caused. I wouldn't blame her if she didn't understand. I don't fully understand my own explanation.

I kept on with normal things – school, church, horseplay with other boys. Wendell and Miss Mitchie each had their concerns and friends, no inclination to spy on me. Dad tried to discourage my far wanderings but was busy with his teaching and efforts to win farther advancement. He could hardly see what I didn't realize myself at the time, that I was drawing guidance and strength and purpose more and more from basic nature, less from other humans and from institutions.

Life went on. One January day in school I saw snow falling past the windows and went to look closer. Miss Rowe persuaded the principal to declare a special recess. We had a great time trying to catch flakes, but nothing stuck to the ground. One April day the school shut down so kids could help farmers with harvesting made urgent by 100-degree heat.

I chose radishes and wore Dad's old straw hat. We worked under time pressure in dazzling sun – not pleasure exactly, but I enjoyed at-home feelings from the land and crops. In that dry air a person tolerated high heat, your sweat evaporating, cooling you as milk was cooled in our kitchen's desert cooler. I pushed a basket along the row as I worked ahead, pulling and tying the colorful radishes. You pull with your right hand and accumulate in your left. When your left can't encircle any more, your right reaches into your pocket for a tie, already cut the right length. You wrap two or three times around the narrow part of the radish bundle. Deftly then, with the right fingers alone, or maybe with one end of the tie in your teeth, you make that special knot. It has to hold through all the transporting and displaying until the customer gets the bunch into the kitchen.

School resumed after a few days, but heat kept worsening – no air-conditioning then – and enthusiasm for study didn't fully revive. Official temperature reached 125 F in the shade before school let out on May 26.

I found an old pith helmet inside an abandoned mine tunnel, probably left by a prospector years ago. It enabled me to increase my miles-long hikes on shadeless mesas and flats and in the red-rock canyons. On each return I hung the helmet again in the tunnel, not wanting to appear odder than necessary in town. I hiked farthest on Sundays when Dad, Wendell, and Miss Mitchie were most occupied in church. I did still attend Sunday School fairly often, understanding that if I didn't I'd be hurting Dad. Some Sundays there'd be a hike at dawn and an afternoon-evening hike – Sunday School and our midday dinner being sandwiched in. I learned the bright constellations in the desert sky and still enjoy them.

Strange tracks in sand or mud intrigued me, and I saw reptiles, including venomous snakes and one Gila monster, also many kinds of birds, rarely a speedy roadrunner – no coyotes, though, few mammals of any kind. I discovered diverse wild places – rugged peaks, fantastic shapes of colorful rock, low coves where vegetation was green-green with water not far underground. I thought of building a rock shelter where I could stay days and nights if I chose – or I might close in an old tunnel and live there. But our Overton time proved too short. I never found the right companion, girl or boy, to hike in that hot desert with me.

I'm remembering Wendell and me cooling off in an irrigation canal near town, a place screened from outside by trees and shrubs, so bathing suits aren't needed. Boys gather in a two-foot-deep upper pool and splash each other. When you build up enough courage there, you float head first, facing toward "the slide" where the water speeds down a moss-lubricated concrete incline into a deeper pool. We pause there, bodies under water, eyes checking whether girls or adults are in sight. If none are, we climb out and run along the bank to the upper pool for another slide.

Most keenly, though, I'm remembering a special day, a Sunday, a dip and a slide after Sunday School, then a sudden idea – trying to recruit Wendell, then just any boy, to walk with me to the Colorado River and explore the old Indians' "Lost City," and, not succeeding, going anyway alone. Picking up my pith helmet not far out of town, not having eaten since an early breakfast, I short-cut across open desert. After several hours, though – hungry and without my water bag – I realize the heat and frequent ups and downs, not noticed from a distance, are defeating me. I remember that pond we'd found when Dad drove us to the river, and I go there to cool myself. Older boys and girls are parading and swimming. I hide my helmet before showing myself, and I think no one notices how I arrive – no car, no friends, just walking in.

My only skill in water, learned thus far, is an awkward dog paddle, working my hands under the surface in quick short strokes. I haven't mastered breathing in splash situations. I don't do anything with my legs and feet. Older boys see me and laugh and say, "Why don't you swim out to Big Island? That'd be easy with the skill you've got." I try to laugh off the challenge. Big Island must be more than 200 yards out there, near the middle of the pond. But I do head for Little Island 30 yards out. Several boys and girls watch me but soon get distracted by a battered rowboat abandoned on shore.

Nobody seems to notice me climbing out on Little Island. I rest, then paddle back to shore. With confidence restored, I talk myself toward tougher adventures. I decide to circle the entire pond, 20 feet out from shore, without touching bottom. If I can do that, then I'll try for Big Island - and not be laughed at any more.

I dog-paddle, then experiment with longer strokes, even lifting my hands above the surface and stretching farther ahead to grip the water. No problem. I'm gaining speed. I'm a fourth of the way around the pond and not even puffing hard. Shore swings away from me, making a bay, and I shortcut across the bay's neck. I notice waves on the open water ahead. A whirlwind crossing there? The waves splash into my face, my mouth and nose. I choke and cough and feel myself sinking while I can't stop coughing. I paddle harder to stay afloat - and stir a constant splashing into my own face.

I'm not breathing, and I'm still sinking. But okay - I'm *intentionally* sinking. I lower my feet, reaching for solid bottom from which to thrust myself up to the air. But I can't find bottom. I dog-paddle to the surface but still can't breathe in the windswept waves. I think of calling for help, but I'd be teased endlessly for that. I think of praying but can't feel I'd be heard. I sink again, no excuse this time, no hope of finding bottom, unable to stop sinking. I paddle with all my strength but don't find the top of the water.

Then, somehow, as if paralyzed, I'm not paddling. I'm conscious, but I don't know what's happening. Some instinct maybe has taken over – or I'm remembering forgotten advice heard long ago. I seem to be soaring in space. I'm relaxed. I'm breathing. My eyes open and I'm lying on my back on the surface, looking up at the sky.

This near-drowning is one of the great, rewarding adventures of my young life, teaching me that, though nature can be deadly destructive "she's" much more often my dependable friend. As I float, resting, these words echo in me – not so much from the *Bible* as from Mother: "The Lord is my shepherd. I shall not want..." I feel happy, feel responsible for myself, feel at home in the water, in the desert, in Moapa Valley, among the desert mesas.

I'm not angry now about the "shepherd" words as I was when Mother died. I feel this Psalm joyfully again most of the time. But I remind myself too that normally I'm my own shepherd – with many part-time helpers, including Dad, Grandma, Uncle Harry, Uncle Roy, Miss Rowe, Wendell, church members – and maybe a talent for pioneering that runs in the Lambert-Seymour blood. But the feeling's still incomplete. Maybe the Lord really *is* my shepherd – as the *Bible* and Mother have told me – but He works through nature and through my limited knowledge functioning sometimes automatically ("instinct?"). Anyway, floating now on that pond, I feel good, grateful, happy, strong. (Responsible? Within tight limits, yes.) It's partly, anyway, a spiritual feeling.

Dad was active in educational organizations and, as a Democrat in politics, hoped for special notice by the Nevada superintendent of public instruction. He took Wendell and me with him to Las Vegas to attend a regional conference of teachers and educational administrators. He believed we'd learn important lessons there, and I think we did, though different ones than he foresaw.

He arranged an excursion for the day after the conference. We three and two lady teachers – who might, Wendell and I guessed, be potential wives in Dad's mind – would go in a motorboat on the

Colorado River through rugged Black Canyon where a giant dam (called Boulder Dam or Hoover Dam) was to be built. At intervals through the years I re-experience that surprising adventure as it continued to shape and illuminate my life:

We start before day to avoid the awful heat. One of the teachers insists on taking her car, a Studebaker with a "California top" that's a rigid structure, canvas-covered, from which you pull down shades with isinglass windows to fasten on the doors for keeping weather out. She drives well on the surfaced highway, but when the route becomes a dirt road, she brakes and holds her hands up off the steering wheel in surrender, asking Dad to drive. He walks around the car in the pre-dawn dark, and she slides over on the front seat to let him get under the wheel.

He's used to such roads, but there are branches, equally obscure, and he admits he's not sure from what he sees in the headlights that he's always choosing the right branch. After an hour of nothing but wild desert, more like the Overton mesa than the tall sagebrush, the owner-lady says, "Perhaps we are lost." Dad says, "Let's look on ahead another few minutes." Daylight's beginning. Instead of dropping toward the river, the road is climbing, and then we reach a ridge top with a view. Dad brakes. He and I get out. The dimly glowing sky reflects as a wide glow in a canyon down ahead. Daylight gains quickly, and we see the motorboat speeding from Arizona on the far side of the wide river. The road ends in sand where we can't quite see the river. The bank is hundreds of yards away, but the car would get stuck in loose sand there. We walk over what may have been a moving dune but now has cactus decades old.

The boatman says he's short of gasoline because an expected supply wasn't delivered, but he'll risk the trip as planned. We decide to risk too. The motor's powerful and noisy, and we're speeding – downstream. But is the motor strong enough, and will the fuel last, to bring us back upstream against this raging current?

The brown river between high dark cliffs towering maybe halfway to the sky is thrillingly awesome, and we forget our worries. We speed through the narrows, trying to believe humans can really block this great stream with concrete and steel anchored in these black cliffs. The time comes to turn around in this overwhelming flow. The boatman grits his teeth, and we all, I guess, gasp, and the raging water almost throws us over. We straighten and settle, though, and struggle upstream. Full power barely moves us against the current, and it's hard to imagine a supply of gas in the tank adequate to carry us within walking distance of the car.

We get there, though, before ten o'clock when the sun is expected to become unbearably hot. The boatman pushes off for Arizona as we start walking. The sun's already dazzling, probably has been for an hour. I wish for my pith helmet. While climbing the dune, we hear hissing like strong wind, but there isn't any wind. We see the car - *on fire*! We all run toward it, but then Dad stops. "Gas!" he yells. "Stay back!"

The ladies moan while Dad studies the fire from a distance. I feel his thoughts – the boatman lacking gas couldn't save us even if we hailed him – without the car we'll die in the sun trying to walk 40 miles to the highway where help might or might not be quickly available – the fire isn't near the motor or gas tank – it's mostly up in that California top that must have caught fire from the torrid sunshine.

I get an urgent responsibility-hope feeling, and I'm already bent over scooping up a double handful of sand when Dad yells, "Sand!" Maybe it's telepathy or maybe I recall snuffing out campfires no longer wanted, using sand to save water. Wendell seemed to get the same message and is already scooping. Dad and I run, one on each side of the car, throwing our double handfuls onto the fire as we pass. It's cooperation. It's also the strength of numbers. Wendell is scooping sand on the far side of the car, and now the ladies are too, not moaning now. We all scoop and run and throw sand into the flames. Black spots appear on the flaming top. We keep scooping, running, throwing.

The fire dwindles. We dare get closer. We throw handfuls up into the compartments where the shades were rolled. We throw till we're gasping, rasping, with our breath. Incredibly, we've put out that fire with dry sand. Together, we've saved the car. Fire burned only part of the California top and dropped blackness onto the back seat. Where there's still smoke rising, we rub with sand. Numbers of people co-operating can save what one can't save. But —using sand? I don't quickly find meaning – just thanks. But somehow now, almost a lifetime later as I'm re-experiencing, odd words push in: We're learning unity with Earth, dreaming harmony, striving for harmony, "making ourselves at home."

Dad's a hero. The lady teachers, taking turns, embrace him, put quick kisses on his cheeks. My eyes burn. But I think Dad's face is even redder than the fire could have made it. Could either of these ladies become a mother to Wendell and me and our sisters?

The car-owner lady gets into the front seat beside Dad. The other sees how charred the back seat looks. It might ruin her dress! She gets into the front as the owner-lady slides over. We boys sweep with our sandy hands at the black on the back seat; it's loose stuff fallen on; the seat was never on fire.

When the car, running well, lurches on the uneven curves, the owner-lady can't help being thrown against Dad. Wendell and I, in back, watch and hope.

Chapter 5 – Wicked Mining Town 1927-33

When we were moving to our next town, Dad told me to stay away from the main street (Aultman) or if I must go there to walk only on the south sidewalk. He repeats of late that he trusts me to be responsible for myself, my own behavior – and I'm ready to do so – in my own way. So my first exploration isn't to the nearest wild place (wild nature) as usual but to the region of "evil." The "city" (population about 4,000) is Ely, Nevada, where copper mining and smelting have expanded for 20 years, ever since the railroad branch (Nevada Northern) was built and trains started hauling ore from the big open pit at Ruth past Ely within easy hearing-seeing distance, to the smelter at McGill. Copper employs 2,500 people, and Ely is the commercial center. A six-story hotel is now being built.

Our Ely home is our worst yet – but temporary, Dad says. We three live in one bedroom on the second floor of a house occupied by others. The house is the second one away from the grassy grounds of the copper-domed court house. I'm considering this big lawn our front yard and trying to feel good about our one-room home. We eat at Crystal Cafe that has a Chinese proprietor.

Dad's office is in the bottom of the court house. I sneak on the lawn to a window and look down on him at his desk, feeling reassured by seeing him there but also resentful for his trying to control my life. What would he do if he caught me on the north side of Aultman Street? He's deputy state superintendent of public instruction now, with a 19,000-square mile territory - one human for each two square miles. He says he'll take Wendell and me out of class sometimes when he goes to inspect distant schools – "but you've first got to prove to your teachers you can keep up with assignments."

I'd wave at him, but he doesn't look up, so I walk down the long slope of lawn. I'm sure it's northward; I nearly always know north. I reach Clark Street, that's only partly for cars, its middle occupied by a railroad branch that's used mostly by passenger trains, not the ore trains that pass continually on the slope of Squaw Peak along the north end of town. No traffic's on Clark now, and I cross, looking through the county park's trees at White Pine High School. Dad says Ely Grade School, where Wendell and I will go, is up past the left end of the high school, north two blocks, then one block to the left (west).

I walk between the county park and the tan-brick Plaza Hotel and stand on the southeast corner of 8th and Aultman – just across the street, I suppose, from evil. I look across and see a drug store, a bakery, the Masonic Temple, and the Collins Hotel. But what's behind those short swinging doors made mostly of slats, two short doors that a man is pushing open and letting swing back together behind him?

Here on the south sidewalk I'm passing stores and offices and an appliance repair shop. Across north I see stores too, but saloons are frequent, though not by that name. They're clubs. A block or two farther along are wide clubs, each with two sets of swinging doors. Does it take all that space for a few miners to drink whiskey – few now in the morning, anyway, maybe more after dark?

I don't like men drinking whiskey, but I'm pulled across Aultman. One set of doors on a big club is stuck wide open. I hurry past and look in, like fighting that car fire by the big river, hurry past so it doesn't burn you. The room, as big as a church, has a bar with a few men drinking but also green velvet tables and a wheel full of numbers that spins around clicking. Six or eight men and two women are playing slot machines. Dad ought to know I wouldn't think of going in there – unless I could be invisible and just spy.

I pass more clubs, and far along where Aultman is becoming Highway US 50 to Reno, I turn right (north), looking for a street leading east to the grade school. I think I'm finding it, but there's another club kind of place called Big 4 – and some cabin-like structures with red lights – and doors open on the upper half and fancy-painted women with breasts not fully covered. The women seem on display like what I've heard about creatures in a zoo.

This may be something even Dad doesn't know about. I want to look closer, but mostly I'm scared, and I run block after block without stopping till I find the grade school and fenced playground.

As in our other towns, a few weeks of growing familiarity with Ely reduced my resentment of being uprooted. The wild country here was like that around Metropolis – high-altitude semi-desert. I felt almost at home in it, almost at home in school too. The teacher told us Nevada's academic standards shared first place in the nation with those of New York State. You really had to study, homework every evening or, if you went to a movie at night as Wendell and I occasionally did, home work from dawn to breakfast. I didn't tell anybody I loved books and writing, but I was secretly eager for most of the subjects in school. They fitted my wish to learn how to cope with everything in human society or in nature all around the world – as I believed my Uncle Harry could.

Dad did take Wendell and me on school inspection trips. We spent the night over next to Utah at the ranch home of Dad's friends Jim and Birdie Robison (parents of Elwin who'd become a partner with me, much later, toward creating Great Basin National Park). I liked the animals and fields and haystacks of the Robison ranch. We also visited Lehman Caves National Monument, walking underground passages by candlelight. My glorying in the fantastic cave decorations and in the majesty of nearby Wheeler Peak – that I'd read about in one of John Muir's books – foreshadowed my decades of scenic-conservation effort that combined in due course with Earth-wide environmentalism (my word *earthmanship*).

Dad arranged other bonus education. Each day for an hour I left seventh grade and learned touch-typing at high school. Before the end of the year my speed surprised the teacher by climbing to 135 words per minute – approaching the world record, she said. The next year I took shorthand. In April, Dad took me out of my eighth-grade class entirely to get practical experience in a court house office. I enjoyed that, but in late May I failed the eighth grade test in reading. I'd overlooked two books they'd studied without me. Several classmates had failed too, so the following week the teacher gave a second test with different questions about the same reading. Having now read what I'd missed, I passed okay, but I told Dad he was expecting too much, doing too much for me, trying to make me "responsible" too fast – for what? He'd reform, he said – but denied favoritism – he'd do such things for any student with the motivation and ability, or again for me – "if your teacher doesn't keep you busy enough."

Dad knew I wasn't exactly a "bookworm," though I did enjoy books about wild nature. I enjoyed basketball too – and got quite good with it, though not as fast and skillful in the game as Wendell (who'd later be on the state-champion team going to Chicago for the national tournament). In Ely Grade School too, there was a better basketball player than I, a Shoshone Indian named Bruce Adams – who could usually beat me too at long distance running, and beat anyone else in the school too. Bruce and I became friends and often ran together far out into flats and up into canyons where we once discovered a great site for a log cabin hideaway we hoped to share. Bruce taught me the Shoshone way of eating pine nuts. After you've put the nut between your front teeth and cracked the shell into halves, the tongue and lips quickly eject the shell halves, leaving the meat for chewing. I thought of lending Bruce my *Two Little Savages* and inviting him to be a savage with me in the mountains, doing Indian things – but would it feel right to him?

My interests were changing anyway – stronger in girls. From eighth-grade time, I remember "Spin the Bottle." A soda pop bottle is laid on its side. About ten of us form a circle sitting around it, often on the floor. A player spins the bottle – end to end, fast – and it gradually slows. You might be both scared and hopeful. My spin came to rest pointing to Nellie Thompson. The rules say I must kiss her on the mouth and she must let me. The kiss is in front of everybody and brief, yet for me anyhow it was an event. I couldn't forget the impact. I wanted to repeat the kiss, alone somewhere with her.

Our family changed. Dad, after asking support from Wendell and me, married Luella Owen, a nurse at Steptoe Valley Hospital. She was resigning from the hospital, and we'd live temporarily in a rented house. She and Dad would drive to Utah to get the girls before school started again. Wendell and I couldn't call her Mother or Mom (death of our real mother was still too recent), so we called her Aunt Luella. She was good to us but emotionally unsure. We didn't know either how to express love for her, and Dad couldn't tell us. We tried to keep the room we shared neat, and we volunteered to help around the house or with shopping and carrying. She seldom accepted our offers or thought of jobs for boys, but when the girls came they had household tasks. Aunt Luella continued, though, to do everything important herself.

She was as dedicated a Mormon as Dad, and I guessed I could help the family best by taking hold of church and firmly resisting Ely's aggressive evils. Surprisingly, in this town that had the major Protestant churches and a Catholic church, the "anti-mining" Mormons held the lead in numbers and influence. As elsewhere Mormons had no paid leaders. Dad was a high priest along with other mature men ready for responsibilities. He taught Sunday School class and took other assignments from the ward's bishop.

Soon I was ordained a deacon, and with other lads having this rank I passed the sacrament Sunday mornings. We used regular white bread (homemade then), broken into bite-sized pieces and passed on plates, and plain water in tiny glasses carried in a fancy metal holder. Where many people sat on benches close together, one deacon would start the sacrament hand to hand along a bench and people would take one piece each and pass the plate on. At the far end a deacon would start the plate back along another bench.

When 15, I was ordained a priest and shared basic responsibilities, arranging who'd bring the bread and what deacons would be called upon. I got down on my knees and blessed the sacrament before handing it to the deacons. Being a link between God and people gave me a heady feeling. I became secretary of the Ely ward Sunday School and stake secretary of the YMMIA (Young Men's Mutual Improvement Association), the stake being an organizational division including many wards. Also I became an active teacher in the Primary, with children under 12 meeting on a weekday, and a Boy Scout member, scouting being a class in the Mutual (boys 12 and older). Aunt Luella and Dad praised my church work.

I felt most at home in Scouting, advancing as fast as the time-minimums allowed, from Tenderfoot to Second Class, First Class, Star Scout, and Life Scout. The next rank was Eagle, that Dad said testified to a better education than did a high school diploma. I earned all the necessary 21 merit badges, but another year of service was needed before the Eagle rank was given.

Though the family home became by far the best it had been since Mother died, I still dreamed of a secret personal home in a canyon near a stream or spring – the imagined site, I guess, of my first poem at age eight. A fellow Scout, Keith Vowles, wanted such a hideaway too. We tried an abandoned mine tunnel west of Squaw Peak, its entrance hidden by twists of a rugged-sided ravine. The main tunnel went into the mountain 200 feet and had four branches, unexplored, except we'd tossed rocks into them, and listened, and from sound-evidence believed none was more than 50 feet long and none had shafts we could fall into.

Keith and I told our families an almost-but-not-quite-lie: that we'd be camping with another scout Saturday night and would be back Sunday in time for church. We took food, water, and blankets and approached roundabout to throw off spies. We cooked on a campfire inside the entrance. We slept a few feet back inside from the fire – tried to sleep anyway. I imagined rattlesnakes crawling into our blankets. We ought to seal up the entrance with boards or mortared stonework and a locked door. When daylight came we located some old boards that might help, and we started stacking flattish stones in position to be mortared later.

Next Saturday, when we returned to our secret site, some vandal, human or wild, had pushed much of what we'd gathered down the waste dump. The place just wasn't secret enough, and we kept delaying. High school was keeping us busy. By next spring, though, we had a better site – and after discussion and worry decided to let another friend or two into our project, building a hidden log cabin.

I'm thinking of myself as the responsible manager but worrying about getting friends to work hard and remain friends. I get up in the dark, not using a light or making a sound. I don't want Aunt Luella, of all people, to know what I'm doing. Taking my .22 rifle, I climb out the window. Though Ely in its canyon remains dark, the mountaintops glow. As I walk up-canyon, I see white quartz against blackness and pick up a piece to help make fire without matches. I climb a long slope and rest on a mountain shelf.

Earliest sunshine is reaching the far part of Ely near the valley's edge. Most people are missing the morning, but I see smoke rising from the Shoshone village. Indians tend to rise with the sun. This wilderness with brush gradually giving way to pinenut trees has cottontail rabbits. I kick a clump of low brush and one leaps and runs zigzag. I'm accepting the kill-to-eat idea now. Looking above the rifle sights, ready to tighten my aim, I follow the rabbit. He stops. I pull the trigger.

Carrying the rabbit, I go deeper into the mountain and find our hidden site. Keith Vowles and I and two other scouts have leveled a space, felled and dragged in a dozen logs. I gather and rub cedar bark, make a nest of it and add charred cloth. With the back of the big blade of my pocketknife, I strike glancing blows on the quartz. Sparks fly. The charred cloth smolders. I blow, with my lips a near-circle, and there's flame that I quickly feed with dry sticks. I cut up the rabbit and drop it into the iron kettle we keep hidden here. I add water and put the kettle over the flame. I worry about our water source. So far, a tiny spring trickles from a cliff, but it may go dry in late summer.

I feed the fire with lasting wood, find my ax where I hid it, and climb the ridge to the next pine I've marked – among the few that are straight enough to use in a cabin wall. I risk blisters chopping, then trim off the branches and drag the log down the steep slope to the cabin site. The rabbit smells great, almost done. I give the fire a little more wood.

My friends, including a Shoshone (not Bruce Adams), come silently behind me. Keith lifts the lid of the pot. "We ate before we came, but I'll sure try that rabbit." The four of us eat it all and are ready for work. Everyone finds his secretly borrowed ax, and we race each other up the steep slope. All marked trees are where the log can slide to our cabin site. Little muscle required. We each choose one.

But there's a shout, "Rattler!" I hear the sharp, brittle sound and see the thick snake coiled. Keith throws rocks at it. The Shoshone walks closer, saying, "It's good eating." With a heavy stick he neatly crushes its head, but the body keeps writhing.

We cut and trim trees and slide the logs to our site. The Shoshone brings the snake. I build a new fire, showing off my sparking white quartz. The Shoshone grins at me and says, "Indians make fire with Whiteman's matches." The Shoshone cuts the snake into sections that we roast on sticks and have fun eating.

My youngest sister, Marta Jeanne, was born in March 1929. Dad and Aunt Luella decided the family should have a new house. Ely was adding a street, higher on the slope than any existing houses. Our lot was nearest Ely's second largest Shoshone village. Again as at our ranch and at Grandma's, I might escape unseen directly into the wild.

An experienced carpenter named Madsen, from the Mormon town of Lund, south of Ely, supervised Dad and us boys technically in putting up a prepackaged "Alladin House." I remember carrying boards and being sent back by Mr. Madsen when I brought the wrong ones – and hammering nails and being scolded at first for not getting them straight. The friction was slight, though; good will prevailed. There were even bits of comedy and laughter now and then – such as when Mr. Madsen sent me for a "board stretcher," and I searched and searched, not wanting anyone to guess I didn't know what a board stretcher looked like. When everyone started laughing, I managed to laugh too, though my face was burning.

By winter we were comfortable in the new house. Aunt Luella was enjoying the space and convenience. The family seemed in accord with that great song that sustained the "Saints" crossing the Plains and Rocky Mountains with handcarts or wagons – "All is well! All is well!"

And another great song – not a hymn exactly but among our favorites – was also sounding inside me, "... Be it ever so humble, There's no-o place like home."

My work with Mr. Madsen helped me solve problems in constructing the secret cabin. My interest persisted. I kept climbing up there. The little spring kept flowing-seeping, and I dug enough of a well to have fresh water during the dry autumn when many days were ideal for cabin work, but somehow I couldn't pull my partners up there any more. After school started, other interests wedged in for me too. Nellie Thompson lived two blocks below our new house, and we often walked back from White Pine High together. Sometimes I carried her books.

Snow and more snow came in December. Coasting sleds got so numerous on sloping streets in our neighborhood there were near-collisions with cars. Eager to be a responsible hero – a trait that kept surfacing in me, though I usually fought it back – I began to build a coasting trail on empty slopes above our house where no cars threatened. Try-outs with my sled showed that the natural slope was too fast for safety, so I laid out and graded a course with long slants and fancy curves – gradual enough for a Flexible Flyer to be guided around. Nobody seemed to look up to catch me moving soil, rocks and snow with pick and shovel. I planned to surprise everyone when all was ready.

Spring came suddenly, though, and the snow melted before I'd had a chance to invite anyone and to glory in the magnificent, sweeping thrills I'm sure could have happened there. I seemed always leaping from one project to another now, neglecting the old. The secret cabin above Ely was never completed, and nobody ever really used my splendid coasting trailway. I would someday have a log cabin hidden in a canyon, though, and I'd initiate projects significantly involving humanity in nature. One such project sneaked in unrecognized as I was failing to win fame as a trailway engineer:

Elwin Robison, a fellow student at White Pine High – my brother Wendell would later marry his sister Alpha – persuades Wendell and me to camp with him near Lehman Caves (that we'd already visited) and climb Mount Wheeler (on maps "Wheeler Peak, 13,063 feet").

Dad is soon visiting Elwin's father Jim again at Robison Ranch. We young folk drive up Lehman Canyon, and when the angles are right I'm watching the great peak of white snow and tan rock that crowns the confusion of forested ridges. As we get closer, the peak sinks behind closer ridges and soon we're at "Robisons' Camp."

Horses will shorten our hike. We ride easily up the trail along the sun-dancing, gurgling stream. I notice large trees, and Elwin says they're yellow or ponderosa pine. Next I notice short-needled evergreens – white fir and Engelmann spruce. High flats of sagebrush amaze me; I thought sagebrush flourished only in foothills and valleys. So much seems unpredictable. We see extensive stands of mountain mahogany, large territories of quaking aspen, vaster, darker forests of spruce. Quite soon we're at a higher elevation than the summit of Trout Creek Mountain where, with Harry Thurston long before, I'd felt outside the known world.

My sit-down feels sore from friction with the saddle's hard leather. But the soreness is forgotten in the exhilarating action and brisk air and the increasingly spectacular views of rock pinnacles and high snow that play peek-a-boo through the side canyons. Elwin has known these mountains since he was a small boy, helping to herd Robison Brothers sheep. He tells us about eagles and other birds we're seeing and about the mule deer, bobcat, coyote, cougar. We reach Stella Lake, a reflecting mirror of bright water near timberline. The rising slopes are open now, rocky, lots of small flowers, but not entirely treeless. A massive limber pine is on the far side of the lake – and a scintillating grove of aspens with white trunks glowing.

We leave the horses and hike up a zigzag trail to a ridge top. Elwin identifies places miniaturized below us in Spring Valley to the west, toward Ely, then landmarks even farther below us eastward, green patches that are shade trees hiding ranch houses, and farther yet one mountain range after another on toward the Wasatch Range in Utah. The far views and the climbing challenge intoxicate me, and I go leaping from boulder to boulder, half running, half dancing, avoiding patches of snow that get frequent. I don't know why the elevation speeds me up instead of slows me down. I breathe in rhythm as if to the beat of my rock-dancing toes.

On the summit before the others, I slowly turn the whole 360 degrees, seeing farther through the unbelievably clear air than I ever saw anywhere else. Wheeler is surrounded for hundreds of miles by mountain ranges, trending north-south, some with late-summer snow patches resembling those on this range, some forested almost as abundantly as the below-timberline levels here. These ranges and the forever-intervening valleys suggest waves and troughs in still pictures of the ocean - taken during a hurricane, I suddenly think, with the bigger waves snow-capped. Surely this scenery is among the most moving on Earth. It should be a national park – Wheeler and other peaks of this range, anyway, from which the vast majesty can be encompassed by the eyes, though not quite completely by the understanding. I feel joyously at home here and wish I'd been born an eagle or a mountain sheep – or an Indian before the Whiteman came.

But no thought grew then that my "responsibility feeling" could ever get so exaggerated as to involve me personally in a third-of-a-century effort to create such a park – and deeply impress First Lady Barbara Bush. You don't go anywhere different or difficult just by deciding, even urgently feeling, that it *ought* to be done – or even feeling you'd dearly love to do it. Serious conservation is one of those things that isn't just mentally adopted, or just learned; it takes time, years, even decades, to grow into deep and persistent emotion, into a firmly sustained course of action, perhaps against adverse complexities and the resistance of long-time friends, including most ranchers and miners or prospectors.

Dad's long and more developed fixed-feeling – not conservation but his ingrained tendency to follow his grandfathers' insistence on "fighting to the last ditch" for long-held principles, lost him his position as deputy state superintendent. Favoring the under dog – part of the two-family reinforced tradition – he blasted Nevada Northern Railroad for boycotting local merchants because they saved money by trucking merchandise into Ely instead of shipping by rail – and thereby lost his school superintendency. Railroad officials had vigorously attacked him – undermined him with the Governor (no longer his friend Jim Scrugham but a man who'd defeated Scrugham).

We moved abruptly to Salt Lake City where Dad hoped to get a suitable job despite the worsening Depression. Again, I resented moving. I complained to Dad he was snatching me away before I could receive my Eagle Scout badge that he'd so strongly recommended. Other accusations, all petty or false, were hinted. Looking back, I feel a more substantive regret: The move was even worse for Aunt Luella than for me. In Ely she'd been growing successfully into the role of loving mother. In our green suburb of Salt Lake City, with Dad no longer ten feet tall but chronically unemployed or underemployed, she shared near-tragedy with him and couldn't regain the degree of rapport enjoyed in our Alladin house. Most of her savings, along with Dad's, must have gone into the down payment on our rather handsome brick house on the southeast edge of the city.

I became a junior in Granite High School and rode the school bus. A Mormon seminary class was compulsory - which irritated me because I no longer fully believed the doctrine. I didn't feel at home there, or anywhere. I'd have to be more persistent in being my own "shepherd" and reaching an appropriate future.

The school year at Granite would end a month before that at White Pine. With my Granite credits and those I'd earned in Ely, I was only slightly short of qualifying for graduation. Wendell would be graduating at Ely; he'd stayed there working part-time for a store. He could get me a job when I graduated, as well as a full-time one for himself – in merchandising. White Pine's principal would welcome me to try. If I passed the final tests in two required courses, I could graduate with Wendell. I got the textbooks in advance, and by the time I'd finished at Granite I'd read them. I hurried to Ely and attended classes for a month and did graduate in 1932.

I worked as Ely area distributor for Standard Brands Inc. Wendell and I together bought a Model A Ford coupe, with rumble seat, and I used it to deliver Fleischmann's yeast, Chase & Sanborn dated coffee, Royal gelatin and puddings, baking powder, and other merchandise to businesses. Yeast came not only in small cakes but also in one-pound size for bakeries. Packages sometimes arrived broken. I liked the taste and munched as I drove between towns. Though I doubt I ate more than two pounds in a year, my weight climbed to 155 – and stayed there 20 years.

Dated coffee was popular at first. The date was printed on the paper label glued to the tin can. It was supposed to be the date the coffee was delivered to the store. Often, with permission, I put the cans directly on the store's shelf. When the time expired, the unsold coffee was replaced by new coffee. People asked me what happened to the old coffee. I told what I knew – I shipped it back to headquarters – and what I'd been told – they put it into paper packages and sold it for less. Suspicion continued, though, and sales of dated coffee dwindled in my territory.

An adventure at Data Brothers store in the small town called Kimberly focused my dislike of being a commercial agent. I'd brought in dated coffee and yeast cakes and was waiting for owner-manager Data, age about 50, to sign for them. He came in front of me, very close, which isn't unusual with people from southern Europe. He took the paper and held it between us, while underneath his right hand was feeling in my crotch. Two fingers and a thumb found my penis through my pants and caressed it while he questioned me about the delivery. Erection started. He told me softly, "I know a beautiful young girl who'd like to meet you – now – upstairs."

"Not today, thanks," I said. But I couldn't afford to alienate him. My supervisor in Salt Lake wouldn't understand if Data Brothers suddenly turned against our yeast and coffee. When he kept caressing, I pulled away a foot or two, taking the paper from him, spreading it on the nearby counter and holding a pencil toward him. "Sign here, Mr. Data," I said. And he did.

I hadn't succumbed to the Ely area's evils, but my confidence was low. One night I sneaked toward the Big Four. I found a hiding place across the street and for two hours watched those women showing off to men – as I might watch squirrels or badgers or cows and bull in daylight. I felt pulled but didn't go in. Dissatisfied with my job, though, I was getting lazy, feeling useless, a failure – empathizing pessimistically with Dad's feeling of failure in Salt Lake, his best abilities unwanted. During the same period, though, I played basketball on a town team, practicing almost every evening, sometimes helping to win. I became a physical fitness nut, reading, for instance, *Vitality Supreme* by McFadden and doing prescribed exercises to make my muscles bigger.

A winter snowstorm stalled the train from Salt Lake; my yeast and coffee failed to arrive, so I couldn't deliver. I went hiking in deep snow up to the abandoned log pile at my old hidden cabin site. According to the diary I was briefly "keeping," I stripped off and sun-bathed there, lying on the snow, feeling sorry for myself but deter-determined to win through. This Spartan tendency, this torture, this exaggerated way of being part of nature seemed for a while to compensate for my staying useless in bed so often until nearly noon. What else could I do now to feel more at home, more worthwhile?

    Maybe I *should* meet that girl at Data's store. Or I could get bold and actually enter the Big Four. When still short of deciding anything, I discover Nellie Thompson is back after a long visit elsewhere. She seems almost to avoid me on the street, and I guess she has a boy friend who'll soon be in senior rank with her at White Pine High. We do speak, though, and I act the grown-up man, coping with the world. She agrees to go riding with me in my car and maybe hiking with me to Garnet Hill to search for semi-precious gemstones.

    I drive around the deserted back way, saying we can thus reach the best garnets faster. Starting out from the car, I tell her to watch for rattlesnakes. The thought doesn't scare her, and she goes ahead of me, stepping lightly among scattered low bushes. She's almost as tall as I. Widening at the hips is noticeable, and the muscles behind tense up and relax rhythmically. I follow to one side of where she's just searched, and my eyes, though looking for garnets, also see a profile of her right breast bouncing a little.

    Rain fell recently, and she finds a garnet from which the pinkish soil has half washed away. "A beauty," she says, rubbing it. She drops it into the palm of her left hand and holds it toward me. I bring a hand up and move her hand to get a different angle, testing the sparkles from the facets, testing the electricity our hand contact generates.

    We keep finding garnets, discarding those with the worst flaws, wondering what to do with the good ones. Cost of setting them into jewelry might exceed their value. I think of having a bracelet made for Nellie but also think of Dad's need for money. Nellie seems happily excited just looking at the facets scintillating in sunshine in her hands or mine.

Back in the car, she accepts a few of my garnets but declines the best. I reach around her shoulders, pull her toward me, and kiss her lips lightly. "Darwin!" she says with protest and pleasure mixed. She moves back, looking into my eyes, then puts her face forward and kisses my lips. I'm stirred up and guess she is too, but I'm also scared and guess she is too. We may be remembering the teachings of our traditions, Mormon and Catholic, or using common sense – all of which agree on male-female morality. She gives me a kiss that's magically delicious, though light and short, and she says, "My parents are expecting me home."

While I drive, she questions me casually about my work with Standard Brands, as if she has a mild, not urgent, wish to know if my position is permanent and financially substantial. I tell the truth more directly than I supposed I knew it, saying the job's *not* related to what I want and expect to do with my life.

I don't kiss her on the way back to town or at her door, but our four hands all come together and give quick squeezes before she goes in. I feel we like each other and might get together in the future, or might not, and either way it won't be life-or-death. We're not ready for life-or-death. The mild emotion goes along with the way everything feels to me now, neither deeply depressing nor deeply rewarding.

I'm waiting, waiting – for what?

Chapter 6 – Mormon Capital 1931-34

Taking all my belongings, I drove the Model A Ford from Ely via the Bonneville Salt Flats to Salt Lake City. Dad and Aunt Luella and my four sisters welcomed me, but all I could think was, I'd failed them. The money I'd been sending would be sorely missed. I explained that I and my boss had recognized simultaneously that I wasn't a salesman. Dad, mostly unemployed too in the unrelenting Depression, put an arm around my shoulders. "I'm no salesman either, Doc," he said.

I told him I'd find a job and keep providing my share of the budget. He helped me get invited to demonstrate my typing and shorthand skills in offices, but weeks went by with no job offers. My morale seemed non-existent. The continually cloudy weather further depressed me. I'd volunteer for household tasks, but Aunt Luella always declined. Dad was different. He'd order me with exactness to hoe or pull weeds in certain rows of his garden, or to feed and milk our one cow, or to clean the right or left half of the chicken coop. I'd make efforts but often do little – or I'd push work far beyond his orders. I'd conquer every single weed, no matter how small, in every row where he was raising vegetables and strawberries for sale as well as for family meals.

But my action mood would then run out. I'd dream an additional garden of my own and start plowing the land with a shovel – but soon I'd catch myself idle, incurably lazy, and in daytime I'd go to bed and try to read – but stop reading and just lie there and hate myself – or dream of naked women (or half-naked as at Ely's Big Four). I'd try masturbating – and hate myself more. A diary I started writing there, but with long gaps between entries, reveals: "Have been praying at night lately and thru this help have made progress against a bad habit I've been trying to avoid." Prayer seemed plausible to me as influencing the person praying.

The diary recalls other things. Not far from our house I discovered a secluded ravine where I could be alone. It had a spring trickling from moss-covered rock that looked ancient. Close to the cliff on the north side the sunshine came through the tree canopy in mid-afternoon, allowing me to sunbathe. Once when I was quite naked, a wren landed on a ledge within reach if I'd raised my arm. It sang liltingly and cheered me. In wild nature I felt strong and good.

My diary shifted from my own doings to morale-building quotes, some I got from clippings long-ago saved by Dad:

> Open the door of your heart, my lad,
>   To the angels of love and truth;
> When the world is full of unnumbered joys,
>   In the beautiful dawn of youth.
> Casting aside all things that mar,
>   Saying to wrong, "Depart!"
> To the voices of hope that are calling you
>   Open the door of your heart.
>   –Edward Everett Hale

The notebook also has a record of my first climb of Utah's Mount Olympus that would influence my life. It's a sample of my prose from the time I first felt I might become a writer as well as a naturalist:

> Mount Olympus is a rugged peak of the Wasatch range that towers just above our house here in Holladay. It has two peaks almost the same height. It rises far and suddenly from the valley floor. I've heard the Ute Indians worshipped it as the home of their gods...
>
> Today Bob Farrell, a neighbor lad, and I have challenged each other to go all the way up. He's not ready as soon as I am, so I start alone and don't stop running until I reach a beautiful spot where the trail crosses Tolcate's Creek. I enjoy the wild stream and wild trees and shrubs while waiting...

Our feet dislodge boulders, and they roll noisily down... A large boulder is bounding, soaring in the air, hitting other rocks and sending out a puff of dust and a crashing sound, then bounding and soaring again. A smell suggesting firecrackers reaches us...

The furor has been strangely satisfying... but there's a stab of regret... I think of Bob's sister Peggy who'd wanted to climb Olympus with us and wasn't invited – but could have decided to climb by herself, below us. I tell myself not to roll rocks – ever again...

I steady myself enough to start a real project – raising watermelons, some of them to sell. First I remake the soil from heavy clay to sandy loam, playing creatively with the nature of Earth. Remembering an 18-inch layer of sand where I'd obeyed Dad and dug a trench as part payment of our water bill, I dig beside my garden plot. The sand layer's as deep in the ground as I am tall – reminding me of the well I dug years before to help save our ranch from drought. I use long days mixing sand and clay on my melon patch. I also mix in dried manure and grass clippings. With persistent labor, you can make an approximation of sandy loam (best for melons).

My sleeping late stops; my morale builds. I'm out at dawn making hills six feet apart and planting one hill each of Kleckleys Sweet and Tom Watson and three hills of Winter King. A week goes by and no plants are up. Impatient, I probe with my fingers; white sprouts are coming from the seeds. Tenderly, I give each seed a drink and cover it in the finest loam. I can't fail, must not fail. This crop *must* succeed.

In the hot summer the vines lengthen and the leaves multiply and yellow blossoms come. I'm irrigating in depth twice a week. I watch each blossom, watch the bees both dancing and sleeping among the stamens, then visiting the female organs (pistils). I notice the swelling at the blossom base expanding as the petals fade and dry, shrink and fall. Every day I count the melons and weigh them with my eyes and pet them one touch with my fingertips.

As they're nearing maturity, local gossip scares me, saying teenage thieves are raiding watermelon patches. I can't stand losing even one. The slide-action 16-gauge shotgun is on the wall pegs near the cot in the basement where I sleep. I take the gun in my hands. I put it to my shoulder and sight along it. I pull the slide-handle and open the chamber. The gun's empty as it's supposed to be.

I take three shotgun shells from the box. With my pocketknife blade I pick at the folded-in cardboard that closes the shells. I loosen and remove the little round lids, pour the heavy lead BBs into an old dish. I fill the shells where the BBs were with rice and salt and pepper, then replace the cardboard circles and fold the cylinder-ends back firmly. I push the shells into the gun – but none into the firing chamber – and put the gun back on its pegs.

I'll need an alarm to warn me of thieves. I encircle the melon patch with black thread running through notches in the tops of little stakes. An end of the thread is anchored on the stake farthest from the house, and the other end I bring to the house. Now what? Tie the thread to a metal pan lid resting on the chair by my cot, so if a thief enters the patch the lid will clang on the concrete floor? No. The thief might hear and be gone before I get outside.

The alarm itself, over my bed now, is a one-by-three-inch board, three feet long, hinged at the low end and latched vertical until a tug on the thread pulls the latch. The board then falls across the cot on my covers, alerting me without a noise. But a trial run doesn't work. The thread needs tension – which I supply with a two-foot-long strand of linked rubber bands. A small pull on the thread in the patch now trips the alarm onto my bed.

I feel anger already. I'm a mixed-up kid, maybe. But here, I feel, I've got a clear-cut case of responsibility. These melons are mine – exclusively mine. Through the system of nature, I created them; nobody else helped me. It's not like partial responsibility – a citizen's responsible for his country (along with millions of other citizens) – a citizen's also responsible for a healthful environment (along with millions of other citizens). But here with these watermelons – I see looking back from my old age and asking myself how much right I really had in that youthful situation – I conclude I had a clear right and duty. I'd done more work per melon than anybody else I ever knew about – remaking the soil, weeding, watering, weeding and watering again and again.

I resume re-experiencing: I'm not asleep when the board comes down. I have my tennis shoes on. I take the shotgun from its pegs and climb the stairs. I go silently out the front door and sneak on the soft lawn around to the back. I have a flashlight in my pocket but don't need it. There's a quarter moon, and I see bent-over shapes in the patch. I pump the first shell into the firing chamber. The sound is sharp, and the three shapes gasp and run.

They seem about my age. I let them run a few seconds, then I fire once at each retreating bottom. The youths yell and falter, then speed again as if surprised they can still run. They separate. I put the gun down and chase one thief. I grab an arm and spin him around. He seems dazed. I tell him he'll survive. I bring him back to the patch with me, and in fear he shows me where he'd left the melon he'd stolen. He doesn't know whether his associates had yet picked melons. I let him go.

My summer's work is a financial success. Though there's gossip about the shooting, no one – not even Dad – speaks to me either in praise or blame.

A surge of socializing involved me in group hikes and field games such as one-old-cat or rounders (simplified baseball) and inside games – word-forming, charades, card games (with Rook cards, not what Dad considered "instruments of the Devil"). On the last day of September 1933 six of us – Bob and Peggy Farrell, Mary Job, Ruth, Ona, and I – were having another indoor party. One game was over and another not yet started when an impulse hit me to organize (for a purpose). Enthusiasm erupted for this new game. Suddenly I was acting chairman of the first meeting of what would become the Pals of

Olympus Club. We defined Pals as friends enjoying wholesome companionship, and our focus was on the trees, wildflowers, and wildlife of the intriguing mountain near us.

Among early moves were drafting a constitution and choosing a club flower. All six charter members had seen the oxhead flower on our Mount Olympus but nowhere else, so it was voted in unanimously. Peggy and I, elected vice president and president, were often together ex officio – which we enjoyed. Photography was soon involved, also writing, both of which tended to become playfully creative in recording our activities. Fake dramatic poses characterized the pictures. The record – which I've held onto through the decades – shows we played "Newspaper Extra," "Who, Where, and What," and "Wills" (what are you leaving to whom?) at our first Halloween party. Then we told impromptu stories, while listeners enjoyed open-faced sandwiches, cocoa, and pumpkin pie. Peggy and I planned some, but mostly the fun was spontaneous.

Paralleling the socializing, I was continuing in secret my fight against "evil." I read church books while agonizing over my inability to believe the churches' teachings. I started a "good" notebook. Among items typed into it are the Ten Commandments – that appealed to me not only from the church angle but also as reasonable helps in maintaining human health and harmony. I kept adding to my store of inspirational verse:

> The night has a thousand eyes,
>   And the day but one;
> Yet the light of the bright world dies
>   With the dying sun.
> The mind has a thousand eyes,
>   And the heart but one;
> Yet the light of a whole life dies
>   When love is done.   – Bourdillon

>   If I can stop one heart from breaking,
>   I shall not live in vain;

> If I can ease one life the aching,
> Or cool one pain,
> Or help one fainting robin
> Unto his nest again,
> I shall not live in vain.
> – Emily Dickinson

I appropriated nine sheets of my loose leaf notebook for what I called "the philosophy of happiness." Here are a few quotes:

HOPE – Something to hope for is an essential of happiness. Without hope we will not care what we do.

EDUCATION – I speak of education as knowledge and the power to think...
With education you can act more intelligently and therefore in a way to promote your happiness. You will know how to live in accord with the laws of nature.

HEALTH – Vastly increases the power to enjoy anything...

OCCUPATION – Something worthwhile to do is an essential of happiness. Purposes of occupation: to make a living – but making a living now occupies only five or six hours a day, so our occupation can include whatever will increase our health, education, love, appreciation of beauty, and harmony with nature.

LOVE – Someone to love is an essential of happiness...

BEAUTY – Appreciation of beauty adds much to happiness...

NATURE – We must live in accord with nature or we will be punished by the basic reality. Living in accord enhances happiness.

DEITY – My present idea: Belief in God can strengthen good and add to happiness but can have adverse effects too. The laws of nature are his policies... The divine inspiration many of us have felt may have been the awakening of some previously unexamined corner of the human mind.

I got a part-time job at the Utah State Road Commission's offices in the Capitol Building, uptown Salt Lake, and it gradually became full-time. The work, though tedious, mostly typing complex right-of-way descriptions, was more congenial to me than selling products. The job might not last, though. When I learned of an examination for beginning levels of civil service in Washington, D.C., I signed up.

Pay for my first month of full-time typing in the Utah agency was $81 ($3 a day). The family – including Owen Carlyle Lambert, born August 9, 1933 – needed most of it. Wendell, who'd been contributing from work in Ely, was going to the University of Utah and needed more than he'd saved. The older girls needed money for school too. I felt better working regularly and paying my way. Dad showed more respect for me, so others did too, and I was strengthened in fighting "evil" through respecting myself. A new problem-opportunity opened, and I re-experience it now.

My conscious feeling for Peggy has been growing friendship. I'm 17, and she's 14. We're neighbors, fellow officers of the Pals, our being together spontaneous, bordering on the accidental. Now she invites me a full week ahead to attend a party at the home of a relative outside our usual circle. I mention it to Dad, and he's almost his adventurous self of pre-Depression times. He challenges me – or teases me – offering his Chevrolet sedan, much better than the old Ford coupe.

The party borders on a date situation – boy-girl couples arriving together. But then five girls come together, followed by three boys. Another two boys are expected but never come. We play games as individuals – some with dice or playing cards ("instruments of the devil" to Dad) – but I feel the people are as good as those at our Mormon Sunday School party last week. I see no alcoholic drinks or kissing games. In bobbing for apples, I win a squeaking mouse and give it to Peg.

After dropping off four guests along the way home, I stop at the Farrell's door, uncertain how to say good night. Peg seems similarly confused. She thanks me for taking her, and I thank her for inviting me. We're wordless a few seconds, then agree we've had a wonderful time. She opens the car door and says, "Good night, Doc." I reach to pull her back, but she's already too far. "Good night, Peg," I say.

Our club keeps meeting Saturday nights, and we six are often together in between – for hikes, or movies sometimes. We exchange clever little nothings at Christmas. But in addition I buy Peg a 16-jewel wristwatch with two diamonds, chips, I should say – regular price $50, but I get it for $17.50. I don't present it to her at the club's Christmas party; I mail it to her, though she's just across the street. I feel it should be secret, and she seems to feel the same. But it does, after a while, become known.

I can't stop thinking about Peggy, and in late January I try for a partial remedy, planning how to spend my time. I'll get up at 7 a.m.; my trouble getting out of bed is long gone. I'll allow 15 minutes for breakfast, then practice the harmonica 45 minutes. I paid $4.75 for a chromatic harmonica, and I'm going to learn to play it if such learning proves possible. After work, I'll spend 30 minutes at supper, 30 minutes on the harmonica, and 30 minutes on my diary, poems, and notes. Then I'll read for two hours and walk alone 15 minutes before going to bed. I think Peg's also trying to tone us down before we become incurable.

In early spring I recondition my garden by digging more trench and adding more sand and humus. I have plants growing in a hot bed under old windows - tomato, cabbage, cauliflower, artichoke, and celery. Dad's impressed. I'm avoiding watermelons. I haven't used church books or prayer or inspirational poetry to fight "evil" since last fall. Those approaches didn't work in me. I tell myself I'm saving my energy for stronger happiness in a marriage later on.

One Sunday morning, instead of going to church, Peg, Ruth, Bob, and I are hiking up Mount Olympus. Together we reach the place where the trail crosses the creek. Bob doesn't cross but starts up toward a waterfall. Ruth follows him. Peg crosses the creek and continues on that trail. I call softly to her and ask if she wants company, and she says, "Yes," shyly. We go up the wild trail together. We come to an exposure of boulders surrounded by bushes, and we sit together on a flattish boulder talking about how pleasant this place is. She says she'd like to stay forever. I say it's wonderful to be here with her, and I'll stay as long as she wishes. We look into each other's eyes, and what we see makes us stand up. My right hand and her left grab each other, and we run together back to the creek crossing and up toward Bob and Ruth – as if a bear were chasing us, except that, as we run, we laugh joyously together.

Almost everything in the spring and early summer of 1934 includes Olympus and Peg. She, Ruth, Ona, Bob, and I start for the summit together at 4:30 a.m. on Sunday, July 1. Bob will soon be going to New Mexico to work on a truck farm. I've been offered a permanent federal job in Washington, D.C., and must tell the Civil Service Commission the date in August I'll report for duty. We five Pals go in the Ford to the foot of the trail.

At eight o'clock we eat breakfast just below the old pine. From there on, the mountain's steep, and we climb slowly, getting to the top eight hours after we started from home - the first time to the top for Peg and Ruth.

I help Peg on the way down – as I did, a little, on the way up. I don't know if she needs help, but I want to touch her, and she seems pleased. Sometimes she holds my hand even after the difficult part is passed.

Everybody is hot and thirsty – and slower to get going after each rest stop. We didn't bring anywhere near enough water, and while resting too long, saying it's too hard to stand up, at a most comfortable stop, we get to talking about our tongues feeling dry, no saliva. I say I'm not tired and will go down into the canyon and get water. It's farther than I'd guessed. When I finally find good water and start climbing back with filled canteens, I feel near exhaustion myself. But I've often wanted to be a hero, and here's a chance, though minor league. I keep struggling upward. The way Peg and the others gulp down water rewards me.

About that same time there's another mountain adventure, also significant in my feelings about wild places and the planet – and more definitely scary. In my summer of not knowing how soon or late I'd be returning to the Great Basin, I'm saying good-by to Grandma and Uncle Roy and family at Kamas. And Walden says this might be our best chance ever, maybe our last chance, to carry out an ambition we've nursed, to climb a persistently challenging peak near the western end of the spectacular above-timberline part of the high Uinta range. I re-experience:

Walden and I hike through Engelmann spruce and open meadows, mostly with small lakes or ponds at their centers. We look up at the peaks of bare rock. In a friendly way, we repeatedly aim our eyes at each other and say without words, I bet you don't dare try climbing those cliffs. Ahead of us, Mount Agassiz may be the highest by a few feet, but Haydens Peak pulls most powerfully. Miles of its rock layers show as cliffs alternating with talus at the angle of repose, rocks ready to slide. Haydens resembles a giant's shoulders thrust above the less shapely rock, and higher still the giant's lofty head.

The easiest approaches might be to climb the main ridge where it's lowest, either far left or far right, then follow the ridgetop to the peak. The shortest route would be straight ahead. It looks impossible, but we're too young to accept that. Both of us at once say, "Straight up this side of Haydens." Our eyes meet in commitment, and we're racing. I'm carrying a canteen, raisins, and a candy bar, plus Dad's camera.

We reach another grassy place. The sod suggests canvas resting on gravy. It sinks where we step – until we're climbing into forest again. Trees shrink as land rises. At timberline the spruces are bush-size; above that, mere doilies on the vastness of rock. The angle is high, and above the talus towers a rock face so steep it seems to hang over us. We consider the first cliffs, maybe no more than 50 feet vertical, and guess which crack-lines might be easiest. My choice is straight ahead; Walden's, a bit to the right. We go our own ways, relying on personal perception of the nature of the rock and of gravity and our own muscles and ability to cling and to balance. It's a test of something fundamental but not accurately defined.

An hour later, yoo-hooing, we find each other above those first cliffs. The way was strenuous, we agree, but not dangerous. We head toward an opening in the second line of cliffs, a continuous talus slope actually. The small boulders slide at our touch. We climb side by side. When boulders move, rumble and roar, we separate and run fast at a slant upward. Our footing keeps shifting and sometimes there's a moving swath far downslope, but we're always stepping from rocks just starting to slide onto rocks still stationary. Success has to come from instinct, or experience in physical pressures and movements. Though the energy cost is high, we both keep gaining altitude. We aim for the next protruding bedrock, where we'll rest.

The main cliff-face ahead is at least 400 feet high, almost exactly vertical. If we had ropes and pitons we'd work together, but we have no climbing equipment except what nature gave us. Walden chooses a fissure to our right again. I pick one to our left. We lose sight of each other but supposedly could still talk by shouting.

My fissure isn't narrow enough to help me with bracing foot- or-hand-holds. I try the right wall. With one foot firm, I feel upward with my fingers. Near the limit of reach there's a two-inch ledge with depressions, and I grasp it with my right hand. I lift one foot onto a ledge previously spotted, then with the other foot feel for a still higher foot-hold. The rubber soles of my basketball shoes are solid now against rock. My left hand reaches for a ledge higher than my right is holding. You need always a hand grip on the cliff to keep from falling backward, outward. Hand-holds must slant downward inside or have finger grips of some kind, or, if your chimney doesn't serve for sustaining pressures, you need hand-holds around corners of rock. Problems are too many to think through. You decide by feel.

Each combination of holds seems so precarious I don't get around to voice-checking with Walden. I worry. But after a while I reach a level space a yard wide. Feeling firm, I call Walden, though not so loud I'll scare him if he's unstable on a cliff face. There's no answer. Maybe he's gone around too many corners to be reached by my voice.

I climb again, keep climbing. At last I sense above me what may be the real top of this cliff, though I can't get my eyes far enough from the rock face to be sure. Another 50 feet might bring success. My left hand has a good hold, a solid edge with a depression behind it, and my right toes and ball of the foot are supporting most of my weight. But I can't see or feel any place for my right hand, or any for my left foot. They grope and dangle in space, finding vertical smoothness everywhere. I begin to tremble, first in my stomach, then in my back muscles.

I try finding holds immediately below me. My cheek is touching the cold rock. Gravity and my own nerves say the cheek has to stay there or I'll lose balance. I can't see details either above or below me. My feeling hands are only good for up, no good for down. With this realization, my left arm and right leg, my anchors, start trembling too.

I tell myself that if Walden were me, he'd pray, and the prayer would help because he believes. I reach in my mind for the Lord my Shepherd. If I find him and feel He cares, I'll whisper my prayer to Him. But He isn't reachable. I think of Mother – she knows the Lord and could speak for me. Mother comes – her image as if alive. But the image weakens, fading, all except the eyes. Mother's eyes say to me clearly: You can do it, Darling. Then the eyes are gone.

Inside myself I attack the trembling. I tighten the muscles just a little, and they're steady. The trembling stops in my stomach. I stretch my whole body and somehow reach higher than before. Fingers find a ledge, find loose sand and pebbles, flick them out, and get a grip. I'm climbing again. I preach to myself, imagining Mother doing it: When you're failing, keep trying a little longer and a little stronger than you ever thought you could.

The natural holds are on the cliff, and I find them. Soon Walden and I, almost simultaneously, are on the talus rock, racing toward the peak, keeping apart because the rock tends to slide. But our eyes meet, and I feel each knows the other has passed a crucial test, the initiation. Now – looking back through the decades, I see we'd grabbed another big chunk of responsibility – taking care of ourselves at least, surviving. And it would gradually grow and embrace at least part of our environment, our homes, places of beauty, sources of pure sparkling water...

Atop the peak, Walden and I shake hands but don't talk. With the camera I've carried on my back, we take each other's pictures signing the register that's kept in the summit cairn.

Back home in Holladay, as my first good-by to the Great Basin gets closer, I fight believing Peg and I will be thousands of miles apart. I want to be with her, but I'm not sure I dare be – without a third person present. But when only two weeks are left before I have to start the trip to Washington, I do dare. I ask Peg to spend the whole July 24 holiday, Mormon Pioneer Day, with me alone. She tells her parents, and they don't say no. We drive up Cottonwood Canyon and hike toward Lake Desolation. I have my arm around her as we walk, and I feel her muscles move. Once I say, "Gee, you're sweet!" and she says, "I'm glad somebody thinks so." I say, "You'd better look out or I might kiss you. Aren't you scared?" She says, "Oh, you'd hardly dare do that." It's light-hearted on the surface but underneath, as down from our viewpoint on this trail, is the deep dark beauty of Lake Desolation that both thrills and mourns.

We eat our lunch in the car and drive on to Brighton and hike to Twin Lakes. Dare I kiss her? I've never kissed her. I kissed Nellie in Ely and nothing drastic happened. To kiss or not to kiss Peggy wouldn't have been a big problem six months ago. But here and now it's the toughest problem I've ever faced. I want to kiss her. I think she wants me to kiss her. But the old casualness is gone. We've passed beyond the region of pals and don't know where we are now.

I think of the judgment-book angel that I've supposed I don't believe in any more. I feel Peggy is too sacred for me to touch seriously. She's 15 now, too young even to get her driver's license, though I've been teaching her to drive, and she's skilled enough. I'm also too unsettled for commitment. We'll be apart, maybe forever. I think of the churches' teaching of chastity. I think of my "philosophy of happiness" in my loose leaf diary. I try to think of everything, including our feeling now and future. And just as she, seemingly so lightly, suggested, I don't dare kiss her.

The next Sunday, my last here, Peg's to go to her Aunt Marian's for dinner. I watch, as it seems I've always watched, for glimpses of her. She leaves with her family. Soon, though, she's back and tells me her Aunt invites me. It takes me less than five minutes to put on suitable clothes. It's a nice dinner. About three o'clock the situation is right for us to escape.

We drive to Mount Olympus Spring Water farm, park there, and hike up-canyon. I'm carrying the camera and ask her to let me take her picture. She seems to agree, but time after time, when I'm about to press the button, she turns and starts off. I go after her, putting my arm around her and bringing her back. It's a game, I guess, or maybe it's the core of life, and she's asking just how strongly I want this last (for a long time? forever?) lasting picture of her. Finally, after my many tender pleases, she stays, and she foregoes the Pals' tradition of inane dramatization in the camera's eye. Then she takes a picture of me.

We walk farther and come to the headwaters spring. We sit on boulders watching the miracle of water forever flowing from Earth.

For a long time we don't say anything. We wander off a side trail and stand a while together, holding hands. Somehow, then, the worst seems over, the hurting inside insulated, the error of timing of our move from the pal relationship into a dear and tender love regretted but accepted and our lives surviving.

On Monday night the Pals stage an official party to bid me goodby. They give me a five-year diary, in which each Pal has written a little verse or copied one from the masters. After all the games and good wishes and the others' goodbys, Peg and I walk out to the street together. I want to get her into the Ford and run away with her to Washington. But we stand as if paralyzed. At last I let go of her hand and kiss her other hand and say goodby. We promise to write to each other. She goes into her house and slowly closes the door. I walk down the dark street, away from the house, away from the lights, and can't see at all where to put my feet. The tears that have waited and waited flow down my face as I feel my unseeing way.

I'm numb in our family goodbys. Wendell wrote wanting me to deliver the Ford to him in Rock Springs, Wyoming, where he's working temporarily at a store of the chain he'd worked for in Ely. My sister Joyce rides with me as far as Ogden, where I leave her with Aunt Jane (Seymour). I go on alone up the Weber River that heads near Haydens Peak in the high Uinta. The river is swollen from a cloudburst in the mountains. I pick up Ruth at a relative's home and take her to Kamas where we visit with Grandma and Aunt Lorraine. I want to talk with Uncle Harry, before going out to cope with the unknown world, but he isn't home.

At 50 miles an hour, I see the last sign reading "Utah US 30." Wyoming looks like a desert here though I see streams with trees along the banks and hayfields farther out with tall derricks. Green River is wide and, yes, green. Cottonwood trees grow by it, and the crowding cliffs are colored and of shapes resembling castles and cathedrals. I help Wendell an hour at the store before we go in our jointly owned Ford to the lodging he's arranged for me.

At 5:30 a.m. I leave the car with him and board the eastbound bus. It travels at 55, if the speedometer I see from my seat is working right. We're passing cars. Mostly I'm watching the land swishing by, too fast close to me for my eyes to focus but moving slowly farther out, showing range cattle grazing and a herd of sheep stirring dust. Far to the south in a blue haze I see the rock-and-snow-crowned Uinta Mountains. I feel goodbye to my home territory as to my family and Peg, with similar pressure behind my eyes.

I try to drink the unknown into me through my eyes and to tell myself it's the same Earth in only slightly different clothing. We cross the Continental Divide at Sherman Hill, highest point on Lincoln Highway. The green forest is marked by great boulders balanced one on top of another. I feel I'm accepting the land, nature, as all fundamentally familiar. I worry more about the strange cities I'm heading for, the milling crowds of unknown people.

The US 30 signs shift from Wyoming to Nebraska, and the mountains shrink to hill-size, then flatten as rolling plains. The land is all green now. White-faced cattle graze on fenced rangeland. I notice foreshadowing of the corn belt, though this first cornfield looks water-starved. Dairy cattle replace beef cattle. Darkness falls; the bright stars shine down on the Great Plains. The patterns of the stars are familiar to me. I relax and sleep as the bus rolls on.

Iowa is greener yet. It's corn and more corn with pastures alternating – and hardwood groves closely confined. Stacks of shucked corn ears are held by chicken-wire screen. Where no streams flow, windmills pump water for livestock. Darkness again brings sleep, but at midnight I wake. The king of rivers, the Mississippi, is below us. Lightning illuminates the expanse of water. I'm thrilled but also mourning and don't quite know why.

Light comes in Illinois and shows mills, factories, tall smokestacks. Cities are replacing corn, trees, pastures. I see the skyscrapers of Chicago, and at 6:30 the bus stops in this second largest city of the

United States. I mobilize myself and boldly register at a hotel that looks inexpensive, then stroll around the shore of Lake Michigan toward the "Century of Progress" World Fair. I like Adler's Planetarium; inside its dome is the familiar night sky. The rotation and change in position of the planets in relation to the star constellations look natural to me, reassuring, as if I'm still in the Great Basin, looking up.

Though I walk the city and the Lake Michigan shore during three days and nights, mostly I'm at the Fair, enjoying, say, the Ford exhibit showing transportation from the old Persian chariot used before Christ to the modern automobile, or Ripley's Believe It or Not Odditorium, or the advanced metal-and-glass construction of buildings that are magically air-conditioned inside. Sally Rand dances naked in dim light, skillfully hiding the views with an immense white rubber bubble. I think of masturbation fantasies, and of Ely's Big Four, though Sally Rand and the fair are grander, maybe more artistic.

Moving again on the bus through South Chicago and Gary, Indiana, I see everything looks dirty. Across Indiana and Ohio, though, I feel a touch of home again – farm after farm, cornfields, pastures, cows, horses. Night comes in central Ohio. Before I sleep I watch a ship with many lights, floating, not going anywhere, on the Ohio River. In Pittsburgh, just after midnight, I wake briefly and see a 40-story skyscraper that's smoke-dirty and a new post office building that's white-clean.

Morning – and we're in mountains again – and I feel better again. The mountains, though not high, are beautiful in their clothing of forest. The pike, as the highway is called here, leads up several ranges. From viewpoints where we stop briefly, I see Pennsylvania, Maryland, West Virginia, old Virginia. I see markers of historic places I've learned about in school. I get off the bus in Washington just after noon, the day before I'm to report for duty. I walk from the bus station to start exploring this magnificent capital city – and soon, I feel quite sure in my surging enthusiasm, to explore the whole great world.

    These words written in that goodbye diary the Pals of Olympus gave me before I left Salt Lake City keep marching through me as I walk:

> Not enjoyment and not sorrow
>   Is our destined end or way
> But to act that each tomorrow
>   Finds us farther than today.
>   Good Luck – Peggy Farrell

Chapter 7 – United States Capital 1934-36

I'm walking to explore Washington when misty drizzle starts falling. I defy the drizzle, turning my face up into it. And there, high ahead, is the white dome of the Capitol. The vision lifts me back into my world dream, yet reality keeps interrupting. The small Astor Hotel here on North Capitol Street has a sign offering rates lower than I'd expected – and I must be responsible now, to take care of myself, at least. I go in and pay $5 for one week. I now have a place to sleep and still have $65.29, not bad for a kid in the Depression who's come two thousand miles, but not so good either when you have to buy your meals.

The Capitol dome seems higher as I get nearer. People I'm facing along the sidewalk stare at my lifted eyes. Few adults in a city look higher than the approaching person's eyes, so, as a newcomer, I conform. On the Capitol grounds diverse trees from around the world are labeled at eye level with their names – a quick gain for a prospective naturalist.

I climb the long flight of steps toward the main-floor doors of the Capitol. Before going in, I turn and stare at the 555-foot-tall needle of the Washington Monument. Its pointed top, incredibly high, is half-hidden in the mist. I'm not totally sure it's real, but I'll investigate it later. I go inside the Capitol, and again my ability to believe is strained. The interior of the dome is so far up, a sky in itself. The colors glow. George Washington is there as a god of liberty and victory – so says a pamphlet I've found – surrounded by symbolic females representing the nation's original states. I feel invisible in this vast inside space, yet I really am here and will never again be the same as when I left Utah eight days ago.

Early in the morning I locate the Civil Service Commission in a heavily fancy building of dirty marble occupying two city blocks.

When employees are arriving, I walk in along wide dark halls and find the agency's examining division. At eight o'clock I'm sworn in as a messenger – $1080 a year. My key function is to rush lists and supporting papers of certified eligibles for government jobs to be filled all around the capital. Three persons are certified for each job, and the relative standings on the register are to be considered before hiring anyone. The densest concentrations of government offices are within five blocks of the Capitol or the White House and along Constitution, Pennsylvania, and Independence avenues. I fear I'll never learn my way around this complex city, but my supervisor says she'll mark on my map whatever location I'm uncertain about. She knows I can type and asks me to demonstrate. There'll be office work for me on rainy days, she decides. Messengers unable to type will go out in the rain.

After work my first day, I walk out Pennsylvania to the White House, then circle back by the Potomac River and climb steps into the Lincoln Memorial. The giant statue sits as if alive. I feel Lincoln filled with love and loaded with responsibility feeling, yet mischievously playful too. I read his words on the walls and resolve with him that "government of the people, by the people, for the people, shall not perish from the earth." I write faithfully but briefly in the diary the Pals gave me. These samples show me getting started:

> August 16, 1934 – Thursday – Used typewriter some. It's raining hard and has been since before noon (now 7 p.m.) I am lonely in my hotel room. Nothing to read or do here.
>
> Friday – Typed most of the day. Went over and saw George Washington University. Much of it looks like old shacks.
>
> Saturday – Worked an hour overtime mailing out circulars. Saturday's normally a half day. In afternoon, visited Washington Monument and hiked up its 898 steps. Scary views.
>
> Tuesday – Moved to YMCA. Haven't tried the pool and gymnasium yet but will tomorrow. Sent transcript of credit

blanks to Granite and White Pine high schools for admission GW University.

Thursday – August 23 – All is well. Peggy sent a very nice letter. I was sure glad to get it. Will answer tomorrow, I guess. Kind of tired tonight.

Friday – Very little sunshine in this place. Seems cloudy or raining all the time. Not very hot since I got here.

Sunday – August 26 – Walked in Virginia. Went thru Arlington cemetery. Saw Custis-Lee mansion, also Tomb of Unknown Soldier. Walked thru Clarendon, Virginia Heights, etc. –about 20 miles in all.

Tuesday – Posted letter to Peggy. Book *American Poems* – 50 cents. Am studying John Muir. Have his *Stickeen* – and *Steep Trails* again. Also *Alaskan Days with John Muir* by Young.

Muir has been bolstering (confirming?) my feelings about nature for years already. I return to him for wild glimpses and feel homesick:

Through a meadow opening in pine woods I see snowy peaks about the headwaters... How near they seem and how clear their outlines on the blue air, or rather *in* the blue air... for they seem to be saturated with it. How consuming strong the invitation they extend! Shall I be allowed to go to them?

My night school days at George Washington started at 5:10 p.m. and continued until 10:10 or, on two evenings, 11:10. I signed up for enough classes so that in one year, including summer, I'd earn as many credits as a regular day student. My classes included botany, geology, English composition, and psychology. I often studied until midnight, feeling strongly responsible for myself, at least, in this confusing city, keeping busy so "each tomorrow" would find me "farther than today" – but also constantly busy to dilute my longing for Peggy and Mount Olympus and Dad. I had my eyes examined and got glasses – $14. I also had five teeth filled – $9. Tuition was $35 and books $11.45. I felt less than half effective without a typewriter, so I bought a used portable for $20.

Washington was even more crowded than I'd feared. Traveling the 14 blocks from office to classroom between 4:30 and 5:10 seemed impossible. An office friend, also going to GW, invited me to ride in his car. Theoretically, 40 minutes was more than enough time, but even in those days there was a "rush hour," and we sat still with the motor running much of the time (opposite of rush?). We never reached class before 5:20. My friend won grudging tolerance from his professor. Mine, though, said if I couldn't get there by 5:10 I'd be dropped from class. I tried street cars, but they never made it on time. I borrowed a bicycle and even tried a taxi - only 20 cents then - the driver meeting me just outside the door at 4:31.

The taxi averaged better but was never quite on time. I did at last discover the way. I walked. I could go into the gutter to get around crowds. If that didn't work, I could keep up speed dodging among the stalled cars. I even had time on the way to eat peanuts and an apple so as not to get too hungry. Mrs. Abrams fed me any time I finished classes; she mothered me, took some of my self-responsibility load, reduced my loneliness, often sitting and talking with me.

My classes were awakeners. I'd thought of botany as identifying wildflowers and trees, but it broadened. Soon I was tracing the life histories of ferns, pines, mosses, wheat, and other plants through a microscope and learning the influences of soil, water, temperature, sunlight. I drew details. Recently I found such drawings in my old papers and barely believed I could have done this professional-looking work.

Geology astonished me. I hadn't known so much of the land, even mountains, had been under water, so much rock deposited as sand or silt brought by streams and later cemented into sandstone or other stone through heat, pressure, and chemical reactions. Equally amazing was the history of life on Earth recorded as fossils in rock layers that could be dated, even back into the hundreds of millions of years. Earth and life, I gathered, hadn't been created just a few thousand years ago. I wondered if Dad or this Dr. Brossard at the church here would agree. The psychology classes let me know I was far from the only one who couldn't be sure just why I did what I did. There was this tug between genetic instinct and learning experience as the main cause of behavior. I could go on believing that instinct (heredity?) dictates the direction to go, while details may come from conscious learning. For English composition and literature I produced papers that enable me now to re-experience myself in Washington in the fall of 1934:

> The sun is shining! The long rain is over! I can't remember that I was ever before so glad to see the sun. He seems like an old friend, a dear and intimate friend, just returned from a journey... I run swiftly, joyfully toward the river. The sunbeams reflecting from the reddish brown stream flash me a glad welcome.

The paper that brought highest praise from the professor came from a long-continued strand of my life:

> Modern men laugh at savages who carry dried lizard skins to keep evil spirits away, but these same people place faith in crosses and certain kinds of clothes... Savage worship, integrating people and nature, may actually be better than anti-nature forms of Christianity... Many people of the past have been happier because of religion. But aren't many of us today able to throw off the now almost transparent mask of supernatural mystery and to see the true reason for living in accord with moral codes? ...
>
> Do unto others as you would have them do unto you.
>
> Love thy neighbor as thyself.

Thou shalt not kill.

Thou shalt not steal...

I see these commandments as rules of happiness... I shall be generous, honest, virtuous, and thrifty to the extent I'm able – not because I want to get into heaven but because I want to be happy.

Here's another glimpse of me in Washington, doing what I've often done, going for a walk:

It's Christmas Day. A thin sheet of pulverized snow has spread itself over the streets and sidewalks and the old brick buildings, and a cold breeze is blowing it into tiny white wisps of mist... The Potomac is bound already in the icy chains of old man Winter. The wind has blown the snow into ups and downs and ripples on the ice, and the once-mighty river lies silent and still like the desolate stretches of a desert of sand... I throw a heavy rock far out on the ice, and it bounces and rattles and skids along... All alone I watch the sun turn to a ten-dollar gold piece. It's so dazzling I can't look at it, so I look at the ice, and there's a shining trail leading toward the sun...

Spending Christmas alone, I rediscovered myself as more nearly at home in wild nature than in city crowds. Washington wasn't and couldn't be my home. How long could I, should I, stay here? At the very end of 1934, I wrote this plan for myself:

Continue at Civil Service, making every effort to gain promotion. Practice shorthand so you can pass 120 words a minute (senior stenographer).

Continue at school, paying special attention to Nature Study and learning to use English. Get advice from Dr. Yocum [biology professor] about being a naturalist. Get acquainted with people in Biological Survey and National Park Service and others involved with nature.

There was a longer range plan too. By January 1, 1940, I should have graduated from college; be working at a salary over $2,000 a year in some government agency concerned with nature – forestry, biology, geology, astronomy, meteorology; have knowledge of natural sciences much greater than would necessarily be gained through graduation; and have ability to write and speak so as to gain publication and attract audiences to lectures. I'd decided not to move into the colony of Mormon lads.

During 1935 I'm teased by a confusing tangle of trails leading, just possibly, toward my "dreams." After completing my six-month probation as messenger, I reach for more money – $120 a month instead of $90. But what I become is a file clerk confined to a vast room without windows. The artificial lights are bright enough, but there's no sunshine, no view of sky, no natural greenery. We file clerks find the papers of persons being certified for positions and pull them out for lucky messengers to carry in open air.

Geology at the university shifts favorably, though. We're outdoors on weekend afternoons, directly studying sedimentary, igneous, and metamorphic rocks. Down in an old quarry we see the inside of limestone that was metamorphosing into marble. Some of the quarrying steps there, though neatly solid, are 20 inches down. A girl behind me hesitates on the brink after I, not having forgotten the mountains, had leaped smoothly down. I watch as she's deciding how to cope. She's lovely. She has coppery brown-blonde hair and an eagerly intelligent expression.

Spontaneously, I hold up my hands to her. She studies my face a moment and steps confidently into my arms. I lower her carefully to the level I'm on, and we're friends. She's Barbara Closs, and her main subject is art. We talk geology first, then realize we're also in the same French class. I'm taking French because I did in high school so have some chance of reaching fluency. Oddly, I don't think of Peggy or of Nellie Thompson in relation to Barbara – they're so different – yet I think of Eloise back in Overton. The angle of view in

French class is the same as it was with Eloise in my sixth grade. Barbara's cheek and ear play hide-and-seek with me as she tosses her hair or turns or tilts her head. Sometimes I see the rounding of one breast in her sheer blouse. She must have several blouses almost alike, a different one each day. Barbara is grown up; she'll be getting her B.A. next year.

The teacher of French, Professor Protzman, has poison ivy on his face. He keeps it bandaged, out of sight, but it must irritate him. Though he doesn't show attention to the ailment, his concentration on the lesson sometimes falters. The bandages grow day by day and hide all his face except the eyes and mouth. When he enters thus masked, we don't know whether to laugh or feel sorry. Barbara turns and looks questioningly for cues on other students' faces. My glance catches hers, and we seem to agree: He's a brave fellow capably launching the day's lesson, and we should focus on that. The whole class pretends all's normal.

Barbara and I feel alike about many things. We enjoy walking, and when our free time coincides we explore the city's parks and art galleries. Barbara teaches art at the Marjorie Webster school far out toward the Maryland line and lives in that vicinity. One night we tease each other into walking all the way, six miles. Street lights and crowds are soon scarce. We're not uncomfortable together or puzzled how to behave. Our swinging hands touch as we walk. They grasp each other, and all those six miles they hold, the arms swinging rhythmically together, our lilting strides continuing unbroken, except there's an extra-strong spring over the curb after we cross a street.

Barbara's home is the Finger Lakes region of New York State. She graduated from Pratt Institute in Brooklyn, a respected school in the art world. When we reach her quiet subdivision off 16th Street, it's near midnight. She shows me the Webster school on its lushly landscaped grounds and the rooming house where she lives. There seems no sex tension or questions. We're friends. Our hands come unclasped, and she finds her key and opens the door. "See you in class," we say.

In the second term my composition class studied diaries, and I started my "Journal of a Young Naturalist" in a blank book with lined pages. I soon abandoned handwriting, though, and typed – which was faster. I planned to keep all the sheets in order in a file folder but was soon sorting by subjects, including humans, not just "natural history":

> February 9 – I walk along F Street on my way home from work after noon on Saturday and have difficulty getting through the crowds... On impulse, I forget the rooming house and start north toward the most solitary place within walking distance, Rock Creek Park...
>
> It's fine to be alone in a beautiful place like this on a beautiful day like this.
>
> It's warm; the snow is melting and water is running in little rivulets down the road... I see a gray squirrel digging into one of his storehouses... about 50 yards away. He's digging in snow, then in the ground. As I sneak closer... he runs off and climbs a tree near the creek bank.
>
> I examine the exact spot where the squirrel dug. He penetrated two inches of firm snow and one and a half inches of hard-frozen soil. I take my pocketknife and start probing...
> Less than a half-inch below the deepest part I find a large acorn.
>
> How could that squirrel know exactly where to dig? He must have placed hundreds of nuts last fall, and he didn't make a map... Perhaps the answer is instinct, but if so, instinct must be more wonderful than reason. I must find out about this, try to think it through.

A week after my concentration on the squirrel, according to my money notebook, I bought my personal bicycle ($17) – to speed and prolong my escapes from crowds, a lifelong need. One Saturday in June I labored faithfully in my file-dungeon until noon (four hours on Saturday is the custom). By 12:05 I was heading for the Potomac

River and far beyond on my first trip to the Blue Ridge Mountains. Along with food and my blanket roll, I carried the 926-page *Gray's New Manual of Botany*: A *Handbook of the Flowering Plants and Ferns* and a little booklet, "A Key to the Flowering Plants" by Robert F. Griggs, professor of botany at GW with whom I was beginning to get acquainted. I wrote about the trip in my Young Naturalist series:

> The ride into Virginia is easy and fast for 40 miles – until the Piedmont Plain steepens toward the mountains and I, of course, am tiring. The bicycle has no gears to shift, and I go slower, soon even getting off and pushing the bicycle up the steeper grades. Just after dark I'm crossing an unusually low but wild Blue Ridge pass (usually called "gap" in this region) at 1150 feet elevation. Satisfied for Saturday, I roll up in my blanket beneath a rugged black locust tree. Fireflies flash-flash in the warm darkness, the flashes surprisingly bright, demonstrating the local name, "lightning bug."
>
> Early Sunday my eyes open and see the sky colored pink. The air is cold; the pink turns gray. I wait for my friend, the sun. Finally, he peeps over a far hill, faintly, where I wasn't expecting him – in the northeast, says my sense of direction that I've considered dependable. I hide my bedroll and bicycle and walk southward along the Appalachian Trail, soon feeling warm.
>
> I find plants I haven't seen in the wild before – evening primrose, some *Scrophulariaceae*, and unknowns. I try to key the flowers – little success. The flattish ridgetop pasture abandoned years back is covered with white blossoms I do key out, *Rubus villosus*, Lucretia dewberry...
>
> I resolve to practice strenuous bike riding and take more trips to the Blue Ridge where, I'm told, a national park is being established.

After another trip or two, consulting with Dr. Griggs, I adopted a botany project that demanded many more hours of work. I'd collect "all the wildflowers" of the proposed Shenandoah National

Park – before the park was officially established and frowning on wildflower-picking. I bought a second-hand Ford V-8 and started taking annual leave that I'd earned. Skyline Drive was partly constructed along the crest, so I could drive deep into the proposed area. Six miles north of US 211, I found a dirt road that would get me closer to Devil Stairs where I might photograph scenery while collecting specimens. I won a bonus that day – 13-year-old Winfield Sisk, who'd volunteered to guide me, took me to meet his family, one of nearly 500 mountain families who lived in the proposed park and were a worry to the National Park Service and to Virginia State. Winfield's mother, Daisy Sisk, invited me to dinner. Also at home were three girls – Marie, going on 12; Coty, age nine; and Anna ("Annie" then), seven – and one boy, Athey, five.

The father, Newt Sisk, came in tired from the corn patch that was out of sight beyond a section of forest. Newt had red whiskers. He shook hands cordially but didn't talk. We ate green beans cooked with pork, using newly baked corn bread as pushers. Halfway through the meal Newt opened up, telling about wild creatures he'd observed and sometimes hunted. He invited me to spend the night – and "all summer or more if'n it fits you."

The Sisks felt like family, congenial to me, and I lived with them often while botanizing. They had a dog and pigs, and they milked two cows, part of a herd grazing on pastures intertwining with forest. Many mountain residents had owner-tenant mutual-help arrangements for generations, Newt told me, though others owned land (as he had "until that house burned down" and he couldn't make payments).

The youngsters helped me find new species, and they laughed when I told them Latin names. Mountain laurel (*Kalmia latifolia*) was ivy to Blue Ridge people, and the hemlock tree (*Tsuga canadensis*) was spruce-pine. Wormseed (*Chenopodium ambrosioides anthelminticum*) was vermifuge; it helps you "get shed of worms,"

Annie said. Daisy and the girls worked the vegetable garden and gathered wild berries, nuts, salad plants, and medicinal herbs.

There was porch sitting late in the day. Newt and Winfield asked questions about situations outside the mountains. I did my best with the answers, knowing the family must soon move "out into the world." The girls sometimes broke the silences with light-hearted tricks. One might say, looking at me, "I bet I know what you're studying on." And I'd say, "I bet you don't." And she'd say, "That chee-er (chair)."

Relationships with wild nature seemed more basic and permanent than relationships with society and its economy. There was faith in the productivity and relative dependability of nature - if you worked with it as these people had learned to do. Most Blue Ridge people loved the mountains – with the ever-renewing abundance of fuel for heating and cooking, the ever-flowing clear cold water, the air so fragrant and free from poisons, the ever-productive soil, the surroundings they knew as home. I felt much the same, though the world (human society) had more handles on me than on them. I'd try to emulate them. I'd wish their way of life could continue.

I remember sitting with Newt as sunset faded. He smoked his pipe, looking at the mountains he loved and trusted. "I reckon I wouldn't be much 'count outside," he said. He wanted me to say he wouldn't have to move. But Washington insiders said the U.S. Supreme Court would approve the park, thus putting to use the funds Congress had already appropriated for staff and operating costs (for such costs if and when the park became an official reality). "You'll be as capable out there as you are here," I told Newt. He kept staring into the darkening distance and blowing short puffs of pipe smoke.

Another evening he suggested we go night-hunting for raccoons – their furs should "bring a price now." His hound named Brook, who'd acted lazy all summer, quickened with energy, ranging out ahead in the dark. Newt and I followed, carrying lighted kerosene lanterns. Newt heard with an educated ear when Brook sounded off. "Fox, I reckon," he said. "Trail's considerable faded, way old Brook talks. He'll give up d'rectly." The baying did stop. Later it came from a different angle. "That ain't coon neither," Newt said. "Possum maybe." And it was opossum, three hanging by their tails in a small tree. Newt stretched and got one down to show me, holding it by the tail. He let me hold it, and it hung limp. Newt had no use for possums but agreed to our keeping them overnight so I could photograph them in the morning. We kept them in a burlap bag; they went to sleep "balled up" in there.

My longing to live and work in the Blue Ridge soon becomes so strong my behavior seems irrational to Washington associates and to Dad. My job with the Civil Service is supporting me and partly supporting the family out West, while enabling me to get a university education. Yet four months after I was appointed file clerk, when I learn of a vacancy as clerk-typist with the National Park Service, I jump for it. Though Shenandoah National Park isn't involved – the work is in Washington – I'll be a step closer.

Barbara Closs and I enroll for the fall semester at GW, and I invite her to explore with me in the V-8 on Sunday along Skyline Drive and hike on the Appalachian Trail. The wild forest intermixes with grassy meadows, the rounded mountains, and the haze that gets bluer with each more distant ridge, everything mysterious and emotionally magic. We start up the Marys Rock Trail where US 211 intersects Skyline Drive. Barbara's not a botanist but knows wildflowers I still don't know; the flora of New York State where she grew up is more like that of the Blue Ridge than is the flora where I grew up. Sometimes she sketches while I key out flowers. If I'm slow finding the species, she might make a painting; she's fast with watercolor.

The view from the cliffs of Marys Rock has a magic glow. The depths of Shenandoah Valley seem another world, hazily unreal. We must explore down there, perhaps have dinner in some romantic place before driving back to Washington. Our appetite for mountain and valley and for each other's company continues to escalate. We climb other peaks or descend from Skyline Drive to dashing waterfalls. When we're thirsty and come to a natural spring, she holds her hands as a bowl and dips a drink for me. We joke about her having me eating out of her hands. Our feelings grow. When a trail is easy, we walk with arms around each other's waists, hips and thighs pressing. The best way is for my right and her left legs to move together in contact. We cuddle in the car after dark, and sometimes we stop in secluded places for kissing. Breasts become okay to fondle sometimes – briefly – but farther liberties are strictly forbidden.

I tell Barbara of my dream of being a naturalist at the proposed park. She's pleased. I tell her of the obstacles. They're not staffing yet, because the appropriation is still frozen while the U.S. Supreme Court puzzles over the land condemnation's constitutionality. A state-bought strip allows Skyline Drive construction with Depression emergency funds that President Hoover arranged while in office. The Civilian Conservation Corps crews, building camp and picnic grounds and trails, are made possible through Depression funds arranged by President FDR. Both presidents ordered the work after getting acquainted in person here on the ground, so it's hard to believe the park won't become a reality. Barbara sympathizes as I do with the Sisks and other mountain folk who'll have to leave the mountains, but we still favor park establishment.

After a year of suspense, the highest court decided the land acquisition was constitutional. Residents could continue a while in their homes if they signed an Occupancy Permit issued by the state, agreeing to move out when a federally built "resettlement homestead" or other appropriate housing became available. By Christmas all the needed permits had been signed, except by four families out of the 465, and those four had been evicted by the state through county sheriffs. As earlier provided by Congress, the Secretary of the Interior then accepted Virginia's gift of the land, and the park officially existed.

On March 1, 1936, the first National Park Service employees would report for duty. A clerk-stenographer position ($150 a month), for which I had the qualifications and would barely have the requisite six months of service in my present position to allow transfer, was among those announced for the park headquarters at Luray, Virginia. The way things fitted both thrilled and scared me. Though my applying couldn't affect the destiny of mountain families – and I'd have no responsibility for the families anyhow – or influence – other reasons to hesitate sprang up. Barbara, whom I was dreaming of marrying, though I hadn't yet proposed, told me pointedly what I already knew, that she was at GW primarily to get a B.A., because it would be important in her future. She suggested a B.A. at least would be important to me. The Luray opportunity sounds great – but – "Can't you wait for your degree and then get a better position?"

I realized also I'd be violating my own long-range plan – "continue at school, paying special attention to Nature Study and learning to use English." In life's swirling currents I might never get back to college. I wrote Dad – and find now an old letter from him, advising me to continue in Washington and get my degree. The arguments made sense – I recognized that – but the pull of "wild nature" (already implying that humans are nature too) continued powerful. A news item in the *Washington Star* – seemingly unrelated but to prove deeply related to my long-range future – delayed my decision:

> Eddie Cantor, America's popular radio, stage and screen comedian, has taken war talk seriously and ...will award a four-year scholarship and complete maintenance at any American college to the person who writes the best letter on the subject, "How Can America Stay Out of War?"

In a brief flash, I felt that war was almost as anti-national park as humans could get. War wastes natural resources, destroys and kills soil, forests, wildlife on large portions of Earth, as well as people.

I guess I was *feeling* at first, not *thinking*. I'd been feeling myself as a citizen of the whole United States, somehow confirmed by my traveling so far to Washington, and now with Cantor's challenge I felt I was a budding citizen of the whole Earth. I felt a strong hint, at least, that I was in some degree responsible for mankind and our home planet. Only much later would growth from these feelings put me among the first to combine Earth-citizenship with environmentalism. But already the feelings were grabbing and confusing me. I hated what Hitler was beginning to do, but I also hated the thought of Americans helping again to destroy Europe in order to protect it from Hitler.

I believed I had an answer – which I've continued ever since to advocate. I wrote Cantor I was "a young man just old enough to be drafted" and, though I believed much of what war-advocates believed, I further believed that: "abundant means for the insurance of enduring peace – with protection of life and homes and resources and landscapes – are at hand awaiting the wise cooperation of people...

> Permanent peace will ultimately be secured by a world federation controlling a land-and-sea police force superior to the armed forces of any one nation. With such a force operating, nations would reduce their own armies and navies...

> During the trying years before a satisfactory federation can be perfected, let us hope that wise administration of neutral policy will save us from conflict and destruction...

I actually thought I might win. The man heading the judges who'd choose the winning letter was one I greatly admired, Robert M. Hutchins, president of the University of Chicago, who encouraged people to educate themselves and encouraged universities to award degrees to students who could pass the examinations, whether or not they'd attended classes. If I won the Cantor-Hutchins prize, I could quit clerical jobs forever – so I fantasized – and in a year or two of all-out effort win a degree from the University of Chicago, while continuing to help my family in Salt Lake. As I received my degree – the fantasy continued – the park service would be adding a naturalist to the Shenandoah personnel list.

But neither reason nor fantasy is conclusive in me. There's a hidden gravity or magnetism, perhaps instinctual, that works best in silence and solitude. Sometimes instantly, sometimes after unexplained delay, it steadies my inner compass for confirming or changing the direction I'm to go. And that compass would prove stubborn!

Darwin's Campsite
Woodcut, 1930s or 1940s by Barbara and Darwin Lambert

Chapter 8 – New National Park 1936-37

The Sisk family and I wake before sunrise the day I'm to start working in Shenandoah National Park. I hear Winfield beside me putting on his clothes and Daisy already in the kitchen stirring up the fire to cook breakfast. She's adding firewood and putting the frying pan down on the iron top of the black range. My 20 years of life have been a preparation; though I've played and worked and studied in nature, this will be my first direct link with conservation.

I've left Washington in defiance of the best advice and my own mental reasoning – perhaps from "instinct" – and my move must succeed or I'll look stupid. I worried about the Sisks, if they'd feel hurt by my joining the National Park Service (NPS) that now controls the land the state of Virginia bought through condemnation. But when I arrived yesterday afternoon Daisy embraced me as if I were a son who'd won an honor. Newt thumped my back in support. After breakfast, Winfield and Marie run with me up the quarter-mile trail to my car beside the CCC fire-road. Though I'm early – the drive to Luray takes 40 minutes at most – Winfield and Marie can't wait to see me speeding into my new destiny. I stop at Skyline Drive overlooks to enjoy morning views, but still I'm parked across the street from the office ahead of time.

At last a young man unlocks the door. No uniformed park rangers are in sight – the first two are said to be transferring today from another park. I see a man of dignity going in and guess he's the engineer-in-charge of the Civilian Conservation Corps (CCC) program, expected to become park superintendent. I follow. But he's not Ralph Lassiter; he's T.T. "Ted" Smith, the CCC chief clerk. He takes from his desk what must be a personnel file on me. He calls others – four of them – to stand with me as witnesses. I'm swearing to perform to the best of my ability and swearing I've never advocated overthrow of the United States Government. Because the Sisks waked so early, I'm the first NPS person sworn in for the Shenandoah staff.

We go through an open doorway into what's called Homesteads Office, and Ted introduces me to L. Ferdinand Zerkel who's creating new homes for the mountain folk. Zerkel looks at me as if wanting to talk, and I want to ask him questions – first, about the Sisks' likely future – but behind us Lassiter is arriving.

"Glad you're here, Lambert," Lassiter says, shaking my hand. "We'll talk after you've learned the main ropes." He shrugs off formality the way my Dad does. He says to Ted, "Show Lambert the current files and the project's financial summaries and leave him to study them. There's a Washington guy coming to show him how to operate that new machine for NPS cost controls and accounts." I've imagined conflict between the CCC management and the usurping NPS management, but now I feel it won't happen. Both sides will do what Lassiter says – he looks so instantly through camouflage to essence. I'm soon deep in the files, stimulated, feeling I really might contribute significantly here. So much is going on that's new, not already cut and dried, organized.

Luray people spoke to everyone on the streets, strangers or not, as if wanting them to feel comfortable, at home, and I wanted to be at home in town as well as in the park and the mountain culture. While I was exploring at lunchtime, eating an apple and roasted peanuts direct from their shells, dropping the shells into my pocket, a woman carrying packages told me that Brown's Restaurant, "right there," served good food at low prices. Two men, walking the opposite way, agreed. One added, "Jim Brown can tell you about Luray Caverns and other sights to see."

Main Street then was bordered by trees over the sidewalks. A slow-flowing creek crossed under a concrete bridge, and I paused there near Brown's, watching reflections in the water. The next person who spoke to me guessed I was "a new park man" and asked if I'd found a house yet. I told him I wanted only a room. "Closest place, I reckon, would be Ashby Foltz's on top of the hill there." He wave-pointed up past the park office. I read files until quitting time. Then two supervisors came down from the mountain to confer with Lassiter. "Sit and listen, Lambert," Lassiter said. "Best way to learn what's going on." So it was after six when I rang the Foltz doorbell. Mrs. Foltz opened the door, and her eyes searched my face and clothes. "Why, son," she protested as if she were my mother, "you're cold. You've got no coat on. Come right in here and get warm." She ordered me to sit next to the hot-water radiator. I obeyed and asked if she had a room to rent.

"We've got two ain't rented." She guided me upstairs and showed the big front room, saying, "It ain't much, son. The trucks coming by make noise and smoke. You going to be in Luray long?"

"Years maybe. How much is the room?"

"Oh. You work for the park. Well – tourists pay a dollar a night. But it'd be less for staying longer. What can you afford easy, son?"

She tried to lower the price and I to raise it. We settled at $12 a month. I figured I'd live mostly at the Sisks' in good weather and mostly in town when weather discouraged driving.

Sleet was falling a few evenings later when I started to Brown's for dinner. Mrs. Foltz called me back. "Hey, son. You eat with us tonight." She guided me into the dining room. "Just an ordinary meal, but it'll save you catching pneumonia."

There was fried chicken, mashed potatoes, three vegetables, milk, and bread.. Soon I felt full. "Pass son the chicken again, Old Man," she said to her husband.

I said, "No, thank you," but she insisted. She also put more potatoes and vegetables on my plate. When dessert time came, I was too full, but she gave me home-canned peaches and frosted cake against my protest, and I enjoyed them. We moved into the living room and listened to the radio. After a time – apparently his regular routine – Old Man excused himself, saying he was going next door to Campbell's service station and plumbing, to visit.

Mrs. Foltz turned down the radio and asked, "You got a girl, son?" She didn't – I'm 99% sure – have the slightest idea she was opening a subject related not only to a young man's dreams but also (a secret from me too until I started writing this life story) to my increasingly central concern with nature and my coming dedication to conservation and environmentalism – a connection that seems at first hard to believe but would prove in my case both intrinsic and powerful. My own mind is still somewhat vague on the connection, because it's mainly through emotion – which doesn't easily find words for itself – but my feeling keeps growing and finds these thoughts again: Protecting and enhancing the environment of home territory is stronger in a female-male combination than in one person and stronger yet when there are children.

Thinking of my artist-teacher girl-friend who'd been enjoying this new park with me, I said, "Well – I went with a girl in Washington."

"You in love with her?"

"I – I don't quite know."

"If you ain't sure, you ain't in love. We got nice girls here."

"I've noticed already," I said to dismiss the subject.

"Now, son, you listen," she came back strong. "Don't go on looks alone. You might as well get a girl with money. For instance, there's Dr. Spitler's daughter, a sweet black-haired girl just outa high school. Her father's got money." She identified others too whose fathers had money.

From Mrs. Foltz's and from the park office, I look up at the Blue Ridge and feel called to conquer it – not fighting, though, but loving. I've wanted work and play and wild nature and home all combined. I know the park's highest point is Hawksbill Head (4049 feet above sea level), but it's Stony Man (4010) that looks most impressive and keeps teasing me. I think of Mt. Olympus in Utah, about the same distance from where I was living – and a similar angle upward – and I think of Wheeler Peak in Nevada.

I've been at the Sisks' on weekends and some week nights, but this Saturday I eat a roast beef sandwich at Brown's, then stroll past the post office and turn on a country road toward Stony Man. The mountain's beard, nose and brow – the profile when seen from the north – are cliffs and steep forested slopes from this angle. The road ends at an abandoned farm house. Evergreen mountain laurel bushes are thick on the slope. Dried oak leaves cover the ground. A cottontail zigzags fast, rattling the leaves.

I find an abandoned wagon road beside a brooklet that's mostly lost under moss-covered boulders. Polypody, spleenwort, and Christmas ferns grow on the half-dry banks. Higher on the slope I look hard at different kinds of rock, identifying origins. I feel the botany and geology course at GW prepared me to tell some of the interesting facts about Shenandoah National Park. The wagon road becomes an uncertain trail that's closed often by tangles of mountain laurel. A downy woodpecker drums a gnarled oak. A brownish-gray hawk – I haven't learned eastern hawks yet – circles above the tree canopy. The sun, when I can find it, gets lower toward the horizon, and I doubt I'm yet halfway up this mountain. I try to climb faster. I wish I'd brought food. I wonder what I'll do when dark comes.

A dirt-and-gravel dugway appears and winds upward through the hollows and over the ridges, perhaps the Luray-Skyland road, now closed. It gets steeper, the curves sharper. A faded sign says, "Shift to Low Gear." Far up ahead a cottage perches on a peak, surely part of Skyland. Kettle Canyon must be on my right. A stream roars and splashes there, out of sight.

When the sun's an orange disc touching the misty Massanutten Mountain behind me, west beyond Luray, I'm climbing into Skyland resort – dozens of cottages but no place occupied or open for occupancy, no humans anywhere. The business doesn't open till spring. The valley I left seems another world. A pond deep in the dimness glows red with reflected light. The sunset has faded to violet and on to gray. A star, maybe a planet (Venus?), appears and keeps getting brighter. Chilly and hungry, I hike on.

I know I'm on Skyline Drive when my boots clap-clap. Soon, beyond the Drive eastward, an open fire glows. There's a CCC camp. I find the army captain in charge. He invites me to breakfast and a chat in the morning but doesn't want me sleeping in the barracks with "the boys." I wonder why. He suggests "Ye Lion-Tamers Clubbe," the big room where forest technicians and foremen eat and sometimes drink. A Mr. Talbot there says, "Toast your shins at the stove." I do that. I don't say I've had no dinner. Confessing I got pulled so far when not prepared can't help the standing I'd like to achieve in the park.

A group of us discuss wildlife, trees, mountains, and springs. They say bobcats are numerous, ruffed grouse often seen among evergreens, and there's danger from timber rattlesnakes and copperheads. I'm invited to sleep in the bed of a work-projects foreman who's away for the weekend.

Next morning, after breakfast with the captain who talks about discipline problems with some of "the boys," I ride with a fellow named Shifensk in his pickup, seeing sights northward on Skyline Drive. We pass the turn-off to the Sisks', but I don't mention it. Fog alternates with sunshine. We visit three additional CCC camps before returning to Camp NP-1, the oldest CCC camp in the entire national park system. I ask Shifensk to let me off where I can climb to the peak of Stony Man. He wants to climb with me. We follow a trailside arrow to Glen Beulah below Stony Man cliffs. From below, the cliffs look impossible – maybe they're the nose. Pretending confidence anyhow, I head straight up and am surprised at finding a blazed (paint-spotted) trail on the cliffs, leading quickly to the top. The 360-degree view reaches magically far among shrinking concentrations of fog. I feel coordinated inside now, ready for anything.

Lassiter often grinned over my obsession with "the mountain," which meant the whole physical park. He'd ask where I came from now, or where I was heading, and I'd tell him the Sisks', or a CCC camp, or a waterfall, or an early spring showing of wildflowers. He didn't hike and denied knowledge of wildflowers and trees and wild creatures, though he approved of hiking and knowing. The park's rapid and massive development needed a good engineer, and his appointment as superintendent came through. I was his secretary at first, but after letting me prove I could use shorthand, he never dictated. He preferred face-to-face talk – on the mountain with project supervisors and foremen, up there or in his office with Washington engineers, landscape architects (often called "landscrapers"), and executives who liked to drive the 85 miles or so to visit him.

Routine correspondence went to the chief clerk. When Lassiter wanted to originate a letter or answer one personally, he'd jot brief notes to me, or hand me the papers, saying things like, "Tell this guy we're grading the old road, and he can drive across that strip of park." Letters, sometimes almost illegible, kept coming from park residents, asking permission to clear new ground for a garden, or to cut firewood, or to move from one house in the park to a better one just vacated. Lassiter would ask me to read the handwriting to see if I saw the same words he did. Then he'd ask, sort of like my Dad, "How would you answer, Lambert?" I'd write the letters, and he'd sign them – or, once in a while, mark them up with corrections.

The mail brought inquiries about the natural features and about the human history. After the first few weeks, all such letters came to me. I'd dig for the information in books or elsewhere. I learned that CCC foremen were knowledgeable in one subject or another – forestry, botany, wildlife, Indian lore, Appalachian folk, or Civil War history. I'd call them and get reliable guidance. Where appropriate, I'd name them as sources, and they liked that.

Commonwealth Magazine (Virginia Chamber of Commerce, Richmond) invited Lassiter to send an article with pictures setting forth the new park's attractions. He handed the letter to me, saying,

"Tell this editor we don't have personnel yet to handle interpretation or publicity." I suggested I could write the article to run under his name and we could get fitting pictures from our CCC "landscrapers," one of whom (George Knox) was taking dozens of good pictures every week. The resulting article filled such a general need that reprints were distributed in quantity as the public's main source of Shenandoah park information.

To improve our interpretive output, I personally wrote older national parks and soon was receiving "Nature Notes" and other publications issued through volunteer organizations working with naturalists and rangers. A half-dozen of us park and CCC people organized Shenandoah Nature Society. I was elected president, probably because I'd contribute the most free time. We began preparing articles for a quarterly to be called *Shenandoah Nature Journal*. Researcher-writers would present programs at the society's weekly meetings, to which the public was invited. Soon we printed Vol. 1 No. 1, with 16 pages. Wildflowers, wildlife, and Blue Ridge geology were described and illustrated by qualified CCC supervisors and a park ranger. I wrote the article introducing the park and our nature society, also short pieces to go with photos by Knox.

Much earlier than I'd ever planned or hoped, I was a naturalist (with lots of help) telling thousands of people about animals, flowers, streams, wind and weather, scenic forests and mountains. My decision to leave Washington looked good so far; I was wielding influence before I was old enough to vote. Yet my influence was information only, with no direct bearing on conservation policy or action, no official responsibility for the park's resources – yet a vague slow- strengthening feeling deep inside (no clear words for it so far) that the scenic beauty and lasting healthfulness of this national park in some degree depended on me. Though not legally or officially responsible, I felt something resembling responsibility growing in me.

I fly high while half-consciously worrying that flaws in my doings or writings will show and bring me down. The cost of living is lower in Luray than in Washington. I trade in the V-8 on a new

Plymouth. The family in Salt Lake is doing better financially. I invite Dad and Aunt Luella to visit this park, after which we'll go in my car to the nation's capital, to New York City and New England, then see the sights across the country back to Salt Lake. They accept for the last half of August. We'll visit all the national parks near our route, and I'll pick up ideas useful at Shenandoah.

Meanwhile, I study this park in every way I can, deepening my knowledge of natural history, of the mountain folk and their ways of life, of the ongoing conservation work and its effects, and of all the attractions that bring visitors. Still, my life is far from all work and no play. I soon have Luray girl friends, though none yet from the wealthy families recommended by Mrs. Foltz.

One is the sister of a friend I took home to put on rough clothes for a bushwhack with me to discover a rumored waterfall. She's in the living room, and he introduces us before he disappears. She shows me an unusual ring of carved red stone that she's wearing. Her hand rests on mine as she shows it. When she finally withdraws the hand, her fingertips and nails travel my palm. "You should see the words inside," she says, her voice whispery. She pulls the ring off and puts it in my hand. She sits on the arm of my chair, her hip touching me. I'm not seeing the ring. I'm feeling her breath and smelling perfume. I grab her and kiss her. "Could I see you tonight?" I ask as I hear my friend coming in his hiking boots. "Yes," she whispers.

This girl doesn't like hiking or even sightseeing. She sits so close that when I steer around curves my right arm feels her breast. On a country road, I stop under overhanging elms. We kiss, and she doesn't terminate the kiss. I don't know how to terminate one myself without offending the girl. And a kiss builds up power. You're soon light-headed, unsure which way's up or down. But the kiss ends somehow, maybe from my feeling that's close to fear, and the blood must be flowing back to my brain. I look out into the dark. Lightning bugs flash out there, lightning bugs in the trees and between them and high above them, lightning bugs in the grass – the *females* in the grass, trying to draw the *males* down from the sky, according to insect books I've studied. The bugs are engaged in reproduction – and I'm definitely not!

I feel caught – and vaguely upset. But when kissing time comes again, and the girl doesn't resist when my hand slides down inside her blouse and holds a breast, my "thinker" goes dead. After a time she reaches up and unbuttons her blouse. There's no brassiere, and she picks up my other hand and puts it on her other breast. That's more maybe than I can stand. When I take her home, she says, "We had fun, didn't we?" And I can't help agreeing – but with a gnawing dissatisfaction that lacks words.

Afterward, I turn over and over in bed without sleep. I want this girl sexually just once – an experience I haven't had. I feel this is what the girl wants too, only maybe not just once. Maybe she'll start coming to me where I work and where I live. Best not to get involved. And there's this thought – wouldn't it be wonderful if the girl were one I could admire in every way, one I'd want as a lifetime mate? I want my true mate to be a virgin, and it would be fair and most rewarding for us both if I were the same. Can't a person plan, and follow the plan that's likely to generate the most happiness in a lifetime? Is the physical in humans stronger than the mind?

I sleep at last believing I'm capable – planning and control are so reasonable – but I wake still wanting this girl. After office hours I drive to a neighboring town, across the Massanutten Mountain where I won't be recognized, to buy a condom. I'm conscious, as the girl climbs into my car, of the little tin box in my pocket. She might feel it there and laugh with scorn, or maybe kiss harder or unbutton her blouse sooner.

Almost instantly, kissing, we're to hands on breasts. We shift position and start another kiss. My right arm is around her neck and my right hand holding her left breast while the whole arm tightens her against me. I touch her knee with my left hand, and kissing her, squeezing her, I work upward along her thigh. I feel quivers along my spine. My mind no longer functions. I'm sensation, I'm desire. I grip her thigh, pull her leg against me. I squirm my fingers under her panties and touch the center of everything. There's a shock, like electricity, like an earthquake.

Then, inexplicably, my mind functions again. All my thoughts, all my plans, all my resolution of the sleepless hours last night, accompanied too by an undefined fear, flood back on me. I seem to hear my father talking about the judgment-book angel. "I'm tired," I say, "exhausted maybe."

She goes rigid. Maybe she'll cry, maybe she'll slap me. "Why? Why?" she demands hoarsely.

I can't answer her Why? I don't honestly know – yet. But I say, "I never had intercourse. I don't want to now."

"What?" She's angry but laughing at me. "You've never *done* it?" I can't read my own feelings, but I start the car and take her home.

Another Luray girl I knew slightly heard I was writing a guidebook to the park, and she wanted to explore with me – by car or hiking or even bushwhacking. We set goals to reach (peaks, waterfalls) or otherwise to achieve, such as through identifying 20 species of trees. When we were alone in wild places, she liked to hug and kiss as I did, spending as much time at it as we had left after reaching our goal. This could add up to hours, but she terminated early kisses before they got scary. She repulsed farther advances that were obvious, but she accepted body-to-body contacts and pressures. I'd help her up vertical rocks, for instance, or carry her across streams. We felt free with each other, accepting each other's wish to avoid the sex act itself.

We simulated, though. The first time, we'd been resting side by side fully clothed on softly thick grass. We reached for each other, embraced and kissed, and the full length of our bodies touched. Our pelvises began almost imperceptibly to press each other, press and relax, yet moving so slightly we could pretend it wasn't happening, but the slight pelvic rhythm continuing, continuing, continuing to a climax – for me anyway and maybe for her too as both of us would be so quietly tender the rest of the afternoon. After that day, we avoided lying down together but found the same thing could happen with a long kiss and hug while we were standing clothed. Inside my mind, secretly, I made excuses for us. I told myself we were finding pleasure but enjoying it "responsibly" – doing no likely harm to each other or anyone else – no pregnancy, no disease transmitted. But I wasn't quite sure my Dad (or his "judgment-book angel") would agree.

My interest in Luray girls dwindled when there was communication again with Barbara. One difference was that Barbara pursued a goal of possible significance in the world. She was making a meaningful effort as artist and art teacher. Another difference was she recognized potential importance in what I was doing in the park – the nature journal, the nature lectures our organization was arranging, usually featuring university professors. I might marry Barbara if I could win her. Then I'd tease Mrs. Foltz; I'd have a girl "with money." Barbara's father was a banker and a mayor in New York State; both her parents had incomes from stocks and bonds. Barbara had declared her independence from that money, though; she was insisting on proving herself financially as well as artistically by succeeding on her own in the nation's capital.

In August Barbara would be vacationing at her parents' home in the Finger Lakes region. I'd be her parents' house guest – as Dad and Aunt Luella would be staying at nearby Palmyra, a Mormon shrine. On visits to Shenandoah Park with me, Barbara had completed half a dozen watercolors, and now she offered to draw illustrations for *Shenandoah Nature Journal*. The first would go with an article I was writing for the winter 1936-37 issue, "Meet Mr. Coon," the text mostly adapted from my mountain friend Newt Sisk, a long-time coon hunter who'd made part of his living selling furs.

The two-week trip with Dad and Aunt Luella inaugurated my adulthood – so I felt. Dad recorded:

> On the 17th Darwin took us in his car and showed us Shenandoah. The tree-covered hills with many varieties of trees (and Doc knew them all), the mountain people and their farms and the green valleys – and in fact everything out of doors – interested me.
>
> In Washington I showed them the Capitol, White House, Washington Monument, Lincoln Memorial, and Mount Vernon (actually out in Virginia).

Then, on to New York via Baltimore, Delaware, New Jersey. Dad recorded in apparent amazement, "Darwin drove us all around the great city." He listed many places I somehow managed to find – to my own amazement – then commented, "All were so wonderful to me – who had to wait until his 50th year before getting a chance to go east." We then discovered Yale University, historic places in Boston, and Acadia National Park, Maine.

Here's more of Dad's diary:

> We went to the Joseph Smith farm at Palmyra, New York, for the night. Darwin stayed with a lady friend and family at Canandaigua... We slept in the room where the angel Moroni appeared to Joseph.

Barbara's arms closed around me as mine did around her as we kissed. Her parents were friendly but not forgetting they were members of the "Yankee" establishment and I was a blend of Wild West and Virginia South. Barbara guided our sightseeing around Canandaigua city as we'd walked in Washington. I felt she'd marry me if I pursued her with both romance and practicality, but I wasn't financially ready.

Dad emphasized experiences he found most memorable. Niagara Falls, Ontario, Detroit, and Chicago made two sentences. Then he recorded and stressed his church enthusiasm:

We saw Carthage Jail where Joseph Smith and Hyrum were killed. Hyrum's blood still stains the floor. Called on Millard Lambert, my cousin, at Ferris, Illinois. Saw Nauvoo, a major city in Mormon history. We stayed at Estes Park, Colorado, two nights. Darwin climbed Longs Peak, elevation 14,252... The Rockies are grand... (Gone 17 days. My first real trip. Traveled 7,000 miles, traversed 22 states. A total cost for the two of us of $112.)

My cost was higher but not great. Prices during the Great Depression of the 1930s stayed incredibly low.

From Salt Lake I drove to Ely and visited Wendell and his bride Alpha (sister of Elwin Robison with whom I'd climbed Wheeler Peak and would later work to establish Great Basin National Park). Alpha's youngest brother George and I drove on to California where I wanted to see Yosemite and Sequoia national parks and gather ideas for improving the Shenandoah Nature Society's work. Yosemite was amazing to me. I learned a lot, and I thought about John Muir – who'd been largely responsible for establishing this great national park – and I gathered enthusiasm for NPS naturalist programs. I was told such programs started in California – as nature walks with knowledgeable leaders in natural, wild places.

Our nature society had advanced without me. A thousand of the first *Nature Journal* had been distributed, and sales were continuing along Skyline Drive. Within the next few months the society's constitution was adopted and an election held. Re-elected president, I invited more lecturers from universities for our public meetings – incidentally educating myself. The quarterly increased in size and circulation. Mail subscriptions increased as did retail outlets in Valley and Piedmont regions. Responding to pressures from readers, and with no one complaining, the title *Nature Journal* embraced the nature of Indians who'd lived here and of White explorers and settlers and of mountain folk. Sometimes it included the nature of park visitors enjoying and learning from wild nature. In February 1937 we started a radio show on WSVA, Harrisonburg, Virginia, and it blended history into nature successfully. I felt nervous speaking for the first time to an unseen audience. Others, including Frank Judy, CCC educational advisor and the society's vice president now, were experienced. The broadcasts multiplied attendance at our monthly meetings in Luray. I was writing a park guidebook on my personal time, and there was a proposal I become full-time executive on salary to cope with the growing business.

Dad and others questioned my proposed resignation from "assured lifetime security" (Dad's words) to adventure in full-time writing and publishing. He wrote, "If you stayed with the government, you could handle that magazine and the guidebook as a sideline, could you not?" But I was seeing an opportunity to be my own boss, doing what I most wanted to do – strengthening national park conservation through interpreting park meanings. The fateful change happened in the summer of 1937 while my first published book (*Beautiful Shenandoah*, 130 pages, illustrated) was being printed. I was publisher of this guidebook and now of the magazine that became simply *Shenandoah* (and would later be *Travel Lore*). I was publishing short stories and poems in addition to articles, photographs, and drawings. Two fiction writers, two poets, five nonfiction writers, three artists, and six photographers were represented in the 36-page issue that first carried The Lambert Co. name. Ross H. Benson, double my age, was selling advertising; Winfield Sisk was selling subscriptions and distributing the guidebook to retail outlets, proving a mountain lad could cope in "the outside world."

In the middle of the big change, Barbara answered my "long ago letter," saying she was in Virginia as arts-and-crafts teacher at summer camp on Bear Trap Farm, one hour by car from Luray. She'd come through a difficult school year in Washington and been offered re-appointment to all the positions "with enlargements." Six of her paintings, one a scene from Skyline Drive, were in a professional exhibit. On her days off from Bear Trap, we explored more of Virginia, cuddling and singing together, hiking wherever a trail attracted us.

Then she resumed her busy teaching schedule in Washington, and I was catching up with publishing projects. I missed her, and I was feeling encouraged financially. I proposed to her in a love letter, and she answered, "Darwin, you darling! Yes!" Later, though, she asked time to think. She told me about another boy friend, who was older, strongly established in his career, and, I guessed, had re-entered the scene after an absence.

She seemed to be asking confirmation of future prosperity. I tried to be honest, admitting I couldn't predict my income as a writer, editor and publisher. The park guidebooks were currently bringing in approximately what my government job had paid. Ross Benson was selling several hundred dollars a month in advertising, but his commission plus printing and distribution costs would be deducted. I expected income also from freelance writing and lecturing and producing folders for travel businesses. But, I had to conclude, it's all too new to be certain. The whole plan could fail, I wrote – "but that wouldn't destroy us, would it, Barbara?"

Early in November, writing from Washington, Barbara put herself convincingly into my picture – rather, into an enlarged picture of the two of us together as partners in life, in love, in business and, strongly and definitely now, in conservation.

> As to our big, and wonderful plans, dear – Let's say June; we can wait until then, don't you think? I can wait until this Christmas for the ring, to give you more time. Things aren't quite as bad financially as I was afraid they might be. I'm glad you told me... Oh, yes. We will spend hours of our lives working together. I'm so glad you want to.

She reacted favorably in her letter to ideas we'd discussed the last time we'd been together in Luray – a less expensive park booklet in addition to the guidebook, adding locally produced crafts to our distribution line, also paintings. She said her watercolors were worth $60 – "I am selling them for $25 to get a start. Drawings are less –

and maybe little ones, if you wish, much less." She said the music of the "bells of Luray" (the new Luray Singing Tower carillon) had greatly pleased her – "I wish they'd broadcast that music on the radio." And she praised the town and the world-renowned Luray Caverns – "They're extensive but intimate." She was already thinking about silverware and linen, having starts of each "at home put away." And she concluded: "The Lord watch between me and thee while we are absent one from the other always." Love, Barbara.

Candid Portrait of Darwin Lambert
Drawing by Barbara Closs Lambert 1939

Chapter 9 – Wife and Children and War 1938-43

Barbara started the year 1938 by sharing with me a letter she'd written ten years before to her later self. Her father had become mayor "at the tick of twelve" that earlier New Year's Day, and Barbara had her "first experience of seeing the New Year in" at a "young people's party." Her earlier self advised her later self, "Never forget the beautiful, thrillable times you have had... Perhaps you are married, but that matters little now if you get a prospective before you are 27," the next year now.

At her classes in Washington, she was showing her engagement ring. We were seeing each other often and exchanging letters. She completed two illustrations for a ghost story of the Blue Ridge and thus raised the year's first *Shenandoah Magazine* to a new high in reader appeal. The income was growing but not rapidly. So, for an additional project, we two were producing a scenic-historic map of four states surrounding our park, with drawings on the map of special attractions. Advertising manager Ross Benson was selling overprinting on the map in red ink to tourist business names at their exact locations.

The wedding was set for July 14 at the home of Barbara's parents. The ceremony would be in the flowery yard, the nearest to my preference for wild nature the family considered feasible. Barbara was struggling in Washington to fulfill her complex commitments for the school year (until June). On weekends we helped each other. Her classes recessed before Easter, so we drove to Canandaigua. She wanted to show me all her "childhood haunts ...that no one else in the whole world would understand but you."

For weeks after Easter, both of us worked 15-hour days, partly on the 25-cent "Lambert's Guide to Skyline Drive and Vicinity," a 68-page special edition of *Shenandoah Magazine* (vol. 2 no. 1). The cover was credited to both of us. Barbara was credited for two lively illustrations of a personal experience piece I'd bought, evoking the woman author's years-long experience with a mockingbird. Barbara and her parents liked and encouraged the nature-conservation tone of the magazine and business. The advertising would launch our marriage with a small surge of income. The wedding was my first experience in "*Society*." I tasted champagne and either a Manhattan or a martini. An hour before sunset, rice-pelted, we headed east toward Syracuse. The highway had deep ups and downs, and we watched several sunsets – I, in the rearview mirror –Barbara, her breasts touching my arm as she turned, watching the bright clouds through the back window, the sun disappearing when the highway dropped but rising as we climbed.

We'd long agreed we wanted children, and the prospect strengthened our nature-conservation feelings. She'd painted an appealing panel of children and playthings; I'd praised it. More recently she'd written, "Oh, Darwin, I love you and can never forget your wistful look when first I showed you those drawings, suggesting we reproduce them for our children's room." We didn't want a baby immediately, though, and we had trouble that night from lack of experience, losing erection while trying to get the condom on. The problem disappeared, though, before we slept. Our honeymoon continued into Maine and included swimming and laughing together, naked, in a moose pond when the moose were away.

I'd rented the ground-floor apartment of the Foltz's two-story duplex. Mrs. Foltz welcomed Barbara as a queen. We were almost-celebrities. Many Luray women brought tasty food. "We know you're a 'damn Yankee,'" one welcomer told Barbara, "but here in Page County now we're putting that old war behind us."

Our apartment was also the office of The Lambert Co., Publishers. We tried to keep business out of the living room, but papers overflowed. Winfield was in and out from dawn to bedtime. Benson was a prolific generator of ideas. When talk was needed to put a new one into action, he'd be with us. If discussion persisted past quitting time, we'd invite him to dinner, and he'd delay leaving. Soon he and Barbara were enthusiastic together about rummy. I might be reading, or editing manuscripts, maybe resenting the disturbance, but I'd convince myself, usually, that they'd more than earned the recreation. Barbara and I began teasing Benson, suggesting he catch himself his own wife. We saw signs he was trying.

The lady was Julia Coleman, a laboratory technician dressed in white, who suspected germs everywhere. Benson had been less than the world's neatest person, but suddenly he was shining his shoes daily and wearing the whitest of shirts, fresh each morning. The new Benson was good for himself, good for Julia, good for The Lambert Co. I arranged more frequent waxing of the company car. We all, I think, saw the business as a stepping stone. Barbara was getting attention for her art, hoping for exhibitions in prestigious galleries. I was winning recognition for my writing while expressing my view of natural history and conservation and the human condition. I put some of my small stories into our magazine, hoping a great editor would discover me.

Someone from Boston did praise my fiction as "strikingly different." But she, Elizabeth Shaw, was neither an editor nor critic but a retired vocational psychologist working on a novel. Perhaps, she wrote, we could help each other find markets. She came to Luray, and her influence through the years has been significant. In her novel, tentatively called "The Smith Myth," she was creating parables related to my own theme, escaping the civilization of greed, furthering conservation. "People *must* escape from the earth's surface," her manuscript declared. "They must go in *airtight* motorized homes and workshops, air-conditioned, and remain ... so high ...that no racketeer can reach them ...more than ten miles up." She wanted me to revise her handwritten manuscript to make the story more accessible to typical readers. She'd pay for my time. Though she probably wasn't wealthy, she went on from our conference to a high school in Kentucky where she was regularly donating equipment and supplying information on chemistry and physics not yet in textbooks.

Miss Shaw analyzed me by mail, free. Her orientation was Freudian, but she recognized Freud had worked with people in deep psychological trouble, so his findings weren't directly applicable to a normal person, which maybe I was. She told me to choose time and place with interruption least likely, sit at a table with plenty of blank paper, write the date and time, then the word *rain*.

> Imagine a voice asking monotonously, What does rain make you think of? And what does that (2nd word) make you think of? and on... and on... Make it a chain of single words (no sentences or phrases) and pull it in link by link, hand over hand, *without thinking about it*, monotonously, mechanically... Note P for pause if a certain word comes slowly and E for emotion if a strong feeling hits you.

This first process was to provide clues to my mind – and to emotions (in which I was illiterate).

Then came radial association, all around the word *rain* itself. What does *rain* make you think of first? What does *rain* make you think of next? and next? and next? Then I was to try chain association (first process) from each of the words marked P (pause) or E (emotion) and after that, radial association from each word I'd put down. Pauses and emotions from marked words could lead to revelations about my life and maybe about human life in general. The word-probing did bring enlightening surprises leading into pinpointing of my "main factors of selfhood," including my growing tendency to see and feel myself inside nature.

One factor she stressed was how memory works. To aid remembering, review circumstances leading up to what I'm seeking. Another way is to approach the hidden memory by thinking of physical things close to it. What mountain was it on? What tree was it near? What house? Which room? Exactly where in the room? Exactly where on a printed page? This is using photographic memory, which she found I had strongly. I also have a disc memory – if I can't get it clearly right now, sometimes within 24 hours it will come around under my phonograph needle of consciousness and I'll grab it. In relation to my tendency (that may have come from Mother's advice) to win by persevering longer than I ever thought I could, Miss Shaw commented, "Success comes from 2% more effort than others can or will expend." We probed for the origin of my reluctance to try selling things.

Miss Shaw confessed she had the same trait. Both of us made deep-seated declarations of independence early in life – independence from other peoples' opinions but not independence from basic reality, nature. In probing this independence, I summarized for her the plot that I'd used in a short story called "Brave as Anybody," portraying me in my teens:

> One night our neighborhood's early teens including me saw a bonfire on a high wild mountain and watched humans crossing in front of it. We were impressed. No one who spoke thought he'd be brave enough to be way up there in the dark. The next evening I climbed to the same place alone to show I was brave enough. As darkness came I lighted a fire, but just as it began to burn, the thought came that it was showing off, and what did I care anyway? I knew within myself I could do it. So I threw snow and wet dirt on the fire, putting it out before it could show.

Another aspect of my life is working with boys. Before the end of my first year as a park employee, I become Scoutmaster. I pick places in the national park for the boys to camp, furthering my own wish to learn more about this park. We camp one weekend near Old Rag Mountain, the parents driving us to the trailhead and agreeing to pick us up on Skyline Drive. Hiking up Nicholson Hollow in heavy rain, after the mountain climb, wrecks the morale and energy of one small scout, and I carry him on my shoulders the last mile to the vacant "castle" where the "King of Free State" once lived. The boys pretend to see the ghost of King Aaron (Nicholson). Next morning we visit the nearby home where descendants of Aaron still live – the George T. Corbin family – whose log cabin is saved to this day as a hikers' shelter. George's son Virgil (my age, 20) tells the scouts about life in the mountains (and has been my friend ever since – until his death near the end of the millennium.)

Back to re-experiencing the late 1930s: I add to the scouting a recreation project sponsored by the town and federal WPA to help keep troublesome teenagers out of mischief. In boxing one day a lad of 18 threatens to beat the teacher "to a pulp." He proves skilled. I've always been weaker in boxing than in wrestling. After three rounds I fear I can't keep going. But I evoke my method of trying longer than I suppose I possibly can. My challenger, it turns out, is a smoker. In the fifth round, breathing heavily, he quits – "But I'll knock you out the next time, Mister."

A worse trial comes on a hike. With ten boys I'm crossing an abandoned pasture. Those ahead, including a husky lad who's maybe 16, reach a small creek before I do. The water is low, and I see it comes through an active farm with livestock. I call, "Don't drink that water." The husky lad yells defiance. I'm hurrying to hold control when he grabs rounded pebbles from the creek, yelling, "This guy's bossed us long enough! Let's rock him!" He begins throwing, and his aim is good.

I think I must run out of range, but if I do I'll never control this group again. By instinct, I guess, I catch the first rock in my bare hands, wishing I had a mitt, and throw it back. Already the lad has thrown another pebble well-aimed, and I catch it too and throw it hard as straight at him as I can. He runs – and is laughed at. He's sullen but not defiant the rest of the hike. Three months later he's chief helper, bringing in other boys and taking leadership in making a high jump with a sawdust pit for easy landing.

Barbara and I wanted a boy of our own but not till our business was stronger. We'd shifted from condoms to diaphragm; soon her periods ceased. We fumed over our budget but felt tenderly happy. For family space we rented a secluded house called Mount Prospect. The walkway passed between tall spruces. There were rooms for separation of office work from home living. One big room was allotted for storage. Soon, though, we'd rent it to Ross Benson and bride Julia.

Dr. Long (George H.) found Barbara healthy and strong. We planned birth at home, the doctor's office being only a few blocks distant. A nurse who accepted private assignments would assist the doctor and help Barbara during the first week. I re-experience the event (and try not to remember births of creatures I'd experienced on our ranch years ago).

The big bedroom on the second floor is ready with everything the doctor told us we'd need. The pain starts. Barbara, unafraid, phones the doctor. He calculates he won't be needed for an hour. "Call me," he says, "about anything unexpected." I phone Mrs. Burgess, the nurse, and someone there says she'll deliver the message. The intervals between pains shorten as expected. The severity surprises me, though, and I phone Mrs. Burgess again. No answer; we don't know if she ever got our message. I phone Dr. Long, and he says, "If she's delayed, you can assist me, eh?" I guess he's teasing but then I know he's not. Barbara and I laugh nervously, imagining me as delivery room nurse.

The doctor arrives, and we wait for the nurse. Barbara's face is alternately smiling and contorted. At last the doctor gives me a hand-sized cotton wad and a bottle labeled chloroform. "The idea," he says, "is for her to breathe in enough to subdue the pain but not enough to lose consciousness. I'll signal. And you keep the cotton away from your own nose. We can't have our nurse collapsing."

Barbara sounds off when the pain is bad but doesn't exactly scream. The doctor signals. I put the cotton against the mouth of the bottle and tilt. The damp cotton chills. I hold it close to Barbara's nose. The doctor says, "Closer." Barbara is quieter, and I don't know whether it's from chloroform or a pause between pains. The doctor's hand tells me to lift the cotton. He's calm, and I'm trying to be calm. Barbara watches the doctor, then her eyes find mine. I'm trying to smile.

The sequences repeat and repeat. I don't know how much time is passing. The doctor's expression says: All is well; and Barbara's says: I'll do it somehow! I see what must be a small area of the baby's head and fear there's not a chance the whole head and body can ever get through. The doctor catches my expression and waves for more chloroform and after only a second waves it away – the action maybe for my benefit, not for Barbara's.

Chloroform. No chloroform. Chloroform again. Not too much. That's plenty now. Barbara looks at me, then looks at the doctor, then shuts her eyes, then opens them. She stays conscious but not fully conscious, and I think I know before she does that the baby is coming through.

"Put the chloroform down," the doctor says, "with the cap tight. And give me a clean towel." The baby is moving its arms and legs. The doctor lifts it, and I see its face, shiny with moisture, somehow wrinkled. The mouth opens with an angry cry. Barbara relaxes then, and I know she knows the baby's born. Her face shows both pain and happiness. The nurse arrives at last, dressed in white. I hold Barbara's cheeks gently while our eyes say congratulations. Feeling weak and dizzy, I flee. The boy, born two days before our first wedding anniversary, is named Harvey Wendell, after Barbara's brother and my brother. While he's too young to talk or walk, or even crawl, I imagine him as one of my boy scouts. We do keep him sometimes in our office and speak to him at intervals, which he likes.

We're re-doing the park guidebook, *Beautiful Shenandoah*. This second edition is our joint production – as was Harvey – a child of our minds and emotions. It's a work of art that could become a collector's item. The front is a photograph printed in color, rare in those years; the back, a glowing watercolor by Barbara of autumn foliage and the newly built Big Meadows Lodge on a clifftop.

My pen-and-ink drawings of animal tracks and tree leaves, labeled by species, decorate endpages. Type inside is dark green; photographs, sepia.

Barbara and I engraved the map plates on type-high cross-sections of hard maple. We similarly engraved 14 moody woodcuts, including a full-page "Impression of the Ghost Forest" (pewter-gray chestnut trunks and branches). We'd even let ourselves go with decorative renditions of the round earth against far-flung curves of the universe, of nonhuman and human life integrated yet competing for living food, and of man upon Earth rising into the starry universe with advancing technology – that's creative nature.

The new guidebook starts off selling better than the thicker first edition, enabling us to take care of our growing family – Sylvia Amy born 19 months after Harvey, Laura Evelyn born after another 19 months – when confusion and war are planet-wide.

After Pearl Harbor the park's visitor count shrinks until The Lambert Co. can no longer afford Ross Benson and Winfield Sisk. They move on to other work, Winfield soon into the military. The war is life-shaking, pulling and pushing everyone. Rationing of tires and gasoline tightens. The magazine is endangered, and we're losing one car and struggling hard to keep the sedan that we call "General."

Much more than General's value is owed to us for advertising. Tourist businesses say they can't pay because the war's wiped out their income. Barbara and I drive to Culpeper and Fredericksburg where many accounts are unpaid. I park near the office of a motel-restaurant combination. Nobody in the office, so I go into the dining room where I'm told the boss will soon return. I wait – and watch Barbara waiting in the car. Tables are mostly empty. Waitresses slink with glum faces. The boss strides in and talks with the cashier. He glances my way as if she's telling him I'm here. I rise to greet him, but he spins away and out the door. I follow. He sits in the office and acts busy. I explain my problem, and he swings on his swivel chair and explodes at me. "Your maps are worthless now, and I'm not paying!"

"If you actually can't pay, I'll try to understand," I say. "The war's hurting all of us. But we delivered our part of the deal and think you should deliver on your signed agreement."

"Worthless! Worthless! Everything's worthless!"

I think he's feigning. I see Barbara in the car, hearing. I can't let him bluff me. I hold one of the maps toward him, saying, "Please point out anything you think isn't as agreed."

He whirls and jumps like an angry dog. "Get out of here! Can't you hear me? Get out!"

I stand still. He grabs me and tries to spin me around. I grip his upper arms and shove him back.

"I'll call the police!"

"I'll call them for you." I lift the phone.

He snatches it, repeating, "No, no, no," as if sobbing.

I leave him that way, maybe a nervous breakdown. Barbara takes my hand as soon as I'm through shifting gears.

We do save the car and do pay what the publishing company and we personally owe, but our business is dead. The news from the Pacific and from Europe seems always horrible. I can't ignore appeals to enlist, especially one saying a young man can become an airplane pilot and an officer at good pay. I've always wanted to fly. Barbara feels as urgently patriotic as I, insisting she'll be proud of me as a pilot and can take care of the children.

Miss Shaw reacts quite differently (by mail):

> Your strong points seem to be patience, thoroughness, careful observation, some power of analysis – not the swift intuitive kind but following contemplation. Also reliability, steadiness. None of these qualities ...is at all typical of airmen... who would enjoy living their working hours at 300 miles an hour.

I drive to Richmond anyway for testing. At 3 p.m. they say I've made the highest score recorded there since Pearl Harbor. But then, as I'm about to sign, someone rushes in with orders to reject me "for sugar in the urine." Back home, I arrange for thorough testing at the nearest medical center. They find no sugar in my urine during a 24-hour period and so certify. Still, I stay rejected. Later, by chance, I meet an officer who explains that, though I'm within the announced age limits, they really want jet-fighter pilots, dare-devil 18-year-olds who'll dash into conflict instantly.

The national park hires me as a seasonal ranger, April to September. I dress in the uniform with badge, polished boots, and hat with a stiff wide brim, but instead of protecting and interpreting the park's wild creatures, trees, and flowers, I'm to collect 25 cents a car from people passing the southbound entrance station at Thornton Gap. Here's the count on April 22, 1942: 56 cars total, 13 from New York, 10 from Massachusetts, only 3 from Virginia, 2 from Canada, and the rest from other US states. One motorcycle. The biggest day I record is April 26 – 311 cars, 1156 people, 26 of them "colored" (a category briefly kept separate in this park, in race-conscious Virginia). More than two-thirds are from Washington, D.C., Virginia, and Maryland, but 27 states are represented. The trend's down and down. On the back of work sheets for May 2, 1942, I scribble my stream of consciousness:

> I wish there were a million cars. I wish Barbara were here and we could go out on a trail... God and God's love... Finally, another car! ... God is underlying principle, spirit. God is the sum of things as they are, the way they work. The Great Disillusionment, men calling natural phenomena, such as storms, earthquakes, etc., manifestations of God's will, His orders. Now – disillusionment! – they are of God, and natural laws apply to life also. (P) So natural laws – the way things are and work – are God... The supernatural, telepathy, seeing ghosts (like *Aurora borealis*, etc.) will prove of natural cause. But are also God...
>
> Another car: Packard. The end of the Great Disillusionment should, for us, have been on Dec. 7, 1941, when our God failed to punish the Japanese. God doesn't affect us (I

mean, He doesn't take the initiative). We, somehow (part of the undiscovered natural laws) get in touch with God... perhaps analogous to lowering our lips to a spring of water and drinking...

One more car. 25 cents, please. Thank you. And God is not always what He seems, for there are laws that come to light through a long view of a life or a culture, through direct contact with God on receptive natures, through experiment and thought, which do not agree with the obvious. And if you seek happiness in the ways that seem most immediately promising, or perhaps if you intentionally seek it at all, you won't find it. It may come instead from what would seem the exact opposite, for happiness is not ease or comfort or security or the satisfaction of appetites, nor even a combination of these things...

I'm on duty the required hours, while travel drops toward zero. In enforced idleness here, my mind and my writing fingers go beyond strict control. Working at home on freelance writing, mailing manuscripts out and suffering rejection slips, is quite different, though still mostly frustrating. I sell a few pieces, fiction and nonfiction, but none brings significant money. The work with Miss Shaw and her manuscript continues intriguingly but brings no measurable success to her or to me. What good am I?

As my frustration grew, the park superintendent and the concession manager dreamed up a bold plan. The high shelf called Skyland, with the park's largest development, was empty – no business expected for the duration of the war. Men hired as guards repeatedly "chickened out." I was seen as a person who felt at home in the mountains. I could become a "permanent" ranger at better pay if I and my family would live at Skyland. The concessioner would furnish a splendid cottage (named Hepburn) rent-free. Further, the company would pay utility costs, including heat, a forbidding expense in winter because of 40-mile wind.

Barbara, though just home from the hospital with baby Laura, was interested. We all drove up in late September 1942 to see the cottage. The big door opened into a hall about 12 feet wide that soon spread wider as the main room. Fifty feet ahead you could see the picture window, a rectangle of sky, 30 feet long and seven feet high. Barbara handed me the baby. She and Harvey, then Sylvia, hurried forward. Even from the long sofa, ten feet back from the great window, no foreground showed. We were hanging in the sky 3,000 feet above the valley.

"It's a palace!" Barbara said. We moved in as autumn brightened the forest – endless miles of reds and yellows, yet an eerie feeling from lack of autumn crowds, the joyous clamor of praise for the unbelievable colors, the bumper-to-bumper traffic. Weird. Sad. Scary?

Barbara tried the kitchen while I tested the furnace. Walnut-sized coal automatically fed into the firebox from a bunker, heating water that circulated in pipes to radiators well-placed to warm the whole "cottage." The coal supply seemed vast. We'd brought many boxes and sacks of food. We sat down to our first clifftop dinner, feeling like royalty, yet startlingly alone.

Before bedtime I explored Skyland's roads and trails with the German shepherd we were keeping for the park engineer who'd gone to war. I carried a long-beamed flashlight, so my glimpses were narrow fingers probing the dark. The dozens of lifeless buildings and the labyrinthine extent of walkways and roadways surprised me. The dog listened with erect ears and sniffed everywhere but stayed calm – no bears, no other humans. The situation stirred memories of ghost towns in the Great Basin. I wrote in a letter:

> I walk the trails and think that these mountains, which have almost completed an earth-man-earth cycle, may be quieter now than they've been for 10,000 years. The Indian hunters and gatherers are gone. The mountain folk are gone. Wildlife has partially recovered. Because of gas and tire rationing, the Skyline Drive is empty; Skyland is deserted. The

park staff is curtailed; the Civilian Conservation Corps (CCC), gone, abolished.

Though Hepburn wasn't exactly a cabin by a stream, in essence we'd been handed my lifelong dream of home – a comfortable hideaway surrounded by square mile after square mile of wild nature. I had a loving wife and healthy children. When in rare moments I could forget the war, I felt at home, temporarily anyway, and I was now a *genuine conservationist*. Yet conservation of nature wasn't the whole of life; everything intertwines. The disharmony from war news on our radio – which we *had to* hear – weakened enjoyment.

I'd expected the scenic inspiration to lift me into success in writing – in free time when there were no ranger duties. I started sharpening my storytelling skill by mail with instructor-collaborator-agent Thomas H. Uzzell of New York City. He classified the high-pay big-circulation stories – that kept teasing me – as either character or complication. A character story shows one trait of the hero or heroine in one action after another until the trait determines the story's outcome. A complication story has a clever and complex plot with a twist at the end to surprise readers. Every word of every story has to help generate one emotion, the same emotion intensifying all through the story – pathos, horror, patriotism, romance, any emotion the typical readers would feel strongly. Perhaps most important – in my contrary case anyhow – never violate the basic value system of the editor and his readers.

I learned many such rules. What I didn't learn was how to force myself to obey. I'd calculate a story by the rules, then toss the calculation into my mental-emotional mill (that's partly unconscious) and expect something there to energize it. But the energizing wouldn't happen unless I let the story flow as it insisted – never exactly as I'd forced myself to calculate mentally. Uzzell said my method wasn't adequate for the big money.

We searched out story materials – that is, people, situations, and actions I'd experienced or witnessed. I stepped up what I do anyway, quickly typing character sketches or happenings from real life, such as these words about the most-real conservationist I'd yet closely known in real life:

> District ranger Hopper is one of the most considerate men I've ever run across. He brought us milk, mail, etc. today, including notice of my winning the prize for September short story in *Salt Lake Tribune*. And Hopper just called up offering to have his helper stop here and get a package Barbara's been eager to mail. Some people must be afflicted with a super-sensitivity to the desires and feelings of others.

Hopper was a tough ranger, but in matters not connected with his job he was a boy scout looking for good turns to do daily. Would this trait make a character story?

One day – because Hopper hadn't let new snow deflect him and had put on chains to come into Skyland, bringing our milk – Barbara and I were able to fight well for our German shepherd. The dog went into convulsions beside our portico. I'd seen rat poison spread in buildings where mattresses and quilts were stored. Some could have dropped on open porches.

"If it's rat poison, what can we do?" Barbara asked. My glance fell on the milk Hopper had brought so recently, and I remembered something I'd read. "Milk!" I said. I held the big dog's head up with the mouth open, and pushed the narrow end of a bottle between the teeth and poured. The milk seemed to dull the dog's pain, so we gave him another quart. He vomited – the whole content of his stomach. Then we poured a third quart into him. He was soon his usual self.

I tried to plot a timely story from this incident – blaming a Japanese or German spy that the dog ferreted out, hiding in a Skyland building – who secretly commuted to Washington for his dirty work. Uzzell thought the story was possible. I tried, but my writing effort put me to sleep. The characters, other than the dog, were too remote from my life; they couldn't engage my emotions. I write well only from my own real life.

Even in wartime I read nature and conservation – and copied words I liked or felt I needed repeatedly – among them (which I confess I might have copied several times):

> When in the Course of human events, it becomes necessary for one people to dissolve the political bonds which have connected them with another, and to assume among the powers of the earth, the separate and equal station to which the Laws of Nature and of Nature's God entitle them, a decent respect to the opinions of mankind requires that they should declare the causes which impel them...
>
> – **Thomas Jefferson**, *Declaration of Independence*

And he gave it a name – the Law of Nature – and said Natural Law is the Law of God – interchangeable names for one and the same thing. – **Mark Twain**

How can one know that the natural is not really of man and what is of man is not really natural? -- **Chuangtse**

Things which are said to be made by nature are the work of divine art. –**Plato**

His judgments are in all the earth. He remembers His covenants forever... – **The Bible** (Psalm 105, 7-8)

One of the first conditions of earthly happiness acknowledged by everyone is that man's union with nature should not be infringed... Men confined in prison feel this deprivation more than anything else. But consider the life of people who live according to the teaching of the world: the more they achieve success according to the world's teaching the more are they deprived of this condition of happiness. – **Tolstoy**

We civilized ones ... are potentially as helpless as canaries in a cage. The ability to cope with nature directly – unshielded by the weakening wall of civilization – is one of the admitted needs of modern times. – **Benton MacKaye**, father of the Appalachian Trail (that passes north-south two miles from Eileen's and my Blue Ridge mountain home)

President FDR said government workers, more than ever in wartime, needed renewal in the harmony of nature. NPS Washington insisted we maintain roads and trails in top condition. The main approach now was the bus from Washington. Get off at Thornton Gap, where US 211 crosses Skyline Drive, then hike through scenery and stay overnight in a hikers' shelter. Okay – we rangers cooperated. But then came 19 inches of rain in five days, wrecking the trails. With the CCC gone and many NPS maintenance men in the military, trail repair seemed impossible. Heroic efforts in trail work were hard to generate when radio waves kept humming with our fellows' life and death struggles to stop villainous Hitler, Mussolini, and Tojo. Nearly every day I drove in a government pickup from Skyland ten miles to the maintenance center at Big Meadows, where I helped coordinate by keeping track of available crews, equipment, and materials.

Conscientious objectors to the war filled part of the gap – and became the closest people to Skyland, based at Pinnacles five miles north, where CCC Camp 10 had been. Their work – officially of "national importance" – embraced "construction, improvement and maintenance of park and recreational facilities, including roads, trails..." Most of the 150 CPS (Civilian Public Service) men were 25 to 30 years old and married (though no wives were here), while a few were young and single, more like the former CCC boys.

Longing for home, men of both categories visited us. Barbara and I liked them, even began to wonder if their protest against war might not be as valid, at least, even as "responsible," as our distant patriotism. I included CPS in my story-search notes:

> Today a CPS "boy" here had an impulse to write to his wife. (A group was sheltering with us from rain that was freezing as it fell.) I lent a pen and gave him paper. Other boys teased him asking what his wife's first name was.

He answered evasively, "Mabel... Ruth... Anna... Carrie... Nellie Mae..." The boys went silent then, doubtless thinking of girls they knew by those names, or thinking of girls generally. When the men talked again, they spoke longingly of "home," and I felt a powerful love of place, associated with but separate from love of wife and children. This love of land is occasionally strong enough to carry a popular story. The mountain folk who had to leave the Blue Ridge here so felt. Few people ever forget their joy in the scenes and events of childhood... The longing for the old home place might rank with love of the opposite sex or with fear of death in literary appeal, also as catalyst for responsibility.

I was talking here to myself a little but mostly to my instructor Uzzell, and I told him about these CPS boys – who could be models for fictional characters. Our CPS people were members of pacifist Christian churches – Mennonite, Quaker, Brethren – that paid all expenses of the camps – except working tools and the park service's supervision on work projects. The Church of the Brethren had been strong among families of German derivation in our county since the first white settlements in the 1700s. Brethren, a camp leaflet said, were part of the "movement in which draftees serve our country in civilian work" – while other members work elsewhere, even abroad, teaching peaceful living, aiding war sufferers, trying to counteract "imperialism, racialism and extreme nationalism..."

Herbert Zim, well known now through the best-selling Golden Nature books, was a CPS man here during the big war. The desire of these people not to kill or even hurt others seemed firm and honest. It disturbed me, partly because, though I'd actually tried to enlist in this war, I'd also read the words of Jesus and interpreted them as anti-war, and I'd also entered that Cantor peace contest and proposed world federalism as peacekeeper. I made notes with instruction to myself to "develop a magazine article" bringing in conscientious objection:

> *The Pacifist's Dilemma.* The teachings that form the basis of pacifism are predicated on a way of life utterly different from modern materialism. We can't maintain our various

"rights" if we literally follow the teachings of the Prince of Peace... The trouble is that the objectors are required to follow the way of Jesus only part way; they're not required to submit to the tyrants, to be made slaves, to turn the other cheek literally, because they're protected from these things by non-objectors, including police and soldiers...

Here I was in a mountain paradise admiring conscientious objectors, while also itching for more direct action and responsibility in putting down our enemies, and, further, struggling to work out characters and complications that would make stories high-paying magazines would buy. I was reaching in a dozen different directions – so keeping myself too far off balance to concentrate and make decisions.

I inched forward, though, toward a possible bonanza. These CPS pacifists – doing conservation work now – were the same breed as the Brethren farmers, descended from German-Pennsylvania-Dutch stock, who had a church at Ida, Virginia, at the edge of the Blue Ridge, where 20 families of the non-pacifist mountain folk, of British origin, had been resettled from the national park. With this realization, I wrote Uzzell what he instantly called, by telegram, my "best short story idea yet! Man, your fortune is made if you will exploit the character opportunities in that combination of opposites!"

Appalachian mountain folk were born fighters and sharpshooters, joining military services in higher proportion than almost any other group. No mountain man I'd known would "turn the other cheek." The opposite modes of behavior could lead into hundreds of short-story-type complications and conflicts. Uzzell summarized, "If you do not immediately set about the closest possible study of these people, you'll be missing the chance of a lifetime."

The idea could be worth a fortune, but something in me resisted. Maybe big-pay writing didn't really fit into my pursuit of happiness. Though I admired pacifists, I couldn't become one. Though I admired mountain folk, I was far from a born fighter. My writing is my life, not something I invent or play lightly with. I excused myself to Uzzell as committed to the ranger job until spring. Then, maybe – my "fortune."

I got prodded, though, by a competing "chance of a lifetime." Whiting Willauer, working with President FDR, phoned from Washington, wanting me to join a civilian mission being sent to Chungking, China. Barbara and I would have to think hard – and fast. Willauer would wait only two weeks for me to decide.

Darwin's wife Barbara with their son, Harvey and daughters, Laura & Sylvia
Photo by Peggy Stewart 1943

Chapter 10 - Round Earth 1943

Barbara and the children would live a few blocks from her parents in Canandaigua, New York, while I was on World War II assignment. We said goodbye on the railroad platform there. The clicking of the rails during the long hours punctuated wild emotions in me, and after I'd rented a room near George Washington University where Barbara and I had met, I wrote her I'd just been told I must spend several weeks training in Washington before I could start for China, and I confessed to her:

> As long as I live, darling Barbara, I'll never forget you standing there outside the train window sort of reaching for me as I was reaching for you, wanting to rush back and take you in my arms – and never, ever leave. But of course I was committed – too totally; I was prohibited from leaving Washington – except en route to China.

I think now, looking far back, that my involvement in the war was one of my few major decisions – like involvement in church or moving to Washington as an 18-year-old – when the controlling factor wasn't my "instinct" or "nature" but a flood of "social pressure" forcing my own inner pattern out of shape. Yet there was potent adventure in responding to my fellows' all-out dedication – in this case for victory over Hitler, Tojo, and Mussolini. Barbara and her parents and just about everyone else I knew had encouraged me, and of course I did want us to win.

China may seem, at first glance, outside and separate from my life's central theme of nature and conservation, yet my re-experiencing will show that the China years deepened and expanded my appreciation of nature and my determination to cherish and protect and work with Earth.

President Roosevelt and Whiting Willauer were sending economic warfare teams, mostly headed by industrial executives, to all our allies. Chief of the China team was Walter Fowler, furloughed from his railroad-car-manufacturing company. Second in command was Harry Lucker, a lawyer and businessman with decades of China experience. Lucker sucked cigarette smoke deep into his lungs with audible hisses, but I spontaneously gripped his upper arm while our right hands were shaking when he said I was the same age as his son who'd been in Tientsin when the Japanese invaded and was believed to be a prisoner in Japan.

Fowler and Lucker were taking off for Chungking with top priority to establish working relationships with Generalissimo Chiang Kai-shek and his economic czars H.H. Kung and T.V. Soong. The rest of our team would follow as we completed our training. Our travel would be slower. We lacked top priority because pending invasion of Italy had shifted fast transportation to military officers.

In our world training sessions, the only other China-team person was Johnny Waldron, age about 45. He'd manufactured rugs in China, with a Chinese partner, for 18 years, and he'd learned to speak the language from his "sleeping dictionary." Professors, businessmen, and diplomats stirred us daily with impassioned views of an ultra-prosperous and benign world the Allies would build through cooperation once the evil power was broken. The only speaker I now remember by name and face was Buckminster Fuller, an early planetary conservationist/environmentalist (among other talents) – a person I've gradually come to realize has had lasting influence on my feelings and doings. He spent a full day with us there in 1943, picturing the world as what he'd soon be famous for calling "Spaceship Earth," a delicately balanced, fragile, yet wonderfully productive planet. He said humankind's home could be destroyed forever, if we failed to take care of it – first, by saving it from the destructive Axis.

Barbara and I, trying to adjust to the reality of years apart, were exchanging daily letters. Pressured by the training and by fever-producing immunization shots, I may have dug too deeply. I suggested that maybe she shouldn't be telling our children so confidently – as she wrote me she was doing – that "God will take care of you." I wrote:

> In God all things are possible. But we must use the forces of God; we must make the advances. God is here but does not take the initiative... Through us, love must become the universal principle; we must control the evil and expand the good. We must shoulder the responsibility...and not pass the buck to God.

She replied:
> I believe that every man, woman and child should feel and believe in the security of God's love. He does take care of us regardless of what physical or material things happen to us. As parent-in-charge temporarily it seems distinct to me and separate from their physical care... Just one more thought, about immortality. Darwin, the love waiting for you here in my heart and in the hearts of the children is only a drop in the bucket compared with the infinite love waiting in heaven, especially for as godly a life as yours.

My Dad wanted to see me before I left, "perhaps never to return." I saw a chance of getting together in the middle of the country – Des Moines, Iowa – and, surprising me! – the strict supervisors authorized a rush-rush visit. No flight was available, but a fast train fitted just right. Dad and my sister Joyce took turns driving his car from Salt Lake. Our brief visit was great, but the goodbye hurt. After finding my seat, I watched Dad and Joyce on the train platform, as so recently I'd watched Barbara and the children. Dad and Joyce were trying to act normal, not looking exclusively at me, pretending to see other things through the tears. I was similarly blinking, waving every time they turned toward me.

Dad wrote Barbara when they got back to Salt Lake, including these words Barbara read to me by phone:

> Darwin has changed and developed from a round-faced lad in the seven years since I'd previously seen him... I have always had the greatest admiration and respect for him. He has a keen intellect. His honor and character are of the highest. There is no greater man in America than he.

My start to China had been delayed again. Supposedly, Johnny and I would go by "air to Buenos Aires, Argentine ship to Cape Town, air all up Africa to Cairo and from Cairo to India and India to China, leaving Buenos Aires the first week in June." We had to catch that Argentine ship but weren't yet released by Washington's paperwork. Heat, pressure, and excitement escalated. I kept sending Barbara glimpses of Washington, D.C. – for instance:

> BLACKOUT 9:20 to 10 p.m. Great sirens; other sirens in chorus, various pitches. Heels clicking hurriedly in street. Giggling from upstairs – "Turn it out, Jane! Turn it out!" Wardens' whistles in the street. Darkness... Sirens again, broken wailing, seeming to answer each other like many great weird birds in a forest.
>
> Man upstairs across the street:- "Hey! Hey, warden!
>
> Lights in a tall building over there! Two *bright* lights!"
>
> > Then, "Hey, warden! A whole tower lit up
> >
> > > on a building over there! Two blocks over.
> > >
> > > > *Whole tower* lit up!"
>
> Silence .... Darkness ... and silence.

Johnny and I arranged our own commercial flight to Miami for June 2. It was the hottest day I ever felt in Washington, or maybe I hurried too hard or my fever resurged from inoculations. Johnny commented, "It's hellish weather to be heading south in." We slept in Miami's Belfort Hotel, then spent the morning getting our baggage through Customs. The Navy claimed to control all but six of Miami's hundreds of hotels; effects of war were everywhere. Hardly any men wore suits. Hardly any women wore stockings; about half apparently wore no brassieres.

Johnny and I tried to guess how many had suntanned legs and how many used leg makeup. We couldn't come close to agreeing but we picked up a leg makeup story. A Miami man, afraid he'd be late for work, shaved in a hurry, reached for his lotion and soothed his face. He arrived breathless at the office two minutes late and was stared at and greeted as never before: "Hi, Chief!" "Hm. Heap big chief, eh?" He couldn't understand until he looked in a mirror. That shaving lotion had really been his wife's leg makeup.

With an advance arrangement we couldn't believe until take-off, we continued southward in a Ford tri-motor plane called Clipper, that functioned on water as well as on land and in the air. Wings and fuselage looked like galvanized iron. The nose and each wing had a motor and a propeller. The roar and vibration were strong. So was the smell. The plane's assignment connected with a significant product of Earth's nature; it was to fly crude rubber from Manaus, deep in the Amazon jungle, to mainland America. The Japanese had stopped our shipments from the East Indies, so every pound of rubber we could persuade Brazil to gather and ship would help our war effort. This project, centering at Manaus, was part of our economic warfare. We'd launch projects with similar aims in China.

The great island of Cuba was flat where we crossed, divided into plots growing sugar cane. There was a jungle too; palm trees stood out from it like greenish mushrooms. The Caribbean came under us again, and we saw reefs, some above water at the moment, some below, the coral vari-colored. Off Jamaica the sea looked dark metallic blue, then the crew covered our windows from inside – this action insisted upon, we were told, by British intelligence, so no pictures could be taken of defense installations. In a building beside the airport at Kingston, British hostesses served us punch. Eager for glimpses of scenery including a 6500-foot mountain, we tried to step outside but were turned back by armed soldiers. Otherwise, Jamaica was cooler than Miami.

We splashed down on Lake Maracaibo in oil-prosperous Venezuela and slept in Maracaibo city. Next splashdown was on the upper Orinoco River – that must have been in flood as the raging water was muddy. Our Clipper nudged a floating platform (held in the current by underwater cables) to refuel and to deliver bags and boxes. The three motors then revved up and pulled us out of the rough water into the wind.

Hour after hour we flew over jungle, seeing no people or buildings. I asked the pilot how deep the jungle was. He said, More than 100 feet – and scattered towering trees, 150-plus. In an emergency, he volunteered, he could land the plane on the canopy. The problem would be getting our people down. Even that wasn't impossible, though. Physically fit persons could "climb" down handhold-size vines. But still – there'd be nobody there to guide us to civilized services.

We crossed the equator, then followed the Rio Negro downstream, a visible path not quite smothered by jungle. Occasionally, along the dark-watered river, we glimpsed boats, piers, buildings. Toward the end of the long day, we saw our river joining the different-colored Amazonas. We slanted down at Manaus. A hard thud jolted us, but we landed right side up. The pilot showed us a deep dent in the metal wing; we'd struck a big hawk. Manaus was surrounded by the world's vastest jungle. In the 1800s it was the original rubber center with a quarter-million people. A five-million-dollar opera house was built. Ships came to get rubber, most of it hand-gathered by natives who deep-scratched Para trees for the juice. By 1910 Manaus was declining because plantations in tropical parts of the Far East had "stolen" the species and were producing more efficiently.

In 1943 with the Far Eastern supply a war casualty, our plane would be loaded with the syrup-thick sap that was raw rubber and head back to Miami. Though we had tickets to fly down river, the

Brazilian airline's flights were otherwise full for the next week. We waited, visiting a house boat community on the Rio Negro and floating port facilities considered remarkable for adjusting the enormous differences between high and low water. We visited the governmental buildings of Brazil's state of Amazonas – that was almost entirely rain forest inhabited by natives said to live in nature with no outside interference.

Leaving overweight Johnny in the hotel, I walked along the busy riverbank, then into the jungle on a narrow trail in pursuit of a recurring squawk. I never spotted the noisy parrot but found the forest pleasant. Where the canopy was but little penetrated by sunshine, the plants weren't crowded. I saw songbirds and a tiny hummingbird but none of the mammals or snakes that had scared me in nightmares.

I met a man carrying a heavy load toward the river and tried to talk with him. He didn't respond to English. I wondered if he and his family lived in the city or in the jungle. I daydreamed living in the jungle, getting to know its wild animals and plants.

With half of me concentratedly careful not to lose the trail here – or Johnny's and my patched-together trail around the earth – I let myself enjoy the adventure toward China as I'd enjoyed my bus trip toward Washington years earlier. The whole country, I'd felt then, was becoming my home. Now, inside me somehow, the whole world. I'd lost the tendency to hate new places, new homes, for weeks or months. That was a childhood thing – resenting Dad's pulling or pushing us kids around. Now, the difference was – I was participating in the decisions – or at least agreeing in advance with them. Yet love of the land is really only a part of feeling at home. Barbara had repeatedly said she'd go with me anywhere and that would be home. Okay. But, still – all parts of my pursuit of happiness plan need to be interwoven – worthwhile work, someone to love who'd love me, hope, learning and achieving, beauty, nature, some feeling I was helping protect or improve the home place... I guessed the problem was too complex – I needed harmony with humanity *and* with the rest of nature. So I gave it up for the simpler task of finding Manaus again.

We finally flew down to Belem, where we caught a U.S. Navy plane to Rio de Janeiro. I'd have picked modest lodging, but Johnny wanted the best, *The Gloria*. Per diem allowed by our government for travel abroad would cover the cost, so we registered. Supposing our ship – reported en route now from Buenos Aires to Rio – would sail promptly, I sent Barbara a cable saying I was safely at the seaport. (Wartime censors scissor-out precise locations.) Then we learned the ship hadn't really even left Buenos Aires, but we should wait here for it. Unable to expect a cabled answer from Barbara, I kept putting my feelings and news into letters:

> I miss you in direct proportion to the attractiveness of the place I'd like to show you. Rio is beautiful. So is this hotel, a place where every man should have a sweetheart and every girl a lover. In my room I take out your picture. I stand at the window overlooking the bay and listen to the waves and watch them coming, reflecting the sunlight, white-capping the rocks. I remember the ocean at Rehoboth Beach... our swimming in moonlight at Bear Trap with evening primroses on the bank ...and that mooseless moose pond in Maine (on our honeymoon).

Later I sketched the view for Barbara – a curving bay, rows of tall buildings, background of hills and "great high rocks...1800 ft. high." I also sent her a handwritten seven-page essay on happiness and illusions.

Bill McGovern, also assigned to economic warfare at Chungking, joined Johnny and me in waiting for the Argentine ship. Bill reminded me of Barbara's father, though much younger. He'd been an anti-trust attorney at the U.S Department of Justice in Washington and had left wife and children with her parents in Maine.

We three – under time pressure, yet with nothing to do – let ourselves enjoy Rio. On the splendid beach of Copacabana, girls' swim suits were briefer than I'd previously seen. Society at the Opera

House dressed elegantly, nearly all the women wearing black, the men too in handsome dark suits. The business districts had sidewalks with mosaic designs built in. Stores were richly stocked with items the war had forced off the market in the United States, fountain pens, for instance. We rode street cars to explore; the cost in U.S. money was near zero.

I explored on foot alone, finding poorer districts where the people were definitely not prosperous – children playing on dirty streets wearing rags that failed to cover even their most private parts. I wanted to go farther out, to see farms and mines, to see how people actually lived on the land, but we never knew from hour to hour when a call might come saying our ship was in the harbor ready to sail.

Our wait seemed so long I began "reading" the newspapers (in Portuguese which I'd never studied). Many headlines were about events expected to happen – not much on what had happened, which would require expensive reporting. I began speaking the language of common essentials. There was often a letdown, though. After I'd struggled strenuously to express something, the Brazilian might answer in capable English.

The Argentine ship (*Vapor Asturiano*) finally did pick us up. Instead of direct toward Cape Town, it sailed along the coast south-westward to Santos, the port for the burgeoning city of Sao Paolo. The ship was normally in coastal use, its weight only 2300 tons. It had 55 cabins, half of them empty. Seven of the 30 passengers worked for our economic warfare agency. Four of these were good-looking girls assigned to offices in Africa. We met at meals but had different interests. I wrote Barbara:

> I walked last night way out the other side of Santos on the road to Sao Paolo. A few buses and trucks and cars speeded on the road; beyond the fence a few ancient trains hissed and snorted and whistled, reminding me of long ago. Up above me to the left a hill rose, almost a cliff, and it was crowded with "cliff dwellings," almost like the floors of a skyscraper.

Forms crossed and re-crossed the lighted windows – men and children with cheerful voices, mothers carrying babies...

Farther along, the stars dominated. All the familiar arrangements in the sky are gone, but there's still a milky way, and the sun still shines, and the moon. And the people laugh and talk; the young men and women smile into each other's eyes and talk softly and giggle not from mirth but from happiness. The mothers tend the children, and the men speak to the babies and poke their fingers at them in play... I feel the world is one world.

Three days more than a month after Johnny and I left Washington, the *Asturiano* – I'm re-experiencing now – sails boldly out into the South Atlantic. The white-painted craft is well built but slow. The captain is capable and smooth but frank enough to confess our crossing of the Atlantic could take three weeks instead of a liner's five days. He uses Spanish with his men and French with us passengers. My French proves inadequate. Only one passenger, a Belgian whose career has included the teaching of French, catches the full meanings, but he dodges full translation.

There's a scary night when word leaks out that German submarines are near us. Johnny, Bill and I notice additional lights being turned on. The white ship must show for miles in the dark night on the dark ocean. We English speakers, all enemies of Hitler, bring in the Belgian to ask the captain to turn off the lights. I hear *Fermez les lumieres* spoken insistently by the Belgian. The captain refuses. He's explaining the lights are our protection. The Germans will respect the clearly shown neutrality of Argentina. Blacking out would invite disaster.

We're thinking the submarine officers have word from German intelligence that Americans are aboard. Johnny, a born showman, begins chanting softly but persistently, "*Fermez les lumieres! Fermez les lumieres!*" But the lights hold bright through all the dark hours and the repeating radio warnings of U-boats. And no torpedoes come, and no U-boats surface to demand surrender of the

Allied passengers. The captain smiles like a gentle father at all of us children. The ship sails on:

> Darling Barbara – Son Harvey's fourth birthday, July 12, 1943 – with our fifth anniversary coming day after tomorrow – You're all much with me as I watch giant waves level with my eyes on the top deck of our tiny ship – that then rises to the crest and falls into the trough.
>
> I haven't been seasick since the first day... I'm reading H.G. Wells' *Short History of the World*. Wells says it's up to the people to do something now to put the world in order before it reverts to total savagery... Did I tell you I'm "Huck" now, courtesy of Bill McGovern who gives two sources – the scientist Huxley, friend of Charles Darwin, and Mark Twain's *Huckleberry Finn*. The consensus on board is that Huck fits me.
>
> Monday morning 7/19/43 – Sweetheart-Darling – We discovered Africa this morning, our 19th day without sight of land. Blue-gray mountains rose from the sea, and they're growing. About a thousand gulls have come out to meet us.
>
> 7/22/43 - Cape Town is a nice city in a beautiful setting of bays, flats, and mountains. Towering above is 3,000-foot Table Mountain. I want to walk up, but there's a cable car that the others want to ride...
>
> A Mrs. Campbell, a South African Scot who was with us on the *Asturiano*, took us yesterday to visit an old farm that friends of hers have fixed up. You'd love it, Barbara. The house was built in 1699. Its sun-dried-brick walls are 18" thick. There's a large living room from front to back through the center – like our Hepburn at Skyland... The 1,000 acres are mostly devoted to fruit-growing – pears, plums, some lemons – but there are cows, chickens, horses, dogs, cats, sheep, goats. There's a 4,000-foot mountain behind the house, streams, and forest – a view lacking only a little of equaling those from our possible sites in Virginia.

The greatest event at Cape Town – for me – was a cablegram from Barbara, assuring me all was well with her and the children. Life felt real again – briefly. The very next afternoon, though, we boarded a massive troop ship and left the harbor in gathering darkness heading straight south where we had no wish to go. The wind got colder each day, and the sky darker until mist turned to ice on the decks, and still we held that course toward Antarctica. No explanation was given – and none either when we sailed eastward, then northward, and ice on the decks thawed. Rumor said we were dodging U-boats. Our ship was British, certainly not neutral!

Wed., July 28, 1943

Darling Barbara – We're in the middle of a convoy on what used to be a luxury liner. Last night from the pitch black on deck, the stars were myriad and brilliant, with the Southern Cross prominent. And up near the bow where the waves splashed into foam the water was sparkling as though with innumerable lightning bugs (phosphorescence?)...

I hear group singing on deck near our cabin as I write this: "Hang my heart on a weeping willow tree..." and "You are my sunshine, my only sunshine..."

Thurs., July 29

I've stood on A Deck right up on top and watched the waves pile up like mountains...and then go on ahead of us... The rain has drifted over the rough water like snow drifting over weeds and bushes and rocks on the old Blue Ridge, while the wind howls and roars in the ship's rigging like the winter winds blowing against our Hepburn... I like storms...

Aug. 9

Flying fish are everywhere now – and BIG. Some have perhaps ten-inch spread of "wings." We time flights up to ten seconds out of the water.

Bombay, India, 9 p.m. 8/13/43

We came into this bay about noon. The name (bomb-bay) and the day, Friday the 13th, seem formidable... The bay is half blue-ocean color and half dirty yellow river water.

Memories of Bombay's Taj Mahal Hotel boil up in me often. After we've registered following a ride in a horse-drawn garry from the pier, three porters carry our bags to our room. We tip and dismiss them, or so we suppose but minutes later an Indian emerges from the closet in Johnny's bedroom and follows Johnny into the sitting room we all share. He says he's Joseph. He wears no shoes but looks clean. He asks each of us, "Laundry, Sahib?" (pronounced like sob).

We gather our dirty clothes, many pieces because a water shortage on the ship limited laundry to three pieces per person per week. Joseph lists the clothes, then shouts out the door into the hall. Our laundry is taken away, but Joseph remains. He goes into the bathroom, and there's running water. Soon he emerges, saying, "Bath, Sahib?" So Johnny bathes, followed by Bill, and then me, each with fresh water coaxed from the faucets by Joseph as if it's a notable achievement. Joseph unpacks our bags, lays out a complete change of clothing, and hangs the rest in the closet.

He tells us he's been a personal servant for 20 years, often traveling with his sahibs, once as far as Europe. He's Roman Catholic, and he gives me a holy picture with his autograph on it. He says he'll guide us to the "Coconut Festival" on Sunday, celebrating the end of the Monsoon (wet season). We agree, but rain keeps coming – and I feel it as an amazing demonstration by nature. Joseph suggests waiting till Monday, then visiting temples with him. The rain still doesn't stop, and sightseeing dies, but Joseph remains, always within voice reach. He protects us, he says, from fortune tellers, jewel merchants, jugglers, magicians, beggars, snake charmers, and all the hordes who want *baksheesh* (money) from the sahibs.

But he fails once, perhaps intentionally. He lets into our sitting room a strange man who says to Johnny, "Corns removed, Sahib?" Johnny blinks and mutters something like, "How could you know?" – then takes off a shoe and shows two corns. The man takes out a dangerous-looking instrument shaped like a screwdriver but sharp as a razor. With repeated strokes the man shaves a corn down to level. He brings out a hollow bone – chicken bone? He puts one smooth end on the corn and sucks the upper end. When the suction is strong, he blocks the end in his mouth with something like chewing gum. The suction holds the bone to Johnny's foot. When at last the bone falls, the man pronounces the core of the corn gone. He makes a show of applying iodine. He repeats the whole process on the second corn.

Johnny seems pleased, then critical, and I guess he's starting already with haggling, a game he loves. The man says, "Thirty rupees" (about US$9). Johnny howls as if wounded, saying the corns will be back tomorrow, probably with "blood poisoning." The man finally accepts 15 rupees. Days go by, and Johnny walks easier than I've noticed before. Maybe – amazingly – the corns are really gone.

We try for passage across India in both American and British planes, dozens of them with unfilled space according to U.S. diplomatic personnel. Military rules make our merely medium priority ratings unacceptable. We try the railroad and get tickets for August 18, 11 weeks since we left Washington.

Our sleeping compartment extends the full width across the passenger car – no aisle; we enter directly from the platform (outside). There are four bunks; the seats are bunks and, above each, a similar bunk can be pulled down from the wall at bedtime. There's a small bathroom, complete with shower, wash basin, and flushing bowl. Two fans help us survive India's heat. Our fourth passenger is a British army captain who considers he's been in India long enough "to know what is done and what is not done."

When the train moves, I look at the Elgin wristwatch Barbara gave me before our goodby. The departure is precisely on time – astonishing in this wartime confusion. Johnny shrugs as if not surprised; he's traveled in India before. The British captain looks smug. Britons, helped by Indians they've taught, run this railroad. The captain boasts of British precision until I open a window to hear outside sounds and get fresh air. The captain says window-opening "is not done," but Johnny and Bill support me. The fresh air is great. But soon the wind turns; smoke and cinders come from the locomotive. We refuse defeat, though; we're continually opening windows with changes of the wind.

I'm watching life across India – the bullock-carts and the *garries*, the men in their *dhotis* (white, ample loincloths), the women in their *sarees*, the babies always carried straddle of a woman's hip, one little leg in front, the other in back, no different position observed in a thousand sightings. I try sketching for a letter to Barbara.

Though it's August, India is as green as a Shenandoah Valley spring – or as a secret meadow high up in Great Basin mountains. But the season of rain is really ending. The rice fields set so gracefully among pastures and scattered trees are yellow-green, almost luminescent in slanting sunlight. Both men and women walk the darker green paths between the wet glows, and they work in the rice, dipping water, bucket after bucket, from adjacent pools, the water spreading, standing, shining.

The men work in the fields with gray-backed water-buffalo pulling carts or the wooden plows that turn the soil. Or the buffalo at rest wallow in muddy ponds, escaping the heat, sometimes with only their noses above water. Regular cows are grazing too – as are goats – with men and boys herding, carrying staffs. I feel the whole scene is *nature* – except for the train and us foreigners inside it. The farm huts may be of mud or woven of reeds on frameworks of wood (bamboo?). Most huts are tiny, hardly tall enough for an adult to stand. Naked children play. Fires smoke out front.

Seen from this high-windowed train, with the huffing-puffing locomotive pulling us dependably along, India is beautiful. I imagine herding livestock here as I did long ago in the Great Basin. I long to stop the train and touch the land. I easily believe the rural and wild places are parts of my expanding home. The rural women in their *sarees* tease my eyes. A *saree*, I see on a nearby streambank where laundry is being washed, is a rectangle of thin cotton cloth, maybe three feet by 12 feet. The legs and hips must be wrapped in the *saree* first. The part covering the breasts seems precariously anchored over a shoulder or even up on the head. I watch woman after woman as we go by, craning after we've passed, expecting to see the insecure breast covering dislodged by the working movements, by the pull of gravity, or even a gust of wind.

We stop in a city, the train taking on water and coal. People gather, more than half of them children, looking up at us. Many are the age of my children. They gather under these high windows of the wealthy. They raise their arms and hands toward us, and they catch our glances with their dark eyes. They cry to us, "*Baksheesh, Sahib! Baksheesh!*" It's not just the children crying; it's the mothers and fathers too. All the voices have high-pitched tones that tear at my innards. "*Baksheesh, Sahib! Baksheesh! Baksheesh!*" I reach for a window. "No, no!" the British captain says. "It is not done!" I open the window anyway, and I throw out the coins from my pockets and all my one-rupee notes. People down there collide trying to catch. They crawl, shoving each other, trying to find what's hit the ground. There's a different tone in the shouting now, and beggars from up and down the train run toward our window. "Close the window, please," the captain says. "Close it, Huck!" Johnny says. Bill McGovern reaches quickly into his pocket, and he throws a bundle of one-rupee notes before the window closes.

On parts of the route across India a dining car is linked into the train. When we stop at an uncrowded place, we open the compartment door and walk along the platform to the diner. The food is good, though Johnny and the captain criticize in sophisticated detail.

Calcutta is our final stop before we must fly – threatened by enemy Zero fighters – over the Hump into China. The train reaches the station exactly on time, and I congratulate the captain. A taxi horn-blasts with us three aboard through streets full of harried people and serene sacred cows. Calcutta is hotter and more humid than Bombay – the worst on our whole long trip – and has countless beggars, partly because Japanese forces have cut off shipment of rice from Burma.

In our suite at the Great Eastern Hotel, where foreigners habitually stay, we're confronted by seven men wanting to be our servants. We drive six out, but the one we've chosen says he can't do this, says when he goes out into the hall he'll be beaten up. I say he should go out at once and join the protest against us; we'll do without a servant. But Johnny assumes the British captain's role:

"That isn't done, Huck," he says. He goes out with our chosen one to negotiate, and the deal is one personal servant for each of us. "These people need jobs," Johnny explains.

We make contacts around the giant city to clear our papers for the border crossing into China. There'll be one day and one more night before we fly to Assam, change planes and climb over snow-capped ridges extending from the giant Himalayas.

In the sea of starvation that's Calcutta, the Great Eastern has everything. Scotch-and-soda and other drinks flow liberally. At the dining table there's a waiter behind every chair, his full-time job standing there watching his guest's every move or mutter, probing the unspoken wish, signaling it to the appropriate watchers near the kitchen door, at the bar, and near the phone. The dinner courses come one after another at the pace the diners set. The menu doesn't appear to have changed for wartime's shortages.

Next day I walk different streets alone. One has open-front shops displaying fresh vegetables and fruits. Family servants, I think, are the most numerous customers, and they pay for what they get. In quantity, though, the sacred cows, who don't pay, could be champions. I watch the smooth, bold beasts – weighing 1200 pounds or more – taking their pick of whatever each shop offers. No one opposes them. There's danger! You could turn the gods against you!

A nearby street has trees and lawn and leads into a spacious park. Well-dressed people walk here, enjoying the greenery and the breeze. A scattering of beggars intrudes, both humans and sacred cows. The cows have the advantage. What poor human could intercede with the gods for the generous giver – as sacred cows can?

An old woman is sitting on a stone at the park's edge. Her body is shrunken, wrinkled, as is her face, though her stomach is bloated. Her eyes aren't quite shiny but still appealing. I long to help but carry nothing that's edible. I give her a rupee note, but it slips from her fingers, and she doesn't see where it flies on the breeze. I retrieve it and hand it to her again, and she closes her hand around it. Yet I know it has come too late. She still sits there, and her eyes glow dully, and she breathes, but death is with her.

In the evening I skip the luxuriously obscene dinner and try to sleep. I turn over and over but cling to the bed until a window suggests dawn. I dress and go out, eluding colleagues and servants. I walk in three-quarters dark, and I stumble on something unseen. It's a body still wrapped in a ragged *dhoti*. Feeling faint, I move back against the building, a food shop now tightly closed.

I hear a motor and moving feet – a truck with a crew of workmen searching the street. When they find a body, one takes hold of the wrists, another the ankles, and they swing the body between them back and forth, higher, higher, and fling it into the truck bed where it thuds. They search for other bodies.

The truck driver looks British – White anyway – and I ask him to explain. "We are cleaning the bloody streets," he says, "before people are about. We are finding three to four hundred bodies every morning."

Chapter 11 – China's Wartime Capital 1943

I'm in a DC-3, a two-engine transport plane, trying to cross from the American base at Dinjan (Assam, India) into China. We passengers have our backs to the walls, sitting on naked metal in depressions called bucket seats. We face the canvas-covered, lashed-down cargo that crowds the plane, rising to curved peaks high enough to block out the far windows, dipping to curved gaps through which we might meet the eyes of fellow passengers against the opposite wall. About half the passengers are Chinese. One is a well-dressed woman with a baby – I guess, the family of a young government official.

I try to guess what cargo is riding with us, so desperately needed by our ally, China, that's otherwise barricaded by the Japanese and in danger of total defeat. Ammunition? Medical supplies? Drums of gasoline? I'd like to ask Johnny Waldron, sitting next to me, what he thinks it is, but the plane's roar discourages talk. I'd also like to ask this old China hand Johnny what he knows about these fearsome mountains. My map shows them as east of the Himalayas but almost as high. There's Minya Konka, 24,900 feet, between us and Chungking, but we'll avoid it, landing first at Kunming where American airmen called Flying Tigers are based. Our plane keeps climbing – now, I feel, even faster than before, the engines straining. My nerves tighten. Passengers look questions at each other, but the Chinese woman is calmly nursing her baby, its head hiding her breast.

A crew member moves from passenger to passenger across the cargo from me, shifting handholds from protuberances of the canvas to taut ropes tied overhead to steady himself. He speaks to each passenger. One grabs his arm and asks questions, but I catch no words. He climbs across the cargo and moves in my direction. He's saying,

"Japanese Zeroes nearby. Keep your seat belts tight. The pilot is heading for thick clouds, hoping to hide."

Johnny grabs him and yells, "You have oxygen for us?" "Sorry," he answers. "But the pilot says you'll survive."

I twist hard to see out the small window behind me. White mountains are below us, a big dark cloud above us – with lightning. I feel sick and probe under the seat for the paper bag. The plane drops, and my seat belt jerks me down. The plane rises, and my weight against the metal bench triples, hurts. I use the bag and see others using theirs. An older Chinese man is bent far over, the bag between his knees. The plane darkens as we enter the cloud. My arms feel prickly numb. The mother and baby make no sound, but their faces seem bluish pale.

We outlast the Zeroes, then glide downward into sunshine, the engines quieter now, the air smoother. We're all sick. Johnny says, "Hell!" and Bill McGovern says, "Amen!"

American doctors and nurses receive the sickest of us at Kunming. The time spent above 19,000 feet worries them. We three walk okay but choose beds rather than drinks and dinner. Next morning we can eat only toast with our coffee, but we fly on northeast to Chungking, the wartime capital of the national government headed by Generalissimo Chiang Kai-shek. I look down on a graceful pattern of curving terraces bright green and yellow with crops – a Chinese soil conservation method for thousands of years – and on the city's buildings shading from gray to black, spreading densely over a hilly triangle where the clear-watered Chialing River meets the mighty, muddy Yangtze.

We land on what seems a sandbar near the great river's populated bank. Inspection of my papers and two small bags, without evidence of wealth, is courteous and brief. I carry my bags down a mud path to water where small boats cluster. A coolie with a down-curved mustache throws the bags into a boat. Johnny and Bill aren't coming behind me as I'd expected, needing Johnny's know-how. The coolie ignores my protest, so I leap into the already crowded boat with him and my bags. The coolie poles the boat to the mainland. Walter Fowler or Harry Lucker of our agency should meet us here, but the strangeness is unbroken. The coolie takes my bags on his naked shoulders and starts up the uneven stone steps. Again I protest in English – without effect – so again I follow my bags. The steps wind among bamboo shacks, steeply higher, higher. Where at last the land is less steep, the buildings are larger and neater, some with plaster over the woven bamboo. The coolie puts the bags down beside a busy street and stands over them glaring at me.

I pretend I don't see him. I need Johnny to interpret. The street swarms with pedestrians in shorts or in silk or denim gowns. Outdated cars and trucks whiz by, horns blowing. The trotting pullers of rickshas shout, "*Dzo! Dzo! Dzo!*" The ricksha shafts and wobbling wheels nudge people but don't draw blood. Load coolies move with springy gait, chanting in rhythm. The poles push grooves into the callused flesh behind the coolies' necks. I don't know what this fellow beside my bags is shouting at me. I hold a US dollar bill toward him. He squints at it and throws up his hands, his voice shriller.

A big but frail man is crossing the swirl of confusing currents in the street. It's Harry Lucker, and I'm afraid he'll be swamped, but amazingly both motor and foot traffic avoid him. "I couldn't meet you down there, Lambert," he says. "Sorry. Those 400 steps are too much for my weight and age." He pays the mustached coolie, and we wait by my bags for Johnny and Bill.

Lucker has a Jeep driven by a young Chinese who horn-blasts us through the massed confusion. Chungking buildings seem grouped, not lining streets. I look for turned-up roofs, but most of the city is a jerry-built hodgepodge of clay-plastered bamboo that mushroomed after Japanese bombing. I think I'm the farthest I've ever been from feeling at home.

Only one letter, of the dozens I felt sure Barbara had written, was waiting for me. Lucker said letters sent in accord with instructions given at the training sessions in Washington were averaging four months in transit; the U.S. Army postal service was proving fastest. But even one letter was so much more than I'd had since leaving Washington 77 days before that I read it over and over and responded to it before I slept:

> Darling Barbara, The wonderful letter that greeted me here tells much about you and the children and is exactly what I need. Nothing was censored in your letter, and despite our worries about that, it's unlikely personal and family matters will ever be touched...
>
> Conditions here are better than expected, Barbara. We live, eat and work in two houses on a hillside. I have a nice small room to myself, and the food is good... We have air raid alarms still. There are dugouts and ledges for shelter in the steep hill just above our houses. Distances, being so much up and down, seem to be measured in stair-steps. We climb 280 above Chialing River here.

I gave her my U.S Army address, also instructions on sending occasional letters by "diplomatic pouch." I found time to write Barbara two letters a week. Here are glimpses from the early weeks of far-out strangeness, of first acquaintance:

> August 20, 1943 – I'm shocked by the amount of laborious service demanded by typical foreigners. All our water, for instance, comes from the river...carried in wooden buckets by coolies. They carry two big buckets a trip, suspended from the ends of poles on their shoulders and base of neck. They dump water in large wooden tubs or tanks on towers behind house, from which it flows by gravity...
>
> Sunday, August 23 – Have just written Dad and Mrs. Foltz... I'm told the State Department has informed you and Dad of my safe arrival. Our office is that department's adopted child... I long for you terribly this Sunday, my first leisure. I want to look at you, to touch you, to feel you warm and real against me... I may learn to like it here... The faces down the street, though still indistinguishable from each other, seem

friendly. The children call after you, "Haow (how) boo haow" (meaning how are you?) and grin mischievously and good-naturedly... When you get caught in the rain as Bill and I and Lucker just did, the people laugh with you, not at you...

9/1/43 – Early morning. Roosters crowing in the distance (a sound of "home" inside me), and down along the Chialing River a Chinese is calling musically, "*Ha-ooh-a-ooh.*" Not far away someone is hammering nails – Does Ya-ya (I assume the pet name's still in use, though Harvey's 4-plus now) get a chance to hammer any nails. He should.

House coolie just came to tell me he'd brought *rih shuay* (hot water) for my bath. Baths are every other day – one wooden bucket of hot water and one of cold. The bathtub is "our" shape but of speckled gray composition, not enamel...

Vegetation here is familiar. There are locust trees, and I bet they bloom fragrantly here in spring. And I quickly notice familiar weeds – lambs quarter and redroot (amaranth).

Sunday morning before breakfast 9/5/43 – Your letters numbers 15 and 17, air mail, came, and they're wonderful! I climb Chungking steps two at a time now... Prices are high here. Paid CN$50 for a haircut. The barber, a small fellow about 20, in plain dirty clothes, came on our request – for several of us... CN$ – Chinese National dollars – for us (special gov't employee rate) are CN$30 to US$1, so a haircut is $1.66 our money...

Monday 9/13/43 – It's moonlight tonight, and the crickets here (as in Virginia and New York State) are singing... Last night I lay awake, and the moonlight was silvery in the folds of my mosquito net. I got up, longing for you, and looked out the window to where trees were outlined on the horizon against the misty moon-glow. You and I together would have stood hand in hand watching.

9/14 7:30 a.m. Went downtown for the first time Sunday...all the stores open. We were looking for a typewriter, as we contemplate hiring our third Chinese typist and steno. I tried out a dozen machines, all second hand – at my "machine-gun speed." People surrounded me as if I were a three-ring circus, or a snake charmer on the streets of Bombay.

Evidence was still to be seen ...of the terrible bombing Chungking went through a couple of years ago. Little buildings keep springing up around the ruins of large buildings like new shoots around the trunk of a cut-down tree. These people have endless vigor; something is felt in observing them and their works that says they'll go on and on, that nothing will stop them, that maybe after our temporary ways or cultures are changed they will still be going on, absorbing some of our best but not really changing. I hope we can absorb some of their best.

From 1943 on through World War II, an average of ten Americans would live and have their offices at the two-house headquarters of FEA (Foreign Economic Administration, only briefly Board of Economic Warfare) at Litzepa on the outskirts of Chungking. Chinese office workers would be roughly ten also, as would Chinese domestic servants. I was administrative assistant at first, setting up files and accounts as I had for Shenandoah National Park headquarters. FEA was to figure out and implement projects – many dealing with nature (natural resources) – that would strengthen the economy of our ally China or damage the economy of our enemy Japan. The Chinese, through their officials in both Washington and Chungking, had their own ideas and were pressing for the nonmilitary help they wanted most, and we were to investigate and advise.

First projects in action were buying Chinese hog bristles and tungsten concentrates and shipping them on return flights to America of planes that had brought supplies to China. These projects put jobs and money into China. They also helped America quite directly. Our navy urgently needed hog bristles for painting metal ships to prevent erosion. Hog bristles are better than the synthetics; they have short reverse branches that hold paint – so with a hog bristle brush a hand-painter can get twice or more as many effective strokes from one dipping of the brush into the paint can, and the distribution is smoother, more even. Tungsten, dangerously short in America, was also urgently needed – in producing tough steel for modern weapons.

For centuries China had been exporting hog bristles that gave brushes superior paint-holding capacity. Johnny and I visited the Chungking packing plant and examined bundles sorted into uniform lengths, some unbelievably long. The supply already available was a beginning. The needed quantity, though, would require long shipments within China, made difficult by wartime conditions. But the bristles did seem possible.

The tungsten, though, seemed impossible. The great mines were in the far southeast, Kuangtung and Chianghsi provinces – inside Japanese-dominated territory, Canton having fallen in 1938, Hongkong in 1942, no ports remaining open to us. Mining engineer Jeff Morris, an FEA team member whose feelings about man and nature resembled mine, conferred with Chinese officials. With their help then, he traveled thousands of miles, often on foot, climbing mountains to the major mines, looking into methods and special incentives. He gave me a copy of his personal diary, August 18-November 5, 1943 (42 closely typed pages).

Jeff's heroic effort – combined with the millions of dollars American industry would pay for the tungsten and with the Chinese government's eagerness for the money and for the cargo the tungsten-hauling planes would bring back over the Hump – produced miracles. Jeff gave his life to this project. The details may never be known, but before we at Chungking knew that vast amounts of the concentrates were being carried across Japanese lines in shoulder-pole baskets by load coolies, jogging alone or in twos or threes, Jeff Morris was missing. Apparently, he died in a plane crash, maybe shot down by Japanese Zeroes, but tungsten continued flowing to America.

Bill McGovern was among FEA men analyzing economic stress-points of the Japanese that might be worsened through Chinese-American actions. Were there, say, crucial shortages in Japan's industry (similar to our tungsten shortage) that could be tightened by stopping production or transportation in China? Our economic intelligence people were gathering facts from Chinese national government executives and scientists *and* from the "government" headed by communist leader Mao Tze-tung, whose forces were battling the Japanese far to the north. The contact was ticklish; Generalissimo Chiang and Mao were quarreling dangerously while sharing homeland defense.

Our mission's railroad mechanical engineer Alexander H. Mitchell was making history. When I'd met "Mitch" at the Yangtze airport, his leathery face was wrinkled by three-score years, and he seemed unlikely to adjust to wartime China. A month or so later we came to know him through Chinese newspapers as the "fabulous Mr. Mee" helping the Kwangsi-Kweichow Railway (KKR) to increase its tonnages and move its trains on schedule. Mitch was a red-tape cutter, sometimes having parts flown from the U.S. manufacturer without going through either the American or the Chinese government.

Mr. Mee had reached Tushan, the largest rail center left on the KKR, as the Japanese were advancing not far away. He found the railroad yards filled with refugees and demoralized Chinese soldiers. In the car used as railway office were 50 soldiers demanding at bayonet point immediate transportation away from the front. Mr. Mee took from his bag a mosquito "bomb," a tiny tank of compressed insecticide. He had his interpreter tell the soldiers he'd explode this new-type foreign bomb if they didn't leave at once. He moved toward the line of bayonets, cursing, holding the bomb in front of him. The soldiers gave way. He turned the valve of the bomb, and it hissed with escaping insecticide. The soldiers fled the car in wild panic.

Mr. Mee found locomotives idled for repairs but the shops in confusion. Workers were too few and what he called "stuffed gowns" too numerous. Educated abroad on technical aspects, the "gowns" behaved as Chinese scholars, letting their fingernails grow, walking with canes, refusing to dirty their hands. Mr. Mee found a gown waving his cane and shouting impatient directions at an unskilled welder. Mr. Mee grabbed the gowned engineer's cane in both hands, raised it above his head, and broke it on his knee. Then he set the astonished engineer to welding, with himself and the unskilled worker as helpers. The job was done quickly and well. As Mr. Mee went through the shops he broke other canes, and his own gnarled hands helped with the hardest jobs.

FEA tried to improve all the basic industries of China. From our Chungking office, we could watch the increasing glare of molten iron in awakened industry across the Chialing River. Our part was sometimes slight, sometimes crucial. Infusions of American capital launched or enlarged enterprises. A most urgent need developed for technically trained personnel. Why not send capable young Chinese to America for apprenticeship, so they could return and help manage new industries with the latest technology? I became a Lend-Lease requirements officer, arranging such training and helping Chinese industries get needed equipment and supplies.

In working out action, we met with industrial as well as political leaders. Meetings, as typical in China, were often banquets or smaller dinners. We economic warriors were invited, for instance, to the home of T.V. Soong, brother of the Generalissimo's wife Mei-ling Soong. A former ambassador to the United States, T.V. was now China's foreign minister and a powerful influence. The Generalissimo could be indecisive or stubborn or enthusiastic. T.V could make the difference. Though my part was small, I felt Soong's thinking, like his use of English, was American. We enjoyed cooperating with him.

In our FEA offices the central Chinese was Joe Chu, son of a wealthy Shanghai family. He'd fled the advancing Japanese with his beautiful wife Lillian and a truckload of personal effects, bought his way through a zone already in Japanese control, then lost the truckload to "false" Chinese friends. He'd expected an important position in the central government. Soon, though, he was finding the government riddled with graft. Believing in America as a utopia – and in all Americans as worthy members – he'd come to work for us.

Joe saw me as a "budding friend" of China and wanted to teach me the language. A graduate of Shanghai's (Catholic) St. John's University, he'd known Americans well, both academics and diplomats. Though he'd been a playboy, he was now serious. Thin in body, with a long, corded neck and a prominent Adam's apple, he exuded sincerity and energy.

No textbook designed to teach Chinese to English-speakers was at hand, so Joe started with the Chinese children's primer, a thin brown paperback. A portrait of Sun Yat-sen was frontispiece, with characters meaning country father beneath crossed flags in colors of the Kuomintang (party flag) and the Republic (national flag). In text and drawings, Dee-dee (little brother) and May-may (little sister) were followed through their daily life.

Joe read sing-song style, pointing to the bold brush-stroke characters and emphasizing the tones of the official Mandarin, "*Ly ly ly. Ly shang hsueh* (Come, come, come. Come to school." I repeated after him – as I'd heard through open windows the children repeating after their teacher in the Litzepa school nearby. Joe's face would brighten when I got a tone right, then cloud up again.

His tones (Mandarin has four tones) came from long-ago learning. I think he couldn't now tell when his voice rose or fell in pitch, so couldn't explain clearly to me. After I'd tried the examples to the point of confusion, he'd become impatient and keep repeating at me until he himself became uncertain. For weeks we had lessons every evening. When neither of us thought I was advancing fast enough, a dinner party encouraged me.

Several of us Americans were invited to the home of K.P. Hu, owner of a cement factory and a chinaware plant, eager to try other industries. He and his wife (formerly a professional singer) and their daughter now in first grade welcomed us. Aware I was studying the language, K.P. drew me into Chinese conversation. I understood little. After dinner, little Lin came to me and said, "*Nee boo shr Joong-gwo ren. Nee tsung sha-ma dee fong ly-da?* (You're not Chinese. Where did you come from?)" Her speech was Mandarin as taught now in schools throughout China, and I knew the words: "*Wo tsung May-gwo ly-da.* (I came from America.)" She climbed into my lap, and we talked for an hour, discussing my fountain pen, the fabric of my clothes, the games I'd watched Chungking children play, the sun, the moon, the animals on the farm, the noises coming through the open window from the street – all subjects from the Chinese primer we'd both been studying. Joe Chu learned of this episode and praised my progress.

Soon, though, Joe got bored with language instruction. He became the Chinese sage, and every day for weeks brought a different book of classics, mostly Confucius-oriented. He read aloud in ancient style. He translated emotionally into English, telling me of the wanderings of the wise master Kung (Confucius) in search of a ruler who'd utilize his plans for an ideal government. At times, I felt, Joe *was* Confucius, too often disappointed when officials failed to recognize his wisdom. His face reflected the thought of the ages, his head thrust forward in the Confucian manner.

Or Joe performed as a modern patriot, stern and selfless, militarily erect. He'd tell again how he'd fled to Chungking, not for adventure or honor or to escape the Japanese but solely to serve his country. He'd lecture on Sun Yat-sen's "Three Principles of the People." His eyes would flash with crusader's zeal. He'd tell me of visits to Chiang Kai-shek's house, of how everyone, including family members, bowed and were silent in the respected presence; of how Chiang bowed in return, repeating "*Haow, haow, haow...*" until his voice faded; and of the harassed leader's lonely walks in the Second Range beyond the Yangtze.

Sometimes Joe would be his former self, man-about-town, hosting banquets, pouring the *huang jiou* (yellow wine from rice) and calling for *gon bay* after *gon bay* (drink the glass empty! bottoms up!) to General "Vinegar Joe" Stilwell (the American military chief in China and India), to China – and to the Japanese Navy, "Bottoms up!" All foreigners were expected to appreciate this joke – and most did. Sometimes Joe was a devout Catholic (he had an uncle who was a bishop), showing me the bombed ruins of St. Joseph's Church and introducing me to the *padres*. Once he took me to visit a son of Chiang Kai-shek, Chiang Ching-kuo, his friend from Shanghai time. Joe and I would create big dreams together, including one of a national magazine for China.

I slip from "high society" to "low society" and more direct familiarity with the man-and-nature relationship. Our drinking water at lunch one day definitely stinks, and I'm plunged into what we call "the *liang ky shuay* problem." *Liang* means cool, and *shuay*, water, and *ky*, boiled. Bill McGovern says, "Huck, you can talk with these characters now. Why don't you investigate?"

I bounce the job toward Johnny, who really *can* talk Chinese, but he bounces it back. I guess I'm as interested as anyone in avoiding the "Yangtze Rapids" and the more serious amebic dysentery and cholera. I take a water sample to be analyzed at the Army hospital. Then I ask our number one boy to show me where our drinking water comes from. He says, "Yes, Master," but he doesn't lead me anywhere. I say louder, "Where does it come from?"

"From river, Master." I don't like being called Master, but I delay that argument. "Who carries our drinking water?"

"Zombi – you Americans call him."

"Let's get him to show us." When there's no answer, I add, "Is it a secret, Feng?"

He's startled but I think also pleased by my using his name instead of Boy.

"No secret, Lan Hsien-sheng (Mr. Lambert)," he says, which pleases me. But still there's no action.

"Feng, " I say, "are you a communist?"

"No, no, no!"

"But you read *Hsin Hua Jih Pao*" – published by communists.

He's jolted, trying to recover – "Yes – good newspaper – most readers not communists." Quickly now, he calls for the water carrier.

This indoor-outdoor coolie – I'll have to learn his real name as I can't use Zombi – is young, maybe 20. At Feng's orders, he gets a carrying pole and two buckets and starts toward the river. I follow. Feng follows me. The coolie's legs, below his shorts, look powerful. He keeps his gaze ahead and moves fast on the uneven path and steps of packed dirt and stone. At the river he dips his wooden buckets where the water is least muddy, a cloudy green. I think sewage but don't smell evidence; most sewage in China is saved for use on farms. Feng and I stand aside as the coolie, carrying, passes us to climb. The water sloshes, gurgles, splashes against the curved wood of the buckets. I count the steps, keep counting; I take 422 steps (280 of them vertical) between the river and the small concrete reservoir set into the ground between our upper house and the separate but adjacent kitchen. Feng says in English, knowing the limits of my Chinese, "Must settle now – two-three hour." The water at this stage doesn't stink.

Left alone, I study the water. Algae, I suspect. With a microscope I'd probably see animal life as well. The top half-inch slowly becomes transparent. I look into the open door of the kitchen. The cook and his wife are busy in advance work for dinner. They know I'm here but don't let me catch their eyes. The kitchen is tiny – bamboo frame and woven strips plastered with mud. Pushing in, I see a built-in stove of clay and concrete with iron top and iron oven. Remaining space has a work table with a wooden bucket on one end. Water in this bucket doesn't stink. The cook's name is Yu, his age 31. He once cooked for an American businessman in Tientsin. He wipes sweat from his forehead and says to me, "*Rr duh hun!* (Awfully hot!) Need fan. Electric." He points to openings in the roof.

"Flies! Need roof fix." He scrapes the earthen floor with his shoe and shows holes at the base of the walls. "Rats! Need floor."

I feel the cook is amused at his own boldness in speaking directly to me instead of through the number one boy. I grin back at his grin and shrug my shoulders, saying *"May yo fa-dze"* - a popular phrase meaning, Yeah, but there's no solution! The cook and his wife laugh, and I laugh with them. I ask them the real name of Zombi; it's Soong Pai. We chat more about the inadequacy of the kitchen. The cook shrugs and says, *"May yo fa-dze,"* and we laugh again.

When Soong Pai returns Feng does too. With a wooden dipper Soong Pai lifts water into a pottery jar. The first dipperful rinses the jar and is poured on Feng's personal garden not far away. Then the jar is filled, maybe three gallons, and taken into the serving room of that upper house, behind the dining room. "Must settle all night now," Feng says.

At dawn Soong Pai empties the pottery jar into a wooden tub half filled with sand. The sand seems clean, no odor. The water filters through and out the spout where it's caught in another pottery jar. I worry about the dipper and jars but believe nothing is crucial – as long as the boiling comes afterward.

A new mystery – Soong Pai takes up a three-foot stick of bamboo, with slits cut into the hollow near the lower end, and I see whitish crystals imprisoned in there. Soong Pai stirs the water with this stick, and I ask why. He answers, but I fail to follow his Szechuan dialect. "Alum crystal – makes water more clear," Feng explains. After the stirring, the water is boiled 15 minutes in the kitchen – with Feng, the cook, and I as witnesses. It doesn't smell bad. Soong Pai takes it off to cool. I go in to breakfast, and the men look questions at me. I don't explain but ask old China hands Harry Lucker and Johnny Waldron about the alum crystals; they confirm this stirring with crystals is customary but don't know why. At noon the cooled water is emptied into a British-made diatomite filter. No stink here. I ask old China hands how the filter gets sterilized. They don't know but speculate – either it's boiled too at intervals or the filter company furnishes chemicals that purify the water without boiling. At lunch we all drink hot tea – strong. Afterward, in the serving room, I watch the number two boy Liu drawing water from the tap of the filter into empty liquor bottles. Still no stink.

Liu opens the ice box in the serving room to store the bottled water until needed, and the stink wells up from inside this ice box. Other bottled water is lined up at the back of the ice box, and it has the stink. One tiny piece of ice, all that remains, is rapidly melting. Meat in the ice box is making the stink, and the water in bottles that aren't perfectly sealed is absorbing some of it.

> Mystery solved – but remedy elusive:
> FENG: Ice not always can get.
>
> COOK YU: Meat the same. Cost high. Must not waste. Old meat tender. Taste good when cooked. You Americans like.

I arrange for our office clerk Tom Chi, fluent in both English and Chinese, to accompany Feng, Soong Pai, and me to the "ice factory" at dawn. It's four miles away, on an alley jammed with coolies, jeeps, trucks, everybody quarreling. Leaving Soong Pai to guard the Jeep, Feng and I push a way through crowds for delicate Tom Chi. We see ice sliding down a chute, being loaded on a truck. We enter the yard past a guard with rifle and fixed bayonet. He threatens but desists when I ignore him. In the office the Chinese manager smiles courteously.

> TOM CHI: We wish to obtain 100 catties of ice, please.
> MANAGER: Do you pay "gold"? (U.S. currency)
> TOM CHI: No. We have a book of tickets.
> MANAGER (smile fading): I am sorry but ice is all gone.
> TOM CHI: But we saw ice coming down the chute.
> MANAGER: I am very sorry. The new batch will be ready at 7 o'clock.

TOM CHI: We must act quickly to protect health of Americans who bring millions of dollars worth of needed materials to us. You do have ice, do you not?

MANAGER: It is reserved for emergency.

TOM CHI: Emergency is what we have – Americans threatened with cholera.

MANAGER: But you do have "gold," do you not?

TOM CHI (after seeing me shake my head): Do you wish to be reported to Tai Li and Generalissimo as operating black market?

MANAGER: Bring your vehicle, please. We always have ice for our great and kind allies.

The ice tangle is solved, and soon the U.S. Army hospital reports that even the stinking water contains nothing harmful.

My small success brought me the scary opportunity of managing our entire domestic staff and board-and-lodging system. I could practice Chinese language and human psychology while experiencing down-to-earth situations and workers typical of the majority. The front problem was Harry Lucker's order to Feng that Mrs. Feng's father and "livestock" must be removed from our compound. The chronic problem was the failure of the water coolie-plumbing system to function as planned – with ample running water always available. The thought alone of being responsible for such complexities (responsibility for environmental health?) started a perceptible trembling around my solar plexus.

Johnny advised me, "You've got to get out of it, Huck. If Harry Lucker knew you threw rupee notes out the train window to begging hordes in India, he'd know you're exactly the wrong man for this job."

"Okay," I said. "I'll confess to Lucker my sympathy with downtrodden people if you'll accept the domestic management yourself. You talk Chinese, and your background's similar to Lucker's – you're lords of creation exploiting the meek – who may be getting less meek."

Johnny's face got redder than normal, and he said, "I wouldn't take that job if it paid a hundred thousand U.S. – instead of nothing." But I felt he was still my friend and would side with me in a test. So I bravely guessed I'd take the risk.

My most crucial ally, though, had to be Feng, direct supervisor of the domestic staff – or, if not Feng, then a worthy successor. There was a file on Feng Fay-bay. He was 46 in 1943. His parents had farmed rice, and Fay-bay helped. Later he worked for wealthy foreigners. He could read enough Chinese to stay aware of great happenings, including the current war. Feng and family now lived in our compound, in a separate small structure typical of wartime Chungking – woven bamboo walls roughly plastered. Feng and now-pregnant wife had a grown son who worked and lived at a downtown photography shop. At home here, they had a girl, age 6 – who played in the yard with a feathered object resembling a badminton bird, that she hit with a wooden paddle. There was also Mrs. Feng's weak and elderly father. The controversial livestock, noisy and messy, were a dozen chickens and ducks.

Feng knocked on the door of my room. I invited him to come in and sit down, which I guess shocked him. He was used to foreigners calling him "Boy!" He read my face, then shut the door and perched on the chair I indicated. "Mr. Lucker say again I must send away sick old man father of wife and must sell livestock." When I didn't quickly respond, Feng mentioned the recent death of a coolie who'd worked for us and the earlier loss of our mining engineer Jeff Morris. "Chinese die," he said. "American die." I felt he meant we're all humans together, and I agreed.

My impulse was to raise his pay from the unbelievable US$12 a month to whatever it took to rent a nearby place for his father-in-law and the fowls, but I said, "I'll talk with the other Americans and try to work out a plan by next week – so you can continue in your job with us."

"Thank you, Lan Hsien-sheng," he said.

My timing was thrown off by the bathroom-water carriers, who must have felt they could gain advantage before I had a firm grasp on my new responsibility. On Lucker's insistence, the three had increased their trips to the river to take care of increasing personnel who lodged, ate, and/or worked here. They'd been regularly filling the tower-tank behind the one-story upper house but neglecting the more difficult tower-tank behind the two-story house. Under Lucker, though, there'd always been water in the reservoir at the tower's base, and when an American yelled "Boy!" or "Coolie! Water!" someone always hurried to the bathroom with filled buckets. Now, though, with me in charge, the basic reservoir went dry.

Should I threaten to fire the men if water wasn't kept constantly in the tower-tank? Should I set a quota of buckets to be carried per man per shift and have each man's performance recorded, then fire the laggards and increase the pay of any who worked well? I told Feng both houses must have running water constantly – and asked him what additional authority or money would make this happen. He said, "We ask carry-water men."

When we did, they said the river was too far, the hill too steep, and the tower-ladder no good for carrying buckets. But they'd do the job for $10 per month instead of the present $8 (these numbers full US dollars). Feng and I wanted to give them the US$10, but I felt we'd need a factual case to cope with criticism from other foreign households that were holding the line at US$8. I persuaded Feng, against his protest, to provide me with a carrying pole and two buckets. The carrying was done at night, so my working along with the coolies didn't create a public scene.

After three nights of this research, I felt that three men in good condition (which I felt I was) *could* keep the two Litzepa tower-tanks supplied *if* the incentive was strong. Waldron and Lucker thought the men would do the full job well at present pay from fear of being fired for failure. Bill McGovern and Joe Chu thought what I secretly thought – they'd do the job a few days or weeks while seeking less strenuous work, then leave unless we increased the pay. I calculated no American in FEA Chungking was paid less than 100 times the coolie's pay. A discrepancy so vast seemed criminal. I delayed decision, though.

Next day, a Sunday, I hadn't gained in courage. I was escaping the puzzle by walking with Hy Hodes, a newly arrived FEA colleague on war-leave from a New York City business. He knew nothing yet about the problem, and I was trying to guess what his reaction would be, before I confided in him. We were watching load coolies, and I commented on what I'd noticed many times, the readiness of load coolies to laugh and sing. I said the Chinese are mostly happy people, compared, say, with typical Americans. Hodes said this couldn't possibly be true – the degree of happiness or unhappiness results from wealth or poverty, "so the Chinese are of necessity unhappy."

A general theory of happiness relativity popped into my mind: When an individual's pleasure is rising above his own average he's happy; when pleasure is slipping below his average he's unhappy. The economic level above subsistence makes no difference. We argued half the day, Hodes insisting, "Nobody getting less than a thousand dollars a month" – somewhere near the American average then – "could possibly be happy." The talk floated outside reality; I didn't confide the facts that worried me. No use. And soon I wasn't quite hearing what was being said. I was imagining I was bravely doubling Feng's salary – from US$12 to US$24 a month (an amount for which I worked less than a day) and was giving 25% increases to cook Wu and the number two boy Liu and to the water carriers including the versatile Soong Pai. But even in imagination the action was scary.

The year 1943 was running out, and our domestic establishment kept muddling along as FEA projects surged, demanding nearly all our energy. I was writing to Barbara just about everything that would pass the military censor, such as these glimpses:

> Did you have turkey yesterday? We did, wonder of wonders... I feel embarrassed from having the unbelievably underpaid Chinese cook and waiters serving us this meal that probably cost more to produce and deliver in Chungking than these people can afford for food in a month.
>
> We went to Thanksgiving service presided over by our ambassador C.E. Gauss... Bill McGovern and I sat near the little organ ...played by a tall American-European (?) woman in a long blue Chinese-fashion dress ...a missionary gone native... I really like our Christmas card you designed and made – the flowers and the V (for victory?), all delicate pink, and the V cut out inside to reveal the Chinese characters for Merry Christmas.
>
> Sunday after Christmas 1943 – Just returned from seeing the Fengs' baby. He's a good-looking little fellow, though he was half awake only and his eyes didn't open for me at all.
>
> Mrs. Feng brought him out of the inner room all bundled up in a little silk quilt which was bright red on one side and bright blue on the other. His face was pink, and he shook his head, or rather rolled it, back against the quilt, but he didn't make a sound. He doesn't cry much, though I've heard him occasionally.
>
> A majority of us Americans voted the Fengs a Christmas present. The family can live here through 1944 at least – but will fence in the ducks and chickens so they won't soil our walkways. Friendly compromise is the course with the water carriers too. We've agreed with them on a minimum number of buckets full a day and agreed to limit our flushing to fit the quota. If residents and office workers increase further and force the total use up, we'll hire additional carriers in proportion. Policy calls for general pay increases for domestic staff

– as soon as we can release ourselves from traditional conformance with scales standardized by diplomatic custom – or can persuade other agencies to increase along with us.

Chapter 12 – Loneliness and East West Love 1944-45

New Year's Day 1944
Darling Barbara – I feel you're awfully far away and mere letters are inadequate as the link between us. How many words does it take to convey one glance, one smile, one touch? I feel I must tell you everything and you must tell me everything, and this may substitute for the glances and touches that spoke without words when we were together... I'm not unhappy exactly. I draw an enduring happiness from realizing I have you as my wife and you are thinking of me and you write to me and are taking care of our children, our dear Laurie and Dilby and Yaya...

Feb. 26, 1944 – There's a faint possibility I may be one of the heads of a large new magazine publishing business after the war. In the event the plan materializes, what would you think of our spending a year or two in Shanghai? All of us? I would be a consultant – with time for writing on my own...

Sunday 3/5/44 – I'm sitting on a boulder by the river, Sweetheart. All around me are smaller stones, gravel, all rounded and polished by the river when it was higher than it is now. From up above where our two houses are, this appears as a sandy beach. In front of me the junks and sampans are moving on the water, and I hear the chants of the oarsmen going downstream and of the coolie gangs who on the bank tow the heavy junks upstream...

It's 12:20 – I've been sitting on this boulder since breakfast. Many Chinese have walked by, and they've stared with curiosity. The sun has been warm on my back and has moved from one cheek to the other. The rock feels hard now – and cold...

4/25/44 – The stars are tremendously bright. I recognize ones I grew up with. Jupiter (a planet, of course) is right overhead. The Big Dipper is up high in the north with the pointers indicating the North Star... I pick up my mattress and bedding and carry them out to the porch and put them down under the stars. I feel less lonely now – more at home – and sleepy...

After work today I'm expecting a young lady to try out for continuing my Mandarin lessons. Her name is Ho Chao-ye. She wants to exchange Chinese for English. I'll report to you...

I re-experience Miss Ho's visits with sharp and tender intertwinings of joy and longing and regret. Actually – I'm not at all sure, as I wait the first time, that she'll really come. The arrangements are disconnected. By phone and in person FEA clerk Tom Chi spread word an American wanted a teacher from Beijing where people speak the official Mandarin. A friend of one of his friends relayed word Miss Ho would come to discuss the matter. I've reached my room sweating from the office and bathed and just put on my khaki shorts and shirt when there's a knock. It's Feng saying, "Teacher come," and she's right behind him. I say, "Just a minute," and I close the door and pick up stray clothes and whatever else might detract from classroom atmosphere.

Carrying a knitted bag by its drawstrings, she comes into the light. Her dress is white with fruit-tree twigs and pink blossoms, peach maybe. The Chinese collar hugging her neck looks stiff, yet the dress moves flexibly as she moves, the cloth not expensive as are Joe Chu's wife Lillian's clothes but not coarse as normally seen in the streets.

She moves past me with small steps into the room's widest space and says, "Please do not close door, Lan Hsien-sheng," barely loud enough for me to hear yet revealing she knows my Chinese name, Lan Da-wen. "This table by wall," she continues, "may it move to center place – with you to sit one side and I other side?"

I place table and chairs to please her, realizing that, without discussion or hesitation, we've mutually agreed the teaching will happen. "I should travel the miles, Miss Ho, saving you the trouble – and danger."

"Trouble comes always with life, Lan Hsien-sheng. As to the danger, I cannot believe in it." An almost-smile plays on her round face. "I must come. My dormitory with other women has no room for the teaching and no welcome for man."

"We're sitting down when Feng comes with a teapot and American-style cups – big, with handles. We sip. She opens the Chinese primer I've put in front of her and says, "Mr. Chi did not inform me you are child. I see now you are Chinese small boy. I am venerable teacher, to be respected and obeyed. So – please to read aloud, Da-wen, the lessons you have learned."

Her discipline has sympathy and humor; it's easy to obey. I hear in my voice the tones of the beginning class in the Litzepa school just below our compound. Soon she directs me to page four of the primer, showing posture. "I see your American soldiers in Jeep with legs up and all around. Maybe happy for them. But Chinese child learns to sit gracefully." She reads the Chinese characters beside the drawing, "*Dzo, yaow dzo haow*," and translates, "Sit, want sit well." She watches with dark twinkling eyes as I place my feet side by side flat on the floor – as hers, with emphasis, remain.

At our half-time point, the Chinese lesson ends, and I'm to improve her English. I say, "You must relax now, Chao-ye."

She meets my glance in shocked protest. "Strange man who is not kin shall not use given name."

"I'm venerable teacher now," I say, "authorized." I also think for English class the name must be American. I repeat her Chinese name, "Chao-ye, Chao-ye. It could be Charlotte. But, no – Kathleen! You may now relax your posture, Kathleen. It is no longer suitable."

She half-smiles and tries. She puts her right foot forward and her left foot back, almost under the chair, the toe of her straw sandal on the floor, the heel up. I accept the posture as relaxation, though she doesn't look comfortable. She mentions English books she's been reading, among them, *Ivanhoe*. She's also been studying a conversation book written by a British professor. I'll take the part of A in the book, and she of B, and we'll converse as the professor considers proper. I tell her to hold the book flat in front of her, and I'll read my part upside down (a skill I learned working directly with mirror-image metal type and an expert compositor putting together my magazine pages on the stone).

I read enough to convince her I can, then start changing the British talk into what I feel is American. She protests but soon cooperates, saying, "The American is pleasant to the ear – better for me to relax with to please present teacher." She puts her left foot forward and brings her right foot back, smiling.

I recommend American books and lend her my current favorite, John Steinbeck's *The Grapes of Wrath*, along with a recent *Atlantic*. She skims the magazine. "What is the meaning – 'man of the world'?" she asks. "Is it, perhaps, you Americans who travel so far?"

In trying to explain, I use the word *sophisticated*.

She quickly says, "It is bad."

"Sometimes, but sometimes not."

"I think it is the trouble with world," she says. "Most foreigners in China are sophisticated. They play with Chinese girls and Russian girls and cannot know the proper relation of man and woman. Many Chinese too are sophisticated. But all these are not so happy as the man who carries loads all day and returns home to eat the rice with wife and children." She's studying my face, and she adds as if surprised, "But you are not sophisticated, Lan Hsien-sheng. You have happy spirit of Chinese child. Many American soldiers too are children. I see them playing together, laughing and singing."

I'd wanted spontaneous expression but hoped it would be in Chinese. I feel she's too far ahead for me ever to catch up.

Each Wednesday and Saturday evening Kathleen and I had three hours together, the maximum time either of us felt we could take from schedules already crowded. She was two years younger than I – 26. She'd majored in chemistry at a university in Beijing and received her degree when 20, one of the youngest graduates in science and, she believed, the only woman in China to graduate that year with a scientific degree. She worked as a research chemist at a government ordnance plant upriver. To come for lessons, she had to walk the first mile always. When the old buses that used charcoal instead of gasoline were out of order (often) and no ricksha could be found, she walked the entire eight-mile round trip. When she left after 10:30 she was never sure she wouldn't have to walk all the way in the dark.

Kathleen – like Joe Chu – dreamed of visiting America. Otherwise, she was his opposite. Joe responded to his own whims, often unrealistic; he acted many parts, most of them only skin deep. Kathleen was always herself. Though she could be idealistic and imaginative, even humorous, these qualities were managed by a strong and steady consciousness.

I asked her opinion of America. "I am sure it is wonderful," she said, "but Americans are mistaken in supposing money and comfort are most important." Then she added – but not, I think, to salve my feelings – "Large numbers of Chinese now also are too materialistic. Perhaps you know some; they cultivate Americans who can influence money or power." She blinked, then gave me a basic assignment. "You must get acquainted with many Chinese – in Chinese language. Because you are child, you shall start with children."

I told her about visiting with K. P. Hu's daughter Lin and promised to talk with more youngsters. Boys from Litzepa school sometimes looked timidly into our open gate during noon hour, and one day I made a welcome gesture. A boy approached and asked, "*Hsien-sheng* (Sir or Mr.), *nee-yo may-yo may-gwo-de yoo piaow*? (Do you have American postage stamp?)"

There'd been a lesson in the Chinese textbook about stamps; both this boy and I had studied it. I gave him the stamp from the most recent of Barbara's letters. He bowed, repeating, "*Hsieh hsieh hsieh hsieh* (Thank you)." The next day three boys came for American stamps. One wore a boy scout uniform. I made the international scout sign, and he did the same. "You're not boy scout," he said in schoolish Mandarin. "Too old." I confessed I was not – currently – but explained, "Boy time I boy scout."

One day when I was out walking, the two great signal balls went up an air raid warning pole. The unusually clear sky would make an air raid easy and effective, and people acted frightened. The boy scout saw me and came running to guide me to a shelter – a cave below an ancient fortress called Fuhsingkwan. We waited a while with others at the entrance, watching the sky. The scout then hurried off to guide others. An interested circle formed around me, and a man asked, "*May-gwo Jung-gwo shr boo shr haow pung yo?*"

It was something about America and China being friends. A man beside the first questioner began scratching English on the bare gray rock: "Are we truly friends?" Everyone went silent.

I said, "*Shr shr* (Yes, yes)." Approval came like cheering.

The signal balls dropped down the warning pole – enemy here! Some rushed into the cave; the boy scout returned with several elderly Chinese. Most of us waited at the entrance, watching. Three planes appeared so far away no one could identify them. Soon three more planes, a different shape, were speeding at the first three – that then veered away as if fleeing. The second three circled nearer. American stars stood out on them clearly. People around cheered louder now. Someone ran into the cave to tell others. People were looking at me as though I personally brought the protecting planes. "*Ding haow! Ding haow!*" they shouted. "Very good! Very good!" said the man who knew English.

Another day, on a climb up the steepening ridge behind our two houses, I found the home of the scout – where Feng had recently bought weeping willow trees, peach trees that bloom red, pink and white simultaneously, and a bamboo to plant in our yard. Steps had been carved into the rock. The dwelling of bamboo and mud occupied the wide ledge of a cliff. The boy and his parents knew no English, but they showed me around, and the boy told the family's story in a mixture of Mandarin and Szechuanese.

Before Chungking became China's capital, this property had had seven small houses. All were bombed away by the Japanese, mostly in 1941. The father had found a paying job, and the mother raised trees and other plants for sale. The whole ledge and the cliff face, utilized by vines held on ascending trellises of dried bamboo and on descending cords or nets, was colorful with blossoms. There were peaches, pears, apples, and a Chinese fruit I couldn't identify, all coming along well but not yet ripe. There were melons and squash and cucumbers.

I continued visiting with children, partly because I missed my own three, but Kathleen and I advanced on other fronts too. We worked through four of the school books. I learned to write simple compositions with a brush and to decipher the news with effort. Though I'd never cope in complex conversation with adults who knew no English, the attitudes and activities of busy Chungking, so mysterious during my early months, became mostly intelligible to me. Kathleen thought my adventures with children and with adults, both educated and uneducated, would help create a "healthy world consciousness."

She exclaimed one day out of the blue, "The citizens of Earth!" She had hold of something she suddenly realized was lastingly important. "At National Central University – which has temporary location upriver from my dormitory – was recently the Earth-wide citizenship meeting, perhaps forming organization. I wished to attend but could not. You, Da-wen, must investigate. I assign you." We laughed at her stretched authority but pursued the subject. Understandings in the world, we agreed, might depend on friendly contacts of "foreign devil" with many kinds of Chinese – and on a small meeting at a wartime university. The course of history – peace or war... We were both talking at once – excited – then were laughing at ourselves. She said, "We two, in conference near Chialing River, are as important for Earth as Roosevelt-Stalin-Churchill in conference – or as conference in China of Generalissimo and Mao Tse-tung. Do you not think so?"

"Of course," I said.

After we'd laughed some more – partly, I guess now, because we couldn't yet cry together – she asked, "Do you know Laotze of ancient time in China – and his belief the basic way of people, which is way of nature, shall outlast the intellectual way and the official way, even the way of emperors?"

In a Chinese school book are lessons about rural scenes, forests and mountains, planting and harvesting grain, setting out fruit trees and harvesting fruit, feeding and slaughtering chickens, gathering and preparing vegetables. I'm thinking of my rural boyhood and of my walks with FEA colleagues across the Chialing River into farmlands, and I say, "I could learn more and remember better if teacher and I were actually out there."

Kathleen's face shows pain. "I too have wished – many times already – to show and discuss with you in open air the scenes and doings of real China. But it cannot be." Then her face brightens. "There is related possibility. We might cook together. When cold comes and you have *huobun* glowing in room, we shall decide what food. I give you list. You buy in market. We learn from life the words with actions."

My feelings leap. I bring them down to "Wonderful!" But the weather's not cold yet, so she moves from nature and farms to nature and Laotze. She hands me a paper on which she's written an English version of a piece from Laotze's famous classic *Tao Te Ching*:

>Without stepping outside one's doors,
>One can know what is happening in the world.
>Without looking out of one's windows,
>>One can see the Tao of Heaven.
>The farther one pursues knowledge,
>>The less one knows,
>Therefore the Sage knows without running about,
>>Understands without seeing,
>>Accomplishes without doing.

"You see, Da-wen," she says, "it is not fatal that we cannot wander freely. The crucial knowledge waits also inside."

"This Tao of Heaven, is it God?"

"Not God. Laotze did not find mysterious beings. Tao is way of universe, of earth, of human, of all life. It is deep of ocean controlling temperature and significant current, not meaningless waves and ripples of quick-changing surface. Human society is small part – and also lives and dies by nature – no supernatural, no eternal life for individuals."

"Doesn't China have religion?"

"What meaning religion? If meaning control by supernatural God, I think China is poor in it. If meaning system of belief and behavior with ethics and philosophy, I think China is rich in it. In beginning of China was respect and love of heaven, earth, and ancestors. As long ago, perhaps, as sixth century before 'Christian era' came Laotze – or compilation from many sages – with great natural Tao (Way) at heart of everything – and Confucius with mature humans behaving reasonably through social ethics for lasting good of all on Earth. In Han dynasty came Buddhism bringing lessons agreeable with Chinese feelings for merciful behavior and reducing selfish desires. Also coming into China were Mohammedanism and Christianity with Allah and Jehovah God – though proportion of Chinese involved was always small."

Still watching me closely, Kathleen concludes with a mischievous smile, "Your name-forebear Charles Darwin may have learned from Laotze. Certainly *Tao Te Ching* was available, already long since translated around world." She hands me her *Tao Te Ching* – in Chinese. "Here is homework assignment. Do you accept and promise?"

I leaf into it and find nothing I can read except numbers identifying short sections of text. "I accept, but – "

"It is teaser of you into language study until hair turns gray." She takes the book back. "For now I shall help. Our discussion of Laotze shall be in American."

"So we're both teachers now? You teach China and Laotze, and I teach English-American language? Neither obeys the other?"

Her eyes twinkle, and she says, "Let us play the English and see where we go. I start with saying China is Confucius on surface and Laotze in heart. I say America is *yang* (male) and China is *yin* (female)." That almost-smile comes and goes. "Laotze speaks of *yin* as Mystic Female, Mother of All Things, Spirit of Valley, and he implies China is low country being Female of World. He says low country absorbs high country. Shall China absorb Japan? America?"

"Give me a week with Laotze, please, before you ask for thinking. I'll find an English version. Right now I'll talk feeling and say you're flying pretty high for a *yin*, acting more like a *yang*, and might get yourself absorbed by mistake."

I learn more and more clearly that Kathleen's a match for me mentally and as enduring physically, though only two-thirds my weight. Her fluency in English grows fast. I'm gaining in simple Chinese and increasing my vocabulary enough to extract meaning from the *Hsin Hua Rr Baow* that Feng lets me have instead of burning it. But I'll never be able to play Chinese as she plays English. One evening Kathleen picks up the picture of Barbara and the three children from my bureau. "Your wife is beautiful," she says, "and the children too." She especially likes the baby Laura, the face and head almost round, the hair no darker than the skin. "Little Miss Ball,"

Kathleen says. "Would your wife let me hold her in my arms, do you think?"

She doesn't wait for me to answer. Quickly we're back to Laotze, speaking American except when she's reading a poetic piece – or we branch into Chinese poetry in general, or painting, or calligraphy, or music, or Chinese drama – that Kathleen says I must attend sometime. I ask if she'll go to the drama with me and interpret. She looks at me somberly, and I at her, and the eyes hold with tongues silent until I feel tears pressing. I'm sure there's something like telepathy. I change the subject by reciting from the Lin Yutang translation of Laotze – "Nature is unkind! It treats the creation like sacrificial straw-dogs. The Sage is unkind; he treats the creation like sacrificial straw-dogs. How the universe is like a bellows! Empty, yet it gives a supply that never fails. The more it is worked, the more it brings forth..." Or she recites something in Chinese so fast I can't catch the words. And thus we glide back to the ground again, resuming discipline and the play with language – until near midnight.

Kathleen says in protest, "It is too late too soon." She puts her things into her bag. In the open doorway she pauses and looks back at me, pensive expression unchanging. I'm moving toward her when, without another word, she hurries off.

A half-hour early on Saturday evening Feng knocks and says, "Teacher come early." As when she first came, I arrange the room quickly before inviting her in. She isn't timid or defensive. She says, "I come early because must leave early. Is it all right? This night I stay at place of colleagues in city where all day tomorrow shall be chemistry discussions."

We gallop through the Chinese lessons and spend minimum time with the tea and dessert Feng brings. For the English, I reach into my not-so-long-ago past and tell Kathleen about Miss Shaw who believed plastics were replacing metal. "Perhaps your chemistry colleagues would be interested. Miss Shaw told me 'the Iron Age is past and steel is obsolete already except to injure and kill people.'

She said, 'Nearly every factory in the USA is a curio filled with curios. The most important duty for us is to keep our minds from becom- becoming curios too.'"

"Miss Shaw is bold," Kathleen says, "but I cannot say she is mistaken. I think little is yet known in China about the plastics. Perhaps when the war stops, I shall go to America to study them. Could I meet Miss Shaw, do you think?"

The plastics and Miss Shaw keep us animated, using fresh words, until ten-thirty. Kathleen says then, "It is, perhaps, 40 minutes of walking on remote trail that is too steep for ricksha – after which there is populated place with ricksha stand. The ricksha hurries downhill." She stands up to go.

"But the trail – can you follow it in the dark and the fog?"

"The trail I have not seen, but I have reliable direction."

"Does it go on the ridge above Chialing House Hotel and slant toward the Yangtze River?"

"How can you know?"

"I often walk on it in the dark after our lesson, while you're going to your dormitory. Almost no one uses it so late at night. May I guide you, Kathleen – as far as the ricksha stand?"

"I fear it is not proper, Da-wen." Yet she continues reading my face. Her eyes are magic. She says, "The trail will be invisible in foggy dark. Shall I not take ricksha, after all, though the road is four times farther."

"My feet know the trail," I say, "and I have a flashlight in my pocket." Below the stairs, across the street from the now-silent school at Litzepa, I take her hand and lead into an alleyway between bamboo shacks that are dark now. Soon there are no more shacks. The trail, maybe three feet wide, slants up the open slope, but we see only fog and each other and grass.

Kathleen's hand, small but strong in mine, stops me. "Let us look and listen," she says. "I feel we are in different world." The only sounds are from the distance ahead where city noises continue, though muffled. She lifts our joined hands into visibility between us. "The hands are alive with good feelings," she says. "I was lonely child and lonely student and have not experienced before."

We climb on. Where the trail steepens and could be slippery, our hands tighten together, but she's too quick and strong to let me pull any weight. "The handhold is guidance," she says, "not motor." At the steepest place, though, below the brow of the ridge, she lets me shift her left hand to my own left and allows my right hand to encircle her waist, steadying.

There's a flat space atop the ridge, and we stand resting. I release her, but she stays close. I hear her breathing. The fog becomes less dense, and I see her face looking up at me, not smiling but, I feel, sacredly luminescent shining on me. On impulse – that I doubt passes through my mind at all – I put hands on her shoulders lightly, bend my head forward and slowly touch her lips with mine, softly and only for a second.

She doesn't move. She's still looking up at me. She asks, "What is it you have done? What is the name in the English?"

"Kiss."

"I think kiss is not approved in China. I shall return it." She puts her hands on my shoulders, lifts her face to mine, and returns the kiss. The fog glows everywhere around us. The universe glows.

She takes my hand now and leads down the trail toward the ricksha stand. "The kisses are wonderfully sweet," she says. "I did not know. I did not imagine the miracle of them, though I have seen in American movies." The ricksha stand is much too close. Moving lights show through the moving fog. Kathleen asks, "Shall you be waiting for me Wednesday evening."

"Yes," I say, "yes, yes."

I walked back the trail to Litzepa school, then up it again, then down again to Litzepa and far up the Chialing past Kathleen's dormitory, almost to National Central University where I now had an important assignment – but for another time. Loving Barbara so much, loving our three children, having repeatedly assured Barbara of my everlasting love, I couldn't believe I felt powerful love for a different woman. I'd told Barbara I'd write to her everything of consequence that happened to me – unless it was something the army censor would pounce on.

A clever plan came to me. I could write honestly about my teacher and me, thus fulfilling my understanding with Barbara, then I could eliminate that part with scissors as if the censor had done it. That would be protecting Barbara. What kind of husband would be so cruel, anyway, as to tell his wife, whom he still intended to live with until death, that he also loved another woman?

I entered the FEA compound before even Feng was up. The first daylight was seeping through the fog. I threw cold water into my face. I shut my door and sat at the table with fountain pen and paper. I'd been writing long letters to Barbara on Sunday ever since I reached Chungking. I wrote – and rewrote – on that August 13, 1944, and, after all my scheming, simply couldn't censor it. I'm poor at tricks. I mailed the whole thing, then tore at myself day and night for stupidity. What she'd almost certainly conclude from my letter, assuming I was holding back, wouldn't even be true. I had no intention of having sexual intercourse with Kathleen, and she wouldn't allow it anyhow. I can't remember my exact words, and that letter is missing from the bundles Barbara saved and has lent me among other supporting papers while writing this book. But there's my next Sunday's letter:

> Darling Barbara, I don't know what you're thinking and feeling about me. My conscience is hurting... But mostly I long for you; I want to see you, to talk with you, to see how you feel, to ask you to keep loving me forever just as I will keep loving you forever...
>
> My teacher and I have been having classes twice a week as before, and we've been good. Miss Ho is by nature honest and good. She has never been intimate with a man. According to Chinese custom there can be only one man for a

woman... and she has better sense than to allow that one to be a foreigner and a married one at that. We've talked it all over frankly, and we're still friends...

I'm reporting an experience in the big wide world ...that I think is of interest to you regardless of the personal angle ...and I'm also telling you that I'm very, very lonely, that loneliness has soaked through me, has penetrated to the depths of me, and that if a fine girl smiles at me and is friendly to me I'll smile back and be friendly to her... I don't feel this is a reflection on you or on the lasting relationship between you and me.

Barbara's reactions began reaching me in late September. She'd welcome me home as soon as I could come.

Darwin, don't worry about the strain of your return. I will use all the patience, understanding, and love in my possession to keep you close to my heart, however changed you may *seem* to appear. Don't worry – you are terribly needed and grieved for. –Barbara

She enclosed this poem, copied in her handwriting:
SHAKESPEARE'S SONNET CXVI
Let me not to the marriage of true minds
Admit impediments. Love is not love
Which alters when it alteration finds,
Or bends with the remover to remove.
O, no! It is an ever fixed mark
That looks on tempests and is never shaken.
It is the star to every wandering bark,
Whose worth's unknown, although his height be taken.
Love's not Time's fool though rosy lips and cheeks
Within his bending sickle's compass come;
Love alters not with his brief hours and weeks,
But bears it out even to the edge of doom.
If this be error, and upon me prov'd,
I never writ, nor no man ever loved.

I answered that I'd known she was a great woman and I'd written believing she'd understand. I now reported:

> Chinese lessons this afternoon (Sunday) instead of last evening. My teacher is planning to take a competitive examination for scholarship in U.S. or Britain and is cramming for it, so between now and then (December) we'll have only one lesson a week. She wants further help from me in improving her English – but must mostly be examined in Chinese history and geography, Three People's Principles (as taught by Sun Yat-sen), and her technical subject – chemistry, both physical and analytical.

In another letter of this same tense period, I wrote Barbara:

> At present my little teacher is my close friend... Of all the people, men or women, I've known, only you and she seem to speak the same deeper language as I. If you were men ...you'd be my friends... Finally, life is – always is – a tragic thing – but it can be worthwhile most of the time.

Barbara wrote me in October: "I'm with you in all that you do and want you to know how much I love and admire you." She enclosed a friendly letter to be given to Miss Ho at our next lesson, wishing her luck with the examination and inviting her for a visit if she reaches America. Kathleen was as pleased as a child with Barbara's letter.

An opportunity comes for Kathleen and me to enjoy Chinese drama together. Tom Chi of our office invited me and three other Americans. I asked Kathleen to help interpret and bring a friend who might also help. Our party of seven is clustered on adjacent seats. I'm behind Kathleen, warm with teacher's pride at her fluency in keeping those closest to her informed about characters and plot. In the dark I give her congratulatory touches.

The play is "Muffled Thunder," adapted from the famous Chinese novel, *Red Chamber Dream*. Miss Ling and Bowyu Chia are in love. They meet in a garden-orchard and gather flowers. Peach petals fall on them. There's also a Miss Shih; she doesn't love Bowyu but wants to be his wife. Marriages are dictated by parents, with the young people often not sure who they're marrying. The protest of the young against the custom is the drama's muffled thunder.

The actors, make-up, costumes, Chinese furniture, and off-stage effects stretch and squeeze human emotions. I feel the thunder in my depths and hear its effects in Kathleen's voice. The wind is powerful inside us too. Miss Ling in her room hears the music of the impending wedding and assumes she's the lucky girl. One of the beautiful maids in the wealthy household finally tells her she is not. Cruelly shocked, she collapses into bed. Bowyu still thinks Miss Ling is his bride. She dies in her room during the ceremony. Too late, Bowyu discovers the veiled bride is really Miss Shih. The thunder and lightning are horribly realistic now, and persistent.

At our next lesson Kathleen and I talk in both Chinese and English about the drama and our own muffled thunder. We kiss gently to help subdue it, but it keeps on. We manage a shift from feeling to the technical aspects of drama, pretending we're playwrights or critics. She says my education can't be adequate until I've also seen the ancient style of Chinese drama.

Near the end of a later lesson, she gives me a ticket and instructions to come to a theater – which shall be our classroom a week hence. I'm to appear at the door ten minutes early, and if I see her I "must not speak or in any way recognize." Okay. I arrive as instructed and am ushered to a seat. Soon all nearby seats are taken except the one on my right.

As the drama begins, Kathleen is settling silently beside me. She leans away from me in her seat, so I lean a little away from her. When action grows strong on stage and dark surrounds us, I feel her hand at seat level. In secret I grasp it. We say nothing and don't look at each other. Our fingers communicate intensities of emotion.

Unlike "Muffled Thunder," so rich in costumes and stage settings, including heavy furniture, this long-ago version of "Lady Precious Stream" is austere. There's no stage scenery and almost no furniture. Two inconspicuous men carry things. One places cushions where actors are to kneel. The other lifts or tilts simple chairs to indicate an opening door. Both hold up a cloth archway with wooden frame to become a city gate for actors to pass through. The dialogue is in falsetto singing, reminding me of faraway sounds heard at night through my window at Litzepa, suggesting a fifth dimension, a lost, ghostly world.

Chungking changed. The drizzle no longer steamed; it chilled. We foreigners put on heavier pants and long-sleeved shirts, and I realized the overcoat I'd brought because it was a gift from my father-in-law could actually be needed. The fog, so rare and glowing the night I walked with Kathleen, turned heavy and long-lasting. The mud in the road varied from liquid to stiff paste, never freezing solid, though I saw frost once on the green-white cabbages that people found space for in already crowded places. FEA offices and dining room had coal stoves for heat, but bedrooms weren't heated. The other Americans didn't have classes or other non-bed uses for their rooms; they sat, drank and visited in the big living room near the dining room of the upper house.

I'd bought a Chinese brazier (*huobun*) with personal money. On Saturday I asked the house coolie to kindle the charcoal and bring the *huobun* after the glowing coals no longer smoked. Kathleen came wearing a gray quilted gown that ended just inches from the floor. She said, "*Tien leng liaow* (cold outside)," words we'd had no previous occasion to practice. Her mood for a while matched the weather. She stood close to the heat and rotated to get warm. I helped when she faced outward, taking one cold hand in each of my warm ones. We needed no discussion of the ancient drama, though we'd said not a word while watching. Its message was simple and strong – and somber – yet also wonderful.

"Your eyes transmit beauty, Kathleen," I said.

She blinked and gave an oblique answer, "It is not solely from wish to teach Chinese and learn English that I come to you through cold and mud, Da-wen." I squeezed her hands, and she added, "Your remembering the *huobun* warms spirit as well as body. Tonight's lesson shall be the shopping for food. You must learn fair prices and the art of haggling. Our next lesson shall be the cooking and eating together." Her half-smile flickered now.

The next Saturday also she was chilled but not somber. She saw the groceries on the table and the bright charcoal, and she laughed and teased. "You do look starved, Da-wen," she said. "I'm starved too. But important things come first." She locked her hands behind my neck and lifted her mouth to mine. The touch was light, but the sensation lingered and grew after she'd turned to her knitted bag and the food basket.

She'd brought an iron basin, a board, a sharp knife (*tao li*), and spices. She handed me board and knife to cut the pork into tiny pieces – "quickly but not including fingers, which would spoil flavor." With the tongs she arranged the charcoal, then put the basin with pork where the glowing mass was thin. She stirred continually, and she added vegetables as I cut them up. I remember both resisting and welcoming tear-pressure caused by this flesh-and-blood woman cooking for us both – after so long a lack of this phenomenon in my life. But I don't remember how she converted the wheat flour I'd bought into firm dough as a flat sheet that I think she called *mien paow*. She detached fragments of the hot mass and wrapped them in sheets of *mien paow*.. "They are *paow-dze* now," she said. "Easy to prepare and to eat with fingers."

After eating *paow-dze* we drank tea and sampled fruits and nuts. Later, she sang a Chinese love song – for educational purposes, of course. "It is about lovers under peach tree with petals falling," she said. "*Nee dee-ee shoong-roong...*" Her voice was high, though not falsetto as in the ancient drama. It soared in the melody, though, in what I guess was a minor key, filled with joy yet aware of sorrow, the song like nature, loving yet with tragedy lurking, like fate, like the sighing and moaning of wind. When she repeated, I sang to her, mastering the melody but faking the words. Again the peach petals fell upon us. And her eyes and my eyes sent unnamed appeals through held-back tears.

"You don't hide Barbara's picture," Kathleen said. "I think it is like Chinese wife and concubine. I think I do not steal love that was Barbara's. Love of her keeps living in you, and our love is new, additional, not taking away. I dream – but do not think – when war is over and peace has come – we – perhaps – could have –   I dream of a 'Little Miss Ball' or a 'Boy Ball' of my own – but it is not now, perhaps never."

"Who can tell?" I said, holding both of her hands. Then, shifting focus, "You must take better care of yourself, Kathleen. You shouldn't struggle to your dormitory in this drizzle and mud. Stay the night safe and warm with me."

"Safe? There shall not be the sexual intercourse – is this right or not?"

"I promise – if you help. We may kiss as we choose – anywhere, everywhere – but always stop when one of us signals stop."

She tightened the pressure of her hands in mine and said, "I promise and agree."

We went out together onto the porch. Through the foggy dark we could hear the other Americans at the upper house, their voices strong with drink. Any servants not yet asleep would be up there too. No one would be outside in the continuing drizzle. I led Kathleen back into my room.

I felt that night and during the following months that all the earth, including China, was my home. Though we never let ourselves consider sexual intercourse, we felt joined forever, living in relation to each other. This living – as Laotze might have said of it – was deep in the human ocean, deeper than the merely physical way, the intellectual way, or even the way of emperors.

Chapter 13 – Barbaria in the Blue Ridge 1945-49

Barbara and I together "designed" a stone house on a hill with natural scenery all around. In the earliest years of our marriage, when driving near the Blue Ridge, we'd point out sites and ask each other for comments. Barbara's sites were a mile or less from town. Mine were farther out where ridges were tall and the forest continuous.

Barbara's letter of February 15, 1944, to me in Chungking, told about a party for Sylvia's third birthday and added:

> I love to celebrate, Darwin. I love people – being hostess and saying something to everyone present to make them feel good – but on the other hand I also like to divorce the public and live just with my family and the everyday tasks ...This idea is as strong in me as in you.

The next significant discussion was in an October letter to her (three months after my Kathleen confession):

> It's true as we've said that we don't need to build for years... but if we can't now save a substantial amount toward the cost I don't know whether we ever will... When I quit this job, I'm going to want to write, and it may be many years, maybe forever, before I again make as much income.

Different futures seemed possible. The dream of a China-wide magazine – originated by Joe Chu and me – was being talked about in Chinese universities and business circles. Joe said his wealthy family would provide the capital, millions of US dollars. Americans would be involved partly because American businesses would buy much of the advertising space. I was to find the American manufacturer who, as soon as the war ended, would quickly produce the most efficient press for printing 200,000 magazines per week in full color. I'd also recruit an experienced American editorial advisor.

For my help I'd receive substantial stock and would delve into basic problems and give both editorial and business advice, dividing my time between America and China. The magazine plan had brought critical comments in Kathleen's delicate but strong handwriting – handed to me instead of spoken, for a more lasting impression, I guess:

> Joe Chu is a good companion to play with but not a good friend to co-operate with... If you want to have your own business in China, I would suggest you shall try to find a job in China and during working here you study Chinese and gradually get acquainted with people, society, place, and everything... I always think you can be an expert on problems of China... You are like a Chinese, so you can understand, and besides you sympathize China, and like China. But don't think you have enough knowledge already now!

Barbara, after seeing a newsreel in February 1945, wrote me:

> Do you think China might be the real purpose of our lives, Darwin? I saw Chungking – the steps from the river, the big junks on the river, the coolies carrying and heaving and ho-ing, the lumbering sail flopping backwards with the turning of the boat, and I saw those leaders who are running China... I want to be with you, Darwin, and feel as you do about these people. Is there anything in America as worth our lives?

I wrote Barbara that we'd talk at length while I was home, and at last I could reveal the time, July 1945. My authorization from FEA headquarters was to "travel by air from Chungking to Washington – to consult with FEA officials... concerning the port program – and to travel by air back to Chungking." Allied forces were expected to take seaports from the Japanese and use them to supply everything the Chinese needed to push enemy forces out.

I'm flying home in memory reel, traveling light. Only after my assignment in Chungking is completed will I pack all my belongings there. I'm quickly over the Hump into India and across to Karachi. Here I stall in a flow of colonels and generals with higher priorities. The airport is surrounded by desert. I'm assigned a bunk in a vast room where other passengers also wait, day and night. I write to Kathleen and to Barbara. I feel marooned; my letters may reach Barbara before I do.

I walk alone before the sun gets dangerous, noticing, as I did long ago under Dad's guidance, how people work with nature to survive. These people seem more Arab than India "Indian"; they're nomadic, herding cattle and goats. Herdsmen wear tight turbans and loose clothing that blows in the wind. The women are veiled; I want to see under the veils. Camels are numerous – caravans transporting merchandise or individual camels pulling rubber-tired wagons.

I walk at night too. The moon approaches full and plays peek-a-boo among sparse clouds. A native man is driving a cow and new-born calf. I understand from long ago and far away. I report to Barbara I'm reading Thomas Wolfe's *You Can't Go Home Again* and getting laughed at by new friends who know how hard I'm trying to go home. I'm really coming, I assure Barbara, but days later I'm still stalled. I spend hours at the edge of the airport, writing and sketching a camel browsing on a rare desert tree and a man riding a long-eared donkey so small he might crush it.

> The wind blows and blows, Barbara, the airplane motors roar and roar, I read and read and think and sleep and eat and write and read and long for you and sleep and crunch sand and take showers and wash my socks or shorts and ask when I might go, and eat and read and watch camp movies and sit on the edge of my bed.

An opening comes – with half an hour to get on board carrying my baggage. I really fly now, losing track of time. The desert slides backward under me – no ocean, though we must come close. We swoop down at Tehran and lift off again, roaring through the night. I sleep in my seat. The pilot wakes everyone by saying it's midnight over Jerusalem. I see lights down there and watch tenaciously, trying to believe the Resurrection.

We land at a Cairo airport, and I'm guided to a bunk within a hundred yards of the plane. At first daylight, we're off again, soaring out from a cliff over the muddy Nile River and crowded buildings – but also agricultural land with people working by hand. We circle and climb and almost hit the Sphinx and three pyramids of Gizeh. Later, we're over the Libyan desert, and I think it's not so dry. Give me a tract, and I'll make a living on it.

We see the colorful Mediterranean, maybe Khalij Surf. We land near Algiers but aren't allowed off the plane. We land at Casablanca by the Atlantic Ocean, and tomorrow's the Fourth of July. Along with friends (met since we took off from Cairo), I try to celebrate at a busy hotel, while also checking hourly for the latest about our plane. We fly again. We're at the Azores briefly and, I think, on Nova Scotia, before landing at New York – two weeks en route including delay at Karachi, compared with 11 weeks to Chungking in 1943. Exact names of places and races don't cling in me now. I feel I know what humans are like – they're like me – and as long as I'm on the same planet I know the places too – they're like Earth.

Barbara was beautiful as always when I found her at the Canandaigua railroad station. We were hungry for each other and hungry to play together with our children. Harvey and Sylvia remembered me but were timid and looked to their mother as the person who'd stayed in touch with me. They came into my arms slowly one at a time. I lifted each and hugged as long as they'd hold still or hug back. Laura, who couldn't remember me directly, was the most confident; she'd imagined Daddy exactly as Mother told her I'd be. Lifted, she kept cuddling.

All three listened with me when Barbara demonstrated parts of what she'd learned in piano lessons. We five sang familiar songs. We went out in the dark and found familiar constellations. I told them I'd seen the same stars from China on the opposite side of the round Earth. Love-making was as mutually urgent and wonderful as before China. Next day all five of us worked together in the yard and garden. Harvey climbed a tree, showing me his progress.

My time in the United States was over-committed. FEA orders were to fly to Washington and confer, so I spent days doing that. Also, not officially, I was to make contacts in New York for the China magazine. Still further, I wanted to discover scholarships or part-time jobs that could enable Kathleen to become a graduate student in America. Barbara and I went by train to New York City. Between printing press and advertising and editorial contacts, we hoped to attend plays and concerts. I remember the immense white rabbit, "Harvey," who was invisible.

On the roaring streets, we kept hearing newsboys shouting strange syllables. I had no time for news, but the syllables repeated, repeated, and while we were eating a steak-house dinner we bought a paper. An "atom bomb" had erased Hiroshima! Even inside government, I'd never heard a whisper of "atom bomb." We read with escalating urgency. A hundred thousand people, the news seemed to say, had been killed by one American bomb. A mysterious cloud resembling a deadly mushroom had grown quickly over the wiped-out city. The world could never be the same again; our children would grow up in conditions we couldn't imagine.

Hidden in my own mind, suppressed there for weeks, a special fear gnawed: The atom bomb will end the war; our FEA program will end too; the Generalissimo and Mao Tse-tung may be at each other's throats; Kathleen's employment at Chungking may end and unpredictable events may sweep her elsewhere; she and I may never find each other again. My FEA contact in Washington knew only what was in the papers. I was called back to headquarters to sit at a desk with a phone but had no work. After several days they let me loose. I could be in New York or Washington but must phone in every morning.

Immediate action on the China magazine might bring quick and great success. Friends in Washington told me William Ashley

Anderson, a top writer and editor I'd admired (*Reader's Digest*, *Saturday Evening Post*, etc.) might be available. He'd already had China experience. Now, his wartime assignment, like mine, wouldn't last. I phoned and next day lunched with him. He was keenly interested in our *CHINESE LIFE*. He said Henry Luce of America's *LIFE* and Barclay Acheson of *Reader's Digest* were rumored to be "thinking China." I telegraphed both.

Acheson – linked into the *Digest's* owning family as well as into the corporation – invited me to Pleasantville. Already publishing in many languages, the *Digest* was, of course, interested in China and wanted to talk cooperation. First, he showed me the magazine's offices and introduced editors at their desks. A music-selection professional was studying results from a just-installed over-all music system. Nearly all the editorial people believed music improved both quality and quantity of their work. Classical music was tentatively preferred. Words in the music were, of course, taboo where listeners were working with words. Another bit of trivia was Acheson's revelation about proofreading. Every issue was proofread by 18 different readers, yet there'd never been an issue in which typographical errors weren't found after the printing and distribution.

Acheson and I agreed the number of magazine readers in China would start low, but we only teased each other with numbers. I had in mind our Chungking-Shanghai group's study by National Central University "for a popular illustrated weekly in postwar China" – considering personal income and results of the government-accelerated literacy push – that had projected 200,000. And another approach in which the university people had listed known numbers of students, in secondary and higher education, as approximately 1,074,000, of teachers as approximately 500,000, of members of other groups expected to read as approximately 1,600,000, then, after sampling, concluded no more than 5% of the 3,174,000 total would "be able to purchase a copy of our weekly." So the maximum would be about 158,700 regular readers in the early stages.

Twenty top editors lunched with me in a conference room. The air buzzed with China and literacy and the urgent need of a new democracy, freedom for newspapers, magazines, and broadcast journalism to inform the citizens. During the afternoon Acheson and I intensified discussion in offices involved with foreign editions. There was general – and open – agreement that no magazine of interest to the *Digest* or to my group was possible without a strong Chinese government giving firm assurance there'd be no political censorship. Further advances in China by communists would "cancel us out." I didn't mention that Chiang Kai-shek – according to Joe Chu – had assured the Chu family he wanted our magazine published.

Kathleen still doubted the Chu family, though wealthy enough, would ever actually provide the capital. As my teacher, she felt responsible for keeping me realistic. For weeks she'd been studying magazines published in China. She wrote:

> Illiterates in China are more than 80%. In recent years the government has enthusiastically promoted a literacy movement, the effect of which, nevertheless, is little. Even if some people have learned many words, to read magazines is difficult for them...
>
> The second difficulty is the poverty. All day and night they strive only for their mouths, so few can have leisure, free mind, and money to spend. We cannot expect a starving person to sacrifice clothes and food for reading... Lots of professors and government employees, supposed to have better income than most people, now have only porridge as main meal.
>
> As to the censorship... being used by officials to control the thought of people, the government has announced it will be abolished when the war is over. I hope this action will be real but cannot feel confident.

Kathleen summarized *West Wind* first, because "it is translating the essence of foreign magazines" and "introducing the lives of Europeans and Americans." She felt it tried harder to entertain than to inform. It presents "new and strange things... even if nonsense." She'd showed me a *West Wind* in Chungking, and I'd asked Joe Chu his opinion. He'd scribbled this memo:

> (1) *West Wind* lacks editorial content about international and national politics and economics that people want to know. (2) It just introduces the west wind but does not relate it with Chinese. (3) We want equal part of our new magazine to be about the Chinese. (4) We want to put in pictures. (5) We want our magazine to give hope and spirit.

Kathleen was trying to correlate the kind of reader appeal with the success or failure of Chinese magazines – e.g.:

> *Hope* is a literature magazine but almost like a generalizing one... The weight of writings on various subjects is rather heavy, and they are mostly of criticism and sarcasm... If someone can aim to whip the dark out of the society, certainly it can inspire the excitement and sympathy...but the *Hope* essay part seems too much for general readers to accept.

Before visiting *Reader's Digest* I'd had such preliminary comments about 11 magazines. After *Hope* came *World Wind*, initiated years before by Lin Yutang but recently slipping in quality and sales. Then *Writings of Universe*, "imitating the *Reader's Digest*" – at first "a lot of readers" but soon fading. Kathleen commented:

> Our photograph-featuring magazine would differ from all other Chinese magazines and certainly would stir up the talk. But the problems of economics, the mechanics of production and distribution, and the freedom to publish as you please will not disappear and could become fatal.

The news is loud with the war's ending: August 6, 1945, atom bomb wipes out Hiroshima. August 9, atom bomb explodes on Nagasaki, vast destruction. August 14, Japanese announce surrender.

August 27, U.S. Forces land in Japan. September 2, Japanese sign surrender documents on battleship *Missouri*. September 5, Chinese government and communists compete in accepting surrender of Japanese inside China.

Generalissimo Chiang appears weaker than communist leader Mao Tse-tung. Communication with Joe Chu ceases; our China magazine is dead. I have to write and tell Kathleen I can't now return to China, and I must hide from Barbara the devastation inside me that my letter (must send!) will duplicate in Kathleen. After final settlement with FEA, I'll have resources to support my family through fall and winter – trying freelance writing at Canandaigua – and enough more to resettle us in Virginia come spring.

I feel I have a wealth of prime new material for freelancing. Though I'm not yet a China expert, I have capable Chinese on my team – by mail if the mail continues – Kathleen first, then Ernest Fan, a well-educated friend now with China Merchants Steam Navigation Co., Shanghai. They'll research as I suggest after I've visited with editors. I'll produce final drafts, and we'll divide the magazines' checks. Surely, I tell myself, after America's long struggle in the Orient and the victory following revelation of earth-shaking atomic energy over there, American readers will eat up both short pieces and books about China.

My agent in New York is soon offering a 4,000-word piece I call "The Mystic Female: An Impression of China." Also, "The American Who Broke the Chinese Canes – and Saved a Railroad." I'm also offering a newspaper column, "Getting Oriented," using 800-word samples I've written. But week after week there are no results. Editors like the writing but don't see the subject as "compelling." I've sent two short stories direct to *Harper's* and *Atlantic Monthly*. If *Harper's* rejects "Men May Come," I'll send it to *Atlantic*. If *Atlantic* rejects "The Parachute," I'll send it to *Harper's*. But when they dawdle, then reject the same day, I change plan and send both stories to *Story*. The editor Whit Burnett writes me they tantalize him but aren't sophisticatedly subtle enough for his magazine. He wonders, though, if I'd like to write a book. He and Dial Press want a novel of World War II in China.

I'm still overflowing with the surging life of Chungking and feeling what I believe Laotze felt – the Tao, the way, the flow of humanity along the course of the universe – *nature*. I'll present an American protagonist, an exaggeration of myself, following the Laotzean way of nature through personal experience and through science, including at University of Chicago an early stage of the atom bomb project, from which he fled in disapproval. He achieves harmony in depth with a Chinese woman who's also following the way of nature (instinctually but also by studying Laotze). Through diverse adventures the hero and heroine become "Earth citizens" symbolizing the oneness of humankind. En route to Tokyo on a secret mission, to prevent explosion of an atom bomb, the hero is caught and imprisoned at the Hiroshima army base. He dies in the atom bombing, and the heroine tries to use his death to help establish lasting peace everywhere on Earth.

I write three sample chapters and a synopsis. Whit Burnett and an associate work with me. We have long conferences in New York City to "improve" my writing. They shake their heads over the new drafts - "Too coarse-grained." I try again but still can't be "fine-grained" enough. I'm interested in the big things more than in precious sensitivity. I feel the drama is in all humans trying to become one humanity. Two outcomes seem equally possible – (1) destruction of the civilized world with possible extinction of the human species, or (2) human cooperation with the universe, its endless creativity enhanced through science, which is research into reality, which is nature – all protected through world law.

I feel I can involve readers in their own greatest adventure through developing American and Chinese characters relating their lives and loves and strivings to world destiny. But after several months I give up on Whit Burnett at the same time he gives up on me.

At Thanksgiving time, part of me froze as with oncoming winter when I began receiving letters Kathleen had written during the last week in October. Though we'd never supposed we'd live together, we'd relied on seeing and touching each other from time to time. Lying awake thinking of Kathleen, I'd keep trying to lie still and not disturb Barbara. She was kind; she didn't scold when letters came from Kathleen.

In September, Kathleen had been visiting her family's native city far southeast of Chungking. She'd given me an address there, and I'd written. She didn't get that letter, I guessed; hers of October 21, from Chungking, didn't mention it. She'd been called back to the ordnance agency, that hadn't moved eastward as expected. She'd been sick. She spoke of "the long painful days I have spent hour by hour as if year by year." With my father's co-operation, I'd earlier arranged for her to do graduate work at the University of Utah, living with American families who spoke only English so she'd get endless practice. She'd thanked me but said she wouldn't be allowed by the government to come unless (1) invited by a job of some importance or (2) awarded a scholarship. "Please try for me to find the suitable scholarship," she'd written. Meanwhile, she'd prepare for the next Chinese government foreign-student examination.

I'd sent her small packages and asked what she'd really like most from America. She'd declined anything for pleasure, but the first October letter suggested "some strong hypnotic medicine," and the letter two days later explained, "The doctor said I need hypnotic medicine to make me sleep quiet." Friends tried to buy it for her in downtown Chungking, without success, so, "May I ask you to buy several bottles and send to me as soon as possible?"
After two more days she wrote again – a rending scream, as I felt it, in the Earthwide dark:

> It seems I have lots to tell you. While holding the pen, I cannot write them... What is the use to tell anything again now? ... I have bought 42 kinds of magazines since July, read one

by one and got a sketch of them... But now the war is over ...the condition is changed. The good also brings desperate misery...

The darkness! The hopelessness! And the painfulness! With tears to wash face every day, I have spent all these days. And the same will be the days which I shall spend too. I looked at the poison. I walked by the river-side again and again. Poison is so bitter and the vast water is so fearful. Both are so terrible. How can I do with my own hand? But the other side will be the terribly long painful days to go through.

Da-wen ...can we look in eyes and touch ever again? Will you always remember the singing, "I wandered today to Litzepa, Kathleen, to watch the scene below ... Where we sat so long, long ago..."?

Early in November, I learned later, she wrote to the business manager who was closing out the FEA occupancy at Litzepa, asking that my personal typewriter, that I'd given her, be released to the messenger she was sending. On November 15 she wrote me again, asking if I'd mailed the hypnotic drug – "Don't forget or delay to mail. I am waiting for that day and night." But maybe, I almost had to feel, she was getting past the deepest crisis. Though she wrote, "My mind is terribly confused just like the confusion of the political situation here," she added:

> If I can concentrate my mind, I shall study again – special science courses and English. Thanks for your having helped my English... Someday I will try to write compositions and mail to you for correction... Maybe I shall find a job in Shanghai.

Barbara asked why I continued so restless, and I showed her Kathleen's letters about the hypnotic drug. Her opinion bolstered mine – Don't send any (and thereby, maybe, approve suicide). In my letters to Kathleen I emphasized my belief we'd meet again, either in China where I'd find a fitting position, or in America where she'd have a scholarship. But not granting her one specific request was – and is – an unending torture inside me.

Barbara was living up to her promise to love me with all my problems. We worked congenially together. We'd take turns reading to the children and, after they were asleep, we'd read aloud to each other. But, day or night, I couldn't forget Kathleen and couldn't feel comfortable in Canandaigua. It was an old New England-type town with elite, churchly families. The Closses had standing, but I had none, not even a job, and no meaningful successes in freelance writing. My day with Barclay Acheson and top editors of *Reader's Digest* had given me respect for a week only.

A letter from newspaperman Ed Lauck, former printer for the Shenandoah Nature Society and The Lambert Co., began carrying us back to old Virginia. Lauck wanted to publish (finance and sell, not just print) a new guidebook to Shenandoah National Park. I went to Luray for discussions - and to renew the search for our long-dreamed home. I approved Lauck's basic idea for a guidebook that he'd wholesale for 75 cents and retail for $1.50, thus giving the park concessioner a profit justifying feature display in all business developments along Skyline Drive. I was glad to be free of the selling task. But I quarreled with his plan to have our writing and art "polished" by an advertising agency.

I bought a second-hand Dodge and went exploring around the fringes of the great park I'd known so well in what now seemed a far-back, previous life. No sky-palace of Hepburn caliber seemed possible for us now, but tentative scouting confirmed we could afford scenic land with a habitable house. Someone mentioned that Lewis Willis, one of the elderly persons allowed to live out their lives inside the park, wanted a tenant to occupy his home while he worked in towns outside the park to replenish his bank account. The Willis house, I remembered, could hold the five of us, and if we moved to his place Barbara could help choose the site for the permanent home we were now calling "Barbaria."

The springtime of 1946 comes back to me vividly. Lewis Willis is a genuine mountain man, yet educated at the University of Virginia and at age 80 still studying. He meets us where his old dirt road intersects US 211. A car will come in half an hour to pick him up; he'll spend April through July working outside, and he'll return, he says, at 9 a.m. on August 1 to resume possession. Barbara admires him instantly. He's lived alone a year now since the death of his wife Ida, who'd attended Smith College in Massachusetts (serendipity to Barbara). As we enter his yard, he tells about bulbs Ida planted along the walkway.

"We'll cherish them," Barbara says. Beside the house the forsythia is already bright yellow, and we call it "for Sylvia," and Sylvia, five years old, dances beside it. Harvey, 18 months older, is more dignified – but not for long. As soon as the car picks up Mr. Willis, Harvey is splashing in the nearby creek. Laura is in the house with us but wanders out when we aren't looking. The house is cleaned in a man's way. Paths are swept everywhere but bordered by stacks of magazines, bulletins, and letters – with a heavy book on each stack to hold down loose pieces.

I spend little time at the Willis place. In the mornings I make sure there's firewood, then I'm off to find "Barbaria." When there's a likely prospect, I show it to the whole family. The naturally watered land, everywhere greening with spring, reaches out for us. We almost buy 12 acres, accessible by public road, in Jewell Hollow, two miles below the Willis place. But the park's blacksmith Ernest Miller, my friend when I was a ranger, tells me a house I'd discovered and admired before Pearl Harbor, a mile up-hollow from his farm, is vacant now. Quickly that old picture glows again in my mind; it's the log cabin in a wild canyon by a dashing creek that I've dreamed "forever."

The sun is shining when I drive the family up the mile of dirt-and-rock road (no public maintenance). The springtime color and the creek are superb, but the house shocks us. Nobody's lived here recently. All the doors and windows are gone, stolen. Cattle have broken through the kitchen floor. Clay-lime mortar is loose between the broad-ax-hewn logs. But even as we moan, we glory in the views. From window openings on all four sides, we see peaks of the national park. And within six steps from the kitchen door, eternal water flows. I bring a tin cup, fill it from the spring, and give it to Barbara. She sips and smiles and says, "This house is rich in character, but isn't it too old?"

Ernest Miller suggests Tom Jewell as the expert on log houses. When we bring him, he looks and thumps, listens, stomps and tugs as if trying to wreck the building. After one last stomp, his 70-year-old face takes on an expression of joy. He says, "I remember this house when I was a kid. If you pitch in and help, we'll have 'er fixed up better'n new inside three months." Barbara and I blink at each other, and she says, "It's awfully remote, darling."

"Yes," I say, squeezing her hand. "*Wonderfully* remote too." I keep her hand, and we stroll toward the creek. Stopping at the edge, watching the water dance over sun-gold rocks, we listen to creek-music, then we read each other's eyes. "I'll be happy living with you here in the wilderness, darling," she says, "if you'll take me out to church on Sunday mornings."

At eight a.m. next day I pick up Tom Jewell in the old Dodge, now nicknamed "The Weep." It has a wooden truck-bed for hauling tools and supplies. We spend the day planning, measuring. Tom says he'll remember everything we decide, but I make notes anyway – rough lumber from a portable sawmill more fitting and less costly than planed lumber; old-time windows still findable; make our own style of windows for kitchen and upstairs hall, get glass cut the size we want; bricklayer's mix with sand okay for "daubing" logs.

Tom isn't bothered by corners that aren't square. He holds a board in place and marks, puts it on the sawhorse and saws. He works deliberately, with full concentration, for an hour or more, then startles me by dropping a board or a tool and shouting, "Wheeeee!" –

which means, Let's have some coffee. Windows and doors are in; a new stairway to the second floor is rising.

I deal with the log walls, working like a dentist, scraping out everything soft or loose, then filling with the mortar mixed as Tom prescribes. Aided by how-to books and advice from qualified friends, I wire the house for electricity and paint the metal roof to stop rust. On schedule, the house is a success – except we run out of funds and time without the plumbing to bring water from the spring. We're packed to move in – and are just leaving the Willis place at nine o'clock August 1 when Mr. Willis arrives to resume possession of his house, exactly as he said he would.

"Barbaria" was more in the pattern of forsythia (for Sylvia) than hinting uncivilized, yet there was recognition of shared nature-romanticism along with the salute to Barbara. I wasn't then consciously analyzing man-and-nature relations or consciously seeing humankind inside nature. I was semi-desperately occupied otherwise. Half-consciously maybe I was re-creating my boyhood – relating to wild creatures, bringing in firewood for a black cooking range, glorying in Earth's continuing gift of flowing water, planning food production from fertile soil – also, the old part, as agreed anew, of driving out on Sunday, from Barbaria to Morning Star Lutheran, the nearest church.

I bought a Jersey cow who reminded me of my long-ago "Old Sweetie." She wandered but always came when called with a loud "Hi-yo-o-o, Quee-ee-nie!" Once we were all outside eating doughnuts when she arrived. I didn't have the usual bran to reward her coming, so I offered a doughnut, which she eagerly ate. Barbara and the kids scolded me for treating her as one of the family, which I felt she was.

Dad came from Salt Lake and spent August 19-24 with us. We had a great visit and upon reaching home he wrote:

> You and your wife are the highest type of American manhood and womanhood. I am sure that you live by faith and optimistic endeavor and not by anxiety and drudgery... You have

your eyes on the mountaintops and ere long you will find yourselves on a hill of security and satisfaction ...and climbing higher.

It was the last time we'd see Dad, and after he died I realized he'd been moving toward my view of nature and supposing I'd moved toward his view of church. I didn't disillusion him. I felt keenly our failure to find a "redbird" that he'd wanted to see – though we'd searched all those five days where cardinals usually lived. I wrote a short story based on this quest relating to nature and church. The words still hurt when I reread them.

Recognizing our somewhat distant connection with human society, I put up a mile of telephone wire, fastening it on glass insulators ten feet up on tree trunks. Our phone was a magneto-type with a crank, and we could hear other subscribers talking. I pruned the most promising fruit trees, put up a privy near an old cherry tree, cut and carried firewood for a wood-or-coal circulating heater that kept us from freezing in winter. Come spring, I dug, and Barbara and I planted, a vegetable garden back of the house.

We liked the people we met at church. Possibly because of my carrying voice, I was asked to substitute as Sunday School superintendent. Barbara and the children persuaded me to become a Lutheran with them, and I was made regular superintendent. I stood up in front and read the appropriate words, and the congregation responded as the book decreed. It was a pleasant social function but bothered me as I couldn't fully believe the words.

My writing place was a table in our front room beside the fireplace. Theoretically, the open fire helped me dream up good fiction. Though not currently in touch with publishers or agents, I still had faith in the Earth-citizenship-atom bomb novel. The three chapters were insufficient to show the full idea and the vivid setting and activity of China. I must write the whole thing.

When I said in a letter to Kathleen that the theme was Earth citizenship, she said *she'd* carried out that assignment she gave *me*, to investigate that "Earth meeting" at National Central University, near Chungking. Chinese and Americans together had organized there to support the United Nations and enforce world peace. I followed through eagerly now and learned that Colonel M. Thomas Tchou of China and America was full-time executive of an active World Citizenship Movement headquartered at Oberlin, Ohio. I remembered I'd entered a peace-advocacy campaign way back in 1936 – favoring world federation. In a gathering of friends at Barbaria, we organized a Shenandoah World Citizenship Council to bolster peacekeeping through Earth-wide law.

Col. Tchou came as our house guest and lectured superbly on world citizenship. Without notes, he held 200 people seriously listening for an hour, then answered questions. Many joined our council. Soon we were working out a sister-town relationship with Luray, France, also inviting atomic scientists and others to give world citizenship programs in various Shenandoah communities. I started copying into my working files my choice quotes with one-earth thinking. Here's **Whitman**:

> Smile O voluptuous cool-breathed earth!
> Earth of the slumbering and liquid trees! ...
> The earth is rude, silent, incomprehensible at first,
> Nature is rude and incomprehensible at first,
> Be not discouraged, keep on, there are divine things well
>   envelop'd,
> I swear to you there are divine things more beautiful than
> words can tell...
> The main shapes arise! ...
> Shapes ever projecting other shapes,
> Shapes of turbulent manly cities,
> Shapes of the friends and home-givers of the whole earth,
> Shapes bracing the earth and braced by the whole earth...
> As in a waking vision,
> E'en while I chant I see it rise, I scan and prophesy outside
>   and in,
> Its manifold ensemble...

Here's **Laotze** from the other side of the planet – words that tease me mightily, though I can't claim to understand them (they just seem to hint right):

> When the people of the Earth all know beauty as beauty,
> There arises the recognition of ugliness.
> When the people of the Earth all know good as good,
> There arises the recognition of evil...
>
> How the universe is like a bellows!
> Empty, yet it gives a supply that never fails;
> The more it is worked, the more it brings forth.
> By many words is wit exhausted,
> Rather, therefore, hold to the core...
> He who knows the Eternal Law is tolerant;
> Being tolerant, he is impartial;
>
>> Being impartial, he regards the world as one...
>> Being in accord with Nature, he is in accord with Tao;
>> Being in accord with Tao, he is eternal,
>> And his whole life is preserved from harm.
>
> There are those who will conquer the world
> And make of it what they conceive or desire.
>> I see they will not succeed...
>
>> He who delights in slaughter
>> Will not succeed in his ambition to rule
>>   the world...
>> The slaying of multitudes should be mourned
>>   with sorrow;
>> A victory should be celebrated with the
>>   Funeral Rite.
>
> He who values the world as his self
> May then be entrusted with the government of the world;
> And he who loves the world as his self –
> The world may then be entrusted to his care...

There was one by **Alfred Tennyson** too, but I can't remember the "dream," and I must have given away that English literature book: Earth-protective "police" flying far to maintain peace (??).

Evidence of our Earth-citizenship work helped revive Kathleen's hope of studying in America. We learned of "Barbour Scholarships for Oriental Women" to be awarded by the University of Michigan. Food, lodging and other essentials would be covered. I obtained and sent application blanks to Kathleen and wrote a recommendation confirming her ability and perseverance. Her morale seemed strong on December 8, 1946, when she acknowledged a letter in which I'd described autumn at our home in the Blue Ridge. She commented:

> A fine country life appears before my eyes – which I have seen in the color moving pictures. Blue sky with white cloud, a garden full of vegetables and flowers... a beautiful wooden house set in the scene and arranged with cement mortar in all the cracks to make it perfect... It is a place to be found only in fairyland – or in old art – or in words of Laotze. Do you not think so?

She enclosed an able composition in English describing the postwar revival of her parents' home town – even as the Chiang-Mao "civil war engulfs North China" and spreads southward. She was pleased that this city "still keeps the plainness and sincerity of a farming community. We can't find the cunning and sophistication of a big city here."

By the end of 1946, letters had stopped coming from two people in China I'd been corresponding with – Tom Chi and Ernest Fan. I told myself the cause was the advance of communism. Even if not harmed by Mao Tse-tung's forces, my friends might be acting out no-contact-with-Americans in self-defense. I received this brief letter in April 1947 from the University of Michigan:

> We regret to inform you that your protegee, Miss Kathleen Chao-ye Ho, was not appointed a Barbour Scholar for 1947-48. Formal notice to this effect has already been sent to her.

I wrote her and said don't be upset, there are other possibilities. But no answer came. Kathleen's beautiful, so-condensed handwriting never graced our mail again. She might have been isolated by communist agents. I kept telling myself she was finding a good life without me to complicate it. But I didn't – and still don't – know.

I kept working regularly on freelance writing. Barbara made numerous sketches and watercolors of the scenery. All five of us enjoyed watching and hearing the many birds, learning wildflowers and tree species. Our youngest became "Mountain Laura" for mountain laurel, balancing forsythia "for Sylvia." Our garden was repeatedly productive, as was the old orchard, and in the summer of 1947 we entertained a "Fresh Air Kid" from New York City, a boy about Harvey's age, for two strenuous weeks.

Barbara never complained about living with snakes or a haughty Jersey or other difficulties here, such as lack of running water (except, as we joked, when Harvey or I ran with a bucket to the spring and back). Though I wasn't feeling exactly at home in my church position, I don't think I ever complained about going to church every Sunday. We kept our Barbaria bargain and loved each other. I sold a few short stories and articles.

The new guidebook to the park was published. Mostly we'd accepted Ed Lauck's ideas, because he convinced us the sales would be double or triple what we'd sold before the war. But I insisted on my personal invitation to visitors – one of my poems, "COME BACK":

Earth eternal is your mother.
Could you truly claim another?
Foster child of street and car,
yet you hear her voice afar,
hear her singing in the trees,

> feel her breath, the fragrant breeze,
> stirring basic memories.
>
> Birth from earth must humans trace,
> not from nation, sect, or race:
> heart's wrong symbols these,
> from half-blindness sprung
> intermediaries
> by half-knowledge sung.
>
>> Come back, she sings to the civilized heathen:
>> come home again to the Garden of Eden;
>> come rest on the breast of life's true mother;
>> come bathe in the warmth of radiant father;
>>> and find your source again,
>>>> your strength again,
>>>>> your joy again.

The guidebook looked "slickly" professional but sold no better than the earlier versions, so money was short. My big novel wasn't becoming a marketable manuscript fast enough to keep us solvent. I began working two days a week as a reporter for a Luray paper. Barbara persuaded Luray High School to inaugurate an art class with her as teacher. She gained satisfaction from her students' progress, but pay for part-time teaching in Virginia was low.

I was promoted to editor of *The Commonwealth Review*, working full-time, and we were surviving debt-free. I enjoyed expressing my opinions and feelings in editorials, and Virginia Press Association honored me two years in succession for editorials and for feature writing. I got paid extra for my column, "Getting Oriented," that ran weekly in Luray and in another paper published at Arlington, Virginia (a major suburb of Washington, D.C.). We were thus clinging to Barbaria but falling short of our long-time dream.

Chapter 14 – The Great Basin Again 1949-61

My brother Wendell calls from Ely, Nevada, where he's now a car and truck dealer. The primitive phone at Barbaria makes long-distance strenuous. Wendell seems to be saying the White Pine (county) Chamber of Commerce wants me as full-time "manager" because he told them I believe the wild places of Nevada can attract tourists and he knows I can produce publications to build travel business. I can have the job if I want it. "Do you?" I think No, the chamber of commerce role seems the opposite of the present me. But the salary offered is more than double what Barbara and I together are making now, and I say we'll talk it over and call back.

She comes in from her peony bed and thinks No too. We've invested here – our dreams, emotions, beginning achievements – and can't just pull up the young roots. But we're not thriving. My novel is stalled by the newspaper's pressures – yet I can't rise higher than editor there, and the paper is financially shaky. Barbara, though, feels her effort to build interest in art at Luray High School could lead "somewhere."

We'll sleep on the problem. When we suppose we've discussed everything, we quiet down, then one thinks of something else. As always, I can't explain well why I like to live away from other people, why I want to stay here with no humans or structures not our own anywhere in sight. I feel at home surrounded by trees and the diverse creatures. I tell Barbara again I feel wilderness as sacred, as much so as church, and I feel nature's my chief guide to the process and goals of living.

"I know about that old Laotze in you, darling," she says, "and he could be just as happy in Nevada as in Virginia."

"Yes – but the question isn't Virginia or Nevada. Here we live inside nature. There, we'll be living the city life – money, commerce!"

"Yes – but anywhere we'll spend *some* time with civilization."

I'm thinking the whole family might enjoy a *temporary* change. I'd like to show them the West. I'm remembering Ely is surrounded by vastly more, and wilder, wilderness than exists in Virginia. I'm wondering if those pine logs are still at the secret cabin site near Ely. We do sleep now on the problem.

Up before dawn, as long ago, I'm milking Queenie, with my head pushing into her flank, balancing me on the one-legged stool, and the possibilities are coming clearer. Recognition of basic reality – and of the potential romance or wonder in reality because nature's so endlessly creative – is more important than a specific place. As the jets of milk zip into the bucket, becoming lower in pitch as the foam thickens, I decide I could accept being away for a few years – even greatly enjoy what I always felt as my home territory – if Barbara can accept the change – to heal our finances, we could validly say, balancing her long-time fondness for the eastern U.S. We'd hold onto the house and the hollow and our joint dreams that grew here.

The Ely businessmen were in a hurry, so we drove fast and long. After we'd crossed the Rockies, I talked about the Great Basin. It's not really a desert, I said, but a semi-arid geographic province larger than New England. It's a friendly place, often a magic place. Fond memories mixed into my present thoughts. But the "emptiness" – that I personally couldn't see or feel – scared them anyway. After an hour on the gravel of US Highway 6 in western Utah, with never another human in sight, Barbara asked, "Are we lost?"

"No," I said, stalling. I'd come this way – a winding route I'd never been on before – because this road was the first problem the Ely businessmen wanted me to work on. Barbara and the children asked more questions I couldn't answer, but luck saved me. In the distance I saw snow-marked Wheeler Peak and knew just where we were. I began telling about my climb up that peak 16 years earlier, guided by

Elwin Robison, now Wendell's brother-in-law. Barbara and the kids listened while we traversed the immense sage and shadscale flats, then hills with dwarf forest of pine-nut trees. Ahead now – I pointed out – were lesser snow-streaked peaks in addition to Wheeler, all deep-forested on their shoulders.

Beginning at the Nevada line, Highway US 6 was wide and smoothly surfaced. We rolled into Ely near the end of the day. Sylvia shouted "Hooray!" Barbara smiled, saying, "I see a church. It can't be all bad." I thought she was making a joke, but no – she was sober-serious. We took two adjoining rooms at a motel, one of them with cooking facilities.

The president of the White Pine Chamber of Commerce & Mines was Cecil Geraghty, owner-operator of a liquor store on Aultman Street. Geraghty had a flair for politics, using first names in telling me about the governor (Vail), the two US senators (George and Alan), and the congressman (Cliff). But even these powerful friends couldn't get grading and surfacing on the last hundred miles of US 6 – because the neglected stretch wasn't in their state. Geraghty doubted a liquor-store proprietor was the right person to influence the Mormons who controlled Utah. But Highway 6 was a national route, he said – actually the longest US route in existence.

Geraghty walked with me to the chamber's office – on the evil side of Aultman, actually a cubbyhole in a front corner of a big "club." He introduced a young woman who'd be my secretary. She looked up from her typing and was strikingly attractive. They'd crowded a desk for me against her desk with hardly room to walk around. Geraghty said with an almost wink, "We're looking for a bigger room."

The chamber was the leading civic organization of the county – that had 9,000 square miles with only 9,000 people. Kennecott Copper Corporation, employing 2,500 people, was a crucial source of the chamber's funding. Its manager for Nevada, John C. Kinnear Jr., who'd graduated from high school here with Wendell and me – realized the once-immense copper deposit was nearly exhausted. He wanted to save White Pine's economy, partly by bringing in more tourists.

Another source of strength for Highway 6 was the cattle and sheep ranchers, traditionally having clout beyond their numbers. John Chachas, owner of the vast Cleveland Ranch and of several travel businesses in Ely, was the chamber's highway chairman, obsessed with Highway 6. He and Geraghty would take substantial time from their own businesses to help. I was expected to provide the additional energy and strategy to win.

An early duty was coordinating an event at Lehman Caves. Mayor Broadbent of Ely was bringing together the governors of Utah and Nevada and their wives to meet with visiting officials of the National Park Service for escalating promotion of the caves and, of course, improving access. Among Utah helpers, joining us Nevadans, were businessmen of Millard County (adjacent to White Pine across the state line on the east) who'd been trying for years to get that last hundred miles of US 6 re-aligned and surfaced. The Utah governor denied that Salt Lake City, situated on US 40, a competing transcontinental route, was blocking US 6 funds. He said the funds went where the need seemed most urgent. He listened now to the Ely and Millard delegations and agreed with us "the missing link" should be built.

I lingered after the others left. A veteran Lehman Caves guide, who'd grown up nearby, mentioned a man who should have been present – C. C. Boak – in his 80s now – at his Tonopah home, on Highway 6 southwest of Ely. He was a great old character with a background in mining; he showed me his mineral collection – big crystals of brilliant colors, Smithsonian caliber. Together we schemed a coast-to-coast Highway 6 association. We shared names of likely helpers and started writing or phoning them, along with chambers of commerce across the West, then continued on eastward building a list of potentially interested people. Utah's Governor Lee arranged a highway engineers' reconnaissance of the Utah gap. In a *Highway 6 Newsletter* mailed across the country, we were thus able to say one million dollars would improve alignment and surface the now-dusty stretch of Utah US 6.

With encouraging responses coming in, we called a national convention – at Glenwood Springs, Colorado. The six states on US 6 west of the Mississippi were well represented, but only one couple came from the eight eastern states on US 6. Nevertheless, we boldly formed the National Highway 6 Association with Geraghty as president, I as national secretary, Boak and Broadbent as directors – and other directors representing the full route (though half weren't present but agreed by phone). The next newsletter carried photographs of attractions along the nationwide route. Soon we had members from all fourteen US 6 states.

The chamber's office – moved now into sizable rooms at the front of Ely Theater – was national headquarters. We hired an extra secretary and launched a nationwide signature drive – that was soon succeeding spectacularly. I was far outside what I'd supposed was my element, but the action and influence were feeding my hungry ego. I must be a charismatic politician with a knack for organizing. Maybe, after all, I wasn't meant to be a naturalist and writer. Maybe I should run for governor or other public office.

I'd earned a vacation, and instead of getting away from it all, I bargained with the chamber for additional time and sharing of cost – so my family and I could explore Highway 6 all the way from Long Beach on the Pacific Ocean to Provincetown, Massachusetts, on the Atlantic – then explore westward on US 50, another route serving Ely, from Ocean City, Maryland, to San Francisco – making friends, taking pictures, stimulating highway enthusiasm. What was happening to me?

The trip was enjoyably educational for all five of us. We visited Barbara's parents not far from US 6 and checked on Barbaria, 40 miles off US 50. Some businessmen and chamber executives invited us to dinners or to weekends. Newspapers and broadcasters interviewed us, and after we'd returned to Ely I wrote illustrated articles that many of the papers carried. Congressional delegations responded directly to the thousands of Highway 6 signatures from across the country. Though allotment to specific projects is normally the road agencies' prerogative, Congress did what it "never" does – appropriated the needed amount specifically for filling the Utah US 6 gap. The construction was promptly done and traffic flowed across the "desert."

The chamber and the national association produced pamphlets and a color-sound movie of Highway 6 attractions – with copies for television and public-program circulation. This experience launched similar publicity for the other two US routes intersecting at Ely. I was soon president of the National Highway 50 Federation and of the North American "Holiday" Highway Association (Guatemala via Ely to Fairbanks, Alaska). All were managed from Ely.

Barbara and I relish the adequate income, but I alternately relish and resent the unending demands of commerce – the continual traveling for business, the so-frequent luncheons, dinners, even breakfasts. We buy a house at the edge of Ely, touching both the busy little city and the Great Basin wilderness. Barbara and the children attend Sunday School at the Mormon chapel, and for a year or more I go with them when chamber-related projects don't prevent it. Soon Barbara and the children are baptized into church membership. I'd been baptized in the Metropolis hot spring at age eight. It got known, though, that I'd been a Lutheran Sunday School superintendent – so, I must abrogate Lutheranism and be baptized again.

I couldn't do that. Though I don't think I made a scene, defying Barbara's urging, I kept arguing inside myself: I'm a member of everything already since everything interrelates. I belong to Rotary, chamber of commerce, Boy Scouts, three highway associations, a state chamber of commerce that I'm currently organizing. I'm already Mormon, Lutheran, Buddhist, and so on. I learn from Confucius and try to follow Laotze, though I'm not exactly a Taoist in the 20th-century sense. Most strongly of all, I insist to myself, I'm a member of nature and want always to embrace, never to exclude. I continue attending Sunday School when I can – but that's intermittent with long gaps.

I keep thinking of connections. I belong, for instance, to the Jaycees (Junior Chamber of Commerce) that's no part of the senior chamber. As a Jaycee I initiated "Operation Landmark," exploring and researching to choose a dozen points of interest in the county. We're building stone pyramids at highway turn-offs to mark access, and I write articles giving the history or natural history for the *Ely Daily Times*. I take the family with me sometimes to explore, but Sundays are often my only available day, so there's pulling and tugging.

One Sunday morning, driving alone for exploration near Hamilton ghost town where rich silver ore attracted tens of thousands of people in the late 1860s, I discover "Wild Bill" Keller, a grizzled prospector-miner. He and an elderly partner with palsy are working "by hand" in the long-abandoned Dog Star mine. Bill entices me into the tunnel and shows veins resembling tight-pressed sand but melting into shiny spheres of metal rolling down the tunnel-face at the flame-tip of Bill's carbide lamp. "Rich!" Bill says. "All I need's a little credit backing to get a second-hand compressor and dump truck. We could haul thousand-dollar loads to the smelter – and all three of us be driving Cadillacs by spring."

I don't want a Cadillac, but I think my pleasure in commercial promotion is past its peak, and I may want funds for moving back to Virginia where three years of uninterrupted work might produce my China-novel masterpiece. With me as additional partner, Bill "maneuvers" inexpensive deals for equipment. I don't have to labor at the mine, but I invite myself on weekends to bring groceries and help muck out the latest blasted ore and rock.

We call our partnership Shenandoah Minerals Co.; incredibly, Bill's childhood home was only 30 miles from Luray. I receive the checks and handle business records. My experience makes me more useful in the chamber's "Mines" program – right now, promoting an ore-concentrating mill at Ely, for all ores except copper, which Kennecott welcomes at McGill. I keep notes about the mining, perhaps to use in a book when I get back to my writing.

I let myself in for different education when I start collecting pinyon pine sap. A giant soap company, with headquarters in New York, wants pine oils called lemonene and limonene, apparently to enhance fragrance. They've come from lemon rinds but are richer in the Great Basin's pinyon-pine pitch. My part – largely on chamber pay at first but more on my own time as I think I might become a limonene tycoon – is to tap 30 trees near Ely.

With turpentine-industry tools I deep-scratch down-slanting grooves. Metal troughs fasten into the grooves, and buckets hang there catching sap. I record time spent and all costs, and a friend who does the distilling keeps similar records. The different "essential oils" evaporate at different temperatures and are caught separately as they cool. The company tests our samples and wants the oils in quantity but offers less than our cost.

We haggle by mail, then I confer in New York where I've flown for highway business and to visit son Harvey at Dartmouth. Harvey and I tackle New England's Mt. Washington together but fail because freezing rain coats the trail dangerously. The soap executives show me endless figures, including prices paid for the same oils from other sources. The scientists admit our limonene is superior. The company's board believes mass production with efficiency gained through experience could create a workable enterprise in the Great Basin where *Pinus monophylla* is abundant – but declines to finance the venture. A solid offer to buy all our production at prices slightly higher than previously offered is put into writing, good for two years. I return to Ely with this teaser, but it doesn't bring the needed risk capital.

In 1954 I run for the Nevada Legislature, as my father did 32 years earlier. I tour populated parts of the county, mostly with Barbara and the children, and write articles for *Ely Daily Times* combining history with present situations and people. While campaigning I think of Dad, who wasn't elected, and somehow in this connection feel doubly satisfied when I am elected.

I seem to be moving by impulse, not thoughtful planning; maybe I'm half-consciously trying my wings at all angles and speeds before settling down to consistent behavior. I introduce a bill to create a Nevada department of economic development – that the Nevada Chamber of Commerce Executives, a new organization I've been elected president of, has been seeing a need for – at the same time I'm also resenting excessive commercialism. I tell myself I want to help launch industries that fit Nevada's resources, needs, and people, and to attract more visitors for purposes other than gambling and divorce. I then meet with state park officials and give them clippings about our "Operation Landmark" sites. Legislative action doesn't directly establish state parks in Nevada, but one of our sites, Ward Charcoal Ovens, soon gains that status. My economic development bill passes, and Governor Charles H. Russell names me chairman of the advisory board.

Lucius Beebe, millionaire author writing about America's elite and member of our board from Virginia City where he's giving new life to the *Territorial Enterprise*, for which Mark Twain wrote long ago, helps mightily but opposes industrialization. In that opposition, he's speaking arguments that are well-developed in me but currently suppressed in favor of Nevada communities too small even to afford a public library. Beebe is haughty, insisting a millionaire should act like one – for instance, by traveling in his own private railroad car "as I do." But he's my friend too, encouraging me to rearrange my life so I can write more.

Partly because of him, and partly because of my growing uneasiness in direct pursuit of commerce, I accept an offer from the out-of-state owner of Ely's two newspapers. I become editor of both the *Ely Daily Times* and the weekly *Ely Record*. The main factor enabling me to make the firm decision was that I'm authorized to write and publish whatever I wish – conservation, natural history, whatever, in the papers' two-column-wide editorial space.

An idea capable of re-uniting loose strands of my life – desire to harmonize with nature, fondness for influence, readiness to interrelate with people and organize-generate human responsibility – reaches public action while I'm still a legislator. This idea of a national park embracing Wheeler Peak and Lehman Caves has been growing ever since I first climbed Wheeler in my high school years. It spread to a dozen other White Pine people in the early 1950s. Now in January 1956 I announce in the two newspapers that it's an official project of the White Pine chamber backed by the Utah-Nevada Lehman Caves Committee, backed also by Weldon F. Heald, an influential conservationist-writer living in Arizona, who discovered last August that a glacier is active, with crevasses, inside the proposed park, notable because the region is so dry.

The National Park Service, though not endorsing, investigates. Our state economic development board, with Beebe among the enthusiasts, adopts the project. Pete Kelley, salaried director, goes to work to boost Nevada's prestige with a genuine national park. Weldon writes articles about the proposal and by the end of the year six of them are published – in *Appalachia*, *Westways*, *American Alpine Journal*, *Desert Magazine*, *Pacific Discovery*, and *Sierra Club Bulletin*. I'm publishing many national park advocacy items and pictures in Nevada – in the papers I edit, also in Reno and Las Vegas papers and Utah papers.

In 1957 photographer Irwin Fehr and I start shooting footage for a color-sound movie of the proposed park, our fourth half-hour movie, following one each for the three highway associations. Barbara and I and the children spend our vacation roaming the Wheeler high country on horseback, camping out. Fehr joins us at photogenic places to capture more of the spectacularly diverse scenery, including gnarled and twisted bristlecone pines on the Great Basin's Mt. Washington and in the Wheeler cirque.

Back in the office, I phone the non-governmental National Parks Association in Washington, D.C., and ask the executive director, Fred M. Packard, for advice on organizing a Great Basin National Park Association. Surprising me, he says, "Arrange a meeting in August and I'll fly out to Lehman Caves and help."

Fehr and I select color footage of impressive scenes – not yet finally edited or with sound added – to confirm the park's quality. Thirty persons come from five states and form the association – to campaign for national recognition and to enroll members throughout the country. I'm frustrated in an effort to get Heald elected association president; the responsibility lands on me. I step up exploration and photography. Alone or with persons who can wield influence toward park establishment, I'm out in the high wild Snake Range most Saturdays and Sundays, making discoveries that rally more converts. While in West Virginia presiding at a national US 50 convention, I'm urgently invited to the Interior Department in Washington for park planning.

In the March 1958 *National Geographic* I find pictures of bristlecone pines with massive trunks of colorful wood mostly bare of bark – like those at high elevations in our proposed park. Dr. Edmund Schulman, who wrote the article, has been counting tree rings in the mountains near the Nevada-California line and learning bristlecones are the oldest living trees on Earth. I phone Dave Brower, executive director of the Sierra Club and long a central figure in wilderness and national- park conservation. I invite him to hurry from San Francisco to hike with me into the deep cirque of Wheeler and see the "desert-bound" glacier and the bristlecones that are even more impressive, I think, than those in the *Geographic*. Busy though this leading conservationist must be, he comes.

I'm thinking a lot about Dave Brower as I'm working on this life-story manuscript in the new millennium. Writing about him in *High Country News* 11/20/00, Bruce Hamilton said, among much other praise,

> "And now David Brower's too-brief, remarkable lifetime is over... The 88 years that he spent on this planet are truly inspirational. His lifetime environmental accomplishments read like the resume of six or eight top environmental advocates – not that of a single man."

Back now to my re-experiencing the hike with Dave in his prime. It's 1958. Dave and I approach Wheeler Peak from the north. My four-wheel-drive pickup climbs a rough road up Strawberry Canyon onto Bald Mountain, which we think might be the "North Dome" of a long-ago report by John Muir. We hike to Baldy's summit and see Wheeler's lofty bulk beyond Stella Lake. Among white-trunked aspens and alternating groves of tall Engelmann spruce, we drop into Lehman Creek canyon between Teresa and Brown lakes and enter the moraine-strewed cirque. I lead leftward toward higher moraine and the most impressive trees I've found. I'd slept one night cuddled against the trunk of a handsome one I call Socrates. A bit higher, on a steep slope, is the bulkiest trunk I've seen, maybe the world's largest bristlecone trunk. With measuring tape, Dave and I encircle it and read 35 feet 8 inches in circumference. We name it "Giant." Not far above, where the rock field is more nearly level is another obviously ancient tree that we think of as "Prometheus."

Dave promises help toward establishing the national park and saving such trees, among other wilderness features and scenery, whenever we need him. He says national-park-type protection is essential, partly to restrain people from running off with gnarled branches and fallen remnants of the beautiful, ancient wood.

In the fall of 1958, noted biologist Adolph Murie is brought in by the park service to help judge whether Wheeler is of national park caliber. He asks me to accompany him whenever I can. His written report helps me now to re-experience his inspection. We're in Snake Creek Canyon. We examine lofty natural walls near the portal, one with a window high against the sky. He takes many pictures. He comments on a distant yellow pine growing over a giant boulder - and then, up a side-ravine, "a huge yellow pine." We span "our arms three times" to reach around the huge one and conclude its diameter is six feet.

Adolph identifies bristlecones on a distant clifftop, even notices the "reddish hue" of the "exposed weathered wood." He's endlessly teased by the odd combinations of southern-desert plants with far-northern plants. We admire (in his words) "a crowd of graceful, slender aspens, so dense they form a wall of whiteness." Still higher, fir, spruce, and limber pine take over, and there's more and more bare rock. Soon we break out of the scattering of dwarfed spruce onto "the grass-sedge meadow bordering Emerald Lake" (also known as Johnson Lake).

He feels so "exhilarated" he won't stop exploring, though the lake was set as the day's goal. He leads up talus mixed with bedrock to the divide where we look into Baker Canyon. That view teases him farther, around a shoulder of Pyramid Peak where we get a better view of Treasure Lake (also called Baker Lake) and the cliffy half-circle of glacial cirque towering behind the open water. Turning, he notices "the desert and a part of the bed of old Lake Bonneville" and Great Basin ranges farther eastward. Then we must climb for westward views "into Williams Creek... and to see far across another stretch of desert" to other Great Basin ranges westward.

In 1959, as a result of Adolph Murie's exhilaration and scientific reports by Adolph and others, our proposed park is declared "nationally significant" by the authoritative board of non-governmental experts advising the Secretary of the Interior. Complex harmony sings in me when I learn the board's decision for Great Basin was made when it met in "my" Shenandoah National Park.

In July, Dave Brower comes to Wheeler country again and speaks inspirationally at the Great Basin association's annual meeting and excursion to Lexington Arch (its opening to the sky six stories tall) and dramatic Big Wash, deep between limestone cliffs. Dave accepts election to our Association's board of directors, and we all feel stronger, though his acceptance doesn't automatically mean endorsement by the Sierra Club, any more than the help given us by Fred Packard meant endorsement by NPCA, but both conservation leaders strengthened us significantly – financially and through bringing other strong conservationists around the country into our effort.

For instance, that fall (I'm back to re-experiencing in Ely and the Snake Range), I drive Adolph's brother Olaus Murie and wife Mardy, recognized national leaders in wilderness ecology and conservation with much experience in wild Alaska and in the nation's capital with The Wilderness Society, up a "forgotten ladder" onto the plateau of Mt. Washington in our proposed park. With this gentle but strong couple, I enjoy sitting in the ancient groves, not speaking, simply feeling nature's timeless mood, even enjoying there a wild high-altitude storm. These Muries also study and praise the different features, including underground wonders. (In due course, Olaus would join others of us in testifying for the park at a U.S. Senate hearing held in Nevada.)

Ranching and mining people I consider friends oppose park establishment. We advocates try to draw the boundary to leave out grazing land and mineral deposits, but our influence with the congressional committees is limited. When a space-age mineral, beryllium, is discovered under Mt. Washington (though not yet proved significant), our most influential friend in Washington, Nevada's senior senator Alan Bible, chairman of the national park subcommittee and a power on the appropriations committee, tells us the park bill can't be enacted immediately – but *"will be enacted."*

Though I clung to my dream of our log home in Virginia and worldwide readership for my writing, I stayed deeply involved in the Great Basin. I was happier as editor-writer and conservationist than when directly motivated by commerce. The Ely newspapers proved primary in my career, a firm step on stairs leading ahead. Significant currents surfaced through these newspapers. Election year 1960 brought opportunities to interview Lyndon Johnson and Richard Nixon in Ely – also Pat Nixon, who was born just across the street from the *Times*. I told them briefly about the proposed park; all agreed it was important and they'd help when decision time came in Washington. So did John F. Kennedy, by telegram.

My editorial essays were central as expressions of myself in relation to my surroundings. They were surprisingly popular with readers. I can't tell my life story without sampling some of the 2000-plus "editorials" I wrote in Ely. One called "Waning Sun" followed a feature story I'd written about Mary Stanton, a 90-year-old Shoshone woman who still healed people through the strength of the sun. In the interview, she'd mourned Shoshone decline through Whiteman's diseases and alcoholic liquors and loss of water sources and rich land to intruding "Whites." So far, though, she'd quipped, "the Whiteman hasn't taken the sun." At this season (mid-November, but maybe she meant this period of history) the sun is weakening. Then she looked sternly at me and insisted, "But our sun-dances will bring it back full strength." I wrote:

> Life is like the seasons, waxing strong and vigorous, then declining into weakness and inactivity... There are cycles ... times of aggressive action and times of waiting or of finishing what has been started or of dreaming and planning new activities. Some of these cycles correspond to the seasons of the year and to the weather... With the waning sun our lives too wane. We are declining, waiting, hoping, dreaming, putting off bold action until a more vigorous season...
>
> Sages from ancient times have taught the wisdom of moving with the seasons, of cooperating with nature. When our plans fit the seasons, the strength of nature is in our strength, and our projects move forward triumphantly... Thinking and feeling along with nature, we do not despair... We know that though the sun goes down it will rise again... though it slants far southward, weakening, it will turn again toward the zenith – and us.

Here's the essence of "Tunneling Through the Night." I was returning to Ely in the dark from a national-park-related meeting at University of Nevada, Reno. As often, the road was lonely:

>...There is a moon, and you can look far out over the mountains and valleys and see their shapes glowing dimly... Overhead, if you'll just move your eyes a little to the left of forward, you can see a fascinating sky, usually with wisps of cloud glowing against the blue-blackness and with the brilliant pin-pricks of stars forming patterns that your mind tends to connect to "see" buildings or people or birds.
>
> If it's entirely dark with clouds and threat of rain, as it was for a time ...you might have the strangest feeling of tunneling through the dark, of digging the tunnel ahead of you with the lights of your car and having it close in behind you as you speed along. The darkness seems to have a substance and a weight and to be thrust aside by the lights, to be held away from you by the lights, and to close in gently when you no longer need the opening.
>
> Occasionally, the tunnel was cut through from the outside, from a great distance, by the flash of lightning, and once in a while another lonely digger of tunnels came toward me, his lights making a small tunnel far out there, then coming closer, the tunnel widening and passing beside me. It's a friendly encounter in the lonely dark, though you don't glimpse the face of the driver or have the slightest idea who he might be other than just human.

Here's the essence of "The Moving Stars" – becoming the essence of my own view and process of living:

>...The moving stars, playing hide-and-seek among the wind-driven clouds, convey the impression of endless space and vast forces unfathomed by mankind, making us feel small and in the presence of omniscient majesty.
>
> These phenomena of nature are creatures of feeling, of moods, and of dreams. Obviously uncontrolled by man, they tell us of the rhythm and movement of vast forces we cannot harness, and they suggest to us that we must compromise with the universe by shaping ourselves to its unchangeable customs

– as well as, proud scientists that we are, striving to modify the universe just a little toward our own desires...

What prompted us to take a look in words at the moving stars is the fact that, while they may be moving, no one can say with absolute assurance whether they are moving or not unless a base point of reference be established. We look through gaps in the clouds, and the stars appear to be moving ...but more accurately the clouds are moving in relation to the stars...

Moral of this rambling about the sky, if brought down to Earth, is simply that neither the universe nor life in the universe is simple. As we learn more of what have long been mysteries, we discover that our subjective impressions of things and processes aren't likely to be complete or even accurate. Thus, from the sky and its phenomena... we can learn both a humility of spirit and a humility of the mind – combining into a vast respect for the realities of the great home on which we live.

Somewhat as "The Moving Stars" looks up (or outward) from Earth, this one called "Lost Independence" looks at modern human society on Earth from far enough out in space to escape control by personal concern:

It's time we realized that something more than left-tending political philosophy and an alleged weakening of moral fiber is behind the increasing dependence of humans...

The organization of society on the basis of complex technology is obviously one of the factors. It is no longer a pioneer society, in which the strong and capable individual can go out almost on his own and make a place for himself. The structure of the economy is such that rewards now go not to the person of independent initiative so much as to the skilled co-operator. Humans have become, through no fault of the individuals, dependents upon society...

We draw from the complex society, and we must contribute to it. As complications increase, we – quite naturally and justifiably – expect more from the government, the unions, the organizations of all kinds. It isn't that we are softer or weaker; it's more that our type of society automatically makes us dependent. Our way of living also contributes directly to the other symptoms which some contemporary social philosophers are fond of calling "disintegration."

This editorial is not an excuse for the troubles of the present age. It is an appeal for understanding of the facts that former restraints, former traditions, former beliefs, former virtues have, in a realistic view, lost much of their validity; that life is now organized on a different basis; that we must develop new standards, new traditions, new and currently valid ways of creative living.

We trust the new ways will involve the maximum of individuality, the greatest possible strength of America and freedom, but we know the goal will not be achieved through blind crying for times and ways that are gone.

Here in "Mountain Mysteries" I'm back where my experience began to go on record as memories. I'm looking toward home, seeking a firm and lasting anchorage:

We Nevadans look up at the mountains, and many of us climb them. Our home is one line of mountains after another, separated by valleys for variety. We might be said to have a feeling for mountains; the typical Nevadan when out of sight of them on some vast plain feels lonely and lost...

There are various approaches to understanding mountains. We might think of them scientifically as they rose and melted away and rose again through the geologic eons. We might think of the forces that thrust them upward, the wrinkling of the crust of the earth, the faulting or cracking of the layers, and the slipping and grinding along the faults as one side moved upward or downward in relation to the other, the pressures of the hot fluid rock beneath them, and the occasional bursting out of the lava.

We might think of their influence on life forms, of the many different climates that mark one mountain range from the desert country to its foot through the changing belts of vegetation to the arctic country at timberline and above. Or we might prefer to think not so much of the climate and the vegetation as of the wildlife – the infinitely varied insects, the birds, the reptiles, and the mammals including the small and seldom-seen mice and other forms as well as the badgers, bobcats, foxes, cougars, coyotes, antelope, deer, mountain sheep, elk, and humans.

Or we might simply think of the combination... and simply enjoy the wind whispering in the trees, the creeks talking in the language of music as they gurgle down the canyons, the views from the peaks, and the stars twinkling so clearly, or the moon seeming to move almost within reach sometimes through the wind-blown clouds.

Here we've entered the realm of feeling, a spiritual realm, that's the strongest meaning of mountains to most people, for the mountains lift our eyes and our thoughts above the ordinary things of life and lead them to the clouds and the winds – and the unfathomed blue of the sky. And it is there that the dark clouds boil as the winds push them high over the ridges, there that the lightning flashes and the thunder rumbles...

So the mountains are not, to those who know them, cruel or forbidding places. They are instead the places of loving warmth of mother nature. They are the sources from which flow the bounty of life. The peaks and the high ridges generate the storms, and down the canyons flow the streams of life-giving water. The mountains are instruments of a kind, though sometimes violent, providence. From them those living creatures who are best in tune draw upon the invisible and powerful current of the universe.

The mountains are the places of dreams. The dreams move upon the breezes of the dawn or the twilight of evening and the slanting rays that touch the edges of the cliffs and the trees. In midday the dreams hide in the deeper forests and even in the caves, but when the light is dim or slanting and the purple shadows stretch far across the folded land, the dreams fly to you from the places of mystery. Sometimes they glow in the colors of sunrise or sunset, and when darkness really falls, and the strong wind blows in gusts, or the rain falls, or the stars and the milky way twinkle and glow, or the moon comes out, the dreams enter into every heart – beautiful and mysterious dreams of unconquerable life, vague perhaps in shape and meaning but carrying always to those of the open heart a feeling of sacred joy.

Chapter 15 – "Darwin, You Can't Love Two" 1956-61

Soon after I became editor in Ely a letter arrived praising my editorials but scolding me for revealing hidden attractions by advocating the national park. The writer, Eileen Affleck, said we who live in the Great Basin are fortunate in having the wonderful mountains, forests, meadows, and intriguing wildlife, and shouldn't invite overcrowding. I published the "letter to editor" followed by a comment saying we park advocates too cherished uncrowded places but believed the vulnerable attractions – nature-sculptured trees, cave decorations, and scarce creatures – would increasingly need protection. A national park would mobilize enough influential friends to make the protection firm.

Months later, Barbara and I met Eileen and Billy Affleck at a dinner given by the Ely librarian, Pat Bulmer, and her husband Don. Pat and Eileen said they turned to my editorials first when the paper came. Eileen understood my reason for advocating the national park. She was taking a correspondence course in both short story and article writing. I said I'd like to see a sample of her work, and she soon brought to the *Ely Daily Times* office a piece she'd written in response to a *Reader's Digest* appeal for personal experiences. Her "experience" was getting lost with her younger son Mike and two dogs in the proposed national park and being followed by a mountain lion. I read it that night and advised her to send it in as it was – really quite vivid and well organized.

Billy, caught in a prolonged strike of Kennecott employees, took the family to California where he could get short-term employment in construction. There must have been a year, at least, when I didn't see Eileen. Yet I sometimes felt I was writing my editorials directly to her. After the Afflecks returned, Eileen phoned, hoping for the newspaper's help in persuading people who'd taken up five-acre tracts along the McGill highway to join in drilling for water and cooperating in other utilities. I agreed.

In 1958 the newspapers needed someone to do reporting and rewriting. Remembering Eileen's flare for writing, I phoned her. She needed work, and I offered her the job – for one year only because my predecessor had committed the *Times* to hire a woman who'd graduate next year in journalism. Eileen worked in a small office connecting with mine. I intended to leave the door open so we could discuss the day's local news and I could guide her in gathering facts by phone. Soon, though, I was closing the door, because I couldn't otherwise keep my eyes off her.

During the whole year we were careful to visit only in relation to the work. She developed skill in reporting and feature writing, especially on historic subjects and profiles of citizens – whom she interviewed in her office or at their homes or work places. A week before she was to leave, I'd been making a plastic plate from a photograph on the "Scanagraver" near her desk where she was sitting in the *Times* Stationery Store, filling in for the regular clerk during lunch time. No customers were present. I was leaving with the engraved plastic but stopped and looked back. Our eyes caught and held and, whatever the great mystery is, it happened. She said as if in panic, "Don't do that!" I hadn't intended to do whatever it was. Something centrally basic had shifted. I was seeing Eileen and me in the center of the world and all the other people of our lives swirling at a distance.

When I reached my own office I knew I loved Eileen. I almost knew what I couldn't know, that she loved me and that the shift in our feelings was irreversible. I don't believe we've been out of love for an instant during the four-plus decades since then. I've felt her in my living fiber, intensifying all my emotions, sharpening my observation, broadening and deepening my understanding. At my desk that day, trying to concentrate on work, I caught myself humming "Silent Night," though the month was June. I don't know whether she heard me through the closed door when she returned to her office or, if she did, knew what it meant. I didn't know – though I knew my depths were singing a sacred song. All during the early months of our love, though we seldom even glimpsed each other, another hymn, "The Lord's Prayer," took turns in me with "Silent Night" – ironic in the religious skeptic I'd become in relation to this skeptic I loved. But I'd never learned any other spiritual language.

That stressful time lives in me as if it's a tape repeating. I wake after midnight. Barbara seems asleep, breathing regularly. I feel her warmth. I'm on my back, both ears receiving, and maybe hear the children breathing too in nearby rooms with the doors not closed – Harvey, who'll be 20 next month and is home after a year at Dartmouth; Sylvia, who's 18 and planning Antioch College; and Laura, who's almost 17 and planning Whittier College. I love Barbara. I want us to go on being productive and happy together. Yet I lie here longing for Eileen. She and I together are magic mirrors, reflecting each other, revealing new depths in each other, confirming and strengthening the essence of each other. For hours night after night I can't sleep. I stare fixedly at the ceiling, which I can't see.

Even as silent tears chill my temples and ears, I shape an idea for restoring contact with Eileen. I envision a four-person partnership to enhance the reputation of our region and help establish the national park, while also selling our creative work. For years photographer Irwin Fehr and I saw the opportunity to combine his pictures with writing for magazines but never found time for it. Eileen has time now and might do much of the writing while gaining experience for other writing in the future. Barbara has watercolors of scenery in and around Ely, suitable for exhibit or publication, and she's eager to sell and produce more.

Irwin welcomes the idea. Barbara does too, even volunteering to go with me to see if Eileen will participate. Great Basin Associates is thus formed and stationery printed. Irwin and Barbara will produce pictures. Eileen and I will do the rest. We list likely markets, mostly travel magazines, and send out queries. Two magazines, *Ford Times* and *Dodge News*, want illustrations in color. Soon we all have work.

Eileen's best time is seven to nine in the morning – after Billy has left for work and before the children, in summer, get up. Separately, we study recent issues of the magazines involved, then by phone discuss tentative text and illustrations. After getting down to specifics, we need to decide which of us will do what writing. I'm involved with the newspaper from eight o'clock on, so I drive early to the Afflecks' new house on the McGill Highway, arriving the first time at 7:15.

Eileen opens the door. We look at each other. Our hands come together in a sudden grasp. Then she's in my arms, and we're kissing for the first time. We push apart and both of us pick up papers I've dropped, and we sit on the sofa with the magazines and outlines between us. We're enthusiastic about the writing, so it's not quite impossible for us to concentrate. We agree on plans. No children appear, so we kiss again and hold each other. Then we're reading each other's eyes, finding fear and sorrow mixing with joy.

Legislation for the national park is pending in Congress. We have oodles of facts from investigations by National Park Service scientists and by researchers from universities. We have scenic photographs and paintings. For maximum effectiveness, though, Eileen must extend her personal familiarity beyond the main canyons on the east side – Lehman Creek, Baker Creek, and Snake Creek where she's often explored while Billy fished. She must visit the high peaks and a west-side canyon or two.

Almost every weekend now I'm guiding influential people to the main points. The first trip to include Barbara, Irwin, and Eileen, along with visiting conservationists, and Sylvia with a boy friend, is up Mt. Washington and into Lincoln Canyon. Here are some of Eileen's impressions:

Soon we're in heavy manzanita and conifers that remind me of California. Wildflowers are scattered profusely – columbine, lupine, Indian paintbrush... We come to the switchbacks. What a thrill! We drive up one rung of the ladder, and the turn is too sharp, so we back up to the next turn, then go forward one and backward the next... We stop to take pictures of the eye-catching gray and white limestone cliffs, and I see my first bristlecones. They're easy to identify if you remember an expression Dave Brower of the Sierra Club coined on a hike with Darwin. He calls them the bottlebrush tree...

These fantastic trees seem to grow right out of the rock. Many have trunk circumference over 30 feet, but they aren't tall, seeming to huddle close to the ground to avoid the full force of the hammering, screeching storms...

The mid-morning sun casts purple shadows into the canyons below. You feel the limitless distance and gaze across the big valleys at the blue ranges that get dimmer and paler in the distance... You see tiny threads that are highways and can imagine tourists bemoaning Nevada's endless sagebrush...

Lincoln Canyon is tucked away and hidden... Tremendously high, sheer cliffs stretch up to the sky on either side, giving a sheltered, protected feeling. There are big yellow pines, a few maple trees, and many shrubs and wildflowers... Blue shadows creep up the walls, and the late afternoon sun highlights towering sculptures... It's with a tinge of sadness that we leave such lovely, hidden splendor.

In similar groups we four visit other outstanding features, both on the surface and underground. Most of the wild caves are undeveloped, no trails, darkness everywhere, strong flashlights too weak to quiet fear. We hike the Shoshone Trail where Eileen and Mike were followed by the mountain lion. From near the ridgetop that separates Baker and Snake canyons, we see the mighty south slope of Wheeler, its naked rock looming above groves of aspen. Here Barbara starts a watercolor, also taking color slides at intervals in the changing light to help finish the painting.

Others of the party explore in different directions. Eileen and I see a fawn leap from its hiding place and run, then suddenly go out of sight, dropping, staying magically hidden. We wait together, watching, hoping. Later, as I'm walking the trail again, no one else near me, the whole happening plays rhythmically in me:

A flash of brown in the aspens,
    it flees from us.
Behind the white trunks
    and the underbrush
    it disappears.
The spirit of the Earth,
    it flashes through the aspens...
        Ah, Darling, it flees and returns,
            teasing.
        It flashes among the white trunks,
            brown and spotted and alive,
        and it lies by a fallen log,
            living, breathing, quivering –
        the very spirit of the Earth
            lying there.
            And then you come to me,
                and we stand together,
                  touching,
                and the spirit leaps
                    from the fawn to us
                    and is everywhere in the forest,
                    living, breathing, glowing –
                    in the fawn and the trembling leaves,
                        in ourselves.
                Ah, Darling, I hold it, you,
                    the spirit of the Earth,
                    in the curve of my arm.

One evening in the next week, I feel Barbara studying me as I sit reading in our library. Suddenly she asks, "Have you and Eileen been having intercourse?" I can't answer quickly. She runs tear-blinded from the house before I can move. She returns after midnight but still won't speak or listen. We'd planned to backpack this weekend into the Wheeler high country, to the bristlecone forest and the glacier in the great cirque. I'm the guide for the party that's to include Ed Lawrence, a geologist from the University of Nevada, Reno. Harvey is home and wants to go – also Eileen's sons, Dave and Mike. Postponing our crisis, Barbara decides she'd rather be present than absent.

Not noticing I'm doing it, I set such a fast pace there's almost no talking, and we're in the high country early. Ed proposes we climb the tall peak before making camp. Barbara, guessing I'll go with the others – as I want to – lags as we approach the crucial fork. Soon, I see, she's crying, then stumbling back down the trail. I run to catch her. I tell her I hope she'll climb but if not I'll stay with her. She comes with me to where the others are shedding their packs to make the climb without encumbrance. We all eat sandwiches.

Barbara and I, left alone, dodge our impossible problem. We walk around Stella Lake, looking for wildflowers. We've been friends years longer than we've been wife and husband. Quite sure nobody's near, we take off our clothes and swim in the cold lake, then warm up in the sun that's hot at this timberline altitude. We hike the half-mile-plus and shed our packs at Teresa camp site.

Then I remember Irwin – I to meet him at Stella. Also, nobody in the peak group knows the Teresa trail. Leaving Barbara resting, thinking about painting, I hurry back to Stella. Irwin arrives and, insisting he can follow the trail and wants to take pictures en route in afternoon light, starts toward Teresa. I watch the dots of those who've reached the peak and are coming down. I recognize the dot that's Eileen, and I watch her, and soon wave. We start together toward Teresa. I feel I must explain the new tension with Barbara; such matters can affect the whole course of life, even public projects, even success or failure of conservation projects or careers. Eileen sees one thing instantly – we two must not reach Teresa together. She runs ahead and catches up with son Mike.

Barbara acts normal as we eat supper, then spread sleeping bags ready for night. Eileen eats little and says nothing. She and her sons spread their beds far down toward the lake. In bed with Barbara upslope, I can't lie still. Angry at myself, I pull on my hiking boots and start climbing in the dark. I can't avoid loosening rocks on the slope, and the noise betrays me. Soon, though, I'm accepting the sound of moving rocks as a message to Eileen – that I care so much I can't hold myself – and a message to Barbara – that I'm *not* down there with Eileen. I defy the danger of unstable rocks – but carefully. Two wonderful women care what happens to me. At last I'm able to return and sleep.

Next morning the route up into the cirque seems all rock, yet supports splendid Engelmann spruce trees. Farther along, the rocks are the size of refrigerators. Wild gooseberries are red and delicious. I want to pick some for Eileen as well as for Barbara. Both decline my offerings but either will pose when asked beside bristlecone giants or in the foreground of distant Great Basin scenes. Barbara stops to launch a watercolor with a gnarled bristlecone in the foreground, a slender pinnacle on the horizon. I walk with Eileen alone, but talk fails to start. We're fighting tears. She asks me to go on ahead.

I go fast, risking boulder-to-boulder leaps. Irwin is taking glacier pictures from a distance. Ed Lawrence hunts for metal stakes he and I drove into the ice last fall, hoping to measure movement of the glacier. Ed finds bent stakes lying loose; an avalanche defeated our plan. Only Harvey and I climb the glacier as far up as the crevasses. I pull myself onto the crumbly cliff and take more pictures of the ice. One crevasse is so deep the bottom is lost in darkness.

The sun never shines on the glacier – the angle is never right – which is why the ice lasts in this 2000-ft-deep cirque. The shadows of the pinnacle we call "The Gendarme" and of Wheeler Peak stretch so long we lose them in the up-and-down landscape, and we hurry out from the bouldery places for safer footing. Before we reach our cars, I walk again with Eileen. We talk about how unfair our behavior is to Barbara and Billy – and how we don't believe in divorce, and she's been married 19 years and I, 21, and of course there are the children. Two of her three are in high school, the other, Mike, in eighth grade. Mine are nearer independence but hurtable. By what could be telepathy, or just reading each other's eyes, we touch the idea of a final goodby. Both of us pull back, frightened. I reach for her hand, not caring who might see, and though our fingers hold for only a few seconds we regain some peace.

    Our morning phone calls on Monday and Tuesday are strictly business. The *Dallas Morning News*, also a Savannah paper we've contacted, and the *Reno Gazette*, aware of the Senate hearing on the park, scheduled for December, suddenly want illustrated articles. I'll take care of the Savannah and Reno papers, and she'll proceed with Dallas. It's photos they want, not paintings, and we'll work separately with Irwin.

    Wednesday morning, though, we stray from business and sink again into the hopelessness of our love and our duty to end it. We don't phone on Thursday, or Friday. That night (Friday) I sit at a tourist committee meeting downtown until ten o'clock, not saying a single word. When it breaks up, I walk, forgetting the car, out of town and up Squaw Peak in the dark through the underbrush and up the not-quite-vertical cliffs. I kneel on the summit shouting to the universe – to God if he's there – to give me guidance. I stay looking at the stars and down along the McGill Highway with its moving lights to where Eileen lives. I sing "The Lord's Prayer" to the unresponsive dark. Almost peaceful at last, I feel my way down the mountain, cautious again now.

    Somehow on Saturday I get the newspaper together. I also watch every one of the hundreds of cars that go by my office window, and Eileen isn't in any of them. Sunday morning Barbara tells me I was crying out in the night. Though I haven't told her I'm trying to follow her advice to "cut with the sword," I feel she knows I am. She hasn't acted angry; she's kind to me, tender. She urges me to go to Sunday School with her and the children. I decline and sit all morning in the library writing phrases and fragments that might be poetry. When Barbara finds me there, I think she wants to hug me but doesn't feel welcome. I reach but can't be convincing. She says, "If a final goodby is impossible, Darling, maybe exchanges of manuscripts and occasional phone calls to discuss them would be best, after all." I feel she still loves me.

Many things add up to what could be guidance. I phone Eileen as early as I dare Monday morning.

"Darling! darling!" she says. "Why did you wait so long?" She could hardly sleep or eat and has lost five pounds.

We agree we simply must keep in contact somehow. Though we've enjoyed passionate love out in the deserts and the mountains and beside the streams, we agree sex isn't our main need. What's intolerable is no communication. We lose all energy except what keeps gnawing viciously inside us. So we'll aim toward something between active love and complete separation. Being close together, with eyes meeting, may be more than we can stand, so we'll exchange manuscript drafts and notes through the Great Basin Associates post office box and phone as necessary when she can be alone at home and I at the *Times*.

We see each other seldom and briefly, always with others present. But our phone talk and our notes soon stretch beyond writing and illustrating. We talk about everything – the phenomena of wild nature, mountains, trees, birds, rainbows, mirages, sunrises and sunsets, drifting clouds – about literature (what are you reading?), art and music, about people and what they do or fail to do and why, about community affairs, war and peace and politics, about our children, the schools, and, yes, about love, philosophical though, nothing about ourselves personally. Her spontaneous words confirm my long-term feelings about nature and organized religion in which I've felt alone. She's a mirror of my natural depths and I, perhaps, of hers.

From the summer visit to Wheeler until winter, we never touch, even hands. In December she's working at the radio station, and I go driving, listening to her announcements and the tunes she plays. Pulled closer on Christmas Eve, I'm driving slowly past the radio station just after dark when she comes out. She gets into the car, and I drive half a minute, turning a corner. It's not a populated place or traffic artery. We park. We kiss, yet without pressure toward seduction. The kisses are questions, not to be answered now but maybe in the coming year.

"I love you," I say.

"I love you," she says. "But how can it ever be?"

"I don't know – but it can't be impossible."

Her family will expect her after she's off the air, and I drive slowly back to the station. She gets into her car.

Barbara's watercolors were exhibited at the U.S. Senate hearing on the bill to establish Great Basin National Park – where proponents and opponents from across the country testified. The paintings went next for exhibit at University of Nevada, Reno. Irwin was making immense photographic murals of Wheeler Peak, bristlecone pine trees, and other impressive features. He sold them for permanent display in stores and offices.

Eileen and I kept writing. *Dodge News* bought her article called "A National Park in Nevada's Wilderness," and she was cover girl (my Kodachrome of her beside a massive bristlecone pine). The article was reprinted in the *Congressional Record*, helping to win votes in Congress. *Ford Times* bought her article about snowshoeing, along with color photographs by Irwin. My article, "Great Basin Sky Island," was published in *National Parks* and a different one in *Ohio Motorist*.

In secret, we were wild with love. At lunch time I'd pick her up and we'd explore another of the little-used roads through the sagebrush into the pinyon-juniper woodlands. Each time we'd find a different secluded place to unroll the sleeping bag. We could hardly believe what we were doing; we *couldn't* be! But the whisper and sigh of wind in the pines became our song. Eating had little priority, but if we felt hungry we'd have a candy bar or an apple while hurrying back to work. We thus claimed dozens of attractive spots within 15 minutes driving time. One spot became our favorite, partly because, while hidden, we had a far view of the only route by which anyone might approach. Love-making in the wilderness celebrated our feeling of sacred harmony with Earth and sun and all life.

I didn't – couldn't – hide the basic situation from Barbara, just the details. I'd always been honest with her. More than I've ever regretted anything else, I regretted hurting her. I can't ever not regret, partly because she never tried to hurt me in return but kept trying to help me. I wished I could behave differently, but I must have been acting out my deep authentic self and couldn't change. I didn't feel shame. The love was too mysteriously wonderful for shame. It's life, I felt – I'm in the heart of life, and by some law greater than society or culture or my own reason, it's right that I be here.

But the situation kept causing tears – Barbara's and Eileen's and mine. After stressful days, worsened by newspaper deadlines, I'd feel pains the doctor called *colitis*. I'd lie down to rest as soon as I got home, and the silent tears would burn and flow. Barbara would notice and cry too. Once she said, "I don't know whether you're crying for yourself, or for me, or for Eileen. Or why *I'm* crying either." She believed – as I insisted – that I still loved her. "But, Darwin, you can't love two!" Though she didn't deny my love for Eileen was real, I think she expected it to fade. When month after month, after more than a year, it didn't fade, she told me one night she might just have to leave.

I didn't sleep that night but kept trying to analyze, to understand. I did still love Barbara, but I longed to spend more time with Eileen, to live until death with her. Eileen was more completely in the same life with me. Our church, our inspiration, our chief guide in living was the universal reality, *nature*, surely God's direct creation and scripture – more basic, more factually genuine, than human writing, society, culture, ceremony. Since childhood Eileen had explored wild places alone and sought acquaintance with different creatures as I had. Once, at least, she'd run away, having accumulated a supply of food. I felt she'd live with me and love with me in a cabin in a wild canyon beside a creek and not need more of human society than I did.

On the phone after that sleepless night, I asked Eileen if her wish for a long-range future with me was still strong, and she said, "stronger than ever." I fought through the day's newspaper deadline, then went walking on Squaw Peak, telling myself to stop torturing Barbara and myself and Eileen and Billy (if he yet knew the situation). When I got home I asked Barbara for a divorce.

She left the house without answering, without taking anything with her. I was soon searching by phone, but none of her friends had seen her. I think she spent the night wandering, lost and alone, and I couldn't imagine how I could have done so terrible a thing to her after 22 years of loving marriage. Before noon the next day, an attorney I knew phoned and asked if I wanted to speak with her.

I don't know how well my memory serves. Maybe, under the tension, cogs slipped in me. I think I promised Barbara I'd love and cherish her and continue our marriage – but if she ever wanted to leave there'd be a quick divorce with our Ely home going to her, our Virginia log house to me. I think I told her I never could say a final goodby – to her or to Eileen. Though maybe, just maybe, I could decide never to touch Eileen, I simply couldn't agree not to communicate. Goodby was an open wound in me, not healable. Over and over – as a child when my mother had little time left to live, and again with Kathleen in China, and again with my father after his heart attack, and repeatedly through the intense years with Eileen and Barbara – I'd asked myself why I couldn't accept a final goodby. Other people apparently do. But even as I write now, I still can't explain. Barbara accepted my inability and chose not to exercise her option for an immediate divorce.

Eileen – who'd accepted a job in Irwin's photographic studio – picked me up near the *Times* office to go for lunch. She was driving her car on a dirt road toward the pinyon pines when I gave her a condensed and maybe confused version of what happened when I asked for a divorce.

"Do you think we should stop touching each other?" she asked.

"I don't want to stop."

"I know. Neither do I. But could we? Could it solve anything?"

"I don't know. Maybe we should try again."

She turned the car around. But we couldn't drive back into town. Both of us were crying. We turned back toward the pines. We parked and sat stiffly, stubbornly, but with her right hand and my left clasping hard between us. When the tears stopped, she drove us bravely into Aultman Street. "I've got to pick up mail at the post office," she said. "Will you go with me or shall I let you off here?"

"I don't know," I said. Then, "Let me off at the corner."

She stopped and I got out. Her face looked stony; mine felt stony. I closed the door and stepped to the sidewalk, and she drove away. I walked blindly to my office, not looking directly at anyone. I shut the door and sat turning over papers.

Soon she was on the phone. "I don't like the way we said goodby," she said.

"Neither do I."

"Enlargements you ordered are ready."

"I'm coming."

She was waiting between the curtains where portraits are taken. No one else was in the studio. I held both her hands, and we looked into each other's eyes. We might have stood as long as ten minutes. We didn't speak, but we lost our rigidity and filled with pulsing life again. She went for my enlargements. Her face was softly tender now, and mine felt that way too.

Though we went on not kissing, mostly staying apart, we talked on the phone and exchanged letters through our post office box that nobody else could unlock. Here are excerpts from Eileen's of late summer and fall 1960:

My Darling, I'm sitting in front of the fire – it does feel good – and have just read for the fourth time your very dear letters. Oh, Sweetheart, they bring you so close to me. Sometimes this separation is almost unbearable. But I shouldn't say that. You are always with me...

It was late afternoon when we jeeped up past the old Kolchek cabin. Oh, the longing I felt for you there. The sun was already down in the bottom of the canyon but was still shining brightly on the cliffs... I've dreamed of a week there alone... but to share it with you would be heaven.

Your thoughts on loneliness are very deep. It seems I've been alone so much of my life, even in the midst of people. I haven't been able to share any real depth of feeling very often. Most of the time I've drifted along the river of life like an iceberg, mostly submerged, and few people have ever wondered if there is anything below the surface. I have felt self-sufficient most of the time, though, and jealously guarded my privacy and felt no need to share. Perhaps I feared lack of understanding and recognized my own vulnerability. Whatever it was, you have penetrated to the very depths of me. You have pricked my little seal of isolation, and somehow I have expanded into a much bigger person.

It's strange, I never felt such excruciating loneliness, such a searing tearing apart, before I knew you, and yet I can never be really alone again. Just knowing you're traveling the same path and feeling the same things is wonderful comfort...

My Darling... I've read your dear, dear letters again. It's almost more than I can bear to think about, that perhaps life will be forever a great longing for what cannot be. Your thought – "a growing realization that glowing life can but tease and fade, like the moon in the driven clouds, destined soon to set behind the mountains" – is so beautifully and tenderly expressed and pierces me to the heart. My Darling, there is this about the setting of the moon or the sun, though –

they haven't actually stopped glowing and shining, they are just invisible to us temporarily and will rise again soon. I wish you could see these lovely pink clouds over the mountains now that promise a bright day.

The final crises came during the first half of 1961. In addition to poems, mostly unfinished, I was writing a narrative, "Trying to Understand," reaching back a quarter century to my early acquaintance with Barbara. Our marriage had clearly been a success. We'd had many happy years, produced wonderful children and given them good starts in life. Eileen and I had been friends for five years now, lovers for three. Though with months-long periods of abstaining in private efforts to save our marriages. Barbara had been part of the struggle for two years at least.

Billy – maybe aware earlier – was now directly informed. Consultations were arranged – separately – with the Methodist minister and the Episcopal rector. We visited the clergymen as couples and individually. They were kind and concerned. One said Eileen's and my love was a sexual aberration that could be repented of in a month or two, after which all would be well – if husbands and wives faithfully attended church together. The other saw far more than sex in our relationship and wasn't sure there could be a quick solution. But his only advice to Eileen and me was: Obey your marriage vows and never communicate with each other again.

Thus, human society and my own reason kept saying Barbara, Barbara. But my deep-inside nature that doesn't explain, but nearly always wins, kept saying Eileen.

I felt the clergymen were doing the best they could; their advice seemed wise. Barbara was definitely pleased with it; she'd been trying all our married life to persuade me to attend church regularly with her. I tried once more to believe what she and my parents and most of my relatives had always wanted me to believe – what the clergymen said and advised. I could grant the likelihood that their advice was wise, but I simply couldn't *believe*.

I remembered a good-natured argument I'd had by mail with Barbara when I was in Washington training for quick departure on the years-long assignment to China. I'd written to her at the war-time home we'd arranged in upstate New York that I was bothered by her putting "too much responsibility" on God for human doings. She was saying with total confidence to our children and me, "God will take care of you." As many years before that, with my Dad, in our lasting confusion about responsibility, I was saying, "We shouldn't simply pass the buck to God. We must take the initiative in using the forces of God and nature." She'd answered that our human love of children, of family, whatever, "is only a drop in the bucket compared with the infinite love waiting for us in Heaven."

It was a small difference, maybe – or was it the most fundamental of differences? Humans managed by God vs. humans taking responsibility for themselves...? Earth and people governed by God vs. people learning and using the "laws" of the universe (nature) and making the hard, as well as the easy, decisions themselves??? I still didn't know; maybe it's not possible ever to know for sure. But the argument emphasized a basic difference – between living with nature and living with deity. I couldn't help feeling that Eileen and I were living the same basic life on Earth, while Barbara and I were trying to live together in different worlds with entirely different basics. The feeling – was it also a thought? – wouldn't go away – and couldn't be totally hidden.

Barbara, knowing Eileen and I were truly trying to be good, and knowing I'd been writing poems related to the problem, wrote a poem to me, "A Flashback From My Love." These lines focus the meaning:

> There is toil, there is work, there are
>   heights to be reached.
> There are pauses renewing our strength.
> But the view from the heights,

>   beyond struggles that bend
> Reveals life, my beloved, as a canvas outstretched –
> There are darks, there's a flash of regret.
> There's a mist of remembering that
>   God's with us still and the canvas
>   still glowing and wet.

A sonnet I wrote to Barbara ends with these six lines:

> The world may be a swirl of useless talk,
> Fast heading toward a swamp of pain and tears,
> And we alike be sliding down the slope;
> And yet while hand in hand we still can walk,
> Within our sphere we conquer doubts and fears
> And look abroad projecting rays of hope.

This really was me at that time, deeply torn, undecided, yet Barbara and I were still walking hand in hand, still sleeping together. Shortly after the clergy counseling also, not knowing of the poetry exchange with Barbara, Eileen sent me without comment a little poem she'd found in a magazine:

> Even to the marriage of true minds
> one must admit impediment:
> words as interpreters of love
> are insufficient...
>
> Speech is slow when the heart is full
> and heartless time is fleet;
> the body is more eloquent,
> its discourse more complete.
>
> Since truth as well as beauty suffers
> in sentences half said,
> better that lovers speak of love
> mouth to mouth instead.
>   – Marybeth Little Weston

Verse, instead of prose, was telling my story as I tried to bring my "Trying to Understand" piece up to date. I realized my poetic (and nature-loving-protecting) feeling had been stirred by five women and persistent memories of them – Mother, Peggy, Kathleen, Barbara, and Eileen. Here are a few fragments from the Eileen crescendo:

>Singing strings as of a violin
>>stretch between us
>>>invisible,
>>>unbreakable,
>>tremulous with music...
>Electric, the unseen strings
>>vibrate and sing with mystic rhythm,
>>>harmonies of heaven.
>We dance and soar to heights
>>all unexplored in space –
>while others see but earthbound creatures,
>>you and me,
>>on ordinary paths,
>>walking...

>>Singing in the distance,
>>>something singing...
>>Far, far sounds of motors,
>>whisperings of nature,
>>music in a pine tree
>>>roaring, sighing.
>>Singing here inside me,
>>>something singing,
>>>>singing...

>It is said to be a joy
>>when you have lost your sight
>to remember there was day
>>before your starless night.
>It is said to help the deaf
>>who always used to hear
>to recall the touch of song

                    upon the normal ear.
I tell myself to feel that way
            now we have said goodby,
but it is quite impossible
            for me to even try...
Your kiss that I shall never feel
                    upon my lips again
can only be a sad appeal
            for that which might have been,
a searing source of endless tears
to fall throughout all future years.
'Tis better far, it seems to me,
if blind to lose your memory,
if deaf to shed one single tear,
forgetting you could ever hear.

                        I cannot tell why,
                    when I find a flower
                    and can show or describe it
                            soon to you,
                    it is a thing of joy,
                            a miracle divine.
                    Yet, my dearest love,
                    when the flower I find
                            you cannot know,
                    it is sorrow and regret,
                            a cup of bitterness,
                            a taste of tragedy.

The moonlit nights send tauntings
        of your laughter,
and on the wind you
        teasing
        sing to me
                and hide.
And then at last
        the contact
            current flashing,
and joyful life wells up in me

>   and dances like a dashing stream
>   under a shining
>   golden sun
>   set in a shimmering
>   glowing sky.

Barbara came into the library when I was turning over pages of half-revised poetry and asked why I didn't have a fire in the fireplace. When I couldn't promptly answer – I was mourning and a fire means cheer – she asked what I was working on. Poor at concealing as usual, I showed her some of the verse, including these stanzas that seemed to summarize:

> Two glances locked, embraced and danced
>   in glowing swirls of haze;
> a seed was fertilized, it chanced,
>   in mystic, blinding blaze.
>
> In soil between this house and that,
>   the seed took root and grew,
> while people in their houses sat
>   and doubted what they knew.
>
> The houses had the strength of years –
>   foundations strong as stone,
> cemented by the hopes and fears
>   of families at home.
>
> The shoot became a thriving tree
>   with leaves of shining green –
> until the blind were forced to see
>   the menace there between.
>
> From flashing clouds the rains came down;
>   from sun, the rays of life.
> The tree drew strength from nature's ground,
>   like iron defied the knife.
>
> The roots twined deep into the earth;
>   the twigs toward heaven rose;

the trunk expanded fast in girth
>   and turned the axes' blows.

The tree between this house and that
>   cracked the foundations' stone;
the people watched from where they sat
>   and trembled, flesh and bone.

Two glances search each other's depths,
>   amazed at what they've wrought,
examine all their lives' concepts:
>   Is it of God – or not? ...

Chapter 16 – New State of Alaska 1961-64

As dark comes on July 1, 1961, Eileen and I and her son Mike, almost 16, are traveling US 93 north on a three-person honeymoon. All belongings for our new life are crowded into Old George the Buick and the Igloo, our 26-foot house trailer. Our destination is Juneau, capital of the 49th state, where I'll be editor of the *Daily Alaska Empire*.

The brief time of final decision was heartrending, yet with a belief the pain would soon decrease in all of us. After the years of hurting uncertainty, Barbara and Billy agreed to divorces. Because houses were unavailable or shockingly expensive in Juneau, we decided we'd take our own lodging, though neither Eileen nor I had ever lived in a trailer. While I trained my successor at the *Times*, Eileen and Mike drove the Buick to Salt Lake and bought the mobile "igloo with handsome pink refrigerator and gas stove, a honeymoon home" (as she reported to me by phone). Now, where US 93 is straight and smooth, Eileen writes in her diary:

> Pale shimmering light filtered through gently moving trees and glorified the hillside garden (of our friend Eli Evasovic, justice of the peace) where we were married with our 18-year-old daughters and two friends in attendance. Maybe some of the shimmering was my unshed tears. How could one body contain such unbearable happiness and such aching misery? How could I possibly leave two of my youngsters? Unnaturally stiff faces with pasted-on smiles saw us through the final farewells, but my tears overflowed as we towed our little home out of town. I tried to gain comfort from my old arguments that those capable youngsters didn't really need me – they'd leave home soon anyway...

We drive long hours each day and soon we're on "Adventure Road," the legendary "Alcan," officially Alaska Highway, unsurfaced but persistent through seemingly endless Canadian forests and mountains. A bear crosses in front of us and disappears. "Wow!" Mike says, "Didn't know they moved so fast." Cars we meet are mud-spattered and have cracked headlights or windshields from tire-thrown gravel. We've been warned and are partly prepared. We tape cardboard over the Igloo's windows and Old George's headlights. We'll have to risk the windshield.

With barely enough time to reach Juneau on the agreed-upon day, we're hit by bad luck when coming down fast from the continental divide. I press the hand lever to engage the trailer brakes and feel no drag. The road's so curvy I don't dare use the car brakes; the trailer could flip sideways. Here's a straight stretch, though, and with the vehicles in line the car brakes slow us down. We do well on more level stretches and find a garage at Fort Nelson. The overworked manager says, "Flying gravel under there cuts your electric control wire. Sleep at this trailer park next door, and I'll do the fixing there." We hear him working under us near midnight, and next morning the brakes work – no travel time lost. Eileen calls it "good bad luck," and the pattern repeats as one beautiful day follows another. People in these remote places – here as in most of Nevada – help each other eagerly.

From Whitehorse, Yukon Territory, I phone the ferry terminal at Haines, Alaska. The once-a-day ferry is the only way to reach Juneau by car. We're to get on at two p.m. next day. There's time to leave our rig to be lubricated and walk down to the Yukon River. Gold-Rush steamboats are displayed on the bank. In the restaurant we pick up an abandoned *Daily Alaska Empire* dated July 1. The print is pale and full of errors, and we feel sick.

The hugeness of this country evokes nightmares of running in seashore sand and getting nowhere. Mountains grow before our eyes as we head southward toward Juneau. The second highest peak in North America, Mt. Logan, is near but maybe hidden in cloud. We pull off near a roaring glacier-fed stream for the last night short of our goal. Next morning we cross Chilkat Pass that's still wintry, and soon we're in Alaska. The road is paved, and we speed confidently. Then Old George's gas gauge warns us.

Service stations seem non-existent. All is wild beauty. A moose lopes along a shallow stream near us; he's horse-sized and amazingly graceful. We're driving slowly to watch him when Old George coughs regretfully and coasts to a stop – one hour before ferry time! Mike volunteers; he goes pedaling madly down the highway on Eileen's bicycle that we'd crowded into the trailer. A pickup stops behind us, and we get almost a gallon from an "empty" drum. With Mike aboard again, we reach an airport only four miles from the ferry, turn in – and fail. No gas here. An elderly couple in a VW camper offers us a drink. We decline and explain. They rush me to Haines and back.

As I pour ample gas into Old George, the VW, also to take the ferry, speeds ahead. Within minutes, as we come over a rise, we see our friends in the VW having trouble boarding, then realize they're intentionally killing their engine, delaying to give us time. But we're still not *in*. All vehicles must back on via a long ramp over deep water – so as to drive off forward at the Juneau dock. I can't back the Igloo and Old George together along that narrow ramp. I can't! Eileen, though, assures me I can. Obeying the ferry mate's skilled signals, I do, and the onlookers cheer.

In a crowded trailer park beside Gastineau Channel, an arm of the ocean, Juneau's midsummer daylight gets us out of bed early. After breakfast, Eileen drops me off across the street from the newspaper building, keeping the car for shopping. The office windows show no activity. I read the proud sign above the second-story windows in paint now faded: *"THE DAILY ALASKA EMPIRE – There Is Nothing Else So Powerful As The Truth."* I start across the street, and two men come from nowhere and block my way. One holds a sign, something about "damn scabs."

I veer up the street toward state office buildings. Both foot and car traffic escalate. I visit casually with anyone who seems to have time. I learn the *Empire's* in trouble, but still has friends hoping it can become a great institution again. I circle back and, ignoring the pickets, climb the steps, and in the office find Virginia Sims, wife of the Associated Press writer. She's been acting editor for a month. I ask her to stay a week more, letting me weigh the situation and decide whether to stay.

The editorial staff – the whole staff, in fact – is transient. A long-time mainstay, Dorothy Pegues, reporter of local news and society, recently died. Betty Jo Barr, a pretty woman from the South, wife of a Seattle gill-netter fishing seasonally for salmon here, was hired to gather social news. Merle Pruitt, older and the most nearly permanent (two years already), does proofreading and gives Alaska information to people in all departments.

Founded in 1912 by John F. Strong, soon territorial governor, the *Empire* was Alaska's leading newspaper. John W. Troy, who also served as governor, owned it for many years. Most readers turned against him when he argued Alaska wasn't ready for statehood. When Alaska was becoming a state, after all, Donald W. Reynolds, owner of broadcast stations and newspapers, including *Ely Daily Times* and *Ely Record*, added the *Empire* to his holdings. Reynolds didn't endear himself when he transferred printers from his home territory in Arkansas. Local printers went on strike and founded the weekly *Juneau Shopper* that continues to skim off the advertising cream the *Empire* urgently needs.

I feel caught, yet flattered that Reynolds hopes I might help break the siege. I spend the morning visiting community leaders, mostly businessmen. All urge me to stay.

At lunch back at the trailer, I find Eileen and Mike intrigued by Juneau. So I feel challenged. I give Virginia Sims the facts for an upbeat announcement of my arrival and write my first editorial to run the next day, July 11, 1961. It contrasts the dryness of Nevada with the wetness of Juneau, then emphasizes shared characteristics:

> Both states have long and important traditions of mining. Both are, in a real sense, frontiers. Both have vast areas of public land with all the problems that go with such land... Both states are growing in population... and now have somewhere near the same number. Nevada is engaged in a relatively new effort, from the state level as well as in various communities, to industrialize and to greatly increase tourist business...

I invite readers to give me guidance "in person, by telephone, or by letter." And guidance comes. Ward Sims, Virginia's husband, takes me to visit Governor William A. Egan. He looks at me as an enemy of unions that backed him politically, but he looks again. "I like your asking for guidance," he says. "Maybe you can help more than hurt." He explains that Alaska's central aim is "to catch up – in airports, harbors, highways, schools, everything. We have land ready for development and people eager to utilize it – but no funds for pioneer access roads." Our natural resources have "hardly been scratched – minerals, fertile land, forests. And the fishing industry – we're building it back after fish traps and all that just about wiped out our salmon."

The problems are even more similar to Nevada's than I'd supposed. I tell the governor I want to work for economic advancement where small communities lack basic facilities – but also work to protect wild species and ample wilderness.

Juneau's mayor expresses a similar need but complicates it with an inside-Alaska conflict that I'll soon find myself engulfed in. Mayor Larry Parker says, "Juneau's toughest problem is how to change this gold-mining camp into a modern state capital while we're in danger of losing capital status to an anti-Juneau movement centered at Anchorage, Alaska's fast-growing metropolis."

Ed Krause, owner of the trailer court where we soon relocate the Igloo, gives me and Eileen persistent guidance. A halibut fisherman for many years – his old 52-foot trawler, the *St. Louis*, rests on the beach beside Juneau's small-boat harbor – he knows what's wrong with our newspaper - and with the city, the state, and Uncle Sam too. He picks us up early Sunday in his Land Rover, and we explore the highway northward and all its branching roads. He tells us what settlements we find are "significant" and why and tells stories explaining the stories everyone else keeps telling. I make pages of notes. On additional Sundays, Ed gives us tours of Douglas town and the Juneau extension on Douglas Island (across a handsome bridge), also of a developing area south of Juneau reached by Thane Road. Ed says the capital-movers' notion that Juneau has no land for expansion is obviously false – an opinion backed by the tax assessor whose figures show a 10% population increase here in just the one year since the 1960 census, now approximately 12,000 in Juneau and vicinity. We didn't really need to bring a trailer; houses are costly but pay is higher too.

Juneau's mining history comes to life for us through L.H. "Kinky" Bayers. Captain Bayers, who worked for the old Alaska-Juneau firm in his younger years, shows us old workings, including deep shafts and extensive tunnels. He takes us on a "guided trespass" through the old A-J railroad shop where locomotives still lurk and through the tunnel where ore was hauled to the great mill on the hillside facing Gastineau Channel. We walk down long stairways, following the ore course through crushing-grinding-milling equipment still there under cobwebs. On beach-level at last, we walk across the tailings, still part gold, now in use as "the million-dollar golf course."

We learn more during an extended "Sourdough Brunch" at the "House of Wickersham" from hostess Ruth Allman, a niece of Judge James Wickersham, Alaska's U.S. Governmental pioneer, explorer, author, and the Territory's delegate to Congress in the early years. From back windows we see the city huddled far below – the harbor, towering Mt. Roberts, and a long stretch of Gastineau Channel. Ruth remembers from girlhood "a thousand miners pouring out of the tunnel, along the track and down, their lamps gleaming on their miners' hats, like so many fireflies."

Through all the concentrated guidance, I'm seeing patterns of human nature and wild nature mixing, and I'm catching them in the editorial column (where I have the same freedom to write as I choose that I enjoyed in Ely). Here's "Memories of Fog":

> It's said in Juneau that fog in the morning forecasts a sunny day, and we wonder if this wisdom is related to the saying that the darkest hour is just before the dawn, sort of a whistling to keep your spirits up...
>
> Fog can be comforting. All is muffled, confined, close and cozy. Morning fog, if you aren't in a hurry to go somewhere...is like being snug in bed when you're up and about. You have your own small world, and though your neighbors are there and people pass in the street, they're shut out by an insulating drowsiness, and the sounds come to you as though out of a dream, gently and from far away...
>
> Fog changes the world to a work of art, a painting, the over-busy detail eliminated. The leaves and branches of the trees are magic silhouettes against the glow. The nearby buildings can be cliffs from oriental watercolors above secluded glens, quiet for meditation. The drifting fog among the hemlocks on the mountainside above Juneau picks out a line of graceful decoration, and the fog over Gastineau Channel tells of a mysterious universe out of which comes a soothing silence broken only by half-known horns or motors, seemingly distant voices, sighs and whispers.

My feet are hardly on the ground at the *Empire* when Eileen and I, leaving Mike with *Empire* friends ready to help or advise, fly to Washington, as I'd promised Nevadans, to testify for Great Basin National Park. First we visit Senator Alan Bible, key sponsor. Then Senator Howard Cannon (Las Vegas) takes us from his office via the Senate's own subway into the Capitol. Cannon's signal brings Vice President Lyndon Johnson from the podium to a private anteroom. Johnson assures us he favors the park, then questions me at length about politics in Nevada and in Alaska.

I'm the leading non-governmental witness for the park. Stewart Udall, secretary of the interior, is the leading government witness. National conservation organizations support the park but would like to weaken Bible's clause protecting mineral claims. Bible tells me the bill might be amended but will pass the Senate.

Eileen and I visit Alaskan senators – who are Juneau Rotarians with me. We also visit Ralph J. Rivers, Alaska's only representative in the U.S. House. All have been reading my *Empire* editorials. Senator Ernest Gruening invites us to lunch in the Senate's dining room. He's proud of Mt. McKinley National Park and hopes I'll soon visit Glacier Bay and agree with him it should also be a *national park* instead of a mere *monument*.

After a follow-up visit with Nevada's Rep. Walter Baring – he'd been at the hearing, of course – we stumble into a serendipitous relation with Baring's chief assistant, Tim Seward. Tim and his wife Pike will save us renting a car. Our mention of a log house in the Blue Ridge intrigues them, and they'll drive us out there next day. It's Eileen's first glimpse, and she can hardly believe such isolation in the East. The last half-mile of private road isn't passable right now, so we picnic on the creek bank, then walk. Eileen's diary says:

> Trees meet overhead and wild blackberries beg to be picked. The road runs between a creek and an immense old rock fence... and there stands an old log cabin...with daisies nodding in the foreground and a huge black walnut tree standing sentinel. An old, old apple orchard is heavy with green fruit. Forested hills rise in back. What a perfect place for a writer to retreat to! My longtime dream home!

The house has been rented but is vacant now. The Sewards trade the needed protection and maintenance for use of the place as country retreat.

En route back to Alaska, we land in Ohio to visit daughter Sylvia at Antioch College and at St. Louis to visit Eileen's father and grandmother. Six days after we left we land at Juneau, bringing thoughts and facts for Alaska, such as:

> The national capital looms larger from Alaska and the *Empire* than it does, say, from Chicago or Los Angeles or New York... Decisions being made in Washington can be matters near to life and death for Alaska – decisions about public lands and resources, military expenditures... international agreements on fisheries, highway and aviation development and control... We are far away from the nation's capital, but in numerous offices there the decisions make impacts on us.

The Washington trip significantly strengthens me and the newspaper. Eileen and I are invited on "guidance" excursions – by the U.S. Coast Guard on patrol, by regional directors of the U.S. Forest Service and Fish and Wildlife Service on a two-day inspection of Tracy Arm Scenic Area in Tongass National Forest, and by the Glacier Bay superintendent on a cruise of several days inspecting the fabulous national monument. I now answer Senator Gruening's question: "Yes, the *Empire* and I will support upgrading Glacier Bay to full national park status."

Son Mike bubbled over with a job offer. "It's Chris Barr," he told us, "husband of Betty Jo, the *Empire's* society lady. We'll be going up near Haines on his gillnetter boat the *Fury* – be gone four days a week. I get *paid* for going fishing!"

We investigated and agreed. The three of us were making ourselves at home in Alaska at an accelerating pace. On the morning of the Sunday when Mike was to report for duty – at high tide in late afternoon – we were on our first Alaskan hike – and noticing houses at Juneau's edge we'd like to live in. The hike made an editorial:

> At least 20 persons used the Mt. Roberts Trail yesterday, and we believe all found what they were looking for... This trail starts right here in the city and goes just about straight up – on easy-to-

negotiate switchbacks... The peaks are about 4,000 feet above sea level... You start among hemlock and spruce trees, lush vegetation of many kinds including ferns and fungi, and you're finding blueberries, salmon berries, raspberries – all ripe now...

We sat down to eat on the grassy top of a cliff, and big black birds, ravens, put on a show of aerobatics, soaring on the rising currents, folding their wings and diving at each other, leaping in pairs from perches on cliffs and appearing to rise directly into the air, and – you can believe this or not, but three of us saw it – plunging and soaring, then doing "wing-overs" while kicking and moving the wings apparently at random and going into an actual tailspin for half a dozen turns before leveling out... Have they played like this from time immemorial?

Millions of people travel thousands of miles to reach such a place, but we have the trail here as a gift.

The *Empire* gained in public favor. We risked buying a house – not only because we dearly wanted more room but also because owning a house removed us from the transient category and improved the *Empire's* image. A six-minute walk from my office brought me to the house – 125 Gastineau Avenue, a street with a boardwalk up 128 steps on the slope of Mt. Roberts. We moved in on Mike's birthday, September 2. We called the windows "television screens."

Among the first shows was Southeast Alaska's Autumn, opening with torrential rains (annual precipitation here, 85 inches). Lifting clouds revealed gold on the mountaintops where vivid green had been. The gold dripped down to timberline as if with the high waterfalls, and under the evergreens and on the beach were paler yellows and flaming reds. Next, the snows started, the peaks a fresh white, then the white sifting down the slopes till it touched the sea. Spring worked at our windows in reverse, the green climbing back toward the waterfalls under the clouds.

In Gastineau Channel just below the house was ever-changing water with boats and ships, float planes, and sometimes icebergs and whales for our entertainment. The tides were dramatic, lifting freighters or cruise ships high above the piers or lowering them almost out of sight. Bird-watching too was endlessly intriguing. Gulls and bald eagles were stars. One eagle lifted a heavy fish and flew powerfully, but almost touching water, landing on a pile-post to enjoy feasting. Eileen could hardly wait to tell me one evening that, in the winter twilight's blizzard, she fleetingly watched a swan flying low with Juneau's electric glow (street lights coming on) reflecting from its breast.

I began using one feature of our house after over-busy months. You go out the front door, turn and climb stairs alongside the house, go around the back corner, and enter a separate apartment. The kitchenette to the left became Mike's studio and darkroom, multiplying his interest in photography. Beyond was my fiction-writing place. I would come home from journalism, eat dinner and, after a short nap, go up there and write my Nevada novel. Phone or visitors couldn't interrupt; Eileen would say, quite honestly, he's out; I'll have him call you tomorrow.

The Juneau Chamber of Commerce encouraged local citizens to invite legislators to dinner on a special annual evening. Our first was Rep. John Nusinginya, an Eskimo from Point Barrow. Along with him we invited Alice B. Schnee and her husband, long-time Alaskans informed about the regions and the people. Alice, newly persuaded to join my staff, was doing detailed reports on the Legislature, giving us exclusive glimpses beyond the AP reports. Snow was deep, and we expected Nusinginya to be wearing an Eskimo parka, but he dressed as business and government men did all across the country, suit and tie. He was in business at Barrow, delivering liquid water, pumping from tank trucks into whatever container his customer could protect from freezing. Water pipes were too difficult there, but he took great interest in our pipes, and was especially intrigued by the "jacket" in our oil heating stove that kept the water hot for our kitchen and bathroom.

Among others we entertained were Rep. Grant Pearson, Rep. Clem Tillion and wife Diana, Rep. Yule Kilcher, and Senator Frank Peratrovich. As Nusinginya represented Alaska's Far North to us, Peratrovich represented the Far South. A Tlingit, born at Klawock, Peratrovich had long been a leader of the Alaska Native Brotherhood. After serving in the U.S. Navy during World War I, he was active on the statehood committee – until victory in 1959.

As Empire editor, I fought the capital-move initiative of 1962. I had multiple incentives – to please (and save) the community where Eileen and I were creating our new life, to help the new state prosper, not wasting $200,000,000 for something it didn't need, and to strengthen Alaskan conservation to avoid the robber-baron pattern of America's past.

Our opponents argued the capital must be moved if Alaskans were to have better government. They pushed this fantastic notion: The new capital could be built with funds derived from the sale of townsite lots. Bob Atwood, editor-publisher of Anchorage Daily Times, a leading capital-mover, was going to Australia to report on that nation's new capital, Canberra. Meanwhile, Juneau and Douglas "and individual taxpayers residing throughout the state" were suing to keep the capital-move initiative off the ballot – because the state constitution itself specified the capital "shall be at Juneau" and the constitution can't be amended by initiative petition. On the Empire's front page, I placed the Atwood news and the Juneau news side by side for easy comparison. For the editorial page, I wrote, "Hold the Capital":

> The city council of Juneau, we think, is approaching the capital-move threat in the best way for the people of all Alaska by asking the courts to rule on the legality of initiative petitions for amending the constitution... The all-for-Anchorage attitude of Mr. Atwood and his newspaper is generally known around the state, and, to put it mildly, not generally appreciated...
>
> Mr. Atwood's arguments for moving the capital tend to disappear upon careful analysis... If Australia is, in fact, happy in

building its capital city in the wilderness, what does that prove in relation to Alaska, especially when, if we are to go far afield, Brazil is thoroughly *unhappy* with its capital move from Rio de Janeiro to a more centrally located wilderness site called Brasilia?...

This snapping back at the most powerful newspaperman in Alaska surprised readers of the *Empire*. It surprised me, too. I was just realizing how much I cared, and the caring would get stronger. The next editorial hailed the inauguration of Pan American jet service as contradicting Atwood's statement that Juneau was "remote and inaccessible." New navigational aids and the Boeing 707 put Juneau within easy reach of other major airports, including Anchorage. I mixed wild nature with politics in describing the inaugural champagne flight:

> The trip...went southward from the airport over Gastineau Channel by Juneau, climbing rapidly, to Taku and up that river... While we flew along the Alaska-British Columbia border, the Juneau Ice Cap was on the left with great areas of white and a few sharp peaks casting strong shadows... Soon Skagway was below us on the right, nestling in the snow on the apparently flat site at the end of the fjord. Haines was underneath us and within a short time Glacier Bay and Gustavus – glaciers, forests, beautiful arms of the sea, and in the distance on the right, towering Mt. Fairweather... A question was repeated often in various words – why should anyone want to move Alaska's capital from a location of such beauty with the facilities that are here and with service of such efficiency and style as is now offered by the jets?

The Superior Court rules against the capital-move initiative, and the statewide argument subsides, but Alaska's Supreme Court accepts an appeal, aiming to decide in August. Eileen and I take the last half of July as our vacation. We'll spend it touring the "Great Land," for enjoyment but also to improve my understanding. We'll visit son Mike who'll be with his Civil Air Patrol drill team near Anchorage. If my nerve doesn't weaken, I'll then call on chief capital-mover Bob Atwood. I'll also be studying a paradox on which I wrote an editorial called "Split Personality," focusing on the fact that many people are attracted to Alaska by the great wilderness but, once settled here, scold decision makers for not erasing the wilderness with more highways and other development. A wise letter comes from my friend Olaus J. Murie:

> This is a problem...not confined to Alaska... Automation is working against us. Fundamentally, we all want peace and beauty. Alaska has a great opportunity for a new look, to cherish the wonderful natural features that can inspire mankind... When I was in Juneau last I was impressed with the humane and high-level thinking I found there.

Olaus not only sees "split personality" but likes all my man-earth editorials. We share a strong belief, as he puts it, that "the beauty of this world" helps us "meet our problems more effectively."

Eileen and I head north via Haines and that evening set up our pup tent in the Yukon Territory's Kluane Lake campground. Heavy clouds move in, and we're barely packed and rolling again when rain pours. I should write an editorial on asphalt vs. gravel highways. The machine-gun rattle under the car rasps our nerves now. The dust turns into mud that splatters our windshield. When we cross the border back into Alaska where the highway's paved, I let Old George speed up. Then – WHAM! We drop into an invisible hole (rain-filled, looking like wet asphalt). We zigzag to miss other pits. Soon I'm driving slower than I drove on the unsurfaced road in the Yukon. Maybe the engineers should settle for easily maintained gravel until they learn to prevent frost-heave pits.

At Tok Junction, with rain-flood closing highways, we stop at a log hotel. Next day we inch farther north among heavy equipment and men working in mud. Then, along undamaged sections without crews, we see moose among trees and ponds. One moose as big as a mule is feeding in water so near we see the droplets falling from his lifting face. We continue toward the Yukon River through historic gold fields and see a hose-stream of white water, guided by hydraulic miners, washing gravel from the slopes and across riffles that hold onto the gold. We aim for the Arctic Circle and will drop back south to Fairbanks. Eileen sees a wolverine. We stop at a state campground and find moose tracks and moose "nuggets" (droppings). Summer is reigning – briefly.

In Fairbanks next day the display thermometers in the business district show 100 F, making weeks of 50 below hard to believe. The city is rich in "split personality," celebrating its "Golden Days" – its wilderness and Native American past, its bewhiskered sourdoughs chasing women in old-fashioned dresses, its forests and wildlife, while also celebrating the big military installations with manpower and money and the fast-growing University of Alaska rich in scientific advances for utilizing natural resources. Bill Snedden, owner-publisher of the daily *Fairbanks News-Miner*, guides us among the buildings of glass, metal, and concrete going up on a hilltop to house an ultramodern research complex for Arctic and sub-Arctic research and development, seeking solid facts for economic gains without damaging scenery and environmental health.

On a touring riverboat, with the owner-operator who's also a legislator we met in Juneau, we contrast Athapascans operating fishwheels in the streams and drying fish in the sun or in campfire smoke – with other Americans so modern they park their floatplanes tethered to the riverbank, scores of planes, perhaps in the back yards of owners' rural estates.

We escape the Fairbanks heat by heading *southward*! Our continent's highest mountain is white on the horizon, a massive shape rising to 20,320 feet. We camp near Mt. McKinley park's headquarters. (Denali is Alaskans' preferred name, for both mountain and national park.) I want to say hello to park officials, but the great mountain and the wild creatures won't wait. We're on the move by 2 a.m., heading watchfully for Wonder Lake on the 90-mile stretch of substandard road. Light is already ample. Dall sheep with lambs look back at us, and moose watch us too as they breakfast on willows along a stream. We search for grizzly bears on Sable Pass – from *inside the car* as park pamphlets advise.

Unbelievably high Denali is clear again from Eielson Visitor Center. We trace the 30-mile course of giant Muldrow Glacier. Clouds gather once more around Denali, yet we still feel its bulk in the cloud-curtain. We camp at Wonder Lake, and, as planned, meet Rep. Grant Pearson, a former superintendent of the park, author of *My Life of High Adventure* including his climbs on Denali. At his cabin just outside the park line, we dig to experience permafrost. Grant points out "drunken forest" caused by permafrost; he says the topsoil thaws a few inches down during summer, allowing trees to grow, but without taproots going deep to anchor and hold. Thawed topsoil sometimes becomes fluid and slides down-slope, tilting trees "drunkenly."

We visit Camp Denali, a marvelous retreat – cabins and meals and knowledge of nature – dedicated to multiplying the friends ready to defend Denali's mountains, forests, tundra, and creatures. Celia Hunter, co-owner, an Alaskan leader in conservation, becoming a national leader, is as close as anyone we've met to harmonizing with nature. Mosquitoes thrust their proboscises into her bare thighs and arms. Eileen and I want to slap them. Celia says, "If you let them drink their fill, they'll suck out their anti-coagulant toxin and the bite won't itch." I like that but still fail on myself to resist my impulse to slap.

We've narrowly missed seeing thousands of caribou migrating; Eileen gets a picture of one caribou. We get to see grizzlies, thanks to learning from Grant and Celia that Adolph Murie, author of *A Naturalist in Alaska* and *The Wolves of Mt. McKinley*, is here studying bears. When we stop at his cabin near Sable Pass, Adolph remembers Great Basin and the ancient bristlecone pines – where we explored widely together in 1958. He brings his telescope and shows us a mother and two cubs. We'd failed by looking for brown; they're *blond* in Denali, like the dried vegetation. The mother lies on her back, and the cubs suckle.

Alaska fitted together like a jigsaw puzzle. Soon I was trying to weld the cracks. Discussion with newspapermen around the state helped, and now I confront capital-mover Bob Atwood. He proves affable as he conducts Eileen and me around the *Anchorage Daily Times* offices, but she nearly bites her tongue in holding back criticism when he shows off his elephant-leg wastebasket. Mutually, somehow, we dodge the capital move. I'm asking myself, Can Bob and I be friends personally while being enemies through the newspapers? We know we can't change each other; it's citizens out there we're competing for.

Some friendliness persists. I publish an editorial about Anchorage, "Los Angeles in Miniature." Bob promptly reprints it and comments editorially that it was perceptive and generous throughout, "considering the fact that it was written especially for readers who rarely hear kind words about Anchorage." Soon my editorial was "One Great State":

> We've heard it said...Southeastern is altogether different and should secede and form a separate state... Fact is, however, if there were a logical dividing line in Alaska – which there isn't – it would go somewhere along the Yukon River, for only the great North and Northwest fit the "classic" idea of Alaska as dominated by ice and tundra...with Eskimos...
>
> We go far north to Fairbanks and what do we find? Talk of forest products. Loggers at work. (And do not the forests also give hope to Southeastern?) We find a great history of gold mining with hope of a revival. (And what is the main factor in the history of Juneau?) Fairbanks is building a tourist industry. (And so is Southeastern.) Fairbanks speaks of its hunting and fishing, its mountains and glaciers, its boat and airplane trips, its scenery. So does Anchorage. (And so does Southeastern)...
>
> We need to understand the tremendous identity...the urgent need for unity among the parts.

In August the Alaska Supreme Court reverses friendliness all around by decreeing (two justices for, one against) that the capital-move initiative will, after all, be on the ballot in November. The Anchorage and Juneau papers go head to head again like rams. The count of my editorials opposing the capital move rises past 50, and I publish dozens of anti-capital-move letters to the editor from all around the state. I can't tell how much the newspaper feud influences Alaska-wide opinion. *Anchorage Times* circulates in far greater numbers. But our Sunday *Empire*, at least, is read by leaders around the state, and many subscribers clip or copy editorials and send them to other Alaskans. On November 7 our top headline reads: CAPITAL MOVE BEATEN. The official count is 32,325 against moving the capital, 26,542 in favor. My adrenalin declines. The real me is catching up with himself, wondering if the *Empire* is really our long-term future.

Eileen and I and sometimes Mike were spending more of our time in the mountains or along the shore or watching the shows through our Gastineau Avenue "television" windows. In my hideaway attic I rewrote my Nevada small-mining novel. Eileen and I caught up with personal correspondence. We'd continued communicating with Barbara, cooperating in the children's educations. Barbara read *Empire* editorials and sent us Christmas cards she designed. A year plus a month after the divorce, she married Robert Richard Gill III, a Nevada attorney. Considerably older than Barbara, he died the next year. She'd continue art teaching at Ely. Later, she'd move back east to New York State and marry a railroad man.

Harvey was commissioned second lieutenant upon graduation from University of Nevada and served with army artillery in Korea, where active fighting had ceased. En route there, he visited us in Juneau. Upon his return to Reno he married Dorothy Wells, daughter of Mrs. H. Edward Manville Jr., and soon was teaching at University of Nevada, Reno.

Sylvia, through arrangements by Antioch College, spent a term at a Mexican university, living with a family, speaking only Spanish, then went to universities in Austria and West Germany and worked in a German children's home. She spent a summer with us in Juneau and often hiked with us. Her aim was to teach languages and cultures, and she married Christian Schneider, whom she'd met in Germany and hiked with in the Alps – and who'd get his doctorate in California and become a professor in Washington state, USA.

Laura, after some while at Whittier, married Eldred "Larry" Rowe of a ranching family near Ely. They continued their education together and graduated from University of Nevada, Reno. Larry would serve as an Army captain in Vietnam and return safely, continuing in the Army and becoming a lieutenant-colonel. Laura would use her specialty in elementary education at schools in diverse parts of America, including Chicago and Atlanta.

My energy surged in an effort to make the *Sunday ALASKA Empire* a lasting force for statewide unity and a uniquely Alaskan way of life. Valuable volunteers shared strongly in the effort. One was Amos Burg who'd adventured for decades in the North and elsewhere for *National Geographic*. His weekly contribution, "Mushin' Alaskan Trails with Sourdough Sam," became popular throughout the state. Another frequent writer was Helen A. Shenitz, an educated Russian who'd escaped the Bolshevik revolution and become a sharp-eyed, sharp-minded Alaskan. Dr. Shenitz saw statewide situations and national-international connections with penetrating originality and kept stimulating statewide discussion. Alaskan artist Rie Muñoz, who'd started drawing cartoons during the capital-move battle, continued in the Sunday edition to prick and prod and entertain.

Our main full-time reporter, Dick North, was a growing asset. He'd worked his way west from New York looking for a wild place "without discarded beer cans." Though his interest was all-engulfing, he favored history of the Far North. He rediscovered a remote cabin where Jack London used to write.

I produced a continuing series of editorials on unique aspects of the Alaskan way of life – such as aviation and "marine highways" making an extravagant highway system on land unnecessary, and tendencies toward focusing education on Alaskan's human and natural resources combined and using environmental science directly in the art of living. I summarized on January 19, 1964, in "Crystallizing a Dream":

> The ideas were grasped in semi-darkness as likely fragments of the Alaskan dream struggling for realization against pressure to establish just another example of what is established elsewhere, struggling against habitual tendencies (even in those who dream the Alaskan dream) to push accepted forms of progress and conform to known patterns... We hope some of the ideas will be of use toward crystallizing instead on Alaskan ground the beautiful dream so many of us carry deep inside ourselves.

I guess I knew the *Sunday Empire* and I weren't going to prove successful in "growing" the dream. At best, we would plant the seeds. I guess I knew it may never be possible to heal Alaska's – or civilization's – split personality, the desire to harmonize with nature vs. the desire for maximum consumption and minimum work. But I'd keep trying. There might never be total man-and-nature unity, but there could be "harmony" as I defined it when I started writing this life-story – "a functioning complexity that goes on sustaining life and creativity while producing more concord than discord."

Doubleday in New York was publishing my novel, *Gold Strike in Hell*. Eileen and I, invited by Governor Egan who appreciated our Alaska-wide vision, were enjoying the six-day "inaugural voyage" of the M/V *Malaspina* – flagship of the state's much-expanded marine highway. The voyage proved an unforgettable demonstration of Alaskan hospitality, scenic magnificence, historic and prehistoric attractions, and easy accessibility. Yet – because newspaper owner Don Reynolds was complaining about the amount of original Alaskan material we were publishing, hinting he'd rather fill the columns with less costly "canned stuff" from the lower 48 – our enjoyment was tinged with a possibility of farewell.

A movement grew that spring to nominate me for a Pulitzer Prize in journalism. Though I wasn't chosen, I treasure Alaskans' words, such as:

> There are few men writing editorials in the United States with the scope, with the maturity, with the perception, with the understanding, or with the morality of the works of this kindly man... I admire...his lovely prose and often poetic expressions of the beauties of nature and the fineness of the human race – the positive approach... Darwin Lambert has embroidered the *Empire* with such extraordinary editorials that citizens see fit to preserve them in scrapbooks.

After my Nevada novel came out, the Upper Yukon River Press Club gave me their "Honest Spike Award, for an honest piece of writing well done in an interesting entertaining way." At the luncheon where the spike was presented, Eileen and I sat next to Lowell Thomas, who'd been skiing on the Juneau Ice Cap with his son Lowell Jr., an Alaskan. We talked about aspects of the North country and of writing as a profession. Lowell hadn't read my book; the club was just presenting the autographed copy. But he said, "Doubleday published it, and I know I'll enjoy it. Doubleday is my publisher too."

I planned months and years of producing more books, each better than the last, but Eileen and I loved our Juneau life and didn't want it to end.

Chapter 17 – Tenting North America 1964

Remnants of hope that, through the *Empire*, I could continue contributing to a harmonious future for Alaska began shattering further when the paper's owner Don Reynolds arrived from Arkansas with what he called a solution. He'd revolutionize the printing plant, discarding old machines. Young women with high school diplomas would operate typewriter-like devices that cut tapes which, when run through another device, produce type for offset printing. Other new machines, also using inexpensive personnel, would do the printing. There'd be no more faded-out effect or smudges; the papers would be neat and clean. There'd no longer be jobs of interest to the printing trade unions, so the strike would fade. Personnel could be hired or let go as work fluctuated.

I agreed with Reynolds, of course, that the business must make a profit. But he bulldozed on into what had been my domain: Front and editorial pages remain free of advertising, but all other pages must be at least 60% advertising. We fill the front page with the world's top news from the wire service; it comes in on teletypewriters as both reading copy for the editor's use and tapes for automatic typesetting. We fill nearly all the small space remaining on advertising pages with features that come in already set up from newspaper services in the lower 48 – with which Arkansas headquarters already has contracts. Fill the editorial page with opinion columns from the lower states, plus cartoons also from outside, and, just occasionally, a local or Alaskan editorial. And, of course, we can't go on publishing many letters to the editor or Alaska-written articles.

I interrupted and said I couldn't go along with "the largely canned and second-hand content – with no room for Alaska." He said, "Don't look at it that way, Lambert. I'm investing in all this new equipment partly because you're here and becoming a genuine Alaskan." I agreed to meet with him again next day.

Eileen and I talked and thought and talked again and couldn't stop thinking and feeling. Juneau and all Alaska had been good to us. Reynolds's plan, though, included little work I'd enjoy doing. That kind of *Empire* didn't need me. Since completing my Nevada novel, I'd often worked at night and produced a readable draft of my world citizenship novel (set in China) that I felt would help keep nuclear bombs from destroying us and help inspire a nature-harmony dream earth-wide. I'd sent the manuscript to my agent in New York. Eileen and I felt this big novel would add reputation and income to what we'd already gained and thus launch us as freelance writers. "I love the log house in Virginia," she reminded me. "We could live there on a small income."

I autographed a *Gold Strike in Hell* book for Reynolds and told him I'd be moving toward other work but would stay, if he wanted me, until we'd sold our house and he'd found a new editor. I didn't say anything to anyone else about leaving, but somehow the word spread. A telegram came from Bill Snedden, owner of the *Fairbanks Daily News Miner*, a far more prosperous paper at that time than the present *Empire*. He wanted me to consider becoming the *News-Miner* editor. Eileen and I admired Snedden; we'd enjoyed seeing Fairbanks with him. We guessed we could learn to love Fairbanks, yet we wanted to distance ourselves again from crowded consumerism, and freelancing kept pulling. We told Snedden we weren't ready to decide, and he answered, "I'm thinking ahead for lasting arrangements. Just let me know when you're sure."

Trevor and Carol Beery Davis, long-time Alaskans and our friends since we arrived here, invited us to go fishing with them again on their *Sylvita*. They wanted me to catch a king salmon big enough to boast about wherever I'd be going. We'd fished in the rain with them the previous June, mostly on Admiralty Island's Green Bay, a fascinating place partly because it holds an old ship that sank with Klondike gold rushers and their gold. Carol had included among her published Alaskan poems one about the dramatic sinking of this old *Islander* after it hit an iceberg. We reread the poem that day, feeling nostalgic tragedy while waiting for a salmon, or even a halibut, to bite.

My second fishing experience, many enjoyable hours of a June 1964 Sunday, also netted nothing worth keeping, zero salmon. The third experience, a few days later, shortly before the Reynolds revolution, I wrote up for the *Empire*:

... Weather was mixed, the sun peeking through at intervals, nice showers in between but hardly enough to wet the deck, the clouds glowing white around patches of blue. We fished faithfully until nearly five p.m... Just as we were thinking about concluding...by going in for dinner that was being prepared in the galley, something took my bait while I was reeling in from the bottom near Point Arden at a depth we estimate as 60 feet. The fish zigged and zagged tentatively down there, then took off in the direction of Juneau, pulling the line insistently against the reel-brake...until less than a quarter of my line was left.

We guessed he might weigh as much as 25 pounds. But then, way off about halfway to Marmon Island, he surfaced, and we guessed maybe 35 pounds. Then he turned around and headed for our boat at high speed... The line of a fellow fisherman, who'd tried to reel in when my salmon struck, tangled with mine but was still slipping along it above water, not tangling my pole.

I think – I can't reconstruct the fast action – the lines disentangled when I stepped back, pulling hard, into the center of the rear deck... My attention was forced, however, to the salmon as he surfaced by the boat, then went under the skiff, threatening to tangle my line with the rope. I fought him and, I think, turned him, but I was swirling around this way and that, about done in, barely holding.

And Trevor got the net under the fish and lifted it, a feat in itself, and it weighed 49 pounds on the hand scales. Whatever it weighs dressed and on the most accurate equipment, we're claiming a record now – the highest average weight of salmon caught over a three-year period of any citizen of the Greater Juneau area.

The official weight was 49 pounds, 13 ounces. *Empire* writer Helen Shenitz soft-smoked this king salmon for us.

Yellow typesetting tape began emerging from new equipment in the editorial office, along with reading copy. I learned to select items of some interest, at least, to our readers – and match them with the right lengths of tape. And somebody in the plant learned to operate a machine that read the tapes to make printing. Reynolds was in Arkansas, and no word came of a search for a new editor. Didn't he believe I'd go? My paychecks kept coming, and the papers kept getting printed and delivered.

Eileen and I weren't exactly in a hurry and weren't sure just where we'd go. Two of our "multiple-incentives" were the need to find magazine-article subjects and facts for our freelance writing and our growing wish to help save wild scenery along with the maximum of healthful environment. An extended odyssey seemed needed. One specific floated up: we wanted to ride mules down into Grand Canyon – when the weather had cooled enough for Phantom Ranch to be comfortable – and write about our enjoyment, while also opposing too-low or too-numerous flights of sightseeing aircraft.

Our house at 125 Gastineau was in good repair, and Eileen repainted it beautifully. We offered it for sale through a real estate firm belonging to the husband of Eileen's animal-artist friend, Josephine Crumrine. Eileen had taken care of Josephine's difficult cat while she took a trip; as compensation Josephine made a splendid painting of our white cat (Chilkat).

The first couple who looked wanted the house at our asking price, nearly double what we'd paid. They wanted it "now," but we didn't want to head south in hot weather. By plain good luck, though – or because Eileen had made friends while working in the Alaska travel office – we quickly found congenial summer work. As with Mike and his fishing three years before, we'd get paid for what we wanted to do anyway – camp in Alaska until Grand Canyon cooled. I gave a month's notice. Here's my farewell:

Once an Alaskan ...

An announcement of the 18th annual Juneau-Douglas Picnic at Seattle came yesterday, reminding us of the many people who once lived in Alaska, or still live here part-time, who gather at locations elsewhere... We've been told by people who man Alaskan exhibits at vacation shows "outside," of the countless former Alaskans who come to talk about the past and check on how Alaska's doing now and dream of their glorious years in Alaska...

The great mountains of rock and snow and ice, the winding glaciers, the icebergs dropping into the deep fiords, the endless tundra of dwarf willows and berry bushes and reindeer lichen and pools, the people who live with nature, the soaring eagles with white heads and tails, the deep forest of spruce and hemlock and birch and aspen... the fishing cruises with restless water confined by high green walls, the wide winding rivers of glacial silt and icy water with gray gravel bars, and the brilliance of fireweed...and always the mountains of rock and glowing snow, and in the keen cold dark the northern lights, colorful, moving, changing – all these memories and many others are unforgettable.

They penetrate somehow, not just the mind but the heart, the fibers, of those who have lived here, and they rise again within to glow and surge. They become a call of the wild, reaching out from the depths of being for the responses of the earth, the forests, the mountains, the wind, the rain, the snow and the sky, the long long days and the nights that come in the middle of the afternoon and last until the middle of the morning. So Alaska lives in those who have known her – and will live as long as they live – the voice and fragrance of the awesome wild, the glories of unsolved mystery, the glow of basic earth insisting upon its natural courses of power and beauty despite the efforts of man to impose his patterns upon it. So those who have known this land and air and spirit, and known the splendid people who are in their element here, do not forget but continue to live, if only inside themselves while far way, the deep-singing life of Alaska.

The memory of our reluctant pulling away lives in me and in Eileen – as if forever. Son Mike chose to remain in Alaska, working in the *Empire* plant. He was nearly 19 and had a very special girl. Both planned further education.
I'm re-experiencing, feeling the emotions and events as if I'm inside them again – Eileen and I in Old George taking the ferry to Haines. She stays at a vacation cabin lent by Amos and Carolyn Burg and produces nostalgic oil paintings of ocean-mountain-glacier scenes, while I'm in Anchorage being trained as an interviewer for a study of camping in Alaska. When I fly back I spend the night in that cabin with Eileen. There's a disturbance under the floor next morning as we're getting up, and out the window we see a mother black bear and two cubs leaving.
We drive north to my first interview site, the Canadian customs station at the Alaska-Yukon border. We're invited to dinner by Ken and Eileen Watts, one of the two Canadian couples who live at and staff the lonely station, while also befriending wild birds and mammals. Ken projects a red fox on the screen – first, small in the distance. The fox doesn't flee, so Ken moves forward with his camera, picture by picture, until the fox fills a whole slide with its living detail, including a fear-denying yawn. We speak a hope we'll find a wild creature so obliging as we survey Alaskan campgrounds. Eileen entertains Eileen at tea beside our tent – that's a quarter-mile into wild woods – while Ken and I do our different work with the motorists.
A discovery at Deadman Lake alters our understanding. We arrive in mid-afternoon. Not far inside this campground there's a concentration of sites around the registration box. That's exactly where we don't want to be. We drive around a full loop slowly, then park where the sites are farthest apart and walk for closer inspection.

Our chosen spot is deep among trees, away from the road, with the lake and nearby shore visible – no view at all of any road or other campsite. After setting up our tent, we walk to explore the wild edge of the lake and watch waterfowl.

My work time starts when most campers have settled in. With survey forms on a clipboard, I walk the loop road. All the far-apart sites except ours and one other near the lake are vacant. Higher on the slope the campers have occupied every designated site and wedged in between. Just below the concentration, I greet tenters with a Missouri license while the man hammers stakes to anchor their home. He's eager to talk. "Your campsites are too far apart," he says. "Campers want to visit."

"But I thought the idea was to camp in nature – fishing or hunting, hiking, exploring – "

"Well, there's that, but most campers are like us. We'd have bedded down by the registration box if there'd been any room left. We're out of it here."

In accord with the survey form, I ask, "What recreation do you enjoy while camping?" Then I quickly add, "Besides visiting?"

"Fishing."

His wife says, "Bob, you haven't fished yet the whole trip."

"But I've got the tackle. I just don't know where the fishing's good or what lures to use in the North. If we were closer to the others, we'd be picking up what I need to know."

The conversation educates me. I hesitate on the way to the crowded place. Eileen and I consider ourselves nature people – but since we married we've been deeply and busily involved in society and commerce. I've been picking up from other people the mass of facts needed for the newspaper. This interviewing job now, I begin to see, is strongly relevant to our odyssey, our wandering homeward. The worlds of nature and of human society are competing inside us as in these other campers. Nature, we feel, is winning in us – but is it really? Or are we only nature snobs – hypocrites?

I walk on, and over and over again I ask the survey questions – and get the impression most campers put visiting with fellow campers ahead of fishing, hiking, photography, birding, botanizing. After I've completed each form, there's freewheeling conversation, and I learn further something that restores my shattered concept – the shared nearness to wild nature isn't wasted; it's a catalyst that enlivens human visiting. Many urbanites don't know their neighbors and may feel friendless in cities but make friends in campgrounds.

A gathering of interviewers and tourism officials, to discuss the findings, concludes the Alaska camping survey. Most of the interviewers are teachers or graduate students. Few seem surprised at my suggestion a main recreation of campers is visiting with each other. The planners and executives, though, blink a lot and scratch their heads.

Eileen and I in Old George leave the captive phase of our odyssey and follow our own route and timing, exploring our selves. We first head for Dawson where the Klondike gold rush pulled fortune hunters from around the world at the end of the 19th century. The camping survey has us feeling wild nature's pull from one side and the pull of human culture and society from the other. We're even surer than before that we'll enjoy living mostly with nature in the Blue Ridge where she fell in love with the old log house.

But we're soon distracted by trouble in Old George – strange noises and unsteady power. We struggle to keep moving and finally find a mechanic at a place called Forty Mile near the Alaska-Yukon boundary. A crucial part of the engine is malfunctioning, and we have to wait for a replacement. We set up our tent out of sight in sapling forest across the road, then explore. Back of the garage is a dog village. Members of the business owner's family are prominent in dogsled racing. We count 34 Huskies, each with a house, collar and chain. The chains allow the dogs to exercise in circles but not to reach each other. We see them fed. They're healthy, but, we think, not happy, not "at home."

We aren't "at home" either. We watch a dog with one dark eye and one blue eye – both eyes watching us. Eileen speaks to him, and he listens with a half-puzzled expression, inching toward her until the chain stops him. We can't reach far enough through the fence to touch him and that seems sad. There's communication, though; we feel this dog and most of the others are really glad to see us – but don't trust us, most likely don't trust any human.

We wander elsewhere and watch birds and search for wildflowers and trees to see how many species we can identify. We look for mammal tracks and find signs of most species we've guessed would be here. Nothing fully engages us. We stroll along the road in both directions. Traffic is sparse. When we see a car or truck we try to guess where the people are going and why. Few of the people are tourists. We don't feel as close to anyone, except each other, as to that Husky with one dark eye and one blue eye. We go back and visit him again.

At least twice every day we walk down the road 15 minutes to the bridge over what we take to be an upper branch of the Tanana River. We think of Athapascans' fish wheels and wonder about fish in this smaller stream beneath our Forty Mile Bridge. Athapascans do live near here. We've seen several in the store and garage. Some drive pickups or jeeps now and if not near roads drive snowmobiles in season. We wonder if they feel "at home" with White-American culture pushing in.

While staring over the bridge railing, we get lost together in our frustration, letting waves and swirls rise to the surface – regret about leaving Alaska and leaving Mike, burning our bridges, wishing we could have done better with the *Empire*, worries about the future, our present non-momentum, powerlessness, maybe directionlessness. We're strengthened by how completely we feel alike, how completely we're a team – so this frustration too will pass. Yet now nothing seems logical. The river down there is symbolizing life – flowing swiftly from its beginning far upstream to the present, where we're watching, and on downstream into the unknown future. But, no – the past must be downstream, because that water is here with us in the present but going swiftly and disappearing downstream never to be seen again, while the unknown future is coming at us continually from upstream and, for the moment while in sight, is our present time. Thus confused, I say to Eileen, or maybe she to me, we'd better go see if Old George's part has come – and stop at our tent to prepare and eat another meal.

The wait seems forever and farther – into a different world where humans and culture are tiny compared with nature and are swallowed into nature, yet humans keep speaking of themselves as outside nature and all-dominating and heading for heaven – or that other place. But our wait isn't forever; the calendar says only five days. When Old George is mended, we drive over high open country and stop to pick Alaska cotton from plants beside the road – though this is Yukon now, and it's goodby to Alaska – until – who knows? We've decided anyway to be freelance writers, and launching such an uncertain career in high-cost Alaska seems unwise.

There's supposed to be a ferry to take people across the Yukon River – maybe we blow our horn and the ferry comes? But today we like this lonely west bank more than what we've heard are the hyped-up tourist appeals of Dawson City. We find an old cabin with roof and walls shingled with tin that we guess was cut with tinsnips from squarish five-gallon gasoline cans long ago. I remember cans like these from my Nevada years. We try to guess who occupied this Yukon cabin, and when, and how he made his living on this bank opposite from the fabulously rich sands of the Klondike's tributaries.

The Yukon heads at a cluster of lakes in British Columbia quite near Juneau and flows northwest via Dawson to the Arctic Circle, then diagonally southwest across the middle of Alaska to the Bering Sea. It's the fourth longest river in North America, 1,979 miles. We decide for no conscious reason we'll tent all the way south to another great river, the Rio Grande, fifth longest on this continent, 1,885 miles – which decision makes us ask, why not tent also from the Pacific to the Atlantic?

Next day we find Dawson noisy and disreputable, yet, after all, genuinely founded on the real but incredible historical gold rush. I'm impressed by a lone man we find at a worn tent beside one of the creeks beyond the noisy "city." He's old and unshaved. He was here as a young man and has come back at intervals to pan for gold. Now he's retired from his last job and has lost his wife and guesses he'll keep searching until he finds the last bonanza, or dies.

Driving the dirt-and-gravel road between Dawson and Whitehorse, we fail to find a campground so put up our tent on an extra-wide shoulder where maybe a road crew parked a trailer for lodging. It's so rocky our stakes refuse to go deep. While we're sleeping a gust blows the tent down on top of us. We aren't hurt or even stimulated enough to crawl out and investigate. We already knew nature could get rough – as well as friendly and hospitable.
The flapping canvas fails to keep us awake.

Some Canadian campgrounds had enclosed kitchens where all campers shared a big flat stove, burning wood. Eileen found the arrangement lifted the visiting aspect of camping to a new high. She made friends from diverse places and acquired new recipes. We were soon moving southward on the graveled Alaska Highway where we'd come northward pulling the trailer. The country was the same, almost scary yet rich in friendly people ready to rescue anyone from bad luck. But there's more society in tenting than in trailering and more feeling of wilderness, wild creatures, weather.

We drove slowly without strain but gradually recognized wishes that tightened our time – more national parks to visit and children and Eileen's mother. And we ought to see my editor at Doubleday and the agent who was failing to sell my China novel, and, yes, we should talk with magazine editors about articles we might write. Living from freelancing wouldn't be easy, even near low-cost Luray. Eileen wrote in her budding journal:

> August 14 – Made coffee on the "marge of Lake Labarge"... Had lunch at Wolf Creek Campground, Alaska Highway Mile 907. Saw three-toed woodpecker, "teeter tails," red squirrel... Stopped at Big Creek Campground, M 674. Beautiful stream. Grilled sirloin, dinner at sunset. Our tent right by creek, big cliff on opposite side. Swallows feeding, darting.
>
> August 16 – Saw gray wolf at M 270... Lovely blue-lavender wild asters and a type of goldenrod along road. A little yarrow and fireweed... Saw many extremely tall slender aspens... Camped by the "Big Bam" (Balm of Gilead tree) by the waterfall where we stayed last time with the trailer and Mike.

While studying a Washington state map, I noticed a town called Ocean City on the Pacific and remembered the same name on the Atlantic. So, yes, we'd tent Pacific-Atlantic. Reaching the next junction, we veered westward and set up our tent in the mist on Ocean City's broad beach. Strange shapes loomed, perhaps oil-drilling platforms or odd ships anchored. Sanderlings raced in dense flocks along the seemingly endless beach, running, flying low, running again on the sand, reflecting eerily in the shiny wetness just after a wave receded. The sun was setting beyond the mist. Eileen whispered, "The water, the waves, look opalescent."

We camped at Crater Lake in Oregon and heard a bear raiding garbage cans, approaching closer and closer, but passing us by. The next night daughter Laura and husband Larry Rowe welcomed us at their small apartment near University of Nevada, Reno. We unloaded enough to make room for taking them sightseeing up to and halfway around Lake Tahoe (they were economizing, no car). Pete Kelley, an early and capable recruit in the decades-long effort to "create" Great Basin National Park, and his wife Caroline, invited us and the Rowes and Irwin Fehrs to their rural home for steaks and conversation about events in Nevada since we'd left and likelihoods for the future.

Ely awakened painful memories. No one knew we were coming. Barbara was in New York state; none of my children were in Ely. Eileen's Dave and Linda were here, and this much reunion was okay. Linda's youngsters, Kim and Judy, were in Eileen's words, "absolutely adorable, Kim a little giant." Dave and Thera, later to marry, were with us at dinner in Linda's home. Eileen showed slides of Alaska. We picnicked in the county park and went swimming at the still-new-looking indoor pool the chamber of commerce and I had promoted. We wanted to camp at Wheeler Peak, but there wasn't time to do anything meaningful for the national park idea – that was still alive in Washington, D.C. At Lehman Caves we met Robert R. Jacobsen, who'd later be superintendent of Shenandoah National Park and, with his wife, Phel, close friends. We hurried on via Cedar Breaks heading for Grand Canyon.

There's almost bound to be fear mixing with the anticipation of the famous canyon's so-vast labyrinthine depths. The colors of the water-and-wind-sculptured cliffs, in their thousand-foot stairsteps of unending variety, are so predominantly fiery, you can feel the canyon is Hades with the roof off. The mules may be sure-footed, but riding one over that ominous rim, even with the trail visible and with the wrangler-guide and others just ahead, can feel foolishly risky. And on the first switchback, with dizzying depths yawning, Eileen's mule stumbled on loose rocks – but recovered!

Eileen hadn't been feeling well but couldn't let herself miss our long-anticipated ride into wonder. Often, though, we wished we were doing our own walking; we'd have rested when we wanted and more carefully studied the rocks and the cliff-crevice plants. Maybe we'd have seen more wild creatures. Eileen felt worse and decided to remain at Indian Gardens where box lunches, brought along on a pack mule, had been served. The whole ride was reduced anyway. Flood had washed out part of the trail, and the canyon bottom and famous Phantom Ranch weren't reachable.

In New Mexico, Eileen's mother guided us in sightseeing – up to 11,000 feet in a cable car over a ski area where she'd been managing the restaurant. The slopes were covered now with wildflowers. She also guided us into Lincoln National Forest where, she said, Smokey the Bear, long-time symbol of forest fire fighting, was born. We saw pronghorn antelope racing across brushland and tarantula spiders crossing the highway, big enough to show well even at 60 miles an hour.

The Rio Grande runs south through the middle of New Mexico. We headed for Big Bend National Park where the river is the line between Texas and Mexico. Carlsbad Caverns held us a while. In our tent just outside that national park's boundary, we were waked by deer gnawing woody twigs, almost touching our canvas. We'd known deer eat twigs but had supposed tender green twigs. Eileen wrote:

> September 5 – Got up about 5 a.m., went to Carlsbad entrance and watched the bats dive into the dark, then took the desert nature trail and the 3+hour walk underground. Impressive!
>
> Got to Big Bend after dark. Labor Day crowds. Spectacular mountains. Special luck getting campsite in Chisos Basin. While slicing roast beef Mom sent along, I saw a beautiful hog-nosed skunk. It came up to me several times for tidbits of beef. Well-mannered skunk.
>
> September 6 – Roadrunner preening on a rock. Took nature hike up "Lost Mine" trail – many unusual plants identified. It rained. Drove down to Rio Grande Campground... Walked at dusk and saw many huge millipedes. Very picturesque campground full of large shade trees – cottonwoods, willows with orchids, mesquites tree-size, cactus, songbirds, raccoon.
>
> September 7 – Waded Rio Grande, knee deep only here now, and in Mexico walked across burning sands to primitive Boquillas village. Had warm beer in cantina. Pigs and chickens in and out of houses. Kids selling rocks. Burros tied to

fence. Boy on horse with big catfish. Real "movie-type" village.

Among memories I don't forget is a Mexican farmer, small with distance – maybe a third of a mile from our camp, past the river, to the stone-and-adobe house up the opposite slope – that man coming out in the early half-light, yawning, strolling among bushes, standing there unselfconsciously in a man's posture urinating, then scouting around picking up dry sticks, disappearing into the house with the sticks – and soon the smoke of a small cooking fire rising into sky. This man could have been my father. He was a universal human, anchored, at home with Earth. He could have been me. I with my raveled sensing of home wanted to be him, wanted to wrap myself in the basics of life, not depending on society or the economy, not struggling for things we didn't need, forgetting all the far impossible ambitions.

Our odyssey continued its emotional ups and downs. From Big Bend we headed toward St. Louis to visit Eileen's grandmother, father, and stepmother. Eileen wrote of our approach:

> September 8 – Crossing Texas, saw fossil bones in national park exhibit ... saw Texas cattle, cowboys, lots of oil wells, crossed Pecos River... Camped at Brownwood Lake State Park, tent and table under big oaks with acorns. Had nice swim... Saw lots of funny scissor-tail birds – flycatchers.

> September 9 – Pretty sunrise... Saw deer. Real thick swarm of mayflies all over tent and trees. Saw dead armadillo in road – hit-and-run victim.

Eileen was telling me – as we crossed Oklahoma and Missouri – about her childhood and later visits with her kinfolk in St. Louis. Her mother, Edna, divorced her father, Leroy Robinson, when Eileen was seven. Edna lived a "liberated life," often absent for work and other reasons, and Eileen was soon living mostly with her grandparents. The court transferred nine-year-old Eileen to the custody of her father, but almost immediately Edna married a man she'd known just three weeks, and the newlyweds kidnapped Eileen and took her to the West, keeping their oft-changing location secret but allowing communication with her father via her grandmother – a sadly unsatisfying contact.

When Eileen and I reached St. Louis, Grandmother, still living in the comfortable home Eileen was born in, seemed frail but happy. Dad and his second wife, Mae, lived six blocks away. We visited long-ago haunts. The great St. Louis Zoo, a favorite place of Eileen and her Dad from her early years, was joyfully nostalgic.

Next stop was Antioch College in Ohio. Daughter Sylvia had graduated in June but was staying for additional studies and because Christian Schneider, whom she'd met at Tübingen University in Germany, had an assignment here. We all picnicked at our tent. They're planning to be married in November at Morning Star Lutheran Church, where I'd been Sunday School superintendent years before, just down-hollow from our Blue Ridge log house.

When getting close to New York, we packed our old tent and other camping equipment as much out of sight as possible. We read a small bit of welcome when, even as traffic became more frantic, we saw whitetail deer browsing peacefully on bushes beside the freeway fence. From previous experience I felt Brooklyn was nearer our taste than Manhattan, so we crossed the rush-rush island and the East River and took a room at the St. George Hotel – that I remembered from 28 years before with Dad and Aunt Luella.

After a bath and change of clothes, we went deep under the St. George to the miraculous subway and soon were at the World's Fair. It magnified the dazzle effect of the city on us denizens of the wilderness. Its advanced industrial and scientific exhibits – as in the Chicago World's Fair I'd seen in 1934 – struck me as statements that man and nature can be endlessly creative and must come together somehow in a lasting home for Eileen and me.

Next day, en route to the literary agent who'd handled my Nevada novel, we wandered in Manhattan and found the Empire State tower. That day we dropped our first agent and found one we liked better. He wanted only books, advising we deal directly with magazine editors. If Doubleday didn't want my China novel, he'd take a look to see if he might place it elsewhere. He doubted that manuscript could bring us an advance big enough to launch our freelance career. We preferred his frankness to unquestioning praise followed by weeks and months of non-action.

At Rockefeller Center-Radio City, we enjoyed the stage show that included the Rockettes. We were approaching Times Square when an ex-cop shot the "doll man." The crowd became a mob. Police on horses – incredible to us but apparently a tradition – tried to keep us all under control. A man behind Eileen whispered hoarsely, "We live in a jungle, an asphalt jungle, and you'd better believe it!" We believed it; in fact, we'd long suspected big cities were less civilized than small towns and rural places.

On Thursday we rode the Staten Island Ferry – 30 minutes for a nickel, our greatest travel bargain, less expensive even than tent camping – then spent the rest of the morning with Harold Keubler, "my" Doubleday editor. He encouraged me to write a novel I described for him and the two of us to collaborate on a nonfiction book that might be called "The New Alaska" or "The Alaskan Dream," but he offered no advance of funds or signed contracts. He considered the China novel too vast and its time-line too confusing. I reminded him it was a world citizenship novel, as well as an American-Chinese love story – and most timely right now – but he didn't change his mind.

With world citizenship alive in us, we visited the United Nations headquarters. In 1945 Barbara and I had been in New York with similar thoughts when the atom bomb wiped out Hiroshima. We'd thought the United Nations would make war rare or nonexistent. But the charter would first have to be strengthened, the big-nation veto eliminated from the Security Council. Now, 19 years later, the organization was still struggling, not really coping, and my world novel still wasn't out there helping.

From the St. George we phoned several magazine editors. Hugh Grey, editor of *Field & Stream*, was intrigued by our continent-wide tenting and bought my unwritten article. Maybe we *could* make a living from freelance writing.

Our final tenting was to be on the Atlantic shore, but there was no campsite near the shore in Ocean City, New Jersey, and I faced the fact I'd never seen or heard of one in or near Ocean City, Maryland, eastern terminus of US 50 where I'd visited half a dozen times. Our log house and the need to start writing pulled us as far as a Maryland state park at Elk Neck – on Chesapeake Bay, which I correctly but unsatisfyingly asserted was the Atlantic. Our night at Elk Neck wasn't good for sleeping. I remembered Barbaria of the 1940s – we'd need a new name for it – and wondered how strongly Barbara would haunt us there. Eileen's thoughts were probably similar, but we talked instead about Tim and Pike Seward.

When we'd written them we were coming home to live, Tim replied in friendly words that didn't quite hide his disappointment. They'd invested themselves, hoping we wouldn't come till I'd retired. They'd seen our freelance writing as an unreal dream. When we phoned their Washington number with an estimated time of arrival, Tim told us politely but maybe ironically, "Make yourselves at home. We'll come for the weekend, and we can talk about everything."

This painting served as a "window" above Darwin's desk for many years.

Mary's Rock, Shenandoah National Park
By Eileen Lambert, 1960s.

Chapter 18 – The Blue Ridge Again 1964-68

We drive with slow care up the mile-long lane that's barely wide enough for the Buick. The rocky creek-bed beside us has no ripples, just shallow pools. "The fish must be dying in this drought," Eileen says. As we turn up from the creek-bank into the yard, she groans. The lawn, though neatly mowed, is brown. No daisies or susans bloom as when she fell in love with the place three years before.

I stop Old George on the barren lawn. Eileen and I look at each other. Complex emotions swirl. We go into the house, and it looks good the way the Sewards have arranged things. I think of Barbara and the kids and me, 15 years back, gathering all our belongings into this living room to load for the move to Ely. Though Barbara haunts this house, she doesn't seem hostile. She coped well with hardships here – no running water, for instance. The "cabin in a canyon" was more my dream than hers, and in our divorce she quit-claimed this place to me.

Eileen too is aware of Barbara – and says, "We should move her old furniture" (heavy oak bed and chest of drawers) "into the guest room. We'll use the brass bed."

We bring in camp equipment and supplies but use the old-model electric range that was put into the kitchen for the first renter. I gather wood for the fireplace. Rain starts falling while we're eating. When it escalates, beginning to end the drought, Eileen laughs and says, "We brought the rain from Juneau – where there was too much." The creek almost roars. Wind whistles between logs. It's chillier than usual in September, and I light kindling and add wood in the fireplace. Radiant heat is soon hot on my hands, but the room temperature doesn't rise. The fireplace is a giant vacuum cleaner sucking warm air. The biggest draft comes from the old root cellar under the floor. It lifts the rug.

"What have we done?" Eileen asks. "Can we really survive here till we're self-supporting writers?" We agree we must save on groceries through vegetable gardening, producing orchard fruit, gathering wild foods – starting with persimmons already ripening on nearby wild trees, but of course testing first to avoid the pucker.

The Sewards, arriving Saturday, gracefully accept us. We thank them for the maintenance they've done here and refrain from asking why they machine-mowed everything, including daisies, susans, and grapevines. Tim is justifiably proud of the stone-and-concrete repair in the front wall that may have saved the log structure. He gives primary credit to Ernest Miller, who's retired from the national park now and works in his own blacksmith shop on his farm where our lane leaves the public road. When Ernest walks up to visit us, we praise the stonework as blending with both the logs and the stone foundation. He accepts repayment for what he actually spent – for cement and sand – but nothing for the skilled work. His joy is in creating, just as in his shop making beautiful things of iron, not in making money.

Some weeks back, Ernest tells us, he came across wire and a green-glass insulator of the phone line I put up in 1946. The old magneto phones won't work now, he adds. We tell him we don't want a phone – or a television – here. At the newspaper jangling phones began upsetting my nerves and digestion. He chuckles good-naturedly, reading my eyes, then Eileen's, and he volunteers his own phone if we ever need it. He also offers to help "daub" the logs, where the wind sneaks in, but I decline.

Eileen and I want to do the basic things directly, personally. The work brings us down to Earth from our free-floating odyssey. In myself I feel multiple incentives harmonizing more fully than ever before – respect for Earth as the source, writing plans to protect Earth, exercise that's good for my health, weatherproofing for the house, and a feeling of accomplishment. With the same worn-out screwdriver I used in 1946, I again mimic a dentist readying cavities to be filled. Everything that's loose I scrape out, leaving mortar where it's solid, also the basic logs and the long wedges of wood driven tight between logs long ago as a base to hold mortar. When all cavities are clean, I paint the wood with creosote to stop further decay.

Following old Tom Jewell's recipe, I mix brick-laying cement powder with sand in proper proportion – in the old wheelbarrow – then stir in water and keep stirring until the soft but stable mass is homogenous. My mortar tray is old waterproofed plywood 15 inches square. Balancing the tray, with tiny trowel stabbed into the mortar, I climb the ladder. Daubing-chinking from a ladder isn't easy – one hand holding the tray, the other wielding the trowel, forcing the mortar in, smoothing, my feet on the rungs and my knees against the ladder's edges that support the rungs and hold me steady and firm, though sometimes the pressure bruises my legs near the knees.

Eileen takes time and energy from her own urgent tasks to carry many tray-loads to me up the ladder. She's busy making curtains, scraping off crumbly whitewash, painting inside and out, harvesting apples, making sauce. Sometimes we entice each other for intervals of rest and enjoyment of the forest's autumn reds and yellows. Eileen and the scenery move me to try for artistic contours in the mortar-finishing. She appreciates – and strokes me with loving irony in return – for instance, "You're always saying a job's impossible, then going ahead and doing it."

The other fixing, though, is merely difficult. I make a concrete base and reconstruct the wood frame for the cellar door, thus shutting off the rug-lifting draft. With cold chisel and heavy hammer I dismantle enough of the stone fireplace to install an adjustable damper of iron to reduce sucking of air. We gain a little heat now from fireplace fires, but the old wood-or-coal heater, here since the 1940s, will be our main winter warmer.

There's running water at the kitchen sink now, and the old pantry is a functioning bathroom – improvements made in the 1950s with funds I sent from Ely. Our bedroom at the back of the frame addition to the house overlooks the vegetable garden area; the ceiling is higher here. The middle room upstairs, also high-ceilinged, is Eileen's – for writing, painting, sewing, whatever she wishes. My writing table and rotating chair (brought from Juneau), along with book shelves and filing case, are in the living room near the fireplace.

Working in the evenings, I wrote the Yukon-Great Basin-Rio Grande-Pacific-Atlantic tenting article. Eileen, always my first reader, made suggestions. I left it a week and then, as would become habitual, improved it. Strange – I never rewrote newspaper items, even editorials; the deadline was too close. But for magazines and books, I rewrite – once, twice, some manuscripts three or more times. "You Meet Such Wonderful People" was rewritten just once, and the *Field & Stream* editor sent a check and scheduled publication (June 1965).

We spent a day in Washington, 85 miles from Shaver Hollow – I attending the semi-annual board meeting of National Parks Association (now NPCA), Eileen visiting the Smithsonian Institution's art galleries, American history, and natural history exhibits with the wife of another board member. A much-wanted designation of vast wilderness in Great Smoky Mountains seemed stalled, and I agreed to go with a staff-man to investigate. Through a quarter-century of service on this board, I'd be most active in relation to Great Basin National Park, Shenandoah National Park, Glacier Bay and Denali in Alaska, and in national and worldwide environmental thought.

The semi-annual board meetings usually included a cocktail gathering or dinner or both with leading conservationists inside and outside the organization. Through the years Eileen and I thus mingled with many people we greatly admire – Supreme Court Justice William O. Douglas, for instance, and Interior Secretary Stewart Udall, and Rep. John P. Saylor of Pennsylvania (senior minority member of the House committee dealing with national parks) – and Mrs. Cazenove (Dorothy) Lee, a fellow board member who'd invite us to her mansion in Washington and accept our invitations for weekends in Shaver Hollow. She loved bird-migration times in spring or fall.

Paul M. Tilden, editor of *National Parks*, invited me to write a piece demonstrating NPCA's interest extending beyond the parks into general conservation. My mind went back to my Alaskan way of life series in the Sunday *Empire*, seeking "a true standard of living, not a statistical one based on dollars" but one actually enhancing human happiness. This seed grew fast, and I wrote:

> Signs abound in America today that the pursuit of happiness is no longer to be identified with the pursuit of perpetual growth; that production and consumption of material wealth should move over for creation and practice of the art of living; that conquest and alteration of Earth should give way to harmonizing with nature inside ourselves and with the nature around us.

I argued that, despite recent advances into space, "Earth is where we live and will continue to live." Population growth resulting from economic growth was becoming "a threat to the good life." I showed people suffering from too much growth, not simply crowding but more crime, more pollution, more accidents, more vandalism, more welfare costs, less enjoyment of living.

> We simply cannot afford to leave the juggernaut of population-economy growth without firm brakes. Times and places where that juggernaut must be halted for the good of humanity are becoming more and more numerous. Were we to grant continuing priority to the perpetual-growth concept, we would be admitting defeat for the good life, the maximum happiness of humankind on Earth, our home.

Paul Tilden published the article in the April 1965 issue with fitting illustrations. Bundles of mail came from around the country, agreeing with my ideas and title, "Let's Outgrow the Growth Mania." A professor in Florida called it "one of the best articles I have ever read." NPCA files showed, "Never before have we received such a flood of congratulations." Thousands of reprints were ordered by readers. The phrase "growth mania" spread fast; Interior Secretary Udall was soon using it in public statements.

Eileen, meanwhile, was selling articles to *Virginia Wildlife*. We weren't getting rich but were getting known – a little.

A week before their wedding date Sylvia and Christian arrived here in a panic. A long-awaited gift of a specially created pattern, with silk from China for the wedding dress, still hadn't come. They'd hurriedly bought a pattern and lovely ivory brocade and brought the problem here. Eileen, though experienced in sewing, had never made a wedding gown. The task was complex, but the gown was completed – with extra help recruited, even mine, to cover numerous tiny buttons with the cloth. Sylvia's closest friends from Antioch College (two of them New Yorkers) felt they'd ventured "outside the world" – especially when Eileen and I investigated noises at dawn and found our back stoop moved and bear tracks in the exposed soil.

The Morning Star minister of our 1940s time here returned to conduct the ceremony. Christian Schneider, the groom, a musician, composer, and former church organist in the Black Forest, Germany, supplied the wedding music. He'd composed the prelude, and he played it "live" on the Morning Star organ. Sylvia's mother, Barbara, widow of attorney R.R. Gill, was hostess at the reception in the church basement. Bride and groom changed outfits at our house, then hiked into the forest, heading for a cabin they'd rented for their honeymoon. Their friends had fastened signs "Just Married" and tin cans to jingle on their backpacks. Eileen and I felt the wedding harmonized with our life.

We adopted a cuddly puppy and named him Sourdough and loved him. Eileen began feeding birds – tufted titmice, chickadees, white-breasted nuthatches, cardinals, white-throated sparrows, red-bellied and downy woodpeckers, blue jays, doves. From her study window, above the dining room, she had suet hanging, and she put sunflower seeds on the sill. Soon she was enticing chickadees into her hand, through a slight window opening. She similarly attracted a curious downy woodpecker, twice.

I wrote between breakfast and lunch. In the afternoons I worked outside, mostly on firewood half the year. My muscle-powered saw bordered on silence while cutting easily through four-to-eight-inch logs. With firewood there were three obvious incentives – exercise, household heat, and enjoyment of wild creatures. I experimented with different kinds of wood; the Blue Ridge has a hundred woody species. I preferred to have only a month's reserve, enough to last through a case of flu, say, or short trips, too little to let me loaf when days were suitable.

Here's my equipment – 30-inch bow saw, ax, wheelbarrow, portable home-made sawhorse, leather gloves. Choose afternoons when there's been no precipitation and the temperature is above 20 and below 50 F. Go up-hollow or slightly up a ridge from the house so you'll be moving your heavy loads down slope. Look for standing dead trees "seasoned on the hoof." Black locusts five to eight inches in diameter will nearly always give the most heat for the least work. Saw the wood into stove lengths and load the chunks into the wheelbarrow, while staying receptive to sights and sounds of the forest – deer, bear, chipmunk, weasel, fox, bobcat, wood frog, many kinds of birds, sometimes at dusk an opossum or a raccoon starting early on his nocturnal rounds.

Two large and long projects dangled enticingly in January 1965. First, Nevada organizations, informed I was here in Virginia, proved ready to revive the Great Basin National Park effort – that had failed in the House after the Senate passed its bill in January 1962. They wanted me as their part-time lobbyist and national publicist. I'd never stopped believing this park would be established. The offer was another case of getting paid – all actual expenses anyway – for exactly what I wanted to do anyway. Our car now was a small Renault that got 38 miles to the gallon, so travel was inexpensive. Lack of a phone was a handicap, but Ernest Miller agreed to take names and numbers for me. He'd put them in the mailbox, and I'd call back from his phone. The main work, though, would be in person.

I contacted key people I already knew in Washington. President Johnson – partly because of my visits with him earlier in Ely and in that Senate anteroom – would ask for Great Basin National Park by name as part of his program presented to Congress. Senators Bible and Cannon would introduce a Great Basin bill identical with the one that had passed the Senate earlier. The people in Ely – Betty Whitehurst, chamber manager, and Burrell Bybee, chairman of the chamber's national park committee – reported that Pete Kelley, long-time friend we'd been entertained by in Carson City when en route from Alaska, would be active in Nevada again. Another small advantage – I also knew the current House chairman of national parks, Rep. Ralph J. Rivers of Alaska.

The White Pine Chamber of Commerce wanted "a national park PERIOD!" – any bill that could pass the House and the Senate and be signed by the President. We knew already what could please the Senate and the President. The puzzle was, what bill could please the unpredictable Rep. Walter Baring of Nevada and still not be rejected by the House committee or by the Senate or by Interior Secretary Udall (which meant a veto by the President). I believed Baring wanted to serve his state but looked on Nevadans as depending on mining and ranching, while the two Senators knew most Nevadans were urban now, looking for outdoor recreation, depending largely on money brought in by visitors.

One way forward might be bringing the three lawmakers together in person. I went often to Washington, probing – and reported to the White Pine Chamber: The Bible-Cannon bill is strongly supported by NPS. I spent two hours with Baring. He's upset, emotional, rather hurt... At the end he'd tentatively agreed to an entirely new approach...in cooperation with Bible. However, Bible hadn't conferred with him prior to re-introducing the park bill, and this gave him a feeling the stage is being set...for a campaign of criticism against him... It doesn't seem he's studied the NPS reports or made any contacts with Interior...as Bible has... There's no advantage, however, in criticizing Baring – in fact, quite the opposite. There's no way for us to win without getting him on our side... Pete Kelley will know how to stir up a letter-writing campaign among Nevada voters, perhaps beginning with the conservation people who endorsed the program before – both Toiyabe and Vegas chapters of the Sierra Club, the university, garden clubs, then chambers of commerce throughout the state, Lions clubs, American Legion ... I talked with Jack Carpenter, Bible's executive assistant. Bible wants to see me on Monday, after he's made more contacts and can spend an hour or two with me.

Bible feared the House committee might look unkindly at his bill after the Senate passed it – and maybe reject the mining and prospecting provision as it had rejected similar wording for Canyonlands National Park, Utah. I talked by phone with Rep. Rivers. He was noncommittal. He'd try to go see the area himself. No member of his subcommittee had seen it.

Pete Kelley and helpers, including the Nevada legislature and the economic development agency, stimulated hundreds of letters and group resolutions and thousands of signatures on petitions from throughout the state. But the opponents matched our effort in Nevada. Baring introduced a bill for a 53,000-acre park – which he knew and I knew neither the Senate nor the President would accept – nor even the House committee. I have thick files of reports I sent to Nevada. My three-page report of April 30 began:

> The last two days I've made 18 different contacts in Washington – including Baring, Aspinall (chairman of the national park subcommittee), Bible, staff persons of pertinent committees, Interior executives, and nongovernmental park and conservation people. The Great Basin...is "on the front burner."

But we were failing. In accord with House tradition, there'd be no action on such a project, affecting Baring's congressional district, without his consent. And his rancher and miner friends persuaded him not to consent. Yet we'd keep trying.

The second big teaser starting January 1965 was the desire of a New York publisher, David McKay Co., for a book about Alaska by Eileen and me. Doubleday hadn't moved with our "Alaskan Dream" suggestion, so we felt the possibility was open. The company's development man suggested we outline a book about our personal experience including my newspaper work with Alaska's troubles, achievements, and prospects, and write three sample chapters.

We might have dashed off a presentation, subject to fuller development after they'd given a contract and an advance of funds. But we had boxes of Alaskan reports rich in pertinent detail. So we bought a special file and labeled folders for 20 possible chapters, then began sorting. We're not fast sorters, because we're tempted into reading. In newspaper work you pick up documents when you can, but there's the daily deadline and you grab for the main conflict, pushing most details aside for study "at leisure" – which never comes. Books, we believed, should be tackled differently. Book authors should know more about their subject than anyone else anywhere.

We put three person-months into the first Alaska presentation and sent it off the end of March. For ages no word came, then the opinion that we really had two likely books – "Alaskan Honeymoon" by Eileen and "The New Alaska" by Darwin. As we found time after taking care of work more definitely in demand, we gambled on outlines and sample chapters in the two-book pattern. But no money was ever paid, no words published, no judgment rendered.

My use of the phrase "conversation with Earth" began here in late winter. Eileen and I cleared intruding vines, bushes, and even trees from the old orchard. By doing that, we began to understand, we'd asked a question, "What will you do, nature, if damp fertile soil in this kind of location is cleared?" The answer came gradually –

I'll send up new plants. Many will be what you call weeds, but some will be berry canes. A few will be baby apple trees.

We were soon engaged in a dozen different conversations. From wild creatures we might get an instant response, *I'm scared and getting out of here*, then a changed response weeks later from, for instance, birds and rodents: *Hey! I like black walnut bits you throw out with the shells. Keep doing that, and we'll visit often.*

I began to understand we were playing science in an elementary way. What is all of science but asking questions of nature and picking up nature's answers? Eileen's and my science was amateurish, as much of emotion as of mind, yet valid to the degree of accuracy we needed here.

We wanted to harmonize with reality in a practical way, not just recreationally or esthetically. We must persuade nature to feed us as she feeds all other creatures that survive. Our income wasn't yet enough even to camouflage the fact that nature – not factories or stores – is the real source of food and shelter.

Eileen put Shaver Hollow-mixed potting soil into half-gallon milk cartons sitting on their sides, the top side of each cut away, and started our garden in the house. For me – I'll be the outdoor vegetable gardener – she started cabbage, broccoli, celery, tomato, and green pepper. For her own outdoor gardening, she started an assortment of flowers.

Instead of plowing, which we weren't equipped for, I dug the garden, and turned the top six inches upside down, with a shovel. The soil was dark and fertile. This plot had been a garden for generations, manured often, I supposed, the humus mixing in depth. I'd fed-in cow manure when Barbara and I gardened here in the 1940s. When I had enough soil dug and raked smooth, I planted radishes, lettuce, and peas, locating the tall peas close to the right edge of the plot (as you look from the kitchen) because the still-so-slanted sunshine touched there longer. For best production, Earth seemed to say, you'll have to cut down that big oak on the south. But how could anyone harmonizing with nature cut down a beautiful tree?

Obviously, we had fine-tuning to do while becoming conscious of living in nature. Individuals, families, and species compete. My interest in Charles Darwin had taught me that, vaguely. Soon I was able to convince myself we have as much right to cut a tree that's hampering our food production as a beaver, say, has to cut trees for his use. With regret, I cut the shadowing oak. Nearly all our vegetables flourished; the plants Eileen started in the house were great producers. We worried then about wild creatures gobbling the goodies. There were deer, rabbits, raccoons, bears, voles, groundhogs, and maybe others. The old fence was down, mostly decayed, but few wild ones are stopped by fences anyway. Our dog Sourdough, growing out of puppyhood, should help some, but our love of wild creatures hampered him. Though he made instinctive gestures, he lost his enthusiasm in our ambivalence. Mostly, though, we got ample vegetables and fruit. Insect pests and pine voles proved worse than the bigger animals. We disliked poisons, so I hunted and killed cutworms "by hand" in the soil where plants were being damaged, and I fought cabbage worms on the plants with eyes and fingers. Both Eileen and I swatted the white butterflies that lay cabbage-worm eggs, using badminton racquets. We fought aphids with soapsuds spray.

Any creature is innocent until proved guilty, we said. Inside the house, we'd kill ants or moths damaging or laying eggs in food and wood borers that eat houses and furniture. Innocent insects we'd catch alive, putting a glass over them and sliding in an old postcard to hold them for carrying. We'd put captives outside when the weather wasn't severe. Through the years, catch-and-release systems, with diverse live-traps, would apply to blacksnakes, water snakes, white-footed mice, moles (they eat grubs and other meat, not roots), flying squirrels, wasps, and spiders.

Lawn-mowing, though our designated area was less than half that mowed by the Sewards, competed for my time and energy. I used muscle-power – no fuel and little noise – and this activity too was bolstered by multiple incentives – smooth lawn, no hiding place for venomous snakes, exercise for me, lawn clippings to mulch the garden to conserve moisture, suppress weeds, feed earthworms, improve soil texture and fertility – and to keep the forest from closing in.

We tapped into wild production for food – strawberries and native black raspberries in spring, followed by wineberries (tart red raspberry-types from the Orient but wild here now), native blackberries producing through mid-summer, blueberries growing on the quick-draining ridge up beyond our creek, and elderberries where the soil's moist – all berries, yes, and black walnuts shared with other creatures who liked them. In fall, we enjoyed persimmons and wild grapes.

We've kept increasing the number of species of wild mushrooms we can identify and trust. Morels ("merkels" locally), world-renowned delicacies resembling conical sponges, grow on our land in April and early May. Our most frequent visitors from the outside in our early years here, Doris and Hank Hansen, were Juneau friends who'd moved just after we did from Alaska, where morels also flourish. She's a poet among other talents; he's a biologist. Eileen's sautéed morels please them, being wonderfully tasty and going well with meat or in scrambled eggs. She dried some, but mostly now she freezes them after sautéing them. From morel time on, there's a diversity of wild greens, eaten raw or cooked.

Food-gathering is a natural rite of the changing seasons. Or let's say simply it's joyful living – as it appears to be with wild creatures. We and our competitors are also replanting and spreading food-producing species. We feel ourselves participating in an all-inclusive harmony. Wild food helped Eileen and me significantly from our beginnings in Shaver Hollow, surviving without regular paychecks, building and maintaining our happiness in the natural world, our fellowship with other species. And we traced this tendency way back with each other. Eileen talked about childhood dreams and growing-up dreams – a secret room of her own somehow hidden in the house, hideaways she and her dog found in Nevada hills, the gathering of persimmons and wild nuts in Missouri, and gathering, roasting and eating of pinenuts in the West – and coveting an isolated house she saw on a clifftop overlooking the ocean. I talked about my similar dreams and searches and imitating Indians' ways of living and hunting and eating. And we remembered how more recently we looked so longingly at the isolated, abandoned log ranch house beside a tiny stream on the western foot of Mount Wheeler (bordering what's now Great Basin National Park) but weren't yet financially ready to buy it. Now in the Blue Ridge we recognized ourselves together at last in a living consolidation of our individual dreams.

After we'd lived joyfully here a year and a half, Eileen went to Ely to attend the wedding of her son David. I took her to Winchester, 45 miles north, to catch the bus for St. Louis. She slept that night at her father's and stepmother's home and the next day drove grandmother Sarah Wood's "Rambler" long hours westward with the 81-year-old lady enjoying it all, reluctant to stop – 500 miles one day, 720 the next.

Eileen and I wrote daily letters of love and longing. She'd left dinners for me with easy instructions, mostly just thawing in advance, then warming. They were tasty, but my main enjoyment was relishing her involvement. Without her actual presence, though, I seldom used the table. I'd eat quickly, standing at the kitchen counter, without formality that would emphasize my aloneness.

I slept the minimum to stay healthy. As almost always when I had work in Washington, I commuted carrying my lunch and hurried home for dinner and sleep. In addition to the park lobbying, I was rewriting a conservation novel, making it more psychological as the first draft seemed thin – little artistic depth and not enough sex or violence to excite basic emotions. I'd about given up on my China novel, convinced it was too complex. Also, while Eileen was away,

The Atlantic rejected "Klondike," a short story for which I'd had high expectations.

I felt better after Eileen's letters started arriving. Dave's bride, Thera Anderson, was "Delightful!" So was the ceremony. Associated contacts were smooth. Her mom was much the same as before, generously pushing gifts on everyone, though she was out of a job, low on money. In Salt Lake on the return drive, Eileen and Grandma visited my sisters Ruth, Joyce, and Marta Jeanne. I met the bus in Winchester, and Eileen made our log house warm and wonderful again.

National Parks was featuring my article, "Over the Years with Great Basin Park." *The Living Wilderness* was scheduling two major articles – "Facets of Wilderness," about wild nature repossessing the Shenandoah park, and "Conversations with Earth," about the meanings and moods of the Wheeler-Lehman country. In Ely, Eileen had visited the *Daily Times* and met the recently arrived editor – who'd given a front-page welcome to Rep. Rivers, U.S. House parks chairman, when he'd come at last to see and judge the park area.

After her return we belatedly learned of an incredible event: In August 1964 a bristlecone pine of planetary significance – in our proposed Great Basin National Park – had been chain-sawed down by the U.S. Forest Service for a graduate student investigating glacial moraine on which it grew. The Forest Service had suppressed the news. My first inkling came through a Luray friend, an alumnus of the University of North Carolina where a brief report was published (Oct-Nov 1965) and where the student, Donald Currey, was to receive a Ph.D. This bristlecone had been by far the oldest living tree confirmed by science to exist anywhere on Earth. Currey and helper counted the rings under low-power magnification from a cross-section – 4,800 and still counting. I checked the facts through the NPS superintendent at the caves, from Currey's own report in *Ecology* (Early Summer 1965), and later through the world's leading dendrochronological laboratory at the University of Arizona, Tucson.

This champion tree – that we early park advocates had named *Prometheus* (without knowing its age) – then made headlines in many countries. A strong side-effect in Nevada and, as the news kept spreading in national conservation and in Congress and the Administration, was increased prestige for our proposed park. Wheeler Peak and its cirque became famous. A public-lands conservation organization (called NORA) with headquarters in Nevada, publicly and repeatedly accusing the Forest Service of anti-park conspiracy, made strong local headlines – after I'd called Nevadans' attention to the basic event. In Washington, the park's major advocate in Congress, Nevada's Senator Bible – at a meeting of the Senate's appropriation committee – scolded the Forest Service chief heavily and repeatedly.

I kept investigating the event and whatever was known about *Pinus longaeva*, the species that produces the longest-lived trees. And I kept writing. Not counting reports in newspapers that must total hundreds of millions of copies, my pieces about the cutting of the world's oldest living tree, published in magazines and books, have added up to 35,000,000 copies in a dozen languages.

A series of happenings in Shaver Hollow concurrent with our mourning of *Prometheus* is rerunning inside me. With our dog Sourdough we're walking down-hollow for our mail as we do five days a week. Ernest Miller and helpers, including his mule, are getting out logs, partly because a contract has been awarded to build the flood control dam down there. We talk with Ernest about the likely destruction – how it seems unnecessary when the entire drainage area above the dam site (2.2 square miles in all) is solidly forested, able to absorb precipitation, and how the work will leave 20 acres of the land naked. "Wish I'd never signed those easement papers," Ernest says.

While continuing to work with the logs that spring, Ernest has a heart attack. He's been so healthy-looking – "the smith, a mighty man is he, with large and sinewy hands" – we can't feel he's in danger. Yet I think more strongly and clearly than ever before how much he means to me, how he represents, say, the pre-modern human dealing directly with life's basics – like that farmer I watched across the Rio Grande – no evidence of ever commercializing to get rich or to consume more than he produces.

Soon Ernest is home, recovering. We visit, and he's cheerful, confident. Then he has another attack – and dies. We can't easily believe – a pillar of home is gone, all is weakened. I write:

A hidden hand has switched off spring...
  enlivened by his vibrant gentle voice
    with words of radiating love
    but thinly veiled by indirection:
    "Cold up your way last night?"
    when he knew it was zero
      and what he sought to learn was,
      Are you warm and well supplied with fuel?
    "Got your garden in?"

    when what he meant was,
    I'd plow it for you and save the spading...
Enlivened by ringing pings on anvil
    and forge fire heating iron
      and hands and heart
    with the glow of near-lost years
      when men were men and not machines
      and hammered themselves into the shape and temper of their work
      with process of creation and not price
        their source of satisfaction...

This place so warm with music of metal,
  with touch and smile
  linking the world with current
    from a reservoir of joy,
      went wan and cold with his departure –
  yet, because he filled it with himself,
    it's sowed with seed to sprout and grow again
    in new and greater springs,
      a richer Earth.

The bulldozers he and we had feared invade the hollow. We walk destruction for our mail and see heavy machines uprooting trees. Eileen cries when a favorite great oak crashes beside the rippling creek. The work continues through most of 1968. Our road is destroyed. We fight for a usable grade up the dam. Eileen brings her camera. The contractor's own trucks can't climb where we're expected to drive our car. The construction supervisor plays into our hands by sending a bulldozer to pull the trucks up the grade. Eileen gets embarrassing pictures to send to Washington, and a more usable road materializes quickly. We feel we've won a little for Ernest Miller too – not just for ourselves.

Yet we have nightmares of bulldozers shattering our own 63 acres of forest. Details differ in Eileen and me, but the feeling is similar. In one of Eileen's horrors, a subdivision is being developed. Furious, she confronts the foreman and drives the crew out. We still welcome hikers but post "No Trespassing" against strangers in vehicles.

Chapter 19 – More Letters to Mentors 1968+

I don't know what to do with Walt Whitman. I never did. As a board member of National Parks Conservation, I could write or phone and *get responses* from *living* conservationists and ask questions or give information or thoughts – or maybe talk with them during the meetings or at cocktail gatherings at Mrs. Lee's mansion in Washington. Relating to conservationists not now known to be active – gone silent or even *gone from this life* – I can organize my thoughts and feelings in "letters" to them and usually get some feeling as to agreement or disagreement that lets me rest.

But it's different with Walt Whitman. I can't feel he'd listen to me or read what I write. In the Blue Ridge here I walk alone in fog while Whitman chants inside me. Trees loom, and I stumble on rocks I can't see. I touch trees, feel their bark with my fingers. Even the identity of species would be something to cling to. One tree, hiding its leaves in fog, has smoothish bark – the ridges not high nor the valleys deep. I recognize it – a tulip tree, the straight trunk reaching tall toward heaven. Though I can't see well, I know where I am and can discipline my thoughts. But Whitman keeps chanting. I doubt if he ever stops – or would pause if I tried to interrupt him. Okay then – since both nature and the human are in him simultaneously, why should he stop? What else is there? He's chanting now, echoing in me from Eileen's and my first winter here when, seeking reassurance in our new life, I'd read much of *Leaves of Grass* aloud and copied out many quotations, so holding some of them in memory:

> Seest thou not God's purpose from the first?
> The earth to be spann'd, connected by network,
> The races, neighbors, to marry and be given in marriage,

> The oceans to be cross'd, the distant brought near,
> The lands to be welded together? ...
> my body no more inevitably united, part to part, and
> made out of a thousand contributions one identity
> any more than my lands are inevitably
> united and made ONE IDENTITY ...
>
> I swear the earth shall surely be complete to him or her
>   who shall be complete.
> The earth remains jagged and broken only to him or her
>   who remains jagged and broken...
> The workmanship of souls is by those inaudible words
>   of the earth.
> The masters know the earth's words and use them more
>   than audible words...

In the fog under the ghostly trees what seemed a key to the whole puzzle sounded in me. It was that piece about the poet standing between quarreling Man and Nature – that I've copied out for a *National Parks* article and will include in the next chapter of this story, somewhat like this: Whitman (the poet) "took each by the hand – which he will never release until he reconciles the two – and wholly and joyously blends them."

The image of Whitman thus holding hands with Nature and Man appeared to me there under the trees in the fog. I felt the image wouldn't leave me – ever. But I found my way back to our log house and my typewriter, feeling I'd had enough Whitman for one visit. I forced myself to concentrate on a "letter" to another man of the same era – who also haunts me but who's less likely to interrupt me before I've had time to ask questions:

Shaver Hollow, VA – 1968

Dear Henry David Thoreau:
Pardon me. You seem a wee bit accessible – which I can't say for your contemporary Walt Whitman – and I feel you have some responsibility to help my wife and me decide whether to continue our life in the woods or to retreat to the busy world (and if we retreat,

how?). We moved here, I feel, partly because of ideas and images advanced by you – grabbed confusedly by me when my cousin named Walden and I read parts of your book named *Walden*. And clinched with what seemed to be understanding through taking turns reading *Walden* aloud with Eileen here in Shaver Hollow. Today, with fog filling our hollow and glowing with unearthly light, I feel you're still with us – somewhere – in the fog or on the far side of it.

Maybe I was too young and uneducated to interpret your language correctly at first, or for my cousin Walden and me to correct each other. And maybe Eileen and I saw too eagerly what we'd strongly wanted to see. Your Pond territory was something like our wild place here in Virginia – though tame compared with what surrounded my cousin and me in the Far West, yet we boys identified with your wandering alone and relished your observations of sun, sky, storms, wild plants and creatures. I wished I could go out on a lake and play hide-and-seek with a diving loon, as you did, and maybe have him laugh because I couldn't catch him.

Through many years, trying through publicity and politics to help save wild places – one especially as a national park – Eileen and I have been finding quotations attributed to you. They've awakened my boy's dream again and again, and they've stirred Eileen's girlhood dream of a wild hideaway. You know, of course, Mr. Thoreau, as shown by your own words: "In Wildness is the preservation of the World. Every tree sends its fibers forth in search of the Wild. The cities import it at any price."

Such words, plus your rebellion against civilization, strengthened our long tendency to rebel. Memories of your building a cabin helped hold me to difficult repairs on this old log house. Your advice to "simplify, simplify" bolstered our divergence from the American "normal." Your dissatisfaction with society heightened our own dissatisfaction. We agreed with you that "the mass of men lead lives of quiet desperation." You've helped keep us – until now – whenever our going got tough here – from being pulled back into the desperate mass. Your fellowship with wild creatures strengthened our fond co-existence with deer and bear and other wild ones.

Might you still help hold us here, Mr. Thoreau? We've been hoping so – and reading parts of your *Walden* aloud again to each other. The reading is fun now, though also serious. Sometimes, though, it's *exasperating*. Or maybe I should say, *puzzling*.

You write, "I lived alone, in the woods, a mile from any neighbor, in a house I had built myself... earned my living by the labor of my hands only." As have countless others, we'd taken these words to mean you lived directly from and in nature, and we'd struggled to do likewise. But now, having made our way together through the whole mass of your "Economy" chapter, we absolve you of full blame for the notion of your *Walden* life prevailing today. Though you seem to tell how you lived self-reliantly in nature, you never quite say you did. We laugh at your joke about beans – how you planted a big patch, labored in it mightily and produced many bushels, but never quite knew the meaning of the enterprise, since it certainly wasn't that you "wanted beans to eat"; you'd never liked beans!

Maybe your cabin and the wildness of those woods are puzzles too. Using a borrowed ax, you "cut down some tall, arrowy white pines, still in their youth, for timber." But you "bought the shanty of James Collins, an Irishman who worked on the Fitchburg Railroad, for boards." In your humorous-sincere way, you lived on the fringes of society, frequently walking to town where you visited and "dined." Between Walden and town you often followed the railroad, learning its pleasures and dangers. You bartered, sold and bought. You worked for pay at "surveying, carpentry, and day-labor of various other kinds in the village."

You were what you were – a savage and a scholar by your own admission, a nature-romantic feeding your soul. Though you grasped bits of real life, you never tried to weave a workable unity – as Eileen and I keep trying for unity with all humans and in the same effort with the rest of nature. We can't agree with you that "nature is more to be admired than it is to be used." We use nature a lot here, producing beans, for instance, which we eat and enjoy.

We're puzzled from another angle too – as we seek guidance on possibly returning to "civilization." You give us an impression of knowing how to return. You reveal that after "two years and two months" of living in the woods you became "a sojourner in civilized life again." At another place you say "civilization is a real advance in the condition of man ...though only the wise improve their advantages." From these words and others we gather a vision of your life as rounded to completeness. You found wisdom in the wild and returned to the world to live it and share it.

Are you sharing it? You say, "I love Nature partly because she is not man, but a retreat from him. None of his institutions control or pervade her. There a different kind of right prevails. In her midst I can be glad with an entire gladness." We like all your words, Mr. Thoreau – *until* we try combining them for the actual living of life. The picture we're getting now is of flight to wild nature, followed by a flight back to the human world, followed by another flight to the wild, and so on – without reconciliation forever. Is this your meaning? It's the flight pattern of many of your admirers today. But doesn't this pattern contradict your "simplify, simplify" and uncounted bits of your related advice?

When our effort toward harmony with nature is all-demanding here, we're strengthened by your jabs at society. We don't exactly disagree with them at other times, but what we feel should be an interrelating pattern keeps splitting in two, refusing to function. Why are you so against reconciling, becoming complete, Mr. Thoreau, being yourself a human, one even returned to civilization? You say, "It appears to be a law that you cannot have a deep sympathy with both man and nature. Those qualities which bring you near the one estrange you from the other."

Can this attitude be sincere or are you making some kind of joke? What do you mean – your life and your words? I'm trying to place you. Or, rather, I'm seeking help in finding (placing?) Eileen and me in relation to varied landmarks (of which you're an important one) and thus finding ourselves in a workable pattern that includes humans along with the rest of nature.

I see people-nature passages from long ago (that I've recently reconnoitered) leading toward you and your work. There's the pastoral genre rising from a Greek and Roman habit of escaping periodically to semi-wild nature. There are the Greek gods inside nature – as my god is (but not yours?). There are Oriental mysticism and philosophy. There's a wide open channel carrying the warmly emotional affair with nature launched by 18th century artists including Wordsworth – which I guess was partly a reaction against the selfish coldness of dawning science, seeing creatures as mechanisms and "nature" as given to humans for production of wealth and power. There's the rising flow of facts from the natural sciences – an earlier stage of which you seem to have been receiving eagerly.

Eileen and I draw what we can from such passages, partly through you and your friend Emerson – and Walt Whitman – and we appreciate your additions such as the idea of national nature-reserves (national parks?) and especially the spiritual nourishment from Walden Pond. Urgently we wish that certain other American "transcendentalists" had succeeded as well in their effort to live socially-economically in nature as you did in your lonely romantic quest – and produced books as eloquent to help guide us now. Or that you had recorded a blending of nature and man (a Whitman goal) in real life. Or, better yet, that you really are somewhere near us now, blending in the conditions of today, able and willing to advise us in our present, most specific puzzle – an intensifying effort in Washington to lure me to a much higher income as editor of a conservation magazine.

History has kept moving, of course. Charles Darwin rooted our species deeply in nature, thus changing people-nature understanding. Science has been proving nature to be an interrelated system in which not only spirit and thought but *all* physical-material things and processes interconnect. The technology and social complication you deplored in *Walden* went on developing (worsening?) until our best hope now could be that you were wrong in saying we "cannot have a deep sympathy with both man and nature." I feel we must grow so we *can* have such simultaneous sympathy. Won't you whom we so much *admire*, agree? *Please*?

But I fear you really can't. I guess, then, you advise Eileen and me to return to the civilized world – and stay split inside. That's what you did. But frankly, Mr. Thoreau, your advice isn't clear for tough decisions on how to live. Still, as you say at the end of *Walden*, "Only that day dawns to which we are awake. There is more day to dawn. The sun is but a morning star." Your double meaning to us, I think now, is your stubbornly penetrating quarrel with a society trying to separate itself from nature and your splendid vision of wild nature that might yet brighten an integrated life for the future.

With gratitude for your aid in exploring literary-romantic channels – Sincerely.

D.L. (year 1968)

My list has a lot more names to thank for guidance or to ask questions of. I'd understand myself better if I wrote to all of them. Only two more, though, seem imperative now – the *Robinson Crusoe* author that I've admired since boyhood – and my Dad, who's been gone 20-plus years but still lives on inside me, telling me now I should accept the financial advantage of that editorship in Washington, then confusing me – as he did so long ago after catching me and a friend hiding in tall alfalfa smoking Camel cigarettes – telling me with emphasis never to smoke, then explaining it's my responsibility to decide and to accept the consequences of my decision.

"It's your life!" Dad seems to repeat now. Then, somewhat like Thoreau, he adds, "Choose one way or the other. You can't choose both!"

But I'll keep trying to choose both, obeying Whitman (and, maybe, imitating Crusoe). I'll keep trying to reconcile and blend "Nature and Man."

Shaver Hollow – Feb 12 '68

Dear Dad:

This morning I waked with your shout, calling me "Jonah," one of those odd nicknames you invent and soon abandon. Is it Jonah because you think I'm dodging a task assigned by the Lord? Or because you've found out I've been studying the Bible? While still half asleep I remembered today is your birthday – and Lincoln's and Charles Darwin's – and your old joking began echoing again, that "all great men are born in February – and *you*, Doc, came three days too soon!"

About the *Bible*, Dad, assuming our old taboo against discussing religion is gone: This winter I've read every word in the order presented – 883 pages, the Old Testament, and 247 pages, the New Testament, a total of 1,139 pages – of *THE BIBLE, An American Translation* published October 1935 by University of Chicago Press. I find your beliefs solidly in this great book, Dad, and welcome them as authentic "you." I also find nature and conservation. I seem to find the main features of Earth's environmental history, past and yet to come.

My purpose in restudying scripture has been reconciliation of spirit and body, of God and nature and people, of YOU and ME – multiple incentives. I hope this letter will clear my link with you so it can energize me instead of continuing to discourage me.

The deep meaning of *one God*, I've come to believe, is one interrelating system, all-inclusive, every part affecting every other part, beliefs influencing behavior, beliefs and behavior affecting everybody and all life. What's been read in Christianity as opposition to nature may be, instead, opposition to paganism, to the idea of many gods working separately, often at cross-purposes. *One God* integrates all.

Other pushes and pulls brought me into scriptures – among them the current surge of blaming the *Bible* for civilization's tendency to "ride roughshod" over what's naturally here, blaming especially the text in Genesis giving us "dominion over" nature. Current advances in understanding the original Semitic language suggest God wasn't granting man "dominion" but urging him to embrace responsibility, "to take care of" other creatures and the land.

During my full reading of the testaments this winter I've marked many passages with environmental meanings. Now I've skimmed the hundreds marked – and typed the most revealing onto 90 file cards (*with chapter-verse references*). After "playing solitaire" with these cards, I've sorted the "history" into five parts – *Earth, Ecology, Responsibility, Discord, Harmony*. Please stay with me a few pages, Dad – knowing I'd welcome (dearly cherish) your comments if communication were possible.

We start by agreeing – as we did from boyhood – that the *Bible's* deep theme is human relations with eternal reality. We further recognize that some biblical language is straight-forward, as when people are told (through Moses) how to treat the promised land, and some is poetic-symbolic, as when we're given glimpses of God creating Earth and life and Adam and Eve, and when Jesus (speaking "figuratively" as He Himself said) taught union with the Father (one God all-interrelating). In this light it shouldn't be hard to read the instructions for getting along with God, winning and keeping His good will, as also instructions for conservation-environmentalism, for getting along with nature, with social and earthly forces, for avoiding potential hostility, winning and keeping hospitality, generating harmony.

In the first part (**EARTH**) we learn that the wisdom and law of God are the wisdom and law of "our" planet: "The Lord by wisdom founded the earth, / By reason he established the heavens... The Lord God molded man out of the dust of the ground, and breathed into his nostrils the breath of life... Then the Lord God planted a garden ...and put there the man whom he had molded ...to till it and look after it... His judgments are in all the earth. / He remembers his covenant forever... There is but one body and one spirit... The kingdom of God is within you... The kingdom ...is like yeast, which a woman took and buried in a bushel of flour until it had all risen... You must love the Lord your God with your whole heart, your whole soul, and your whole mind."

In the second part (**ECOLOGY**) we see how Earth and life work through the one system, the one God: "It is what existed from the beginning... it is the very message of life... We are parts of one another... As the deer longs for the water-courses... my whole being thirsts for God, for the living God... Deep calls to deep, in the sound of thy waterfalls. All thy waves and thy billows pass over me...

"See, I give you all the seed-bearing plants that are found all over the earth, and all the trees which have seed-bearing fruit; it shall be yours to eat. To all the wild beasts of the earth, to all the birds of the air, and to all the land reptiles ... I give all the green plants for food... All flesh is grass...

"I am Way and Truth and Life... My inner nature agrees with the divine law... I am the true vine... You must remain united to me and I will remain united to you. Just as no branch can bear fruit by itself unless it remains united to the vine, you cannot unless you remain united to me... The whole system, adjusted and united by each ligament of its equipment, develops in proportion to the functioning of each particular part, and so builds itself up through love."

In the third part (**RESPONSIBILITY**) – which you, Dad, started growing in me – though a bit confusingly – we're allowed to choose unity with the one system or attempt to deny it or to fragment it:

"See, I put before you today life and prosperity, along with death and misfortune. If you heed the commands ...I am giving you today, by loving the Lord your God, by walking in his ways, and by keeping his commands, statutes, and ordinances, then you shall live, and multiply, and the Lord your God will bless you in the land... The Lord your God is bringing you into a fine land, a land with streams of water, with springs and pools welling up in the valleys and on the hills; a land of wheat and barley, of vines, fig-trees, and pomegranates; a land of oil-producing olives and honey; a land where you may eat food without stint, lacking nothing in it; a land whose stones contain iron, and out of whose hills you can dig copper...

"For six years you may sow your field ...but during the seventh year there is to be a sabbath of complete rest for the land... You must not destroy its trees by taking an ax to them... If you should happen to come upon a bird's nest ...and the mother is sitting on the young or the eggs, you must not take...

"Whoever commits sin disobeys law; sin is disobedience to law... You must lay aside your former habits, your old self which is going to ruin through its deceptive passions. You must adopt a new attitude of mind, and put on the new self which has been created in likeness to God, with all the uprightness and holiness that belong to the truth."

In the fourth part (**DISCORD**) we are warned more specifically of the consequence of sin (*sin* being failure to blend with the interconnected system of one God by obeying its laws): "Does the cold flowing water of the mountains run dry? ... My people have forgotten me... They stumble off their ways, off the ancient tracks ...making their land a horror, a perpetual scorn; everyone who passes by it is horrified, and shakes his head... Before them a fire devours, / and after them a flame scorches. / Like the garden of Eden was the land before them, / And after them it is a desert waste...

"Because you have ruined your land, you have slain your people... The earth is polluted through the touch of its inhabitants because they have transgressed laws, violated statutes, broken the everlasting covenant... They have forsaken me, the fountain of living water... I will set portents in the heavens and on the earth, / Blood, and fire, and columns of smoke. / The sun shall be changed to darkness and the moon to blood... I will exhaust calamities upon them ...till cities lie waste, without inhabitant, / And the houses without man; / And the soil be left a desolation... For you the sky overhead shall be bronze, and the earth underfoot shall be iron; the Lord shall turn the rain of your land into powder and dust; it shall descend from the sky upon you until you are destroyed..."

In the fifth part (**HARMONY**) we learn how disaster can be avoided or remedied by cooperating in the one interrelating system, in the wisdom and law of God and the universe: Our "delight" is to be "in the law of the Lord... For you who revere my name, there will arise / The sun of righteousness, with healing in its wings. / And you shall go forth skipping like calves from the stall... For with joy shall you go out, / And in peace shall you be led; / The mountains and the hills shall break into singing before you, / And all the trees of the field shall clap their hands...

"On that day I will make a league for them / With the beasts of the field, the birds of the air, and the reptiles of the ground; / And the bow, the sword, and war I will break off from the land; / And I will make them lie down in security...

"Men shall rejoice and exult forever in what I create... There shall no more be heard in her the sound of weeping, nor the sound of crying... And they shall build houses, and inhabit them; / And they shall plant vineyards, and eat the fruit of them... For as the days of a tree shall be the days of my people, / And the work of their hands shall my chosen ones enjoy to the end... They will do no harm or destruction / On all my holy mountain; / For the land will have become full of the knowledge of the Lord."

I'm not alone in reading the *Bible* this way, Dad. Your (our?) Brigham Young, for instance, must have done so, part of the time anyway, to "make the desert blossom as the rose." In Italy long ago St. Benedict must have done so. The Benedictine monks tilled and looked after the "garden," producing food and fiber from land that had been useless or had produced malarial mosquitoes. They cooperated with wind and water-flow to run mills. They harmonized prayer and scholarship and physical work in the natural order of days and seasons. And St. Francis, who preached to the sparrows, identified with and worshiped nature. He also identified with Jesus to the point of receiving through a vision (but evident in the flesh for the rest of his life) the wounds of the Crucifixion. He celebrated the physical-mental-spiritual unity of all in the one great system.

This view of the *Bible*, though one of many, goes farthest, I think, toward reconciling discordant elements, toward bridging or healing the abyss. I feel that through it I've come to you (almost), Dad. Can we agree now and be at peace? *Please*?

"Doc" (as you called me for decades)

Planet Earth 1970

Dear Daniel Defoe:

I ask whether you – educated for the ministry but not active in it, a prolific writer as well as a merchant and a political thinker and worker – whether you found time and energy, before starting the word-by-word writing, to plot in detail *The Life and Strange Surprising Adventures of Robinson Crusoe?* I suspect you did not, or, if you did, your unconscious intuition snatched control and guided you where you had little intention of going.

You knew the real-life experience of some castaways, including Alexander Selkirk on an otherwise uninhabited island out from Chile. You added cannibals to heighten suspense. You thought up horrible events for your hero to struggle through for survival. With your writing skill and talent for detail, that novel would have entertained readers and sold well. But you didn't stick to writing that plot. You got caught in what I guess was a largely unconscious current and produced something quite different – that *Encyclopedia Britannica* has called "one of the most famous books ever written."

Literary critics try to explain: "Crusoe has come to symbolize the universal man in his struggle against the forces of nature." Man against nature, or man and God against nature, has been in the human mind for millenniums. Maybe critics guessed it built up in you during your theological training. Though I've failed to find it in words of

Jesus, I suspect you did think of it when you were speedily writing (as was your habit).

But it wasn't struggling against nature that saved Crusoe, Mr. Defoe. It was wooing nature. Such wooing, under whatever word carries it from era to era, has, you know, accompanied wooing of the supernatural from our beginnings – and still does – and still tends to hide in the unconscious. Your Robinson Crusoe first taught the idea to me, though not the word. Wooing nature is as complex as technology, or as poetry or painting. It's both art and science, and it's the heart of conservation-environmentalism-earthmanship.

The basics can be simplified. Stand up in a small boat that's crossways to a strong wind. You and the boat are in trouble. Sit down before you're toppled. Turn the boat parallel with the wind, then stand up in balance with your back to the wind, and you'll be pushed forward. It's trial and error, plus reasoning and willingness to change. Be patient and persistent, and your wooing begins to win rewards – ultimately sailing ships around the planet. In some such way, wooing, agriculture too started millenniums ago. You aren't the boss; you learn nature's ways. And the more you learn, the more choices and freedoms you enjoy.

Let me tell you how, at age 54, I'm consciously reading your book (portions of which I must have been interpreting in my unconscious on my first reading around age 12). I'm seeing three parts now (though this old book isn't thus divided) – *dissatisfaction with the human world, 50 pages; alone exploring the people-nature maze and discovering half-lost instincts for harmonizing with nature, 120 pages; humans and the "civilized" world again, 79 pages.*

Young Crusoe quarrels with his father about religion (as I did with my Dad). The son tends to dislike the timid morality and comfortable security into which he was born. He runs away and has close brushes with disaster, then seems to find himself as a plantation owner. Yet dissatisfaction with the world keeps gnawing, and again he runs away. He's repeatedly "shipwrecked" in life before he's shipwrecked on the ocean. The ocean wreck is temporarily grounded near shore, so he's able to take with him into his new life some guns and other tools and immediately crucial supplies. He thus has time to start tapping the island's hospitality.

Oh, I know, Mr. Defoe, people *fight* forces of nature. Remember, when Crusoe's trying out a boat he's finally managed to build, a storm sweeps him dangerously far out? He fights nature's ocean current and wind, struggling to return to the island, now his home. Yet he's saved – I've reread several times – by a counter-current, also nature's. Even wind and water are more with him than opposed. How else could anyone float and reach desired destinations – as humans quite habitually do?

There might be a hasty contention that Crusoe is struggling against nature when he starts supplementing his food supply: "The first time I went out, I presently discovered that there were goats in the island, which was a great satisfaction to me; but then it was attended with this misfortune to me, viz., that they were so shy, so subtle, so swift of foot, that it was the most difficult thing … to come at them; but I was not discouraged at this, not doubting that I might now and then shoot one." He does, and the meat is tasty and nutritious. Has he triumphed over nature? Not in my language. How, if not through nature, are the animals born? How else do they eat and grow – and help feed Crusoe?

Later, he tames a young goat. He "catched it, and led it home on a string; when I had it at home, I bound and splinted up its leg which was broke… I took such care of it that it lived, and the leg grew well and as strong as ever; but by nursing it so long it grew tame, and fed upon the little green at my door, and would not go away. This was the first time I entertained a thought of breeding up some tame creatures, that I might have food when my powder and shot were spent." Through observing the life of the goats and the wild habitat in which they thrive, he does establish, in a pasture he's enclosed with a dense hedge of wild bushes, a flock of goats regularly supplying both meat and milk, while increasing in number.

Equally crucial cooperation with the "forces of nature" begins when he sees barley sprouting where he must have dropped grain while bringing supplies from the shipwreck. "This touched my heart a little, and brought tears out of my eyes, and I began to bless myself that such a prodigy of Nature should happen on my account; and this was the more strange to me because I saw near it still, all along by the side of the rock, some other straggling stalks, which proved to be stalks of rice." He watches with care, saves and plants seed. His first intentional agriculture fails because he hasn't understood the pattern of rainfall. But he has seed left, and, after studying the seasons and the soil, plants and animals, he chooses appropriate times and places to plant again. The harvest is good. He goes on to get two dependable harvests each year.

Crusoe acts out the basic human drama – which is the wooing of nature, not struggling against nature as western civilization has long supposed. In today's language – this part of it I can approve – he's an ecological realist in living action. He also proves to be romantic as most people have been. Though we don't survive without bread, we don't survive by bread alone. Even as Crusoe cooperates with nature to survive, he finds satisfactions, even fulfillment, even a new (yet very old) natural approach to religion. He sees Earth's beauty; he experiences fellowship; he experiences happiness.

While exploring the island he finds "pleasant savannahs," notices that some scenes are "fresh, so green... everything being in a constant verdure, or flourish of spring." While using nature, he also admires it. He finds an attractive valley. "I descended a little on the side of that delicious valley, surveying it with a secret kind of pleasure... When I came home from this journey, I contemplated with great pleasure the fruitfulness of that valley, and the pleasantness of the situation... I was so enamored with this place that I spent much of my time there."

He "saw an abundance of parrots, and fain would have caught one ... and taught it to speak to me." Soon he does that – with more than one parrot. When he later encounters one flying free and it calls him by name, "Robin Crusoe," he's thrilled and comforted. Though he considers himself, half-humorously, a monarch, he writes of his Poll as a person. He reports himself becoming "so naturalized ...that, could I but have enjoyed the certainty that no savages would come to the place to disturb me, I could have been content to have capitulated for spending the rest of my life there, even to the last moment, till I had laid me down and died, like the old goat" (that he'd found welcoming death in a cave). He felt himself related to all animals – "I always kept two or three household kids about me, whom I taught to feed out of my hand... I had also several tame sea-fowls."

How you reported it all so true to the essence, I wish I knew. Did you yourself ever live in the wild, Mr. Defoe? If you didn't, how could you tell what goes on inside Crusoe as well as outside – how, for instance, his relationship with nature builds his spirituality? Did humans lose their instincts in the Garden-of-Eden "fall" – or is this instinctual short-cut channel to truth and decisive action still open in all humans as my wife and I have found it in ourselves (but too often obscured)? Crusoe says, "I began sensibly to feel how much more happy the life I now led was, with all its miserable circumstances, than the wicked, cursed, abominable life I led all the past part of my days... My very desires altered, my affections changed their gusts, and my delights were perfectly new from what they were... I daily read the Word of God, and applied all the comforts of it to my present state... 'If God does not forsake me,' I asked myself, 'of what ill consequence can it be, or what matters it, though the world should all forsake me, seeing, on the other hand, if I had all the world, and should lose the favor and blessing of God, there would be no comparison in the loss?'"

Crusoe identifies God with the goodness of nature as happy people so often do. He says, "I frequently sat down to meat with thankfulness and admired the hand of God's providence which had thus spread my table in the wilderness. I learned to look more upon the bright side of my condition, and less upon the dark side, and to consider what I enjoyed rather than what I wanted, and this gave me sometimes such secret comforts, that I cannot express them, and which I take notice of here, to put those disconnected people in mind of it, who cannot enjoy comfortably what God has given them." You must have felt, Mr. Defoe, that "God's providence" is the reward for harmonizing with nature..

In the last part of your book – back in the human world – Crusoe feels no such harmony. Though he's wealthy now (because his plantation was saved for him and has increased in value), he longs for his island. He founds a community there. He visits but doesn't stay. He can't feel at home either on the island that's no longer wild, or in civilization. He's come "disconnected"; he's "shipwrecked" again. I wish you could somehow respond to letters, Mr. Defoe, and together we could deepen our understanding of people-nature cooperation in the protection and enjoyment of Earth.   **D. L.** (1970)

Chapter 20 – Earthmanship 1968-72

Eileen and I were feeling menaced at home not only by excessive bulldozer power but also by thickening air pollution. On misty mornings we smelled poisons from industry, sometimes the "rotten egg smell" from the big viscose plant 25 miles northeast. The famous Blue Ridge-Skyline Drive views were turning gray or tan.

We'd read that lichens die where pollution is dangerous, as canaries die in unsafe mines, warning the miners to escape at once. Our lichens still thrived on boulders and tree-trunks, but mountain laurel sickened and specks dimmed the brilliance of red maple leaves in autumn. More from emotion than from science, our main "canary" became morels, spring mushrooms; they seemed to be failing in numbers, size, and range.

A new word, *earthmanship*, had been dancing in me as a defense against the environmental menace. I'd spoken it spontaneously when talking to scientists at Auke Bay, near Juneau, Alaska, back in 1963. It bounced off *seamanship*. So, most simply, *earthmanship* means ability in living enjoyably and sustainably on Earth. I'd been discussing "creative responsibility," reviewing changes in humanity's image of itself in its habitat – from chosen creature living at the center of the universe, through changes from astronomical work by Copernicus and Galileo and biological work by Charles Darwin and others. I quoted the editor of the *Bulletin of the Atomic Scientists*: "Man's is only a small place. Like a cell in an organism, like an individual in a community, like a nation in the human race, so the human race as a whole is but a tiny and expendable constituent of the evolving universe."

I argued, though, that while moving humanity down a notch or two, science simultaneously promoted us. Science studies nature, and as we learn more facts, the natural grows and the supernatural shrinks. We're less the chosen creature and more the responsible creature. We create, for instance, berries larger and sweeter than before, dogs low to the ground, dogs tall and graceful - and atom bombs! With such power, growing continually through our study and use of natural potential, we must, I said at Juneau without conscious thought of the language, "improve the understanding, art, and skill of our *earthmanship* to protect our home planet from ourselves." I connected myself into the process:

> As editor of a newspaper, I'm supervising a basic tool for helping to create understanding ...for helping to build and maintain the best possible way of life. Like science, in a sense, a newspaper is a continuing process of investigation and self-correction for society, of putting up theories, or shooting them down with facts, or of improving and refining them. It's a way of sorting out truth.

The word came out again when I was speaking in Washington at the 40th Anniversary Dinner of the Potomac Appalachian Trail Club. My central focus was the club's far-reaching decision in 1927 "to foster public appreciation and use" of the proposed Shenandoah National Park. I'd considered this park's establishment a significant event in world history, demonstrating that civilization can reduce as well as escalate its strain on the planet's resources. I mentioned forester-philosopher Benton MacKaye's insistence, in proposing the great Appalachian Trail, that "the increasingly crowded city dwellers not only wanted, but needed, time with unspoiled nature, time and solitude and effort in the wilderness." I credited MacKaye and the Potomac club with helping to save our health and emotional-cultural fulfillment, both threatened in the technological-industrial squeeze. I recognized the club's ability to see common interests under surface differences, the ability to agree on, and put into effect, the most generally rewarding and lastingly satisfying strategies of *earthmanship*...

giving us a chance, at least, to work out a life that is at once more secure and more deeply fulfilling than has ever been lived before.

This speech led to articles in print, but more significantly it began to define a way of life Eileen and I were trying to make our own reality. For some while it's mostly a feeling, a love of home, say. But it spreads and deepens until it's under the mind secretly suggesting patterns and details of living behavior. We ask little questions of nature and wait for answers before we start anything big here. For instance, I mow an early swath where a few wild strawberries and violets bloomed. The mowing, perhaps keeping down the competing grass, brings more strawberries where I mowed than where I didn't mow. So – in future springs I'll mow the whole area once, early, then not mow there again until after berries ripen and are picked. It's conversation with Earth. On a sunnier part of the lawn, I recognize daisies and susans when tiny and mow around promising clumps. The many resulting flowers say, among other things, "Eileen, I love you."

I find yellow jacket nests, small holes in the lawn. Eileen and I want peace with the creatures, and various wasps help us by eating harmful flies and worms. But Eileen is dangerously allergic to stings. What to do? I wipe out nests we *must* work near. Others I test by approaching nearer and nearer until the yellow jackets act hostile, then I retreat a bit without getting stung. I mark these nests with stones and mow around them, leaving a lawn-island. The yellow jackets seem to learn. As my mowing gradually gets closer, the incoming and outgoing flights dwindle and cease. Can it be these insects understand cooperation and reciprocate? I've mowed within a foot of the entrance-hole dozens of times – no stings – but we aren't sure enough yet for Eileen to try similar closeness. Other factors, such as individual persons' fragrances, may be involved. More experiments are needed.

We cherish frogs, and toads are *special* favorites, partly because they feed on bugs that harm the garden, partly because of their song in breeding season. I imitate the toad song – a continuing high pitch that rises and falls and makes – I say, though Eileen laughs at me – a dotted line. The ringing note comes waveringly from my throat, and I put the dots in with my tongue against my upper teeth. One warmish night a few toads sing in our Tadpool, then falter into silence. We want more music, so we go down to the pool, and I start toad-singing. Soon we're hearing them again. I keep on, and toads come closer. Soon one is almost at my feet, singing and looking up at me. We're a duet, I feel, while other toads farther away are a chorus. Eileen jokes afterward that I won first prize in toad-singing, ahead of the real toads.

Weeks later, after the singing season, I go out to mow. I'm pushing the mower back of the house, and Eileen's in the kitchen window. There's an unexpected crunch, and the lawnmower stalls. I bend down and see a toad cut almost in two. I straighten up, shocked. Eileen comes out, and I say, "I've killed a toad." We hold each other while tears run down our faces into our clothes. I'll mow much more carefully in future.

There've been other tears – such as for Hazel, a gray fox who first came with her mate Notchy and later brought three puppies onto the lawn. The next winter, February maybe, Hazel came on three legs for dog food Eileen was putting out. Eileen feared now the past feeding – and friendship with humans – made the foxes less wary of traps. Maybe Hazel gnawed off her own foot to escape from a steel trap. No owner of land near us authorized trapping, so when we found illegal traps, we tripped them and called the game warden. Notchy had sometimes carried away a whole tuna can of dog crunchies, and when Hazel didn't come any more, we hoped Notchy was carrying food to her. But we never knew.

I don't recall weeping for snakes, though we've felt sharp regret and repeatedly reconsidered our policy of killing the venomous ones who come near enough our house or frequented trails to be credibly dangerous. I can't forget a copperhead struck Barbara here, and it's said one killed a small boy long before we came. Yet, like other snakes, copperheads can be seen as beautiful. At wild strawberry time once, though we always look carefully before picking, Eileen reached for a red berry, and a copperhead beside it wriggled away instead of striking. I killed the copperhead, and we stood looking at its colorful hourglass design as its muscles kept twitching in death. "It could have struck me," Eileen said, "but – it – didn't."

We can't know exact behavioral details of earthmanship for others. We're feeling our way, studying and experimenting. Earthmanship, we think, has become the main job and privilege of humankind and must remain so if life is to reach far into the future. Our focus is on deep change of heart, enabling us to reject harmful technology and cling to (persevere in) helpful projects. We're guided by what we know, but we know so little, so mostly we're guided by *feeling*. There are clues in mythology, religion, philosophy, law, but for Eileen and me they're most legible in nature. Earthmanship is a process – with living experience, research, and reverence for the wonders of the universe continually helping to improve it. Eileen and I are guided by our conviction that earthmanship is reasonable-logical while also generating feelings of happiness and fulfillment. With us, it's more rewarding than the so-called "high standard of living."

The thinking wasn't thus integrated, though, when I first tried to launch the new word toward print. I was seeing a knock-down-drag-out battle, developer-producer-merchant ravaging nature, conservationists defending nature. The conservationists (and environmentalists) were my buddies; the ravagers were my enemies. Editor Paul Tilden understood my early draft. He was *our* kind – with even his own mountain place across the Blue Ridge crest from ours. He explained, though, that less than a third of his readers were our kind. Two-thirds would fail to understand earthmanship from what I'd written. Many Americans felt that any hampering of development

or production was bad, and they'd feel my key example, Shenandoah National Park, was bad. So I rewrote, pointing out that the material resources withdrawn from production had been small and dwindling, while the recreational-esthetic values of the new park were tremendous, even for businessmen serving the great flow of visitors. The park strengthened, not weakened, the region's economy. Park establishment was thus genuine earthmanship with principles worth applying elsewhere. I concluded in the published "A Running Start on Earthmanship"
(*National Parks*, August 1968):

> This example of conservation-as-progress prophesied that we could ... create more outdoor cathedrals where they seemed the best use of the land, just as elsewhere, with the aid of newly discovered aspects of nature, we might create factories to produce fantastic energy... The Shenandoah park publicly demonstrated that we could refuse the strongly pushed diet of "bread alone" and retain the power of decision across the whole swath of living... The earthmanship task might be most aptly described as involving all mankind in improving the planet as a pleasant home for life, productive of material abundance and genuinely conducive to both physical and mental-emotional health.

It was an effort to plant seeds of earthmanship feeling, to win recognition that the greatest problem, greatest opportunity, greatest drama weren't in personal or even national competition but in human cooperation with the planet. The attitude would guide individuals and groups to the details. Some people listened. Universities invited me to present earthmanship programs. I lectured on *Shenandoah National Park and Earthmanship* at the Smithsonian Institution.

Albert H. Farnsworth, editor of *VISTA* (magazine of the United Nations Association of the USA), invited me to write "Toward Earthmanship" (Nov-Dec 1968) – which would lead to more *VISTA* articles advancing earthmanship – "Dialogue with Walt Whitman" (Jan-Feb 1970) and "In Orbit with Laotze" (Sept-Oct 1971).

William Benton, board chairman of *Encyclopedia Britannica*, wrote the UN association: "Please congratulate the editor of *VISTA* on the piece by Darwin Lambert, the dialogue with Walt Whitman. I read it aloud to Hubert and Muriel Humphrey and my wife, at my home in Phoenix where the Humphreys were visiting us." With Humphrey a Presidential candidate, I felt almost influential. I felt more definitely so as the United Nations scheduled a world-wide *Conference on the Human Environment* at Stockholm for 1972.

Yet, while the needs to protect the environment and to keep the peace were seen clearly, in relation to the future of humanity and all life, I found little recognition of the other half of earthmanship – how working for Earth's health and beauty along with her productivity cuts alienation and despair and generates happiness. Fortunately, there were opportunities to emphasize the joys – among them a magic voyage off the California coast and a different article for Paul Tilden.

Daughter Laura's husband, Eldred (Larry) Rowe, with the army in Vietnam, earned medals for "exceptionally meritorious" service and was promoted to captain. He'd return soon. Meanwhile, Laura, who's been teaching first grade in Ely, Nevada, has time to try tenting with Eileen and me. We pick her up at Dulles Airport. Briefly at home, we sample the earliest ripe Bing cherries and let her breathe some Blue Ridge air before we start westward. Doris Hansen from Juneau, now of a Washington suburb, will enjoy our house.

While rolling in the Renault, we talk earthmanship, noticing places in urgent need of it, then finding and camping at an inspiring example – Kickapoo State Park (Indiana), recently redeemed from mining. Wounds of open pits have become scenic ponds, and the natural forest is regrowing beautifully. In my mind on this trip, our country is marked with negative and positive earthmanship – my emerging basic standard of judging human doings.

Yellowstone reflects earthmanship. The three of us, sharing a viewpoint above the famous falls with a hippie group, hear after a time of silent contemplation – "I find this view perfectly satisfactory!" I endorse this hippie judgment; the American majority recognizes this canyon and waterfall as too grand for power plants.

In McGill (near Ely) Eileen and I visit her daughter Linda and husband and their youngsters Kim and Judy. A day or two before, Linda hung her laundry on the outdoor clothesline as usual, where it was dampened by a drizzle mixed with smoke from the copper smelter's immense chimney. When Linda went out to get the dry clothes, she found the cloth cut along the clothesline, every piece ruined by the fall-out of acid. The company's anti-earthmanship was blatant, dangerous.

In Reno we visit Harvey and Dorothy and my first grandchild, "Lisa" (Elizabeth Anne), the family now in an attractive suburb – made green through artificial irrigation – the good or bad of its earthmanship too complex for hasty decision. Eileen and I drive on to Santa Barbara, where coincidence has placed son Mike Affleck and his wife Doreen, recently married at Juneau, and daughter Sylvia and husband Christian Schneider. The Schneiders had invited us and the Afflecks to sail with them to Channel Islands National Monument.

As we head out, soon beyond sight or sound of cars, the Schneiders and Afflecks report past discussions of my earthmanship articles with each other and additional friends. My mind starts weaving a *National Parks* article laced with seamanship-earthmanship – this sailing craft's power (gentle wind) so quiet and no strain on the planet's oil supplies. The Sierra Club chartered this cruise of the *Swift*, a 90-foot-square-sailed schooner, carrying 36 passengers plus crew. We move quietly southward, the Pacific waves and troughs long and gentle. Conversations keep starting on deck – and getting deflected as wild creatures appear in both air and water. Blue sharks compel attention; porpoises perform; large seabirds are active.

There's a proposal for a Channel Islands National Park, adding three larger islands to the tiny ones, Anacapa and Santa Barbara that now are the national monument. Soon we glimpse the largest island, Santa Cruz, 62,000 acres – ahead but to the right of our course – rising half a mile above sea level. The park would be rich in scenic cliffs, both sandy and rocky beaches, sea caves, rock bridges and pillars, and diverse life. There'd be northern fur seal, Steller sea lion, Guadalupe seal, elephant seal, California sea lion, and harbor seal. Sea otters would thrive.

The Swift anchors at small Anacapa, and we wade ashore from a rowboat. We explore beaches, tidepools rich in life, and a sea cave reverberating with wave sounds. A trail leads us up a sharp-edged ridge with views of island and ocean, including brown-furred sea lions. We focus on an extraordinary plant species along the trail – giant coreopsis, a sunflower relative with woody trunks up to six inches in diameter, no leaves or flowers now but annually reviving in the rainy season and producing golden masses visible even from ships miles away.

We felt the proposed park would be superb earthmanship. But complexities lurk. What present uses of large Santa Cruz – cattle ranching, naval training – might suffer? And how much? We wish for more time but are soon mesmerized by smooth, silent sailing with the wind back to the mainland, watching flying fish soaring over the waves, the dorsal fins of sharks cutting the water, the porpoises so lively, and the sea lions lazily floating.

Back home, I wrote "Escape to the Channel Islands" (*National Parks*, April 1969). Paul had another assignment for me, a month of delving into 50 years of records to produce "Patterns in National Parks Association History" for the golden anniversary issue (May 1969). I'd now had 15 different articles touching earthmanship published in seven different magazines of national circulation, and I was completing two book manuscripts for Shenandoah Natural History Association.

One (to become *Herbert Hoover's Hideaway*, 1971) was my first major blending of history into earthmanship. Ray Schaffner, chief park naturalist at Shenandoah, had driven me in a government car to visit diverse people who'd been with the Hoovers at the fishing camp (or "Summer White House") at the head of Rapidan River across the Blue Ridge from our hollow. Most knowledgeable was Admiral Joel T. Boone, White House physician to Hoover after serving other Presidents. I also delved into records in NPS offices, National Archives, and Library of Congress. The earthmanship came from the lives of President and Mrs. Hoover. As I'd pointedly emphasize in my chapter of another book (*Herbert Hoover Reassessed*, 1981, sponsored by U.S. Senate), this President's linking of conservation and careful economic development helped shape policy decisions.

Reactions to the *Hideaway* manuscript had brought me a contract to produce a man-and-earth book using Shenandoah for illustrative details. The research, photography, writing and rewriting spread through several years. I approach Earth as astronauts might – a small lonely sphere in the vastness of space – and tell how its rocks and soil formed, after which there was life, and much later, human life, and how we draw our living from Earth and relate our physical and spiritual being to this home planet.

Eileen and I live inside this story. There's interweaving of humanity's many aspects – social, psychological, artistic, commercial, industrial, ecological, recreational, religious, all involving Earth.

Eighty black-and-white prints, selected from a thousand negatives I produced, became five picture essays – Air, Land, Water, Fire, Life. Humans show dimly in still waters, in bushes, among flowers, in air pollution, in scenic beauty, suggesting both creative and destructive forces. Technological civilization contrasts with old ways of plantations, primitive mines and iron furnaces, timber operations, isolated mountain homes. The national park concept brings a revolution in the Shenandoah Blue Ridge – nature re-creating wilderness, urban folk visiting. An environmental awakening transforms park interpretation, helping people to harmonize with land, water, air, sunshine, life, through working with, not against, nature.

After I produce three versions, progressively shorter, the last becomes *The Earth-Man Story* (New York and Luray Va., 1972). Noted author Sigurd F. Olson, whom we'd met in Alaska, called it "an amazing achievement... I'll never again see that country without being conscious of this book, or for that matter any other country. The book has planetary scope and should be read by millions!" Sigurd was among those whose writings Eileen and I were reading aloud to each other. I'm reminded of that period's other reading by these samples copied into one of my diary-type-files, supporting our Blue Ridge "experiment in living," strengthening our confidence we were close to the right track:

> **Harrison Brown**: The machine has divorced man from the world of nature to which he belongs, and in the process he has lost in large measure the powers of contemplation with which he was endowed. A prerequisite for the preservation of the canons of humanism is a re-establishment of organic roots with our natural environment and, related to it, the evolution of ways of life which encourage contemplation and the search for truth and knowledge. The flower and vegetable garden, green grass, the fireplace, the primeval forest with its wondrous assemblage of living things, the uninhabited hilltop where one can silently look at the stars and wonder – all these things and many others are necessary for the fulfillment of man's psychological and spiritual needs.
>
> **Sally Carrighar**: Looking out on our urban scenes, we often believe that life is absurd, which is to say without a chance of achieving coherence. Can one reason for our discouragement be that we have divorced ourselves from the patterns and rhythms and the renewals of the natural world? ... The stars are not absurd.
>
> **Aldo Leopold**: There is value in any experience that reminds us of our dependency on the soil-plant-animal-man food chain, and of the fundamental organization of the biota. Civilization has so cluttered this elemental man-earth relation with gadgets and middlemen that awareness of it is growing dim. We fancy that industry supports, forgetting what supports industry.

Joseph Wood Krutch: The naturalist tends to think first of man's place in nature and the consequence of modern man's refusal to accept this fact that he is indeed part of a scheme which he can to some extent modify but which he cannot supersede by a scheme of his own making.

Tolstoy: One of the first conditions [of earthly happiness] acknowledged by everyone is that man's union with nature should not be infringed... Men confined in prison feel this deprivation more than anything else. But consider the life of people who live according to the teaching of the world: the more they achieve success according to the world's teaching the more are they deprived of this condition of happiness.

Laotze: To return to the root is repose; it is called going back to one's destiny. Going back to one's destiny is to find the eternal law. To know the eternal law is enlightenment. And not to know the eternal law is to court disaster.

"Mardy" Murie (in Preface of her book, *Two in the Far North* 1962): I would love to think the world will survive its obsession with machines to see a day when people respect one another all over the world. It seems as clear as a shaft of the Aurora that this is our only hope.

Thomas Jefferson (quoted by **Benton MacKaye** in 1947 letter to Shenandoah National Park superintendent): When we take a view of the universe ... it is impossible for the human mind not to perceive and feel a conviction of design, consummate skill, and indefinite power in every atom of its composition. The movements of the heavenly bodies, so exactly held in their course ... the structure of our earth itself, with its distribution of lands, waters and atmosphere ... animal and vegetable bodies ... it is impossible, I say, for the human mind not to believe that there is in all this, design, cause and effect...

In my feelings and thoughts everything bent toward earthmanship in those years. I recall saying in response to an interviewer's question on nationwide TV, "As long as the morel mushrooms still sprout in our hollow, it isn't too late to try for understanding that can save the planet Earth and human life and morale." A crucial test of Eileen's and my dedication to earthmanship came soon after publication of the 50th anniversary issue of *National Parks*. Paul Tilden decided to retire, and association president Tony Smith offered me the *National Parks* editorship. Heavily urged, I spent a day in Washington with Tony and Paul.

There'd be ample help in the office. My main job would be to initiate or otherwise obtain the best original articles on the parks and on the forefront of conservation. The starting salary would be several times what Eileen and I were spending in Shaver Hollow – living, as I thought of it, "from land to mouth." Leaping back to above-average income had its appeal, but so did being our own bosses in beautiful, peaceful, natural surroundings. We were living as we felt experimenters toward earthmanship should, through working knowledge of how the planet feeds, clothes, and shelters us. I promised Tony we'd "sleep on" his proposal, and we did – or lay awake agonizing over it night after night.

The ample salary couldn't be conclusive. Could hope for fame? Though we hide in the wilderness and don't enjoy being celebrities, I do deeply enjoy having people say their lives have been influenced by my writing or speaking, or by Eileen's and my way of life. So – there's *increased money* – and isn't there also *increased influence* as editor of the magazine?

But we just couldn't do it. Not money, not even influence, could pull us out of our Blue Ridge home. Yet we couldn't explain well to Tony Smith exactly why. The best I could do in my own mind was generality skirting the fringes – the joy of intimate communication with the processes and creatures of Earth, such high points as singing with the toads or exchanging attitudes with birds, maybe barred owls quite near, or occasionally in real depth with our dog or cat, or looking into our spring and seeing clear, cold water rising from the depths of Earth, or when Eileen and I lie together relaxing in the sunshine caressed by a breeze and feeling so at-home, so *totally* at-home.

At last a stroke of luck got us gently off Tony's hook. Superb photographer David Muench asked me to write the text for a large-format book – *Timberline Ancients,* meaning bristlecone pines (to be published by Graphic Arts, Portland, 1972). Tony understood I must grab this rare opportunity. I could do the work at home where I already had much of the needed information. As it turned out, "Wes" Ferguson of the world-famous tree-ring laboratory at the University of Arizona, Tucson, most experienced bristlecone scientist now living, would spend a couple of days with us on his trip east to a national science gathering.

This book became earthmanship too – for instance, where I'm dream-talking with an overwhelming ancient of Wheeler Peak, the one we park advocates named "Socrates" in the 1950s (when we also named the most ancient of all, "Prometheus"). Socrates asked,

"What are you really doing in this wild place, man?"

I answered: Persuading you to go on helping humans understand the basic way of the planet we share with you.

What is it you think you understand?

That the land and water rise and fall, move and change. That life-sustaining temperature, moisture, sunlight and chemicals are dependable within broad limits... That the things and processes affecting you affect humans also. That you and we live together on a small planet floating in space and time too vast to be fathomed, though we reach and reach. That Earth and her whole family of life are interdependent.

Did you need to construct truth so laboriously? Why didn't you simply feel it?

I do feel it – when I'm near you. But we moderns have been taught to separate the intuitive from the logical and physical, not to let feelings blind us.

Are you not thus divided against yourself and forever blinded to the unified truth?

I don't know. Right now I dare to dream of earthmanship, a process of identification in which is conceived an art of living for the planet as for self and all life.

The bristlecone project deepened our acquaintance with magazine editors. The new one at *National Parks* was Eugenia (GG) Horstman Connally. Eileen and I invited her to Shaver Hollow with her daughter, young Lara. GG was already appreciating earthmanship. In the January 1970 issue she implemented a proposal I'd made to Paul in 1968, describing the plan in her editor's note as...

> a series of short articles by thinkers in a wide range of disciplines who will examine various aspects of man's relationship to nature. The series will, we hope, stimulate thought and indicate routes toward developing the kind of man-earth relationship that will lead to creative ecological harmony, thus operating and preserving our planet as a physically and mentally healthful abode for all life.

I would be unpaid co-editor of the series – labeled "Exploring Earthman's World," its identifying logo being a photo by astronauts of the half-earth seen above the moon's horizon.

The launching article identified me as "a budding Earthman, my older identities fading or becoming subsidiary." I defined Earthman: "Body, mind, spirit, environment ... an integration, a symbiosis with the planet, a citizenship." The essay concluded with Walt Whitman's words:

When the full-grown poet came,
Out spake pleased Nature (the round impassive globe,
  with all its shows of day and night), saying, *He is mine*;

> But out spake too the Soul of Man, proud, jealous and
>   unreconciled, *Nay, he is mine alone*;
> Then the full-grown poet stood between the two, and
>   took each by the hand;
> And today and ever so stands, as blender, uniter, tightly
>   holding hands,
> Which he will never release until he reconciles the two,
> And wholly and joyously blends them.

Twenty-six Earthman's essays were published in our effort to concentrate forces for the creative harmony of humankind with the rest of nature. Many of the writers were nationally known. Several, from different crafts or professions, stressed the importance of earth-manship, not only to keep "the environment" in healthful and pleasant condition but also to reduce alienation of individuals or of groups that feel left out, useless, lacking connection into anything basically meaningful.

Psychiatrist Edward Stainbrook, University of California school of medicine, wrote:

> Man has ... conceived of himself as outside of nature. In Western civilization especially, he has considered nature an opponent to be conquered... He has seemed determined to eliminate himself as natural man and to ... despoil unconcernedly the earthly space in which he lives.

Stainbrook then gave details about many psychic and physical ailments caused primarily by anti-nature attitudes and living conditions – and concluded:

> We must decide to work harmoniously with nature, not against her. Otherwise we may mindlessly follow the Pied Piper of our materialism and technology to the desperate edge of our increasingly synthetic existence.

Anthropologist Loren Eiseley wrote that "what increasingly is required of man is that he pursue the paradox of return..."

The axial religions had sought to persuade man to transcend his own nature; they had pictured to him limitless perspectives of self-mastery. By contrast, science in our time has opened to man the prospect of limitless power over exterior nature...

Today, man's increasing numbers and his technological power to pollute his environment reveal a single demanding necessity: the necessity for him consciously to re-enter and preserve, for his own safety, the old first world from which he originally emerged. His second world, drawn from his own brain, has brought him far, but it cannot take him out of nature... He must now incorporate ... an ethic directed not alone toward his fellows but extended to the living world around him.

Theologist Joseph Sittler, University of Chicago, warned against making "a preaching gimmick" out of the environmental crisis and against simply adding this crisis "to the already overloaded agenda of moral imperatives." Instead, the basic doctrine "must be freshly understood." So the first correction, one of language, is that the phrase in Genesis that we've read as "to have dominion over" the earth and other forms of life, is more correctly translated as "'to exercise tender care for'– almost 180 degrees of shift in meaning." The other correction is in "the doctrine of man's independence." Sittler declares: "That man is independent is a plain lie. He comes *from* nature, he *is* by the processes of nature, he lives in every moment in absolute dependence upon nature." Sittler concludes:

> Man must honor and love the creation that is the womb and web of his life. If he does not, he will die. Nature's reprisals are slow – but sure. Nature, like God, will not be mocked.

During the *Earthman's World* period several of my more voluminous projects also flowered in *National Parks*. "Earth's Words in the National Parks" (July 1970) was written to accompany an NPS educational article. The NPS Washington people were so pleased with my vivid account of an environmental education event at Big

Meadows in Shenandoah they distributed thousands of reprints. GG wrote me that NPS executives said they'd been "having difficulty defining their goals, and your article did it for them!"

Another article, influenced by experience in diverse countries – "Personal Testimony on the Standard of Living" (June 1971) – generated even more thousands of reprints. Eileen and I had been off this standard for seven years, receiving and spending about a fourth of the American average, yet feeling happier than either of us had felt before. My most original contribution had to do with "overconsumption vs. human enjoyment and fulfillment":

> Subtly, perniciously, the American standard is eroding key conditions that make our lives worth living – our ability to feel fellowship with all mankind, the satisfactions of using our muscles as well as our brains to create truly useful things... Overconsumption imposes itself between the built-in biological program of the human being – physical, mental, spiritual – and many of the requirements for realization of this program.

Sometimes GG was ahead of me. In the middle of a three-page single-spaced letter, mostly about personal things such as creating a "Japanese garden" in her back yard, she took off thus:

> Darwin, I have an idea I want your reaction to: It is the year 11,970. Earth is a beautiful, clean, healthy planet inhabited by a race of happy, healthy Earthmen... Earthmen reckon their beginnings in the 20th Century during the Foul Age. Back then, *Homo sapiens* was headed for extinction when an important event occurred:
>
> Man freed himself from his Earthly bounds and for the first time viewed his tiny planet from an infinite viewpoint. This experience wrought profound changes... What kind of creature *is* Earthman? How does he live? What is his philosophy, religion, ethic? What decisions did his ancestors make that changed their destructive course?

The questions percolated in me for months. The resulting "future fiction" was published as "Coming of Age on Earth" in

National Parks of April 1971 – maybe the only fiction this magazine ever published. Here's the action line: As the Foul Age worsens and space technology advances, the "teens to twenty-twos" give up on Earth and fly off to seek homes on far planets. This trend-becoming-stampede is the watershed event – so much so that years worldwide are numbered now from the Youth Exodus. My report – I just couldn't span 10,000 years as GG suggested – focuses on YE 55 and YE 56 when old Great'pa – who remembers the whole sweep including two decades building toward the Exodus – is still mentally strong. Great'pa helps his great-grandson Art, who's come from a far planet for advanced education – to make a film about Earth's 75 revolutionary years. Art is teamed in audio and video aspects with Earth-girl Tess – whom he hopes will return with him to his remote planet. She and Great'pa, though, scheme to hold him here.

Great'pa remembers the intolerable condition of Earth's cities that led to the Exodus:

> While our youngsters were speeding into the unknown, we were trying to save them through space-survival research we transmitted to them – yet, after all, largely failing. Quite suddenly then, on Earth, the ecology movement surged again – this time deeper than reason, frantically. We urban people ran away from our jobs and our properties with no effort to recover our investments, and went out to live with nature. Government became useless, helpless. The mass media proved uneconomic; nobody cared to hear or read; disaster was too obvious first-hand... Shortwave hams multiplied worldwide. An Earthmen's council came into being – not a body, you must understand, but a process. A dozen or so of us on each continent were main spokesmen, but anyone could listen in, anyone could speak up. Discussion went on in all languages, with translators seeming to come out of nowhere. An amazing convergence of attitude, a foundation of human values, came into being in this total emergency. We who remained on Earth were reborn as *Earthmen*, inextricably identified with our planet, our home.

People cooperated out of desperation, organizing around a fundamentally different arrangement of population and activity.

Everyone was close to forefront technology and close also to wild nature. Pattern details varied. In China, for instance, the webstrands were often the rivers. In the United States the Web followed the crisscross of the decaying Interstate highway system:

> We began excavating the freeways to a subsurface level of 50 feet - and building the Pipe, a great flattened cylinder of concrete and steel which now carries all our freight, power, and fuel and most of our passengers and communications. Elevators connect living apartments with essential services and supplies and with both short and long transportation, mostly speedtrains, but for special trips, electrisoarers. The arrangement is less costly and more pleasant than the old urban sprawl. No pollution goes into Earth's air and water. Vehicles in local use near the Pipe – for farming and recreation mostly – are electrically powered and regularly recharged from the Pipe.

Art and Tess are filming from an electrisoarer, bringing one strand of the Web into sharp detail – skyscraper apartments with staggered porches; long low manufacturing plants (whose gaseous, solid and liquid wastes are channeled to recycling plants, along with a constant pumping of used air from the Pipe and all sewage and other wastes, to become fresh air and pure water for recirculation, plus diverse products, mostly fertilizers). All sizable development is in the single line called webstrand, bordered on both sides by tree-canopied walkways, parks and playgrounds. Working farms are visible a bit farther out. From every apartment there are views of agriculture in action and, still farther out, working forests. Then, somewhere in every interstice of the Web, there's space for nature enjoyment, picnicking, camping, harvesting of wild fruits, greens and nuts. Where possible, large tracts of untrammeled wilderness are protected for solitary exploration and contemplation. Great'pa explains that the much-reduced population on Earth allows this ideal arrangement – but insists no problems can be considered solved forever. He worries about rising birth rates and increasing volume of back-to-Earth immigrations – as no other planet has proved as hospitable as Earth.

Now, the ancient man explains, there's no wall between rural and urban. There's no wall, either, between school and work. Children as well as adults are always in "real life"; everyone learns and works and plays; everyone (almost) contributes regularly to family and community success; government is our tool, not the manager; education is not compulsory; people find or create their own niches. Great'pa continues:

> We found no need for schools in the old sense... Every apartment building, factory, office tower, laboratory, shopping center and community center has student rooms. Teachers are supplied by business, industrial, scientific, agricultural, or other institutions for helping to train workers the institutions will need in future. All of us all our lives are *participrobers* – that is, explorers, apprentices, learners... When learners begin to produce significantly they're placed on part-time pay and may soon become full-time workers...
>
> Earthlife is more challenging than ever before; learners who shift often may become generalists and solve problems we haven't solved before... We're all *needed*. We're Earth-centered; there's a trend toward spiritual gatherings in open areas, surrounded by scenery or natural abundance of production, harvest festivals, perhaps, as in long-ago times...

In late summer 1972, Eileen and I tented westward and flew to Alaska. We'd been touring the West every four years (1964, 1968), visiting family, scouting for article subjects. We felt better in Ely where we'd met and married – a mildly triumphant return this time, our visit having been announced in advance by the *Ely Daily Times*, with mention of our magazine articles. The old stationery and book store had two of my new books – *The Earth-Man Story* and *Timberline Ancients* – and invited people to have copies autographed. Many did, and there was good conversation with old friends. Some brought their *Gold Strike in Hell* novel, its action centering at Ely, to be signed.

In Alaska we found Mike and Doreen with baby daughter Krystal at home in Douglas across Gastineau Channel from Juneau. Mike was employed by the state to photograph great scenery. Grandma (Eileen) had the privilege of bathing the baby. We picnicked together in our old haunts and found many of our Alaskan friends. Carolyn and Amos Burg invited us to dinner, and again we enjoyed Alaskan talk and Gastineau Channel views. We enjoyed an evening too at the home of our artist-friend Rie Muñoz high on a Juneau hill. Some of our special friends, including Carol and Trevor Davis, were away.

After visiting with Sylvia and Christian in Ellensburg, Washington, where he was a university professor, we headed for Priest Lake in northern Idaho for the annual foray of the North American Mycological Association. Our interest in mushrooms had been expanding from the morels of Blue Ridge springtimes. We'd safely and enjoyably eaten ten wild species by 1972, but we needed more discussion with knowledgeable people. Also, magazines had expressed tentative interest in mushroom articles.

The forest around Priest Lake was evergreen and damp, rich in mushroom species. The campground filled with 291 association members. We were divided into groups and assigned territories, so we wouldn't crowd. In three days, September 29-October 1, we brought 340 species to central tables where experts confirmed or corrected our identifications. Many species were edible and tasty; some were poisonous, from slightly to deadly; most were harmless but not delicious.

Dr. Alexander H. Smith, author of one of our identification books, was foray leader. Other experts included researchers, professors, and well-qualified leaders of mycological groups across the country. We gained confidence in our ability to identify. During the last hours of the foray, before people began taking back what they'd brought in to show, the hundreds of feet of displays were richly fantastic in shapes and colors. We photographed and smelled the mushrooms and visited with mycologists.

I considered the foray an event in earthmanship, pointing our way forward. So many species growing so lushly here indicated that this part of the country, anyway, was surviving in natural good health. Analyzing from a different angle, Eileen and I decided that if 291 people could gather and handle 340 species of mushrooms, eating the good ones and not eating the poisonous ones – all the people remaining in vigorous health – it was certainly possible for humanity to learn what's good for itself and other life, and for the planet, our home – and what's bad or fatal – then apply this learned earthmanship to assure the health and happiness of life on into the future. We tented back eastward encouraged.

Chapter 21 – Feeling vs. Thinking 1972-84

Our dog Sourdough barks to announce *Reader's Digest* editor Edward T. Thompson as he drives into our yard. Eileen and I talk to Sourdough, telling him Ed is our friend. Sourdough reads our feelings and stops barking. Ed speaks to him. I wonder if Sourdough could star in a *Digest* article – but dismiss the thought.

We've prepared for this rare opportunity. We're eager to tell millions of people – if we can reach them – about our living in nature. The *Digest* just bought my article about bristlecone pine trees, "What the Ancient Pines Teach Us," and we've tried to work out additional ideas with similar qualities. Ed's hint by mail was that feeling is the key, not unsophisticatedly lyrical, yet strongly present or implied. But can feeling be duplicated?

Though this June day is almost hot, Ed wants to stroll around our clearing and into the forest; he seems familiar with wild places. Sourdough walks close, and Ed touches him in recognition. When we get back to our log house, Eileen brings lunch to our pool porch. The food is what we've grown or gathered – cold asparagus soup, diverse salad, stuffed morels, peaches, black-walnut cookies. She tells Ed about a black bear coming up through the briers this very morning, wallowing in our Tadpool, then ambling out front, standing on hind legs scratching his back against the power pole. Ed's eyes grow large, and he watches the woods. He sees Sourdough calm on the lawn and relaxes. Eileen tells him about Sourdough chasing bears out of the yard and then in the forest the bear gaining courage and chasing Sourdough back toward the house, where Sourdough gets brave – and the game continuing.

I'm not relaxed enough to propose a Sourdough story spontaneously. We've felt our most promising new subject is the amazing regrowth of wilderness in Shenandoah National Park. The forest Ed sees here resembles that all over the park, with lichen-covered stone walls marking borders of now-erased fields, pastures, and home sites. Wilderness is high in public interest following establishment of a national wilderness system and frequent emergence of proposals for adding to this system. We could show that "Wilderness *Can* Grow Again," focusing on eastern states.

Ed is interested – in wilderness being created by nature under human protection – that is, in the reverse of the much-touted dictum that wilderness if not saved now is forever lost. He says he senses in me the feel of regenerated wilderness – "Describe examples from other states but feature Shenandoah, what you know best." He's a good coach; I feel I can do this piece.

We don't get anywhere with "The Struggle of the American Chestnut." He says, "Your feeling is valid, but unless you can re-create the chestnut forest, it's essentially what the magazine carried long ago." There's a tentative spark for morel hunting in springtime around the world's temperate zone, "The World's Greatest Easter Egg Hunt" (Eileen's suggested title) – facts from different countries but featuring our experiences here. Ed suggests research-scouting but makes no firm assignment.

I suggest an article on earthmanship, saying it's basically important all over the world, but I'd need editorial help to pin down an approach that would put the complex idea into words stirring the feelings of readers. I know I'm close to what brought Ed to see us, but he says, "It's fuzzy, undefined." He coaches along, though: An "inspirational tour de force" on earthmanship "should have top priority for development effort." After a moment, he advises, "Try to extract from experiences living with nature – yours here plus others' elsewhere, or perhaps yours alone – things that can be used in the way of life of the majority. An article, or more than one, could show a different approach to the environmental problem that's of high interest. We've been having one environmental article a month, but are letting some issues go to press without any – for lack of fresh views that will appeal to the increasingly fed-up public."

After he's gone, realizing I have a once-in-a-lifetime opportunity, I restudy the earthmanship articles I've done for other magazines. The *National Parks* kind won't fit. *Parks* readers are already into conservation, at least a little; they aren't the "majority" Ed wants to reach. Something like my approach in *VISTA* might serve. Earthmanship there means mostly world citizenship. As I quoted from Whitman in *VISTA*:

> Seest thou not God's purpose from the first?
> The earth to be spann'd, connected by network,
> The races, neighbors, to marry and be given in marriage,
> The oceans to be cross'd, the distant brought near,
> The lands to be welded together?

But no. The majority isn't ready for world citizenship, won't welcome interracial marriage, won't easily see war as mistreatment of the environment.

Can there be an angle, then, in my "interview" with Laotze? Editor Al Farnsworth was pleased by my use of the old Chinese philosopher's words. But no – Ed wouldn't go for far-out philosophy. What about the *Bible*, then? I feel *Reader's Digest* loves the *Bible*, and I have loads of biblical quotes copied on index cards during my recent cover-to-cover reading (in University of Chicago translation). Neither my "letter" to Dad (see Chapter 19 in this book), nor my 12-page article, "Earthman's Bible," that *VISTA* just bought, used a 20th of them.

This angle seems an inspiration. I summarize in a letter to Ed. No quotes used for *VISTA* will be duplicated, and I'll use no words of my own – just arrange biblical quotes to bring out world peace and environmentalism, elaborating this bare essence (which uses biblical words and phrases but is my condensation):

> **Earth** – The Lord by wisdom founded the earth... His judgments are in all the earth ...You must keep His statutes and commands ... that you may prosper, and your children after you, and that you may live long upon the land.

> **Ecology** – We must lovingly hold to the truth and grow up into union ... for it is under his control that the whole system,

adjusted and united by each ligament of its equipment, develops in proportion to the functioning of each particular part, and so builds itself up through love.

Responsibility – You must observe my statutes, and be careful to observe my ordinances, that you may live in security upon the earth.

Discord – The earth is polluted through the touch of its inhabitants, because they have transgressed laws, violated statutes, broken the everlasting covenant… I will exhaust calamities upon them … till cities lie waste, without inhabitant … and the soil is left a desolation.

Harmony – Thine exhausted and worn-out land thou didst re-establish … He makes wars to cease to the end of the earth… He is the God who formed the earth … for a dwelling place… For as the days of a tree shall be the days of my people… They will do no harm or destruction… For the land will become full of the knowledge of the Lord.

But Ed Thompson's discouragement is firm. He simply reminds me I'm a conservationist, a naturalist, not a preacher, and I shouldn't meddle in religion. I don't argue, though of course effective earthmanship has to include religion and all other strong influences. The value and power multiply through interrelationships.

Eileen and I are pushing earthmanship on many fronts. I'm preparing an NPCA-Smithsonian lecture, also writing the earthwide essence of bristlecone pines to be published in three languages with David Muench's photographs in *International Photo Technic* (Munich), also weaving aspects of earthmanship into articles for *Reader's Digest* and *National Wildlife*, plus adding the Earthman's view to wilderness discussion on nationwide NBC television.

I keep failing, though, to work out the pattern and the feeling for a full earthmanship article to please Ed Thompson. Though he insists he knows Eileen and I aren't pompous, he senses pomposity in our efforts to suggest routes toward human harmony with nature. My ambitious hope is reduced to "We Chose to Live With Nature," hewing strictly to how and why we two live in Shaver Hollow. In it I express a feeling of conversation with Earth, and publication is rewarding (*Reader's Digest*, Jan 1974). Among the many appreciative responses is a letter from James Stewart, long one of our favorite actors – which the *Digest* features as a page-size promotion of the magazine.

Granddaughter Laurie, almost three, and her mother Laura are visiting in Shaver Hollow as the much-transferred military family moves from a post in Georgia to Fort Riley, Kansas. Laurie supervises while I tie a rope swing on a horizontal tree limb and fit in the board seat. I push her, and she swings. "Push harder, Granddad," she says. She swings higher, squealing with delight. Then she insists on pushing me.

After the swinging, we climb a forested slope and see mountain laurel blooming. She laughs when I call her "Mountain Laurie" and says her mother climbed the same slope when little and was called the same name. She's interested in birds and butterflies and frogs, in trees and flowers, in everything alive.

Early on the day they're to fly to Fort Riley, which they've never seen, Laurie comes to me in the garden and grasps two of my fingers. "Granddad," she says, "could I plant a tree?"

It's mid-June, dry and hot, too late for easy transplanting. "You could plant a tree seed," I say. "It will sprout and grow."

"I want to plant a living tree." She jerks my fingers gently. "Please."

We find shovels, hers a small one we carry on tenting trips, and we walk in the forest. She stops beside a tulip tree about her own height. It's leaves are big and smoothly green. She lets me help dig it with soil clinging. With Eileen's and Laura's help, we choose a site and dig the hole in the lawn. Laurie places the tree. She abandons her shovel and puts dirt and humus around the roots with her hands. She tamps the soil with her sneakers and carries water to her tree.

Then, with one hand muddy and the other wet, she grasps both my hands and says, "This is home now."

I return the pressure but with tear-pressure behind my eyes. I feel she's saying her family has been changing residences too fast for her. Is this, her tree, an anchor in an unsteady world that keeps uprooting her? When we return from putting Laurie and Laura on the plane, the upper leaves of the little tree are already wilted. I carry water frequently until bedtime. The tree looks strong at sunup but then goes limp. I keep nursing it, but one by one the leaves wilt and turn yellow, then brown. I prune dead sections of the thin trunk, painting the cut each time to keep moisture in. I finally sacrifice most of the trunk, saving just one live-looking bud.

Twenty months later Laurie's father is transferred from Fort Riley to Germany. Laura and girls (Heather Mary is four months old) arrive to stay with us until their place in Heidelberg is ready. Laurie runs to her tree. The twigs are bare; it's early April. She reaches with both hands to touch the beginning hints of a new spring's leaves. That one low bud has grown faster than Laurie; the tree is already twice her height. Gently, lovingly, she grasps separate twigs and holds them as if letting the tree's current flow through her. She stays there while we unload the car.

Laurie loves this place and wants us to be here forever. She wants to find all kinds of creatures – if possible, to touch them. One day she says, "Grandad, I want to be a naturalist like you and Grandma Eileen." She catches woodfrog tadpoles in our pool, and Eileen puts water in an over-sized brandy snifter for them. Laurie feeds them algae. Soon they're growing legs, and Eileen floats a stick for them to crawl up on. One day – after Easter and the outdoor hunting of hidden eggs – we go moreling, and Laurie finds some of the delicious spring mushrooms. "They grow under the mothers and dads and grandmas and granddads of my tree," she says.

Next morning we're heading for the airport. Up early, Laurie holds a twig in each hand and stands solemnly there alone, but she's cheerful and ready to go when we are. After the flight is called, she takes my hand and looks into my eyes. "Granddad," she whispers. "When I'm old enough to make a home, I'll plant tulip trees – and maybe morels will come under them, like Easter eggs, for my grandchildren to find."

Eileen and I selected friends who enjoyed nature and supported conservation, and we talked quality of life with them but never "standard of living." Our social friends had incomes ranging from quadruple ours on up. We acted as if no difference existed, but once in a while I let the mask slip in my writing, such as in "Personal Testimony on the Standard of Living" (*National Parks*, June 1971), the article on our life with nature (*National Wildlife* and *Reader's Digest*, January 1974), and as a minor thread in *The Earth-Man Story* (SNHA-Exposition, New York, 1972). If friends read these materials, they seemed to assume I was using "literary license" to promote environmentalism, and they forgave me. They noticed we could afford whatever we strongly wanted; they tended not to notice our wants were few, or satisfied without consuming.

The foregoing confesses we're hypocrites. Nearly all humans are; we project images that hide what's inside us. Eileen and I – as individuals and as one (we're in both statuses) – are more what we feel than what we say or think. I recognize different spokesmen inside me. At first there were my "world face" and my "nature face," but the names changed and the personalities multiplied. I wrote a novel called "Rad & Co.," unpublished, the company being half a dozen arguers inside Rad, rendering firm decisions impossible. In me the personalities coalesced into Left Brain and Right Brain, later called Thinky and Feely, and now, with the nervous flippancy fading, become Think and Feel.

My decisions are made by Feel; he appeals to literary writers and readers. Think always argues; he appeals to academic-scientist-type intellectuals. Though Think seldom changes a decision I've made, he worries me a lot before he rationalizes that he made the decision himself.

Meanwhile, the think-feel or feel-think question can break through into "real life." During that "Rad & Co." time the action settings were in Nevada, and often I was exploring the Great Basin again in my mind and emotions. A friend, Charles S."Charlie" Watson, co-founder of Nevada Outdoor Recreation Association (NORA) devoted to protecting U.S. Bureau of Land Management (BLM) lands, was helping and encouraging me. Together, on the phone or by mail, we were remembering extraordinary features and lands in the Great Basin, and I wrote an article for *National Parks*, "Hidden Treasures on OUR Lands" (Dec '74 issue) that *Reader's Digest's* editor-in-chief Ed Thompson had agreed to publish simultaneously in his magazine.

Unfortunately, I'd failed to realize that in those months some wealthy and politically powerful people were at odds with Charlie – perhaps having other prospective uses for those "worthless lands." For some reason, anyhow, the *Digest* canceled out and never published the piece about Charlie and his organization's campaign to protect those lands and their so-attractive resources.

Through the decades since, though, I've been honored by membership on NORA's advisory board, enjoyed a long and productive friendship with Charlie, and been able to contribute a bit here and there to the protection of valuable public-owned attractions in Nevada and, in some degree, throughout "the Commons" around this nation and occasionally world-wide.

Many internal arguments cast light on my struggles between "human culture" and "nature" that continued through a nonfiction manuscript called "Earth Dream." It focuses on man-and-nature relations but also on the near-impossibility of avoiding hypocrisy. "Earth Dream" – Think says the title should be "The Earthman Condition" – ought to become my most significant work, though maybe instead it's now finding its function through helping make this autobiography more obviously significant, surrendering its status as a separate book, no longer being what it's been called by one team of big-publisher manuscript readers, "the equivalent of a dissertation based on a decade of research into ecology, economics, psychology, religion, literature, and philosophy stirred into six decades of living experience."

In its longest form, "Earth Dream" has 1100 pages arranged in three parts: I-Goodby World, II-Inside Nature, and III-Still There, World? The manuscript says we need to understand we're living in nature; it's the whole system of which we're parts. Otherwise, we feel alienated, incomplete, discontented, angry, in despair. It says civilization is mistaken in aiming for less and less work and more and more consumption. It says nature is wonderfully creative and includes all existing reality plus innumerable possibilities yet unrealized. It suggests that generations of humans' relations with each other and with nature (if we see humans and nature as separate) have produced the basic morality for successful living. It suggests humanity's primary function from now on is to keep this planet of life in healthful, productive, and beautiful condition and that happiness and creativity in addition to physical health are most likely to grow in us as we devote our minds, muscles, and emotions to harmonizing our living with the nature of Earth.

Encouraged by Shenandoah Natural History Association and the U.S. Department of the Interior, I agreed to produce an "Administrative History of Shenandoah National Park 1924-76," not for book publication but for use in photocopy by policy makers in the Washington, regional, and local National Park Service offices. The work, using up three years, took me back to my earliest Virginia memories, causing me to wonder again what happened to the mountain folk I'd known personally – the Sisks, the Corbins, and so on.

But most of my research was in the park headquarters attic where old files and maps were collecting dust. I enjoyed rediscovering documents I'd helped create. Solid evidence corrected faded memories. I also probed the Library of Congress, the National Archives, and the Virginia State Library and Archives for parts of the park story that happened before I rode my bicycle to the Blue Ridge. There'd been lots of hearsay about how the national park originated and how the scenic land was acquired from 1300 landowners, including mountain residents.

This project turned out to be one of those dissertation-equivalents I fall into, and this time I even had a professional keeping me in line (James W. Bond, historian, Mid-Atlantic Region, NPS, Philadelphia). There was also a graduate student, D.E. Simmons, working at the same time on his doctoral dissertation, "The Creation of Shenandoah National Park and Skyline Drive, 1924-36" (University of Virginia, Ph.D., 1978). We searched together sometimes and shared old papers, though my work is more detailed and covers 40 additional years, to 1976. My degree, I guess, is the acknowledgment from Dr. Bond:

> You certainly have gone the extra mile in producing the finest park administrative history I have read... It is a model that future writers will undoubtedly look to when other administrative histories are being written.

Life in that busy period continued as a mixture of disappointments and rewards. A park-introductory movie, "The Gift," borrowed much of my history. Then a different movie crew persisted without advance arrangements up our "road" with their truck that had a crane to lift the cameraman skyward. The director and interviewer talked with me in the front yard. Soon they moved chairs into position there, and the cameraman went into the sky, and we kept on just talking and looking up at the ridges and maybe mentioning the birds singing and the frogs chattering and something about blossoms, maybe flowering dogwood, and about this old house that was showing too in the film.

Next winter the Governor invited Eileen and me to the premiere showing of the result, "And You May Find Virginia." We accepted but had to cancel when a below-zero air mass moved in. If we weren't feeding our fire, our plumbing and all the laboriously canned fruits and vegetables would burst. Rumor said I was talking at least five of the 26 minutes, and the film was circulating in New York and other cities. We expected to see it soon, somewhere, but we still haven't and probably, now, never will.

My curiosity about what I said sitting out there under that camera multiplied when Central Virginia Educational Television, Richmond, wanted to launch a television series based on my "astute views of man and his world" as expressed in my book *The Earth-Man Story*. The Science Museum of Virginia was also involved. We (mostly they) put together an HEW grant application. But the competition for limited funds squeezed out our grant.

Another great idea came in a phone call from the Smithsonian's Air and Space Museum. They'd discovered *The Earth-Man Story* and persisted through intricate difficulties in getting me on the phone (Bob and Dorothy Smith's, a mile-plus down-hollow, was best after Ernest Miller was gone). The plan we worked out was announced in a Smithsonian newsletter of September 1978:

Earth in the Universe

An extensive scientific probe of the Earth – and its place in the universe – is the theme of this weekend seminar held in the magnificent setting of Shenandoah National Park. The world is perceived through the body and mind as a naturalist and an astronomer lead participants on invigorating study hikes and lecture-room discussions...

The item filled a column and sounded exciting, but after I'd spent many days preparing, the seminar was canceled "due to the low enrollment." They expected to try again but didn't.

Still another proposal came out of the blue. Ed Merritt, a producer at WAMU public radio, American University in Washington, came to Shaver Hollow to discuss reading *The Earth-Man Story* aloud on his daily program. With him was Neenah Ellis (who's since been active on National Public Radio). They taped an interview to help introduce the book. I felt skeptical. Who'd listen to a whole book on the radio? But early in April 1980 Eileen and I at home heard Merritt start reading. No hitch developed, and the daily reading, that finished the final page (193) the middle of June, did a lot for my writing career and for this national park and for earthmanship.

As a board member of NPCA, regularly meeting in Washington, I kept pressing for action to save world-class natural wonders in Alaska and to develop them non-destructively for profitable tourism. Through *National Parks* magazine and NPCA-sponsored excursions visiting potential park units, we encouraged an earthmanship approach. An Alaska issue featured articles by friends that Eileen and I had made in Alaska. My shorter piece, "The Alaskan Dream," had these words:

> There is a fortunate chance to use in Alaska the wisdom of hindsight and live American expansion into the wilderness again, this time as it ought to have been. The outcome will be fateful – preeminently because it can provide inspiration and guidance for long-range survival and fulfillment on a healthful, productive, and beautiful planet.

Partly as a result of our work, Congress passed and President Jimmy Carter signed the historic Alaska Lands Bill of 1980 – of which our friend GG, the *National Parks* editor, wrote in a second Alaska issue (March 1981):

> This bill is the greatest single conservation act of the century. It more than doubles the National Park System with 43.6 million acres, adds 53.8 million acres to the National Wildlife Refuge System and 3.4 million acres to the National Forest System ... and ... more than triples the National Wilderness Preservation System with 56.4 million acres.

One different note – of mourning: Our good friend of Great Basin National Park efforts, Keith Trexler who, along with Superintendent Jacobsen and others of NPS, tried to save the world's oldest living tree in the Wheeler cirque, had been killed in a plane crash while studying Alaskan lands for national parks. There were consolations, though – not only the new parks in Alaska but stirrings again toward establishing Great Basin park.

Eileen's and my feelings were being stretched by the human world, happily as well as sorrowfully. We got a telephone – mostly for contacts with family members at a distance. We also got a TV – or, rather, Mom sent it to us without warning – "so you can see how sincere Reagan is," she explained when we protested. Further, our environmental purity got tarnished. Worms and fungal diseases drove me to treat our fruit trees with "home orchard spray" at petal-drop time and again two weeks later.

A family project renewed my closeness to four sisters and two brothers, all my living siblings. It produced a photocopied book about our father, *J. CARLOS LAMBERT; A Life in Utah and Nevada 1887-1948 with Clues to Origins and Meanings*. The book was his diary plus recollections of intervals when he'd neglected the diary. We kids added two sections: "His Descendants" (numbering 69 by 1980) and "His Children Remember" anecdotes and character traits, including his determination to do "what's right" for people and the land, even if his insistence damaged his own personal interests. We seven children were all in friendly contact now, though I remained a sort of black sheep in their Mormon eyes.

I held back from mentioning the early confusion caused by his persistent efforts to instill "responsibility" in me while insisting God is responsible for taking care of us, as well as of wild nature. What came clear and strong was his insistence I do everything possible for our own family, our own farm and home, our own livestock and crops.

Nonhuman creatures – the wild ones – are important parts of our society in Shaver Hollow; Eileen and I can't help feeling at least partly responsible for their safety and welfare. Our sharing here is mostly pleasure, though; just a thread or two of duty mixing in. When we put peanuts out on the bird-feeding shelf on the cedar tree after the birds have gone to bed, the flying squirrels glide in from high in the forest's edge. A human-nonhuman understanding develops. If one of us goes out slowly when the squirrels are on the shelf, holding out peanuts, the squirrels will let us put the nuts down within inches of their mouths.

Friendships develop with many creatures, and we think total intolerance of anthropomorphism in biological study is a serious mistake. Geneticists now report a common language in the genes of all life on Earth. Hummingbirds have tried Eileen's eyes and mouth for nectar – mine too one day when I held still a while – and she once persuaded a skunk mother and youngsters to come to her hand for pieces of cooked chicken.

Since settling in Shaver Hollow in 1964, we two have talked often with dogs in our normal language, and they've used varied language – tones and rhythms of barks, whines, sighs, howls, posture, movements, speed or lack of speed, wagging tail, grins, nudges, licking tongue, touch of paw, or more elaborate movements such as walking to a door they'd like to have opened, please, or going to their empty food dish or water dish, then back to one of us. Feelings are the message, but facts slip in – like *there's a* **bear**!

Two out of four of our Shaver Hollow dogs have come to us "out of nowhere." Woodsy, for instance – we hear a puppy crying out beyond our back stone wall, seeming to say, Help! Help! I'm too young to cope. So Eileen goes for him, brings him in her arms and feeds him. He has no collar. Our old Sourdough – who's appeared strongly in *Reader's Digest* and reprintings – acts reluctant, harried by the intense puppy pressure. He's too feeble now even to walk for the mail. But after a week or so, suddenly he's defending the new puppy against our visiting friend GG's adult Boxer.

Soon we're planning an all-day hike over the Blue Ridge crest, guessing Woodsy can keep up with us. He's energetic the first mile, then lags, seeming to say, I can do it if I have to, but why? He's that way until we're approaching the Shaver Hollow hiking shelter. Suddenly, there, he's energized, running with his nose reading the ground. We find bear tracks in the mud near the spring, a day old but obviously fragrant enough in the pup's sensitive nose. He doesn't act tired again till we've been to Corbin Cabin and back home at dinner time. After eating, he sleeps – and sleeps.

Woodsy grows fast and handsomely – black on back and sides, champagne on chest and stomach and legs, black and champagne in a pleasant design on his face. One day Eileen and Woodsy are on the flood control dam, finding wildflowers. As I'm hurrying toward them, Woodsy erupts in a big-dog bark for the first time. Though he recognizes me, he barks again, seeming to say, Hey! Hear! Isn't it great!?

Soon he discovers his wolf howl. It soars in our front yard with increasing volume and rising pitch, resounding from the ridges, and leaps to a still higher pitch, not shrill but tenor, then in a step or two and a slide both volume and pitch decline. I try imitating, and he listens, and then he howls again, and after that he and I and Eileen are singing trio, while Sourdough stares in disbelief. I feel the wolf howl speaks of the miracle of life, summarizing what I've been trying to say about nature ever since I wrote my first poem at age eight.

One day Woodsy is hiking up rugged mountains in the national park with me and Harry Korine, a teenage cousin from Switzerland, here "to learn about nature" from me. When Harry's far ahead, out of sight, no longer a magnet pulling, I let Woodsy off the leash for good behavior. All's well, I think. But then the trail makes a blind turn, and Woodsy goes around it first. There's a swish and a yip. A deer that must have been beside the trail is leaping away, white tail-flag high, and Woodsy's close behind. I call, "*Woodsy! No! Come back!*" But they're gone in an instant.

I keep calling, "*Here, Woodsy! Here, Woodsy!*" I throw in my best far-carrying wolf howl. Other hikers – they're numerous up here – must think I'm crazy. They may report the dog without his leash, an embarrassment to me who sometimes helps train seasonal rangers. But I can't stop calling now. I think the deer has gotten far ahead, even of fast Woodsy, and Woodsy is bewildered, not knowing how to find me. I keep calling, and after 20 minutes Woodsy answers a wolf howl and comes quickly back. He rubs his head and neck on my leg, asking, I think, for the leash.

Old Sourdough dies on Christmas Eve, weary but not indicating pain. Eileen and I bury him at the lower edge of our clearing, with Woodsy nearby watching. We cover the body and stand there in silence. After a while Woodsy points his nose toward the sky and howls. Eileen and I join in. We're mourning, yes, but also celebrating Sourdough's long friendship.

We suspect Woodsy of reading our minds. He knows in advance when we're going somewhere and whether we'll be walking or driving, and if driving whether he'll be invited or left to guard the house. He doesn't easily read our policy on deer, though. We like to watch them and photograph them. In winter they're allowed in the yard anywhere. In growing season, if they're in the edge of the forest, as mostly they are, or on the lawn, that's okay, don't chase, but if they're in the garden or orchard, chase them out.

Woodsy gains understanding, though, and ultimately graduates with honors in a related, unexpected test. We're hiking in the fall to see if the Sisk pear tree in the park is producing. We leave the car beside Skyline Drive. A new sign by the trail says backcountry use is restricted because of high fire danger, but we don't even carry matches. We put the leash on Woodsy, and at his first pull the leather collar breaks – no way to mend it. Still, we go, maybe violating two regulations. We find the pear tree thriving but the pears not ripe yet.

Everything's going smoothly until we're almost back to Skyline Drive. Two ranger cars are stopped behind our car. And two deer are ahead of us, just a few yards off the trail. Eileen says softly, "Woodsy – two deer up ahead. Stay close. We don't want you to chase them." I lift my hand – as if with a leash.

The deer start away from us, walking, then trotting. Woodsy watches – and stays. We walk on up to our car, and he's still on the invisible leash. Eileen unlocks the car and opens the back door.

Woodsy steps in, onto the back seat. Eileen closes that door and gets into her place in front. I stroll over and say hello to the rangers. I ask them about the fire danger and what activity is restricted. "Backcountry camping," one says, "not daytime hiking – unless you smoke." The other says, "Good thing your dog was on a leash. Those deer were close."

Woodsy is a source of joy, but another side shows too. He chases females. One day he disappears with no easy-to-find trace. I hear dog sounds down-hollow and blunder into a pattern of tracks in shallow snow. Some are Woodsy's size. I go home for Eileen, and we follow the Woodsy-sized tracks among the hodgepodge of other tracks in the near-zero breeze. They lead up Tutweiler Hollow, a branch northward from our hollow. They lead far up. Dark is coming. We stop and settle our breathing, then I call as loudly as I can, "Here, Woodsy!" But of course he won't answer this call. If he's up there and persuaded to break away from the pack, he'll just come. We call again and wait.

Then I remember he always answers the wolf howl; he howls along with us. Even if he doesn't come, we'll know he's there. I howl with all the volume and vibrant melody I can muster. My howl fades, and the echoes fade into silence. And then, in the gathering dark, from far away, wavering on the wind, comes the answer, thrilling, prickling along the spine. I wait for silence, then call loudly again – a confirmation.

After a while we hear dogs yipping, snarling. Woodsy comes, and we embrace and hold him. A medium-sized dog, in the clear for an instant against the snow, veers off into thicker forest. We guess she's the female. We take Woodsy home. He complains, but soon the pressure slackens, and he seems at peace.

I've written a short novel about an Indian lad in the Blue Ridge, just before and just after the Whiteman came, and our friends the Ed Smiths and Lewis Firths with second-home farms on the east side of the range have my first readable draft and are ready to discuss it. We take Woodsy with us to the Firth place, that's hidden in forest near the corner of Rappahannock, Madison and Culpeper counties (about 20 straight-line miles from our place). We leave Woodsy outside playing with the Firths' dog McDuff as we've done before, and we take the novel apart and put it together again during lunch and while clearing the table.

When we go outside, there's McDuff but no Woodsy. I call and Eileen whistles. We expect Woodsy to show at any minute, racing toward us out of the forest. But he doesn't. It's December 5, 1984, a degree or two below freezing, and wet, sleety snow is starting to fall. If someone or something enticed Woodsy away, the ice and snow might obscure the scent that could help him find us again. We go out along roads and trails, calling. He doesn't appear. The snow thickens. We get in our car and drive, extending the radius of our search from half a mile to two miles, stopping often to call and wait, to wolf-howl and listen. Nothing. The thought of a female in heat comes, of course, though different ideas are also mentioned – a dognapper who'll sell him to a research laboratory to be experimented upon, a hunter who mistook him in the undergrowth for a deer, a trap or wire snare set to catch a different creature for its fur but capable of choking a dog.

We search all that afternoon and into the night. Eileen and I leave our scent out on the road and every trail to Firths'. We search for weeks, putting ads in newspapers and broadcast stations, putting pictures of Woodsy in country stores, crossing the mountain again and again. All clues fade to nothing, yet we can't give up. On Christmas, 20 days after the disappearance, I write this poem, and we send it to editors and broadcasters:

Here, Woodsy!
Your big ears pointed aloft and cupped wide
   we feel must hear forever – somewhere.
     We remember you've often heard our call
        echoing from the ridges
        and raced to touch us and leap with joy.

Your dark eyes shining with surging life,
    sometimes following high jets or red-tails soaring,
        or rolling to catch our eyes
            and read what's brewing,
        we feel could recognize from afar
        the mountains where we've lived
            from your puppyhood together.

Your black nose so sensitive to fragrances of life,
    lifting into the wind to test all sounds and glimpses,
        finding our hiding places in play
            kissing our hands or faces,
                giving and receiving love,
    we feel could scent the trend of lines
        we've tread in sorrowful search.

Your ready reading of human talk and doings,
    with head tilting to ask questions
        and catch human emotions, intentions,
    we feel could help you correct errors and choose the way.
Your muscles so firm and rippling
    under black and creamy fur,
        lifting you in leaps over stone walls
            or to catch a frisbee from the air
                or a thrown stick on first bounce,
we feel could bring you long and lonely miles
        along edges of highways, on rural roads,
            or through unmarked woods
                over the Blue Ridge
                      HOME!!

Here, Woodsy! ... Here, Woodsy! ... Here, Woodsy! ....

The newspapers all publish the poem, and I hope for invitations to read it over regional broadcast stations. I'll add the wolf howl, spreading our feeling tender and strong over all three counties – so Woodsy will know, at least, we still exist and love him. But no broadcast invitations come.

Chapter 22 – Circling and Linking 1985-94

I re-experience, hoping to catch and record significant emotions: Three score years and ten - the traditional lifespan runs out for me next January (1986). With Helga, our almost-grown German shepherd (successor to Woodsy), I'm walking Shaver Hollow paths at night, feeling Eileen and I are harmonizing well with this home place. But I'm finding my way forward by dim indications – as just now with Helga showing rarely in spots of moonlight. I'm feeling the tease and tug of loose ends dangling.

I don't want to die before writing a history of Shenandoah National Park that some authority might call "definitive," or before seeing Great Basin National Park established, or before gathering once more with my siblings and savoring again our memories of Mother and Dad (for years, Papa) – or without showing more clearly my long-time admiration of American Indians – or while still failing to complete and publish my world citizenship novel set in China.

For what seems a coon's age, the U.S. Forest Service has been studying roadless areas of the national forests in Nevada. Now, late in 1985, there's a bill in the U.S. House to add the wildest tracts, including the central part of our Great Basin National Park plan, to the national wilderness preservation system. It would be a great wilderness – but even greater in a national park. Eileen and I discuss stirring up Congress once more. We're not quite into gear, though, before learning a House committee staffman is ahead of us, digging details from the exploration and study I helped persuade the park service to begin in 1956 and to continue into the 1980s.

The national parks subcommittee considers the NPS reports, along with articles Weldon Heald and Eileen and I wrote, and promptly amends the bill to make the Wheeler wilderness [considerably expanded] into Great Basin National Park. Support re-awakens widely. Congressman Harry Reid of southern Nevada, whose family Eileen knew when she was in eighth grade, becomes active. Chic Hecht, US Senator from Nevada, though not a park enthusiast, invites us to work with his staff on a possible park boundary embracing the main attractions while excluding the best grazing and prospecting land. In Washington we work with Hecht's helper on large-scale maps, showing photographs of special features, exploring use-conflicts. We're called in also by National Parks & Conservation Association.

The battle is uphill as in the 1950s and 60s, but this time the pro-park urban vote in Nevada more conclusively dominates the ranching and mining vote. I testify at a Senate hearing, as I testified a quarter-century earlier when Eileen and I flew down from Juneau. Both pro-park and anti-park people from Nevada and Utah also testify. An amended bill passes Congress, and Great Basin National Park becomes an official reality in October 1986, linking one set of my loose ends.

Publicity for the dedication is worldwide – in newspapers, broadcasts, news weeklies, monthly magazines. As when I saw my *Reader's Digest* oldest-living-tree piece in Chinese, I feel a surge of hope my teacher Kathleen might notice and write to me, rounding out another circle of my life. But no word comes.

Above us in Shaver Hollow the University of Virginia, with a federal grant, is launching acid rain research, mostly up inside the park. Cars crowd our yard and people swarm up the trail and gather where a 100-foot tower, as bundles of metal pipe, is to be lowered by helicopter. We all wait in the spring cold. The spectacle, at last, is extraordinary – heavy packages including an entire equipment building that weighs two tons being maneuvered on ropes through the forest canopy without breaking a tree limb.

Eileen and I reach home shivering, hungry, and unkempt. She makes two fast-fried egg sandwiches, but before we can eat, Charles Kurault's "Sunday Morning" crew is unexpectedly knocking. The spokesman says, "We need plain American language – and common sense – to knit together our sequence of our President and Canada's Prime Minister deploring pollution and university scientists discussing technicalities: "Someone suggested Darwin Lambert." They pull me out into the yard, aim the camera at me and our log house. The showing is nationwide. I come on at intervals between Reagan, Mulroney, and the scientists. In five of those many seconds on the air, they could advance my freelance career by identifying me as a naturalist and historian with books and articles in circulation. But their plan calls for a bystander, so that's my role.

Maybe the media has to be that way, though I tried not to be when I was a newspaper editor. A *World Monitor* crew comes another day; for "Discovery Channel" it's pursuing air pollution with emphasis on Shenandoah views. They ask for half an hour and film me sitting on the moss-spotted concrete of our springhouse roof, remembering the clearer air of the 1930s. Then they film Eileen doing what she'd have been doing "if *we* weren't here," which is setting out basil plants in her herb garden. Two hours gone. Next day – though we're expecting a granddaughter from Vassar and my son and family from Reno – I let them tease me up to Skyline Drive for an additional hour – looking off into the distance and remembering I could see much farther in the 1930s. Okay, true. But I'm only an old man who, half a century before, was a park ranger – no mention of my more significant doings.

Better, but still frustrating, is that piece in *Countryside* magazine, presenting me as a member of "Barbara Bush's Green Team," focusing in text on my perseverance toward establishing Great Basin National Park, but with a photograph of me on Shenandoah's Old Rag Mountain (that name or place never printed anywhere in the magazine). The *Countryside* piece, 300 words, praises my efforts in conservation and environmentalism – world-wide in some degree – and of course I appreciate that, but I'm most grateful just now, with some of my best writing not yet published, for the First Lady's recognition of my writing career:

A series of news stories he wrote in 1965 about the senseless death of the world's oldest living tree – a professor doing "research" chopped down a bristlecone pine more than 5000 years old that was growing unprotected in the Great Basin – brought the first significant ground swell of public support.

Writing innumerable other articles, making speeches and screening at every opportunity a film he had made, Lambert kept the idea alive through the decades. But only when the state's power base began tilting from rural to urban in the 1970s did the campaign gain real momentum.

By 1986, with rural opposition waning, Nevada's representatives in Congress unanimously recommended and soon secured official designation of the Great Basin National Park. For Lambert, the fulfillment of a childhood dream was sweet victory indeed.

The spotlight almost glares on Eileen and me (31.9 million copies distributed) in *USA WEEKEND* for Memorial Day 1992 where we "introduce" Shenandoah National Park. Though we complain about hours lost and failure to mention our writings, we feel partly compensated – by phone calls and letters from friends, relatives, and unknowns near and far. Son Harvey phones from Reno, saying it isn't so much the substance that impresses him; it's the company we're in – Tom Brokaw introducing Yellowstone, Danny Glover introducing Grand Canyon, the Kentucky HeadHunters, Mammoth Cave, etc.

Eileen's mother, Edna Norton, age 84, almost immobilized when a hip operation fell short of success, decided in 1988 to "spend my children's inheritance" while having Eileen (actually her only child) and me with her. Her first plan – "We'll fly to New Zealand" – gave way to less ambitious plans, all infeasible because of her physical condition – until we settled on a six-week motor home tour of the

West, visiting friends, relatives, and national parks. Windows allowed sightseeing while moving, and we two could help her out to her wheel chair and push her for special viewing or in house-guest situations.

From Albuquerque, I drove the "home" she'd rented to the Chiracahua Mountains. Continuing toward the Pacific, we visited my sister Ruth at Mesa, Arizona. We drove up the coast of California to Oregon and Washington and visited Doris and Hank Hansen on Whidbey Island in Puget Sound. Eileen then took off from Seattle for Thorne Bay, Alaska, to see son Mike and recent bride Sharon on their state-land homestead, while Mom and I visited with Sylvia, Christian and Brent at Central Washington University.

After Eileen's return, we found all of Mom's descendants except Mike and daughter Krystal gathered according to plan at Reno – five generations, Mom, Eileen, Linda, Linda's children Kim and Judy and Judy's husband Gary Vance and their baby Ronald, and Eileen's son David Affleck and wife Thera and sons Chris and Nick. Snow wrecked the planned reunion beside a lake in a Reno park. Harvey and Dorothy graciously entertained the five-generation gathering in their home. The spirit, the food, the conversation, and the picture-taking were joyful – and very much in Eileen's and my "nature harmony" theme.

A reunion centering on me had been hinted by my siblings for our stopover at Great Basin National Park. As we began gathering in the morning, we alternately marveled and fumed at the fresh white covering on the Wheeler high country that closed the scenic drive we'd expected to soar on up to 10,000 feet elevation. Soon, though, we were pushing the shallower low-elevation snow off the picnic tables near Lehman Caves where junipers and pinyons grew and carrying the tables onto the empty parking lot. Before noon, asphalt and tables had dried in the dazzling sunshine. Everyone had brought food, and we tried to eat it all. Conversation galloped. The family was pleased that "Darwin's park" was being enjoyed by people from across the nation and farther.

All of my four sisters and two brothers had walked through Lehman Caves years before, Wendell and I anyway carrying carbide flames as well as, on later visits, walking with larger groups through electric-lighted passages diversely decorated by nature. The caves, uniquely snow-free this day, enhanced our visiting, multiplied our pleasure of togetherness. I apologized for not being able to guide the party to the spot where the oldest living tree ever found on Earth had been cut down in 1964. They said we'd all get together some snowless time, and I could guide them to all the features that helped establish the park. I agreed, of course, while feeling that, in fact, even if another reunion happened we'd be too old to hike very far, so I'd never be able to show them why I worked so long and hard for this national park.

My sister Ruth, after a decade and a half of widowhood, married soon after our Great Basin reunion. Her new husband, Thom Barrett, is a retired colonel of the Air Force and a retired professor of soil science, also a good Mormon. He enjoys nature and is teaching Ruth more about plants and animals. They travel a lot and visit us once or twice a year. I feel we four reach spiritually for each other. My moving away from the church was slow, hardly traumatic, and my nostalgia continues. I did feel and believe through the singing long ago in Sunday School. For a time God seemed a marvelous-powerful person. But from that form, gradually, he melded with the universe and became impersonal, became the way of nature – yet without losing any of the marvelousness and power.

The belief that God's angel was recording my good and bad actions in a judgment book didn't dissolve but became a belief that the nature of total reality will somehow reward me for being good and punish me for being bad. As I once hoped to get the angel's or God's opinion in time to correct my earthly behavior, I began studying the ways of reality, began conversations with Earth, to improve my living behavior.

On one visit here, Thom showed me a book about the founder of the Mormon Church, *Joseph Smith As Scientist*. The author was John A. Widtsoe, an LDS church leader and my father's friend who recommended him for the position of county agricultural agent in Nevada. Dr. Widtsoe wrote much that appeals to me – and hadn't reached me through Sunday School or through church books I read in my teens. Here are key quotes:

> Joseph Smith was strictly scientific. He departed from the notion that God is a Being foreign to nature and wholly superior to it. Instead he taught that God is part of nature... The great laws of nature are immutable, and even God cannot transcend them...
>
> God speaks in various ways to men. The stars, the clouds, the mountains, the grass and the soil, are all, to him who reads aright, forms of divine revelation.

So – I'd been reading divine revelation even before I could read words. Smith and Widtsoe had walked many of "my" trails ahead of me:

> This is a universe of law and order... There is no place for immaterialism, i.e. for a God, spirits and angels that are not material... Man ... possesses the power to exercise his will in directing natural forces. Animals and even plants seem to possess a similar power to a smaller degree.

I'm reminded of Laotze and soon find a brief summary by Dr. Moushen H. Lin (in *The Bible of Mankind*, 1939):

> Laotze's view of life is just as naturalistic as his view of the universe. Human life ... is ... natural process.
> This view is similar also to that of the School of the Natural Order, that has its Home Farm alongside Great Basin National Park: The idea ... that there is no truth, reality or substance in matter, must be counteracted and contradicted without equivocation on the grounds that this attitude contravenes the

empirically established facts, leads to psychological inconsistencies which create conflicts, engenders disorders in the psyche, induces trying to function in opposition to the natural structure of the nervous system, creates an unbalanced state, results in a series of psychosomatic maladjustments.

I see a similar pattern in Thomas Jefferson, our almost-neighbor in space and time across the Blue Ridge at Monticello. His phrase in the *Declaration of Independence*, "the Laws of Nature and of Nature's God," fits well.

Eileen is a special ally in my continuing wish to honor American Indians – whether Shoshones and Paiutes of the Great Basin, Manahoacs of Virginia, or Tlingits and Athapaskans in Alaska, or others. Mom hid Eileen's father's Cherokee ancestor until, through buying and selling rugs and pottery in Albuquerque, she came to know Indians well. She then guided us to Pueblo dwellings and working communities, including Acoma on a cliff-encircled mesa, where her friend Frances Torivia, a potter for half a century, gave me a canteen-type pot that's among our treasures.

Mom guided us also to San Ildefonso, where her friend Maria Poveka (Martinez), called America's greatest potter, honored Eileen with a beautiful example of her black-on-black art. We'd meet Maria again in Renwick Gallery being honored by Washington's elite. The dress Maria wore at the Renwick, the great potter told us and others present, was a gift from Eileen's mother. Six months after our motor-home trip, Frances of Acoma came by air with Mom to spend two weeks with us in the Virginia Blue Ridge. Both Mom and Frances were 80-plus in age, neither quite mobile but helping each other. Frances agreed to demonstrate pot-making. We dug red clay from under the topsoil of our garden and gathered tools, including stones for pounding the clay and scrapers to help fingers shape the pots. The clay had to become powder, then be wetted and kneaded. Frances and Eileen made a dozen small pots.

"Indians" are rare in the Shenandoah region, though village sites from the 1500s are numerous where the soil produces abundant corn. Eileen found white quartz arrowheads in a flower bed near our old log house here, also some made of tan quartzite. Vividly imagined Indians first appeared to me in Virginia when we were re-enacting the earliest reported visit of a Whiteman to the Blue Ridge as part of my research for my man-and-earth book. The explorer was John Lederer, guided in 1669 by natives named Magntakunh, Naunnugh, and Hopottoguoh. In villages en route, the intelligence and dignity of the people impressed Lederer – and, through his words, me. Soon after that, in old files, I found a letter from Fred T. Amiss, the civil engineer who'd surveyed land being acquired by Virginia for the national park, telling about an Indian healer living alone near Stony Man Mountain when Whites first settled.

Amiss confirmed the basic facts through family traditions of four families, prominent and well-known in this Page County – Somers, Varner, Sours, and Miller. The lone Indian, called Bright Stony Face, "in robust manhood ... quickly endeared himself to the White settlers by advising and assisting them in their work and administering to their sick." He told the Whites that, as a lad being tutored by an older medicine man, he learned that the most effective herbs came from the high mountains that were hardest to climb – and also learned "that unselfish service to others brings the greatest happiness." The legend ended:

> About the year 1795 Bright Stony Face was missing from his home. A search was instituted by his white friends who, knowing his habits, went directly to the top ... and there seated in the angle of two boulders with a pile of freshly gathered herbs nearby was the lifeless body of the aged Indian doctor and philosopher.

My research confirmed a village site where the four-family tradition said it was; it's described by archeologist Gerard Fowke in Smithsonian Bulletin 23 printed in 1894. The information simmered in me, and I tried everywhere to learn how the medicine man happened to be the only Indian in this village – or living anywhere near – when the Whites settled. Stimulated by my persistent feeling for Indians, my imagination absorbed available facts and took off on its own. Soon I was seeing Bright Stony Face as a boy working with an older medicine man. Then I was that boy – somewhat as I'd been an Indian at age nine when running off from Grandma's house acting out Seton's *Two Little Savages.*

The Blue Ridge Indian boy felt alive in me for several years, and I typed and retyped 150 pages showing him winning "initiation" as the healer the Whites found and called Bright Stony Face (as a boy, Hopato). My novel as manuscript was read and much enjoyed by two fifth grades – in Illinois where daughter Laura was teaching and in Washington State where grandson Brent was a student. I was about to seek a publisher for it when my long-awaited opportunity to produce a human history of Shenandoah National Park knocked irresistibly.

As working title for the new Shenandoah book I choose *Ha'nts* (Blue Ridge word meaning ghosts), because I feel the people of the past haunting these forests and mountains. Eileen pretends with me we're living in long-ago times. We take a field course from archeologists digging beside the park, 20 miles from our house. As we handle tools made from Shenandoah jasper 11 millenniums ago, those earliest American haunts get stronger. I explore inside myself while we two walk old traces in the Blue Ridge. I'm a Paleo-hunter with a Clovis point of jasper on a wooden spear helping to kill a mastodon caught in a bog, yet I'm hungry enough to kill deer when that's easier. After Paleo, I'm Archaic, then a Woodland Indian, then a White explorer and fur trader. Soon I'm a favored Cavalier from England creating a rich plantation with black slaves to work the tobacco, but I run off, preferring to work as a miner and iron processor. I work also at gristmilling, as a leather tanner, a cattleman, a lumberman, and finally I'm a mountaineer, maybe an ancestor of the Sisks or Corbins.

In my own skin I'm seeking the origins of the families living on the park-land when it was bought by the state to be donated to the federal government. I'm tape-recording persons who experienced the last century in these mountains, and I'm remembering myself roaming the Blue Ridge. I'm the 20-year-old first employee of the National Park Service here, setting up NPS accounts and files as the park rangers come on duty and the CCC (Civilian Conservation Corps) engineer-in-charge becomes park superintendent.

I'm re-experiencing too the astonishing completeness of the park's "return to nature." My life and my writing always intertwine, linking and summarizing my behavior in nature and society. This story of Shenandoah (published in 1989 as *The Undying Past of Shenandoah National Park*) is significant in demonstrating that civilization can let nature re-create wilderness, that a free-enterprise system can put restraints on aggressive economics, responding to a symphony of human emotions and values rather than to the economic-financial complex alone.

At age 73, while waiting for the first *Undying Past* books, I'm trying by mail and phone to reach agreement with the Great Basin Natural History Association for producing a similar history of that park in Nevada. I propose starting with the Indians as I did in Shenandoah, but the sponsoring leaders ask, Why not stick to the park's specific genesis, "your real area of expertise"? I answer, "Everything relates to everything else, and the drama is in the tugging of the different threads."

I probe the national-park-history genre. Unlike the "park story" that starts as does James Michener's *Hawaii* with the origin of Earth, rocks, shapes of land, then plant and animal life, the "park history" starts with the first humans. As in *National Geographic* and *Natural History* magazines, the first humans are part of nature, not part of civilization. Then come humans "not part of nature" who greatly increase the use of natural resources in producing wealth, multiplying interference with wild nature, establishing "civilization."

Barely in time to avoid destruction of park values, along comes a lone ranger such as John Muir or Enos Mills, or a conservation-outdoor recreation club, or other agency, insisting the wonder-filled area be defended by persuading Congress to make it a national park.

In my mind, neither Shenandoah nor Great Basin precisely fits the pattern. In parks as elsewhere the division of life and the planet into nature and civilization falsifies reality. Humans in whatever culture are parts of nature. Even before the Whiteman landed, there was no total wilderness. Great Basin park is stronger because Indians left petroglyphs there and Whites raised livestock and prospected for minerals. Humans are among the most intriguing of creatures.

I might have gone on entangling myself in philosophical jungles if the Great Basin superintendent, Al Hendricks, hadn't persuaded the association to send me a $500 check. With that evidence of serious intent, I clear out the Shenandoah books and papers surrounding my desk and start gathering Great Basin books and papers. I join Nevada Historical Society. I spend days at the National Archives in Washington where, along with other valuable papers, I photocopy a detailed report I've never before heard of – many pages about the old forests around Wheeler Peak and the heavy timbering and other exploitation that, the forest expert thought, called for the President (Theodore Roosevelt) to set aside a forest reserve, the Wheeler area's first step into conservation, in 1906.

Before the redbud and dogwood bloom in Shaver Hollow, Eileen and I start driving to Great Basin, stopping in campgrounds when we're too tired to go on. I've pre-arranged research contacts. We put up our tent at familiar Baker Creek, and next morning I'm studying early files of Lehman Caves National Monument. We'll work six weeks in Nevada, day and night almost, exploring state and federal records including Forest Service, voluminous archives at Reno and Carson City, a century of newspapers published at Ely (a crucial five years originally edited by me), and drawers of files of the White Pine Chamber of Commerce (also part of my work years back). And we'll interview persons who've lived through pertinent historic episodes.

Our research goes well – with bonuses beyond my hopes, such as a long-forgotten report written in 1855 on a Mormon expedition to examine agricultural possibilities of Snake Valley and Range (saved in LDS archives at Salt Lake). Several Mormons made the earliest climb of Wheeler Peak by Whites, finding Shoshones using both mountains and valleys. We also learn in detail that my Dad's friend Governor Scrugham, when I was a boy, wanted a national park in our Wheeler country – "which with the mountain scenery and the timber," he insisted, is "equal if not superior to Yellowstone."

We've reserved time for Harvey, Sylvia and Laura and their spouses and children to visit us. Our campsite on Baker Creek is spacious and has warbling vireos nesting in a quaking aspen tree, the male serenading continually. There's no snow on the scenic drive to the trailhead at 10,000 feet. The hiking trail takes us past Teresa Lake and into the cirque under Wheeler cliffs. I remember the weekend when Eileen and Barbara were on the same overnight hike and Irwin Fehr was photographing. Irwin was missing a while that long-ago evening. And now, we all suddenly realize, he's missing again – more seriously. In Reno and Ely, where he's well known, no one we've visited with has seen or heard of Irwin in the last two years. He's a valued friend, and my new history book will need photos from him.

The trail doesn't lead to the stump of the world's oldest living tree (as of 1964), but we talk about that tragedy and find other bristlecones who've lived thousands of years. Our emotions soar in response to these so-venerable trees. Christian – who courted Sylvia in the Alps – is the only one who climbs all the way to the glacier as I did often in the 1950s.

Before Eileen and I start back to Virginia, the Great Basin association's board increases the research grant – in effect restoring all we've spent on the project. At my desk in Shaver Hollow, I sort papers and write and sort more papers and write. After the manuscript's rewritten twice and cut from 500 typed pages to 200, then expanded with a foreword by Superintendent Hendricks, an Orientation by me, a who's who of a hundred continuing characters, an appendix, a bibliography, an index, and 40 illustrations (only two by Irwin Fehr that I'd saved from Ely days in my own files), the book is published in 1991 by Roberts Rinehart Publishers and the Great Basin association in 255 pages with the title *Great Basin Drama.*

    My two park histories, continuing to circulate widely, help link many loose ends. *Undying Past,* listing pre-park landowners and family heads and known cemeteries, stimulates family reunions. Through our friends Virgil and Rose Corbin, I'm invited to bring books to what proves a multitudinous gathering of Old Rag area Nicholsons and Corbins and descendants. Many buy books. Robert A. Nicholson is a surprise double pleasure. After buying the Shenandoah book, he asks what I've written since. I tell him my latest, and he asks, "Could that be Great Basin National Park?" He wants to buy a book quickly; he's visiting Great Basin next month. This Blue Ridge Nicholson owns Nicholson Tool Co. in Ogden, Utah.

    Sisks rediscover us. There's a phone call while I'm not available, and Eileen reports: "It was Annie Sisk. She found us in the *Novascope* magazine, in her dentist's office. Annie told me, 'We all just loved Darwin!' She sounded in tears, and I got that way too." Next, a daughter of Athey Sisk (who'd been a small boy when they left the park) finds *Undying Past* at Big Meadows – and phones. This Dyanne Sisk Holt wants to know "everything" about her Granddaddy Newt. Both Anna and Dyanne come to Shaver Hollow – Dyanne first by an hour, partly because Anna waited for a friend to "bring" her – saving her own Lincoln town car from our rocks.

    Eileen and I are honored guests at the first Newt-Daisy Sisk family reunion – held at Eiselwood, an estate in the Piedmont horse country between the Blue Ridge and Washington, the home of David and Doris Woodward-Eisel, Doris being another granddaughter of

Newt and Daisy. The attendance is near 100. Winfield, my first Blue Ridge friend, and his wife Arlene offer wild blackberry wine. Food is superabundant. Winfield has two sons attending – one, Bobby, a colonel in the Air Force, just now master of ceremonies for an amusing and touching tribute to Newt and Daisy. I participate by imitating Newt's dog Brook sounding off in pursuit of a raccoon and by saying the world needs more people who draw both sustenance and joy directly from Earth as Newt and Daisy did. I feel good in continuing to find descendants of mountain folk prospering.

Different linkings of loose threads happened in Lenoir, North Carolina, when Eileen and I drove there for the wedding of granddaughter Laura Linda Rowe and Dan Jones – just after cancer was first found in me. The church wedding was beautiful; so was the reception in a large room decorated with Christmas trees recycled unused from sales lots. The nature theme, favored by the bride since age three when she planted the tulip tree in our yard, was strong at all the tables in evergreen sprays magically lit by battery-fed stars.

Eileen and I and Barbara and the bride's other grandmother and grandfather, also divorced, chose the same table. We hadn't seen Barbara since daughter Sylvia's wedding 27 years earlier, though there'd been letters. Barbara and I talked about our children and grandchildren, of whom we've always been proud. After her three marriages, Barbara had taken grandchildren traveling to far and exotic places. Often in recent years she'd served as companion and nurse for women older than she. Ever since I met her 57 years back she'd been painting watercolors. She told me now she'd never retire from painting; she was assembling a gallery of her work at her home in upstate New York. I've since sent some of her work from here to be color-photocopied for her gallery, and she's lending me my old letters from abroad and sending books such as Michener's *The World Is My Home*, helpful in my work.

Now, 1992, there's renewed contact, by mail only so far, with the long-lost Irwin Fehr. He's being treated in Utah for cancer (Hodgkins disease). He and his Filipino-Chinese bride, who visited us here before Irwin's apparent disappearance, aren't together any more. Irwin is with his mother who's 95 and can beat him climbing the stairs. Latest word is, he thinks surgery plus chemotherapy and radiation have defeated his cancer. I told him I had prostate cancer, metastasized in my bones. He's impressed and, reaching for his old humor, instructs me, "Don't die till I come to see you, which I'm looking forward to."

Day or night I walk my little trails beyond the lawn into the forest. I carry a walking stick to push briers away or to find venomous snakes before they strike. The shorter walks are me walking the dogs and sometimes the cat too. The longer walks are mostly Eileen and me enjoying the forest and wildflowers, the creek, the wild creatures, or picking berries or mushrooms or picking up persimmons, or going our usual mile for the mail.

When it's dark I carry a flashlight but seldom turn it on. I like the dark; it's so like finding your way through life, being guided only by stars maybe, or shadows. It's meditation – or sometimes adventure. One night our German shepherd Helga stopped unexpectedly ahead of me. I stopped too and aimed the flashlight. Under drooping boughs, as near to me as to Helga, maybe 12 feet, a bobcat with an opossum in its mouth was looking back. The opossum moved (struggled?) in the bobcat's mouth. After a long time (three minutes?) the bobcat crunched the opossum, put it down, and slowly disappeared under drooping boughs of hemlock trees. I approached the opossum and touched it. Yes, warm. Helga touched her nose to it, also confirming it was just now alive.

Eileen once touched a bear in the dark when we were in bed on the lawn watching meteors. She thought it was our dog – but then he barked too far away to have been present. I've had four chances to touch a bear, or get touched. Most recently, one night while plums were ripening, we heard cowbells we'd hung to warn us of raiders. Helga ran barking, followed by Eileen, down our "Inside Passage" as if on the intruder's tail. I went directly to the plum tree to assess the damage. Because, the night before, Helga had found a copperhead there, I had my light aimed downward. I heard, almost felt, a swish and a thump. A bear dropped between me and the tree trunk, a three-foot space at most. I stood paralyzed while the bear scrambled off through blackberry briers.

Next morning Eileen and I checked on the plums (maybe a tenth of them gone). And we kept strolling, asking ourselves what our effort toward earthmanship had accomplished here, or failed to accomplish. "The 19 acres of poor pasture I found here in 1945 – without a single bear or deer or wild turkey – was healthy forest when we arrived from Alaska in 1964," I said. "And I judge all the trees on the present 60 acres of forest have more than doubled in size while we've lived here." We agreed this was good. And I showed her my spread arms couldn't hug and touch fingers around some tulip trees that weren't even here when I bought the place.

We said we ought to sell a few trees – selectively cut – and at least get real estate tax money from the land, but as before when this subject came up, we love our living trees more than money. We're willing, though, to sell two dozen or so oaks that are dead or dying from five years of summer drought plus two years of gypsy moth defoliation, saving a few dead ones, of course, for birds and mammals to feed or nest in. We credited ourselves with killing millions of gypsy moths with an old-fashioned formula (kerosene and creosote) hand-painted on the egg masses.

We've continued being our own judgment-book angels. We worry and mourn mostly now for our hemlock trees, of which hundreds are infested with hemlock woolly adelgid. Biologists fear the adelgid means death to all hemlocks in the Blue Ridge. The threatened tree nearest our house is grandson Brent's, planted by him years ago. We've sprayed it with soapy water, and it's healthier than the others. But we're mostly failing with the hemlocks and half-failing with the oaks. Still, over-all, the forest thrives, gains.

We look critically at house and yard. The old log structure could outlive us – with a caring owner. In the 1980s Eileen and I as a team built a high-roofed portico over the stone floor and a half-circle stone step I'd earlier made at our front door. At the down-hollow (pool) entrance I built a quarter-circle of five stone steps and platform. At the back entrance I built a stone and timber sun room with workbench and storage space. Stone floors and steps are drained by underlying trenches filled with rocks – a "natural" way of preventing freeze-cracking of masonry. Our building materials (except nails and bags of mortar-cement) came from our land.

The two reflecting pools below the house – "tadpools" because frogs, toads and salamanders reproduce in them – created by Eileen with minor help from me – might outlast the house but will gradually become tiny swamps. Also long lasting – but short of forever – will be terrace levels I created as vegetable gardens, avoiding loss of soil to erosion and reminding me of the landscape I admired in China. We'll be leaving near the tadpools a kind of bamboo that grows an inch thick and 20 feet tall, also representing China. And there's a concrete-and-stone cold frame next to the fireplace chimney against the south side of the house – that's produced lettuce through 30 winters so far (1994).

We'll be passing on a rare 1800-foot stretch of powerline right-of-way that's never had herbicide, so is lush with wild berries, hazelnuts, spicebush, flowering dogwood, redbud, and other species that never get tall enough to interfere with the electricity. The homesite has old-fashioned lilac bushes and sweet shrub and daffodils and periwinkle (*Vinca*) – yes, and apple trees and sweet cherry (mazzard), to which we've added trees that produce other fruits.

Through the years Eileen has beautified the yard with flowers and spread them down-hollow. Major successes include a magenta-colored phlox that competes well with wild plants and brightens summers and autumns, attracting butterflies and hummingbirds, and a yellow iris that likes edges of our tadpools and of the flood-control lake down-hollow. Eileen gives big bags of seeds to many friends, suggesting they "fling phlox," as these seeds require no cultivation.

We've done a lot for this place; the soil is more fertile now; the life is more abundant and diverse. Yet the place has done more for us than we've done for it. This land is interwoven with us, with our spirits, bodies, minds, emotions. We've learned multiple incentives and multiple rewards. We share glorious days and nights with birds and frogs, deer and foxes and bears, as well as with other humans, and with trees and the winds that rustle the leaves or sway the branches, and the creek that gurgles in its channel among boulders and carries life in many forms. Here we talk with Earth, are partners with Earth, creating together. We try to learn Earth's ways and willingnesses and harmonize ours with them – and discuss and create also with human friends and institutions to keep learning humanity's ways and willingnesses – to help toward fuller harmony, continuing our social membership without losing our citizenship in Earth.

There's much in our life that can't be explained in words. We seldom try any more to justify ourselves and our ways. We simply feel good inside, feel at home, being our natural selves. Feeling this way deep down, we have no wish to build a fire on a mountaintop in the dark to prove anything to others. Feelings can't be quantified or exactly described anyway.

One of our oddities, though, might be approximately quantified. Our rate of consumption is low in dollars spent, low in strain on the resources of Earth, low in air and water pollution and solid waste. The money we've spent in total during our 30-plus years here has averaged around two-thirds of "poverty level." Yet, as Eileen sometimes says when walking the forest paths with me, or alongside the lilting stream, or when working in gardens or orchard, or when watching and listening to the birds, "I feel so rich!"

Something inside us silently shouts "Never!" when someone asks when we're moving to a convenient apartment close to doctors and a hospital. We feel it's better to keep on here than to be kept safe and secure – if that were possible, which of course it isn't – both of us being on bonus-time now, beyond the three score years and ten, often tired, seldom free from arthritis-type pains, yet still more happy than miserable, still doing our indoor and outdoor work, keeping our clearing open to sun and sky. The plants continue reaching to engulf us, though, and in due course that will be all right. We'd like Earth to absorb us together into nature's endlessly re-creating process. But not yet.

It's spring again after one of this region's most icy winters when courage and special care were needed every time we ventured outdoors – to feed the birds, say, or to bring in firewood. But now the grass is green and our place is decorated with blossoms – apple, redbud, dogwood, daffodils, periwinkle, forsythia, japonica, spirea, wild geraniums, bloodroot, rue anemone, trilliums. The waterthrushes and scarlet tanagers are back to nest. And it's morel-mushroom time. We and the dogs (our older, weakening Helga and a Black Lab puppy she recently found as her successor) start together toward the most likely place for morels.

The trail has been neglected since last spring, and spicebush especially has thrust twigs into it. Eileen has her ever-handy "nippers" (one-hand pruners). I neglected to bring mine, but I nip offending twigs from the trail space with my fingers. Living spicebush twigs are brittle, and I have a special twist that works neatly. When I use it I'm saying silently to the bush, "Okay. Okay. I'll be leaving you. But not yet, not quite yet." And I feel the spicebush accepts being held back from the trail a while longer. It puts such a happy fragrance on my fingers.

Chapter 23 - Loving Life, the Land, the Planet 1995+

My prostate cancer was mentioned earlier – with few details. I didn't want to recognize it. Now (year 2001) our family doctor and the urologist confess they'd believed in 1992 I'd die within six months – but now, "You won't die of prostate cancer." In 1992 my PSA reading was 2,034, almost a thousand times the healthy norm. I had pain in the back of my skull. Complex tests confirmed cancer there and in ribs, pelvis, so many places surgery couldn't possibly cope.

Robert and Phel Jacobsen offered help. Jake had been superintendent of the national monument in Nevada that preceded Great Basin National Park – and later superintendent of Shenandoah here, retired now to a new home built just a few miles from us. Jake mowed our lawn. Next day both Jacobsens were chainsawing firewood in our forest. They'd help us through the cold weather, and we didn't need, even, to thank them. They'd accept a share of our too-abundant dead wood for their house and sauna.

Medical tests kept showing my condition as drastic. The urologist started monthly shots (capsules under stomach skin) of leuprolide acetate to suppress testosterone that – quoting the manufacturer's pamphlet – "stimulates prostate cancer in much the same way kerosene fuels a fire." The capsules aren't a cure, just a delaying action, but the pain dwindled and the PSA dropped to 400, then to 13.5 the fourth month. I resumed my multiple-incentive exercise that in winter was cutting firewood with a bow saw. Soon I was pruning fruit trees, then shovel-plowing our usual garden, and, mostly in evenings and rainy days, writing or revising rough drafts of my life story.

Eileen's and my "simple life" has stayed on course. I've planned an Earth-citizenship novel with a hero who's half-Shoshone and half-White-Mormon, resembling a friend I had in Ely Grade School. I imagine my hero discovering tungsten in Nevada's Snake Range, getting admitted for metallurgy research at University of Chicago, volunteering to help douse the first active nuclear pile (if it got dangerous), later sent to China to buy tungsten concentrates for World War II armament production. Sometimes, though, being elderly, I laugh at my ambitions. When the sun's bright and the sky Nevada-blue, I just walk with our dog – and with Eileen if she isn't too busy.

She and I keep trying to improve our land, reduce our consumption and pollution (not traveling far, for instance, burning gasoline), and otherwise living what we call earthmanship. We've long since terraced the garden against soil erosion, and we keep adding more humus than we take off. We've spread flowers and fruiting plants that wild creatures use. Eileen has fed birds faithfully. We cooperate with wild species – but gently defend our own ecological niche. We've restored many floral species wiped out by humans and livestock – cardinal flower, marsh marigold, skunk cabbage... We want to continue here, to keep welcoming our year-to-year wild clientele, including hummingbirds, who greet Eileen through the window when arriving in spring. Our acreage is a loan from Earth, we sometimes say, to be given back with interest (added beauty and productivity).

We've asked our six children, spread from Georgia to California to Alaska if any would like to live here when we're gone. They say they love to visit but can't stay. They'd sell the land to divide the inheritance. Developers would buy – exactly what we don't want! We could leave it to the national park that's been one of my anchors since 1935 and Eileen's since 1964. Stream and forest would be protected, but the log house would decay or be torn down.

We thought of Corbin Cabin in the national park five miles across the main Blue Ridge from here. It resembles our house in type of construction and is well maintained as a hikers' cabin by Potomac

Appalachian Trail Club. We asked this PATC – which volunteers vast trail work annually – if it would like to inherit our place for hands-on education in earthmanship linked into trail recreation. Club president then was Jack Reeder. He and the governing Council said Yes, and we wrote the bequest into our wills – 61 acres including the log house to PATC, one acre to the park (trailhead uses), and another acre to a trusteeship of our children (camp or cabin site). Jack and Carolyn Reeder became our friends and hiking companions. We discussed the future of our place, including an idea that part of the land could show in action a mountain farm and orchard of pre-park times – the environmental virtues and faults of such land use.

In 1995, with my PSA rising a bit again, we offered PATC immediate ownership of 5-plus acres of forest – hidden from our house and personal trails – a tract where overcrowded tulip trees could benefit from thinning, while giving logs for direct-from-the-earth creation of a hikers' cabin. The Council accepted. Jack brought Charlie Graf, the new president. Charlie embraced the idea and site. Here's a quote about "Tulip Tree Cabin" from Charlie's "corner" in the September 1995 PA newsletter:

> All the logs will be cut on site and hand-hewed with broad axes and foot adzes. We will use draw knives, shaving horses, augurs, etc... and will be building a stone foundation and hopefully a stone fireplace and chimney. There will be a primitive skills workshop.

The project continues in the new millennium. It fits our dream. The volunteers, mostly from Washington and suburbs, are male and female – teens or in their prime or elderly, lawyers, scientists, doctors, craftsmen – a variety stimulating to us.

Eileen and I enjoy watching and visiting, answering questions about trees and wild flowers and creatures. But, not so different from others nowadays, we're pushed and pulled by wanting to do more than we can. So we don't have time or "nerve" to hamper the work over there significantly.

We write. We garden. We have local friends in occasionally for a meal, or go to their houses. We've helped organize a local environmental group, Friends of Page Valley. I answer many phoned or written questions about Shenandoah National Park history. Eileen answers questions about wild mushrooms and about diverse recipes she's served. Every year but one since 1968 we've been volunteer bird counters. We're now approaching our fifth participation in the annual butterfly count – in the park and adjacent Shenandoah Valley. Both counts are to check on how the different species are surviving. Last year, before the count, we had visitors from a distance – to photograph our Baltimore checkerspots, a butterfly species in trouble.

The Baltimore is strong at our place because the caterpillars eat wild turtlehead, a species we've favored until it's abundant. Quite a few plants are "botanical mysteries" to us – names we've forgotten or never learned. One in a swamp near turtlehead patches is a shrub with several "trunks" 3-4 inches thick, some kind of highbush huckleberry maybe. Another botanical oddity is an attractive vine that's become a pest (like kudzu), entwining and smothering our wineberry canes and our roses. The university identified it as Chinese yam (*Dioscoria batata*) but didn't tell us how to "control" it. I delayed joining Eileen in all-out battles to suppress it – partly maybe because it's Chinese and our-also-hard-to-control bamboo (which we harvest for sugar snap peas and other wanted vines to climb on) may welcome congenial company. But now I recognize the aggressive vine as a serious menace and am part of the all-out battle against what we now call "damn yam!"

We've loved our dogs and cats through the years – and tried to protect wild creatures from them – and vice versa. Our current dog is a Black Labrador. Helga (German shepherd) found him on the stone wall out front – half-grown probably, red collar. I approached – his eyes level with mine – and he didn't flinch. I asked, "Are you lost?" His answer was a grin of white teeth. "Are you hungry?" He grinned again, nervous maybe but not hostile. Helga and I started toward the house, and he followed. We couldn't find a clue to his origin. It was February, and we let him sleep in the house. We named him Thumper because whenever Eileen or I moved or spoke his tail thumped.

Helga and Thumper were good friends, both neutered, but Helga's interest in play declined. So did her health. X-ray showed abnormal cementing of vertebrae, keeping her so rigid she couldn't easily eliminate waste. The vet knew no cure. She was most miserable one evening in 1994, though apparently not in acute pain. I lay with her on the floor, touching, and she went quietly to sleep – and never waked.

We buried her beside old Sourdough, mourning with our Woodsy-type wolf howl. Thumper didn't howl – never howls when awake – but in his sleep that night he howled, and we howled with him. It's as though he's civilized when awake but sometimes, asleep, he's wild, and the wolf in him howls.

Thumper seldom barks. If strange cars or hiking humans approach, he alerts us with a high-pitched "yodel." Only if they then act aggressive does he use his heavy bark. I think he senses bears in the forest, invisible. He gives a single bark, then rushes silently. If the bear doesn't go up a tree, he chases, often across the creek out front, then up the steep ridge. There's an occasional bark – three, maybe, per chase – and when his voice sounds remote, I'll shout loudly, "Far enough, Thumper. Come back now." And he always has.

Thumper's long, thick, heavy-boned. Only when on a strict diet does he weigh less than a hundred pounds, yet he's agile enough on our morning walks to jump over the stone wall that's eye-level for me, to investigate the forest beyond. He's treed adult bears twice this summer, calling me to come – which I do, to look. Then I talk Thumper back to let the bear go in peace. I feel it's a game – to dog and bear and me – no real hostility.

On a nearby trail recently, Thumper ahead as usual, he simply stopped, then came back and looked up at me as if asking, what do we do now? A rattlesnake, I saw, was coiled in the trail. I led off-trail and around, and Thumper followed, learning, I hope, never to challenge a rattler. Our way of life feels close to our ideal – what Eileen and I dreamed separately in younger years and have now enjoyed together here 37 years – with possibility looming that house and land will be maintained in our pattern after we're gone. But sometimes, when we catch ourselves too happy, too hopeful, we say to each other, "Knock on wood!" And we do that, wood being always handy around here in this log house and out in the so-near forest.

The year 1996 brought four feet of snow in early January, slowing us to a standstill. Then came too-fast melting, a scary rise in the lake level, and too-sudden cold, with lake ice blocking our road. When we got out at last, we bought a high-off-the-road-center, ultra-capable, rough-riding Jeep station wagon.

There'd been a birthday conspiracy initiated by a daughter, and "big 80" congratulations came from many Great Basin communities plus Virginia, D.C Washington and Far-West Washington, Alaska, and a few from other continents. The central surprise, though, was the party. Eileen had invited friends who had bad-weather capability, plus the whole Tulip Tree Cabin crew. She'd roast a 12-pound turkey and a ham. The wind roared all night and the power went off, so I found the camp stove and gasoline. Eileen puzzled out a "backpack" menu. But Phel Jacobsen phoned asking if they'd need to ski or snowshoe to get here. She learned our power was off, and she over-persuaded Eileen into a "movable feast," the whole gang at the Jacobsens', our turkey and ham roasting in *their* oven. So, turning 80, I drove (as Eileen's journal put it) "our white Jeep leading a parade of 4 x 4s including three Jeeps, on a safari. Fun! Looked like an invasion of the Jacobsens' place!"

Spring and summer were normal – until Friday, September 6. Fortunately, a gang of Princeton University freshmen, "helping Charlie Graf at Tulip Tree Cabin site, had been rescued" Thursday evening by their vans. Some responsible person had been watching the regional weather more closely than we were. And we got surprised again! Eileen wrote – by kerosene light at 8 p.m.:

> Power has been off since about 9:30 a.m. And no phone since around 1 p.m. This is the most rain we've ever seen... Our can-gauge ran over before lunch – but I think we had 9" – plus 5.7 I measured in cans after lunch... The creek was high, brown, and roaring ... like a freight train, and there was a constant sound of big boulders being rushed downstream...

This was Hurricane Fran, though the wind had mostly given way to water that turned much of the ground to gravy, unable to hold tree roots.

Using our battery-powered radio, we learned the whole region was suffering – many families far worse than we. Trees were down everywhere – millions, we guessed in the national park. Our house wasn't damaged, but our water pump was upended in the spring house, the pressure gauge broken, the clean water dirtied. But Eileen had earlier filled jugs. She has foresight, and she has this kind of understanding too:

> Ole Thumper thinks this is all just wonderful. He loves being out in it, splashing around... Catkin is *not* pleased... Carried him to the windows so he could get a better look at conditions outside, then put him out... thinking he'd do his business under the Jeep. But no. He huddled against the door 'til I let him in. Then he used the litter box.

Next morning we walked (stumbled, tripped, crawled) down-hollow on or near what had been our road. It still was okay as far as our land boundary, but from there to the lake area it was a gully three to four feet deep, in places the deep erosion road-wide. The gully held scattered loose boulders, so many we couldn't walk on the bottom. We "climbed" along. The lake level was so high we couldn't see the concrete outlet tower or any sign of a road. We zigged through rocky-brushy forest around the gradually sinking water's edge. Though the dam itself had held, the down-hollow half of the

200-ft.once-level spillway looked like Cedar Breaks in Utah, fantastic shapes and colors. Where the road had slanted down were deep pits and channels of sizes just right to swallow bulldozers that might be sent to restore the lost topography. To the left of the non-existent road, now angry water, we faced a jungle of fallen trees tangled with wild grapevines. We'd brought pruners and loppers and tried to pioneer a path we could follow – and maybe improve – on our way home. Eileen wrote:

> The flood had gone through the gate, bending and flinging it, and taken out the former road. Farther down ... where I always feared the creek would eat the road, it had. There was a huge drop-off from the end of Crist's driveway directly into the new creek. ...

Friends living near our mailbox (Sonny and Louise Williams) offered to freeze ice in their fridge to carry in efforts to save our refrigerated food, and they'd lend us a car to get supplies from town – reducing our backpack carry to only one mile.

Shortly after dawn Sunday, Marcia McFadden of the Tulip Tree crew and I found Roger Miller (son of Ernest and Elva) at his excavation-contractor's shop and asked him if he could make a "Jeep detour" quickly around the major damage so we and trail club workers could use our four-wheel-drives. He said he could certainly make an emergency route far earlier than any likely official action replacing the dam road.

On September 14 the Jacobsens hiked in to check on us – and reported a bulldozer working. The "detour," they said, will have two bad deep-mud places and one "awfully steep" climb. Twelve days after the disaster four-wheel-drives were "possible." We got through and the power company got through. We'd lost many pounds of frozen food but fattened on the best before it spoiled. We bought pump parts and with our own labor restored our water system.

We'd applied to FEMA (Federal Emergency Management Agency) for help in rebuilding our part of the access road – up-hollow from the lake – the Town of Luray being legally responsible from the regular public road up to and around the lake. FEMA "couldn't help" with our road – but would pay rent for us on an apartment in town. We said, "No thanks" – our house is undamaged, our life including our work is here – we need help only in restoring normal access.

A lucky coincidence helped. As Eileen narrated it:

> The trail club crew arrived – with Terry Cummings and his camcorder. Marcia and Terry asked us to go down to the dam area to get some footage. We intended to park above the steep place and walk around. Surprise! A deputy sheriff was below with his 4 x 4 and gestured for us to stop. Said a Jeep was stuck in the mud behind him... a rescue party coming to rescue the Lamberts!

A FEMA man accompanying the Red Cross people now saw what we'd been trying to tell the emergency "copers." But there was still "red tape." We spent time at the FEMA office in Luray. We also contacted Senators and Congressman. The responsibility was complex – several federal agencies plus state and local – but Ernest Miller had signed the easement for flood-control use of his land with the understanding the Town would provide a road around the dam and "above the flood pool to connect with existing roads" and "maintain said road in a passable condition."

We hired Roger separately to restore the base of the section up-hollow that wasn't governmental responsibility. Eileen and I with help from trail club volunteers made "waterbars" on this above-lake section to prevent further washouts. Weeks afterward FEMA changed its hasty decision and sent a check covering our road costs and other Fran damage we suffered. The Town reached for us too, adding five-ft-deep rock-and-gravel fill to a low stretch alongside the lake where even minor floods had earlier blocked traffic for as much as five days at a time.

When the restored road was adequate, we invited loggers to come and take out all the fallen or damaged trees the sawmills would accept (logs ten inches or more in diameter). From parts of our forest their equipment could reach, they hauled out a dozen great truckloads, in the process opening the forest so we could walk in it again – though not perfectly as tree parts less than ten-inch diameter were left scattered in many places and would take years to rot and build good soil again. Charlie Graf of Tulip Tree dealt with the same logger we did, and both of us got paid for the logs.

We've continued for years now heating our house with firewood I've gleaned from cleaning up the Fran mess, and I've only brought in a fraction of what's there. Some of the remainder is beginning to rot now, so doesn't make the best firewood. Black locust, though, one of the very best woods to burn, will last unrotted for decades.

Living threads keep weaving the pattern of Eileen's and my life – partly by inevitabilities from earlier times, and by happiness in partnership with each other, by vibrant nature around us, and by the sustaining influences of both human friends and other-animal friends. Together, Eileen and I welcome and try to honor responsibilities of Earth citizenship. Sometimes we still try through writing or conversation to mobilize the Earth-responsibility of others, though mostly now we don't reach out but feel it's enough if we save and enhance our land for the trail club to take over when we die – a few more years maybe if she and I can be together.

Most of the threads represent both of us now. Our kins blend. Her mother dies, and of course I don't have all the important memories, but I understand quite well. And when a sister dies or a brother-in-law the vivid memories we have of them are equivalent. Grandchildren marry. Great-grandchildren are born. A son designs parts of instruments and containers being sent to Mars. A son-in-law professor still performs on pipe organs in majestic, old European cathedrals. Sons and daughters think of retiring – but not quite yet. One granddaughter writes to us from far parts of the world she visits to enhance health care. And so it goes. Eileen and I feel we're one life; we want to die here and have our ashes scattered together on this land.

Through our children we hold threads connecting in places we've lived. Son Harvey clings to Reno where he teaches mathematics at the university. Daughters Sylvia and Laura teach too – but not where we now feel capable of traveling; their June visits have been high points of recent years. Son David and daughter Linda live in California. Son Mike clings to Alaska – Juneau where we've lived, plus land he's homesteaded farther south. We have kin connections in Europe, but no personal connection now in China (a country long important in my life).

We've been receiving "The Bristlecone," the news and information paper issued by Great Basin National Park (and its natural history association that co-sponsored my book of that park's history). A recent issue confirms that conservation funds compensated ranchers to end cattle grazing in the park (and on Mt. Moriah wilderness that's Forest Service land north of the park) and Congress has changed the law – now prohibiting cattle, as in other national parks.

Family members and our friends visiting Great Basin praise the absence of "cow pies" along park trails and in picnic and camp areas. Eileen and I are pleased too – for park visitors and personnel – but with a tinge of regret. The ranching-mining West is deep in us; range cattle seem almost as natural as coyotes or cougars. Sometimes, when we see the Blue Ridge from a medium distance late in the day when purple shadows are lengthening and deepening, we feel we're in the Great Basin again. We were planning to deliver promised historical research materials to the archives at Great Basin park in person, but now I'm using some of the papers in completing and improving this manuscript. We have an arrangement to ship the boxes by Federal Express when we're ready to let them go. We don't thrive on far travel any more.

And there's another change: On election day 2000, a long-time friend and mentor in the nature of Earth, and in the art of living, Sheldon Wimpfen, guided my buying and learning-to-use a computer for my writing, and I'm moving into the new era with his help through "word-processing" this fourth draft of this life-story manuscript, now nearing completion.

Here at the border of Shenandoah National Park we "dream" what the Appalachian club might do here. We have total faith they'll take care of our land and the old house, maybe even better than we can. And they'll try, of course, to bring fellow-hikers into personal experience with nature, leading into MacKaye-Lambert earthmanship-geotechnics, protecting and improving the habitability of our planet. I hope many will read this life story and Eileen's wonderful journal – to the extent they're available – and find some help here toward living for the future of Earth and life.

Nearing the end of this writing, I catch myself too often pushing the brake. I feel I'm completing my own obituary, and, not being "officially" a "judgment angel" helping guard Heaven against undesirables, I'm putting too-favorable a "spin" on it. Also worrying me – I'm not sure I still have the "nerve" to suggest other individuals and families reduce rather than increase their "standard of living" (rate of consumption) for the long-range health of Earth and, in many cases, for their own maximum happiness. People wisely reducing their consumption, I want to be bold enough to say, add up to urgently needed conservation-environmentalism for the good of the planet and of life.

Most people nowadays, polls indicate, favor conservation-environmentalism. Trouble is, this favoring has traditionally meant approval of certain governmental policies, not changing citizens' way of life. Conservation grew up as a governmental thing – creating national forests and national parks, setting aside wilderness, regulating uses of public land, trying to slow down soil erosion – all through laws enacted by Congress or actions taken by other governmental bodies. The term environmentalism meant more efforts to reduce pollution and other harmful practices – but still mostly by governmental regulation. This life story shows I worked years in government and in organizations designed to influence governments. But now as I write – and read what I've written – I realize I'm saying conservation-environmentalism can't meet the mushrooming challenge unless it strongly and directly influences individual and family living. My re-reading reminds me I began spreading this idea publicly in the mid-1960s, following publication of my article "Let's Outgrow the Growth Mania" (*National Parks* Apr '65). The mentor I call upon now to share with Eileen and me the blame (or credit?) for this initiative is the original planner and promoter of the great Appalachian Trail, Benton MacKaye, who's been one of my chief mentors ever since I met him personally before I was old enough to vote and was just getting acquainted with the idea of saving beautiful wild places "forever."

Shaver Hollow VA March 2002

Dear Mr. MacKaye:

I read your obituary in the *Washington Post* (mid-1970s) and was amazed you'd lived almost a century. I remember our shaking hands for the first time at Skyland in Shenandoah National Park when you were 57 and I only 20, too shy to say anything to such an important man except "I enjoy your trail a lot!"

When you died I'd just discovered, while researching this park's history, a letter you'd written to Shenandoah's superintendent when you were president of The Wilderness Society. While reading that surprising 1947 letter in the 1970s, I seemed to hear our mutual wilderness friend Olaus Murie, who'd recently praised my nature editorials in Alaska, exclaiming, "Imagine words like these in government files!"

Your letter to Supt. Freeland – remember? – proposed a short branch of your long trail with brief signs to help hikers read nature. That first ecology trail became a reality in White Oak Canyon, and one set of signs, where soil erosion showed, said if Homo doesn't stop mistreating the land there'll soon be "**no soil, no plants, no food, NO YOU!**" – eight short words I can't forget. Your letter also said:

Well we've learned, to our dismay and perhaps now to our despair, that man's niche in harnessing natural forces seems filled to the danger line. I need cite but two things (soil matter and atomic energy) on which he has potently demonstrated his knowledge of destruction. The same abilities could of course (conceivably) be reversed a hundred per cent to achieve a corresponding creative consummation.

(Right now, reading the current *World Press Review*, I'd add oil greed, unnecessary travel and transportation, and overpopulation, to your soil erosion and atomic destruction – all of which can be remedied, or at least deeply affected both or either governmentally or individually). I kept probing old files, back then in the 1970s, and soon found your article, "The Appalachian Trail: A Guide to the Study of Nature" (*Scientific Monthly*, Apr '32) in which you said:
> Nature is the source of all our knowledge – the open book of which all others are but copies... The Earth story is told in the Appalachian Range... To know America we must know human history, and to know humanity we must know forest history... It is just a matter of putting this and that together... to learn to read first-hand – on the horizon and along the stream – the big outlines of the primeval drama... even as we already have woven the separate sections of our total footpath.

I felt your lasting dedication, Mr. MacKaye. I felt you exploring humanity simultaneously with Earth, seeking the inner pattern harmonizing with the outer pattern. You're a people-nature integrator, Mr. MacKaye. My feelings leaped to identify your persistent dream with Eileen's and mine. You validate our belief that the nature-conquest thrust – you call it the "machine influence" as opposed to the "primeval influence" – is doomed to failure. You climbed ahead of us out of this and other nightmare pitfalls toward an open web of humanity interweaving with nature for mutual benefit. You advocate "*geotechnics*" similar to what we call "*earthmanship.*" Still digging, I finally found your seminal article - "An Appalachian

Trail: A Project in Regional Planning" (*Journal of the American Institute of Architects*, Oct 1921). In it, you propose, in addition to the long footpath, "a new approach to the problem of living," leading urban-industrial-technological humans "back to the land" – through, for instance, raising crops and livestock here, and through harvesting timber with the conservation-wise guidance of "real forestry." You say, "The ability to sleep and cook in the open is a good step forward," yet "but a faint step... We should seek the ability... to raise food with less aid – and less hindrance – from the complexities of commerce..."

You're practical, Mr. MacKaye, though on a scale too vast for most of us to embrace immediately. You want several kinds of "camps" in connection with the great trail. Among these are "food and farm camps" to "provide a tangible opportunity for working out by actual experiment a fundamental matter in the problem of living."

But when the footpath was being created the hikers weren't ready for the "camps." After World War II, though, they proved ready for your ecological trail in White Oak; it got so popular the foot traffic began causing erosion – that the sign-message condemned – so the park closed the trail. Instead of despairing, you went on saving wilderness (as president of The Wilderness Society) so the open book of nature would still be available.

Perhaps people are more nearly ready now. For years the polls have been showing citizens willing, even, to dig into their pockets for saving or restoring a healthful Earth-environment. The United Nations' environmental program is working in many countries. Some people now actually pay for the privilege of vacationing by doing physical labor in Earth-conservation projects. So it's not too hard now to envision successive teams of volunteers living and working in your "camps," including one in Shaver Hollow an hour's walk, perhaps, below the main Appalachian Trail.

Humanity seems awake again, ready for deep change instead of frequent shallow change. The new attitude goes along with a threatening nightmare of the near future – in which the young men and women, disgusted with the poisonous mess their parents have made on Earth, blast off to find homes on other planets – then are attracted back to Earth by deep and lasting changes their shocked and saddened parents make in Earth-civilization.

One feature of this new civilization is "everywhere school" with branches in the edges of wilderness, also on farms and in factories and homes, in all institutions and functions, the method not academic but learning by living, trying what interests you, finding what fits (my future-fiction "Coming of Age on Earth," *National Parks*, Apr '71).

Eileen's and my dream of the future remains tentative but is lined up for reality-testing here in Shaver Hollow – clinging on the shirt-tail, so to speak, of *your* dream – after we two have followed you into the Great Mystery. One of your most active trail clubs will do the testing, Mr. MacKaye, and we hope will also improve the plan to the point of helping to reverse by a hundred per cent the *human destruction* and achieving – on a part of the planet at least – your *"creative consummation."*

We dream people of all ages experiencing here the combination of land, water, muscle, mind, emotion, spirit – all volunteer, no money aspect – producing and enjoying in symbolic quantities, directly from Earth, the food, shelter, fuel, healthful herbs, scenic beauty, and the music of Earth. We see the people making direct personal connection with deep reality – harmonizing with nature in all the immediately practical ways – and in the long-range practical ways too, such as religion and various forms of art. We see them building the needed links inside themselves. We see them returning to homes, offices, stores, laboratories, museums, art galleries, concert halls, churches, factories, broadcast stations and publishing houses – wherever their wishes lead them – to make the corresponding connections there, Mr. "Mentor," joining what you call "Homo civilization" with "wilderness civilization" in one great Earth-civilization – seeing at least part of the vision you quoted from one of *your* mentors, Thomas Jefferson, in your 1947 letter to the Shenandoah park superintendent.

You and we, Mr. MacKaye, have dreamed and planned and experimented. The trail club leaders of this trial-effort in Shaver Hollow – to help save and enhance life's "home, sweet home" – will need help from many others, too – past, present, and yet to be born.

End

Epilog

Darwin Lambert put this autobiography into book form in about 1995 and made his final revisions in early 2003. He learned to use the computer and presented each of us with a disc of this manuscript on various visits and reunions in the following years. In 2005, he and Eileen realized that they could no longer deal with all the labor of their Spartan existence, so they moved to a small house in nearby Luray, where doctors and a hospital were much easier to get to. Dad's health deteriorated rapidly that year, leading to his death on February 11, 2007. As was his wish, his body was cremated and the ashes scattered in the mountains of Virginia and Nevada.

Separate memorials were held in those two states to accommodate his many friends and relatives at the opposite ends of the country. The 63 acre property he had owned since the 1940's was sold to the Potomac Appalachian Trail Club and is being used as an environmental demonstration and rentable accommodation, much as he had desired. At 91 now herself, Eileen continues to live independently at their home in Luray.

We, his children, have been gathering his unpublished writings with the plan to privately publish as many as we can put into the proper shape (and afford). This will be the second of those; the first was *Talking Waters*, the mostly fictional story of a native medicine man found in the Blue Ridge when the white man first came to the Shenandoah Valley.

Since the three of us live in different states, the process of preparing this book electronically has been long, with much use of the telephone and email. We are proud to do it to continue the communication of his ideas, since we believe they will be important to many people.

December 2013

Harvey Lambert, Reno, Nevada
Sylvia Lambert Schneider, Ellensburg, Washington
Laura Lambert Rowe, Colorado Springs, Colorado

Darwin's and Barbara's children: Sylvia, Harvey and Laura
Photo by Christian I. Schneider - 1988

Darwin Lambert's Family Tree

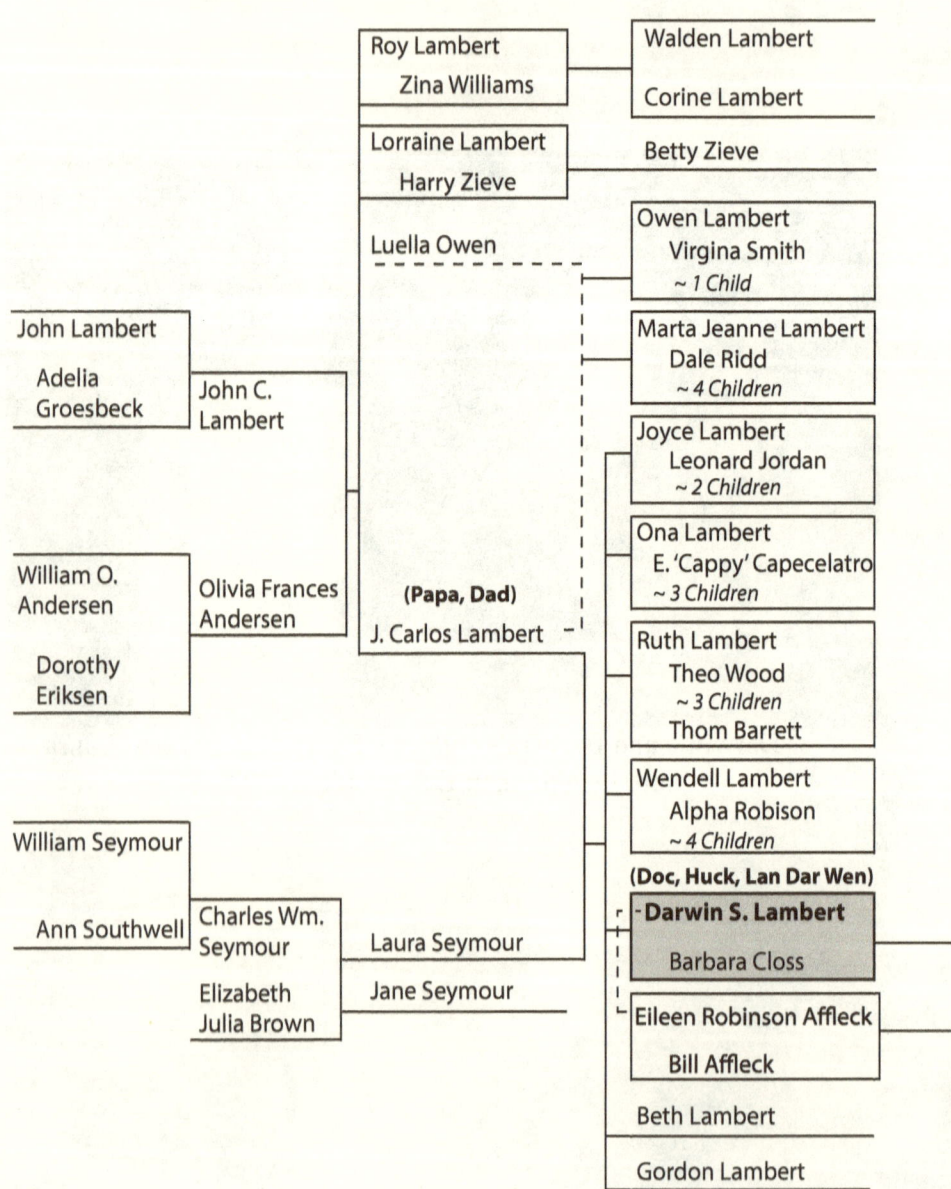

darwinlambert.org

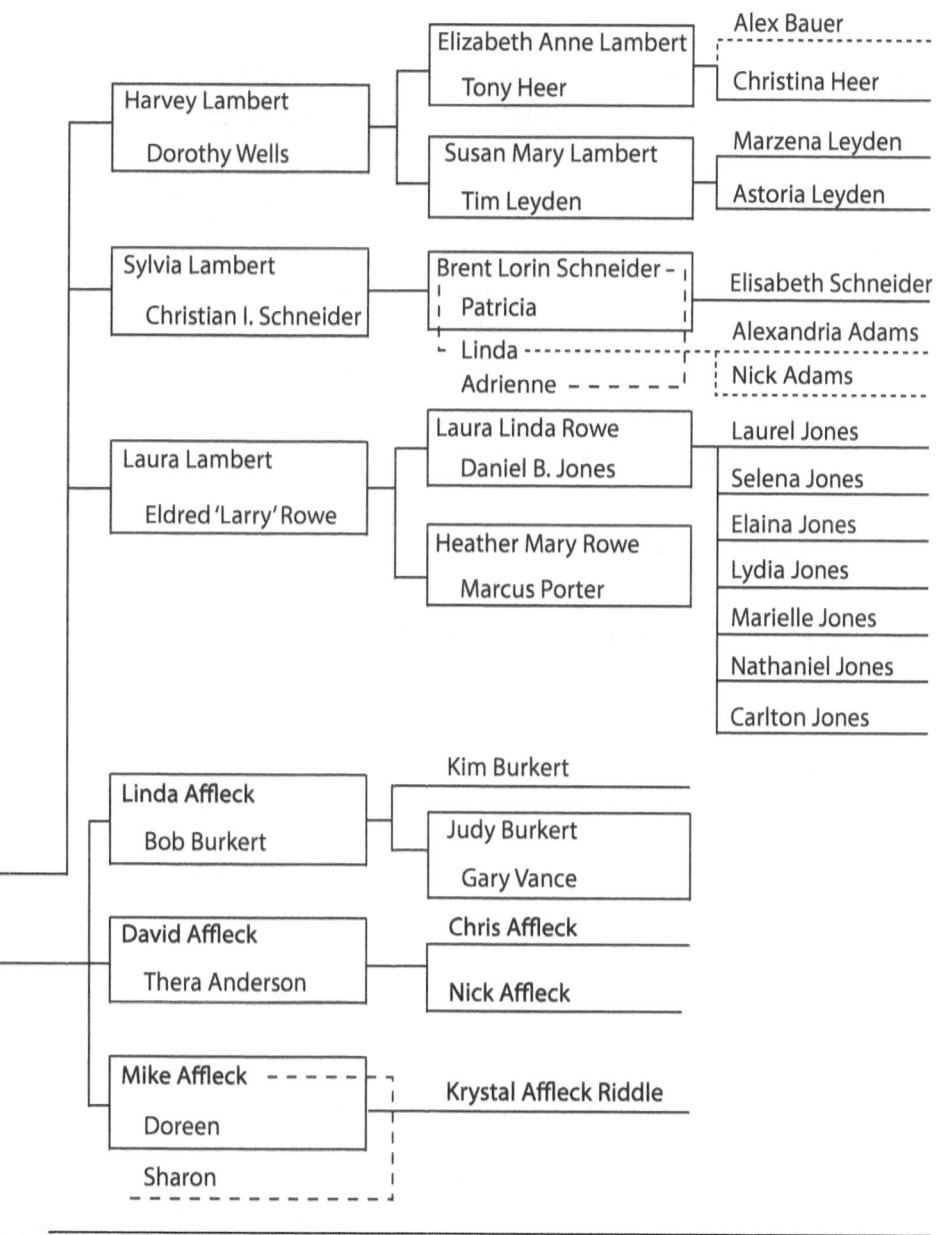

A man of vision, not alone in his ideas, but unique in carrying the idea of Earthmanship (his word) into how he lived. He enjoyed people from intellectuals to the simple man raising his children and scraping a living from the earth, to one walking the highways in search of something better than he had known. He believed in using the rich abundance of the earth, but renewing it and preserving it for the coming generations. He enjoyed nature as a blessing, learning the rhythms of the seasons, the names of plants and animals of varying regions, as he lived in Nevada, Alaska, Virginia and China--the sounds of the owl, the thrush, the whippoorwill, the beauty of the rare lady slipper in the deep green woods, the vista of the mountains from afar, to explorations within their folds.

As a parent, even as in his environmentalism, my father was not dictatorial, but rather a mentor who taught you to think, establish your own philosophy, weigh the consequences of your desired actions, and choose wisely.

The loss of his physical presence on this earth, while painful, is mitigated by the legacy left behind in books, articles, lectures, and the preserved beauty of Shenandoah and Great Basin National Parks.

Laura Lambert Rowe, daughter

People of the Book

Adams, Bruce, a Shoshone Indian classmate of Darwin Lambert in Ely, Nevada

Affleck, David, and **Thera**, son and daughter-in-law of Eileen Lambert, sons Chris and Nick

Affleck, Mike, and **Doreen** (son of Eileen Lambert), daughter Krystal

Anderson, Olivia Frances, Darwin Lambert's paternal grandmother

Beebe, Lucius, (1902-66), author, gourmand, and railroad activist, Virginia City, Nevada

Benson, Ross and **Julia**, friends and business partners of Darwin and Barbara in Luray, Virginia

Benton, William, (1900-73), Senator (D, Conn) and publisher of the Encyclopedia Britannica

Brown, Elizabeth Julia, Darwin Lambert's maternal grandmother

Brown, Harrison, (1917-86), physicist and author who influenced Darwin Lambert's concept of Earthmanship

Burg, Amos and **Carolyn**, 20th century authors, Juneau, Alaska

Bush, Barbara, first lady, wife of 41st U.S. President George H.W. Bush

Burkert, Linda, Eileen Lambert's daughter, children Kim and Judy

Carrighar, Sally, (1898-1985), American naturalist and writer

Capecelatro, Ona Lambert, Darwin Lambert's sister

Chu, Joe, Darwin Lambert's colleague at Lend Lease in Chongqing (Chungking), China

Closs, H. Wilbert and **Jessie**, Darwin Lambert's first wife Barbara's parents

Confucius, ancient Chinese philosopher

Connally, **Eugenia (G.G.) Horstman**, former editor, National Parks Conservation Association Magazine

Corbin, **Virgil** and **Rose**, friends from Luray, VA

Crumrine, **Josephine**, artist, Juneau, Alaska

Darwin, **Charles**, (1809-82), English naturalist and geologist, author of *On the Origin of Species*

Davis, **Trevor** and **Carol Berry**, Alaska friends

Defoe, **Daniel**, (c.1660-1731), English merchant and political writer, author of *Robinson Crusoe*

Eiseley, **Loren**, (1907-77), American anthropologist and nature writer

Farnsworth, **Albert H.**, editor, *VISTA*, magazine of the UN Association of the US

Farrell, **Peggy**, friend of Darwin Lambert in Salt Lake City

Farrell, **Bob**, friend of Darwin Lambert in Salt Lake City

Fehr, **Irwin**, photographer friend, Ely, Nevada

Firth, **Lewis** and **Grace**, friends of Darwin and Eileen, Virginia

Foltz, **Ashby**, Luray family where Darwin Lambert first lived in Luray

Graf, **Charlie**, Potomac Appalachian Trail Club, helped build Tulip Tree Cabin

Hanson, **Hank** and **Doris**, friends of Darwin and Eileen Lambert, of both Juneau, Alaska and Virginia

Heald, **Weldon**, (1901-67), Arizona nature writer, helped explore proposed Great Basin National Park

Heer, **Lisa** and **Tony**, Harvey and Dorothy Lambert's daughter and son-in-law, daughter Christina

Hoover, Herbert, (1874-1964), mining engineer, 31st president of the U.S. (1929-33)

Hodes, Hy, China

Ho, Chao-ye (Kathleen), Darwin Lambert's Chinese teacher in Chongqing (Chungking), China

Jacobsen, Robert R. and **Phel**, former Superintendent, Lehman Caves National Monument, and Shenandoah National Park

Jefferson, Thomas, (1743-1826), 3rd President of the U.S., fellow Virginian and inspiration in conservation

Jewell, Tom, carpenter, who helped Darwin Lambert update his old log house

Job, Mary, classmate of Darwin's in Salt Lake City

Jones, Laura Rowe and **Daniel**, daughter and son-in-law of Laura and Larry Rowe, parents of Laurel, Selena, Elaina, Lydia, Marielle, Nathaniel and Carlton

Keller, Bill, miner in Nevada

Kelley, Pete, Nevada state economic developer

Korine, Betty Zieve, Darwin's cousin, daughter of Lorraine and Harry Zieve

Krutch, Joseph Wood, (1893-1970), writer and naturalist, who places man within Nature rather than outside Nature

Lambert, Darwin and **Eileen** (formerly Affleck), the author of this book and his 2nd wife

Lambert, Harvey and **Dorothy Wells**, Darwin and Barbara Lambert's son and daughter-in-law

Lambert, J. Carlos (Papa, Dad), Darwin Lambert's father

Lambert, Laura Seymour, Darwin Lambert's mother

Lambert, Luella Owen, 2nd wife of J. Carlos Lambert, Darwin Lambert's stepmother

Lambert, Mark, son of Gary and Jane Lambert, grandson of Wendell and Alpha Lambert, ecologist, U.S. Forest Service, Colorado

Lambert, Owen and **Virginia**, son of J. Carlos and Luella Lambert, daughter Stephanie

Lambert, Roy and **Zina**, Darwin Lambert's uncle and aunt

Lambert, Walden, son of Roy and Zina Lambert

Lambert, Wendell and **Alpha**, brother and sister-in-law of Darwin Lambert, children Joan, Gary, Richard, John

Laotze, 6th century B.C. Chinese philosopher

Lee, Dorothy (Mrs. Casenove Lee), National Parks Conservation board member and son Richard

Leopold, Aldo, (1887-1948), American author and environmentalist

Leyden, Susan and **Tim**, daughter and son-in-law of Harvey and Dorothy Lambert, daughters Marzena and Astoria

MacKaye, Benton, (1879-1975), American forester and conservationist, originator of the Appalachian Trail

Martinez, Maria, (1887-1980), Pueblo Indian potter. (Pots signed "Maria +Poveka" indicate they were created after 1959 with the help of her son.)

McFadden, Marcie, helped with building Tulip Tree Cabin, Luray, Virginia

McGovern, Bill, colleague at Lend Lease, China

Miller, Ernest and son **Roger**, wise neighbor, inspiration to Darwin and Eileen, near Luray, VA

Mitchie, Hilda, housekeeper and relative, Overton, Nevada

Muir, John, (1838-1914), Scottish-born American naturalist, author, and early advocate for the preservation of wilderness

Murie, Adolph, (1899-1974), naturalist, author and wildlife biologist, Jackson Hole, Wyoming

Murie, Olaus (1889-1963), naturalist, author and wildlife biologist, and his wife **Mardy,** friends of Darwin and Eileen Lambert

Muñoz, Rie, artist, Juneau, Alaska

Porter, Heather Rowe and **Marcus,** daughter and son-in-law of Laura and Larry Rowe

Reeder, Jack and **Carolyn,** writers, and board member of Potomac Appalachian Trail Club

Ridd, Marta Jeanne Lambert and **Dale,** daughter and son-in-law of J. Carlos and Luella Lambert

Robison, Jim and **Birdie,** children George, Elwin and Alpha, Snake Valley ranchers, Nevada

Rowe, Laura and Eldred (**Larry**), Darwin and Barbara Lambert's daughter and son-in-law

Rowe, Mae, teacher in Overton, Nevada

Sauers, Joy, artist, poet, Luray, Virginia

Schaffner, Ray, former chief park naturalist, Shenandoah National Park, and friend of Darwin and Eileen

Schneider, Sylvia and **Christian,** Darwin and Barbara Lambert's daughter and son-in-law

Schneider, Brent and **Adrienne,** son and daughter-in-law of Sylvia and Christian Schneider, Brent's daughter Elisabeth

Scrugham, James G, (1880-1945), governor of Nevada 1923-27

Seton, Ernest Thompson, (1860-1946), writer and wildlife artist, a founder of the Boy Scouts of America, young Darwin Lambert's favorite author

Seward, Tim and **Pike,** lived in Lambert's Virginia home while they were in NV and AK

Seymour, Charles William, Darwin Lambert's maternal grandfather

Seymour, Jane, Darwin Lambert's aunt

Seymour, Laura, Darwin Lambert's mother

Sittler, Joseph, (1904-87) Theologian and ecologist, University of Chicago

Shaw, Elizabeth, writer, philosopher, and correspondent with Barbara and Darwin Lambert

Sisk, Newt and **Daisy,** children Winfield, Marie, Coty, Anna (Annie), Athey, family living in the proposed Shenandoah National Park; helped get young Lambert oriented as naturalist

Smith, Bob and **Dorothy,** friends of Darwin and Eileen near Luray, Virginia

Smith, Joseph, (1805-44), founder of the Mormon (LDS) church

Stainbrook, Edward, psychiatrist, University of California

Tilden, Paul, former editor, National Parks Conservation magazine

Thompson, Edward T., editor, Reader's Digest (1976-84)

Thompson, Nellie, classmate of Darwin Lambert in Ely, Nevada

Thurston, Harry, friend of Darwin Lambert in Metropolis, Nevada

Tolstoy, Leo, (1828-1910), Russian author of *War and Peace* and *Anna Karenina*

Torivia, Frances, potter, New Mexico

Trexler, Keith, Lehman Caves National Monument

Uzzell, Thomas H., Literary agent, New York

Vowles, Keith, friend of Darwin in Ely

Walden, Johnny, colleague in China

Watson, Charlie, Great Basin National Park advocate

Whitman, Walt, (1819-92), American poet, essayist and journalist

Widtsoe, John A, (1872-1952), LDS church leader, wrote *Joseph Smith as Scientist*, friend of Darwin Lambert's father

Williams, Sonny and **Louise**, neighbors of Darwin and Eileen, near Luray

Willis, Lewis, Shenandoah Park resident

Wimpfen, Sheldon, Luray VA friend

Wood-Barret, Ruth Lambert, Darwin Lambert's sister

Zerkel, L. Ferdinand, Luray friend

Zieve, Harry and **Lorraine Lambert**, daughter Betty Korine, Darwin's aunt, uncle, cousin

www.ingramcontent.com/pod-product-compliance
Lightning Source LLC
Chambersburg PA
CBHW020939230426
43666CB00005B/83